ACTUAL MALICE

A TRUE CRIME POLITICAL THRILLER

Breton Peace

with

Gary Condit

Published in Los Angeles, California, by Ghost Mountain Books, Inc.

ISBNs
Print: 9781939457646
Epub: 9781939457639
Mobi: 9781939457622

Cover Design: Amjad Shahzad
Cover Photo: AP Images
Interior Design and Production: Dovetail Publishing Services,
    www.dovetailpublishingservices.com

DEDICATION

For Chandra and Joyce

FOR THE PEOPLE IN THESE PAGES, however scarred and imperfect, who refused to break to the populist throng, even when doing so might ease their own pain. If there is hope, it lies in your strength. I trust that when you see yourself in these pages, you know you are appreciated, and that readers will take from you the real measure of loyalty.

FOR CC AND CHIEF to tell this story, you had to let me into your most private and painful experiences. Thank you for trusting me to handle these experiences with respect, even where you might prefer to withhold those parts of your lives from the public square. That you were willing to live through this period, again, is both a consequence and a measure of the extraordinary bond you share.

NOTE TO READERS

This publication is a memoir. It contains the opinions and ideas of its author and Gary Condit. It includes Gary's general recollections of his experiences throughout his lifetime to the best of his knowledge. The author and Gary understand and acknowledge that his recollection of the events may conflict with or be inconsistent with the recollections of others. Names, dates, and actions are intended to be accurate as presented. However, some dialogue has been recreated to facilitate flow. This book is not intended to be the definitive account of what occurred, but rather is intended to be a personal reflection of events that transpired from the author's and Gary's own experience and perspective. The author and publisher specifically disclaim all responsibility for, and are not liable for, any liability, loss, or risk, personal or otherwise, which is incurred as a consequence, directly or indirectly, of the use and application of any of the contents of this book.

AUTHOR'S PREFACE

I came to this project as a young lawyer in a large law firm with both the advantage and dis-advantage of growing up knowing Gary Condit as my father's friend.

I say "disadvantage" because I was trained as a lawyer, and as such, I was conscious of my obligation to look at the public evidence objectively while simultaneously having been privy to how the story unfolded privately.

I shared with Chad and Cadee Condit the common experience of growing up in a politi-cal family. Our moms both stayed home to raise their kids despite the trend to the contrary. It was based on these familial connections and common experiences that Gary's kids asked me to help their father tell his story.

I was initially stunned by the overwhelming physical evidence in the case. Chad Condit had maintained and secured every scrap of paper during the tumultuous events. And, after his first encounter with police, Gary and his attorney, Abbe Lowell, had made a critical decision to have detailed records taken of every interaction with law enforcement thereafter. This book would not exist had they not done this.

In writing, I was committed to pulling the story from the records in a way that gives you a sense of the manic pace with which the saga unfolded, as well as honestly depicting the Kafkaesque cast of characters and kaleidoscope of subplots that—but for the body of evidence in my care—would seem too entertaining, bizarre, or tragic to be true.

For every ounce of adrenaline generated by a new revelation of corruption and unfore-seen connection as I researched and wrote, there was a greater dose of sadness knowing that this was not a work of fiction. A sadness that was, and remains today, specific to Chandra Levy, Joyce Chiang, and the other real people that you will meet in this book, and more gen-eral sadness grounded in the recognition that the only closure is acceptance that there can no longer be any.

This is not a redemptive story, and there are no heroes. Laced amid the personal tragedies is a painful truth about a broken system of justice in which so many with power are bent by ambition, indifferent to truth, incompetent, or all three.

Breton Peace

THANKS

This book would not have been possible without support from the following people:

The Condit and Berry families, the Chiang family, Terry McHale, Nate Monroe, Dan Farley, Jason Crowell, Addie Stone, Kaia Los Huertos, John Moores, the Hon. Willie Brown Jr., Bertram Fields, Sonny Barger, Clint Eastwood, Andrew Tan, George and Daniel Mitrovich, Anthony Brigidini, Lin Wood, Abbe Lowell, Mike Dayton, Mike Lynch, Rebecca Cooper, Mike Parker, Rusty Areias, Terry and Marilyn Holum, Deborah Sines, Jay McGraw, Lisa Clark, Carly Stratton, Jon Ford, Jon Peck, Joan Keyes, the whole team at Ghost Mountain, and many others.

My parents for their persistent support.

My wife for her unwavering understanding and encouragement.

Tom Warwick for his guidance and his stubborn integrity.

CONTENTS

Part IV – Judgment   219

Part V – Chief   257

Part VI – Accused   283

PART I
BEFORE A SCANDAL

CHAPTER 1

CONDIT COUNTRY

LOVE, MARRIAGE, LOYALTY

IT WAS AN UNLIKELY SETTING for the harvest of political power.

California's fertile Central Valley is bookended by the cities of Sacramento to the north and Fresno to the south. Here, there are no skyscrapers stretching to the sky. Orchards spread east in parallel lines of bountiful trees until the space between them disappears. Beaches lay not with tumbling waves but rather along lazy rivers that are the community's lifeblood.

On the third Saturday of October, like clockwork, ten thousand people gathered at the Stanislaus County fairgrounds.

Young boys on fake horses roped fake calves under banners reading "Welcome to Condit Country," and church ladies ladled peach cobbler to regular folks in cowboy boots.

"Gary! Gary!" chanted a crowd of thousands as Congressman Condit stepped onto the raised stage dressed in a blue sweater and brown suede shoes.

He had harvested immense political power from them and for three decades had returned it all to them, never giving a reason to doubt his motives or to question his moral compass.

To them, he was still "Gary." The Condit's home phone number was still listed in the phone book, and Carolyn answered when you called. Gary still held his "sidewalk chats" on main streets in and around Condit Country, or in local diners, where he'd spend hours talking with anyone, about any problem or issue they had, so long as they were willing to wait in line for their turn while he sat behind a pop-up table or booth. He remembered them, and the important things about them. They felt they knew him personally, and referred to him not as Congressman or Mr. Condit but "just Gary."

Gary stepped to the microphone and smiled. The thin smile was familiar to many, with velvet edges. An image of an animated blue dog with large yellow eyes flashed onto a screen above the stage.

The crowd roared and barked.

They'd been meeting like this for twenty years. Each meeting was bigger than the last. Politicians from all parties attended the annual Condit Country Jamboree. Local newspapers advertised sales on Condit Country outfits in the weeks leading up to the party.

"This is a great country—is it not a great country we live in?" Gary asked the crowd. His words were met with thunderous applause. "God has blessed us greatly as a people. And you are all blessed because you get to live in the greatest—the finest country on the face of the earth—and you ought to thank the good Lord every day for that."

Gary's voice fell an octave. "Let me tell you the thing we have to do from my point of view. We all have to keep our eye on the ball and not be distracted by a lot of extraneous issues that divide us as a people and as a country."

Dove Condit, Gary's sister, put her hand on her sister-in-law's arm. Carolyn Condit, Gary's wife, spent much of the year organizing the jamboree, making sure every detail was meticulously planned and executed.

"Is it ever hard having to take care of all the details while Gary rides in parades?" Dove whispered.

"Somebody has to clap for the people in the parade," Carolyn replied.

———

Gary's alarm went off at 4:30 a.m.

Carolyn slept next to him, her face calm. He considered the possibility that she didn't hurt while she slept. Nothing fluttered behind her closed eyes or quivered underneath her half-open lips. He hoped that was the case; that sleep brought relief from chronic pain.

He got up, easily, and went to the bathroom. There, he considered himself in the mirror while waiting for the water to warm. He still looked strong. The Cherokee in him had become more pronounced. But crow's feet had formed around his eyelids. Razor-like lines ran down his chin, and gray hair framed his ears.

Distinguished. Its connotations weighed heavy on his mind. Distinguished was just the final step before extinction. Gary spent a lot of time in the gym, knowing that he was fighting inevitability, yet stubborn enough to try. Looking in the mirror he imagined more lines forming around his eyes and mouth, more gray taking over his sandy blond head. He didn't want to look distinguished. He wanted to stay young and relevant.

He turned from the mirror and stepped into the shower. Acorn Lane was silent in the early morning hours. Even after sunrise, it remained a quiet street, in a quiet neighborhood, in a quiet part of California that was far more like Tulsa than Hollywood.

In the front yard, an Australian willow's branches rested motionless on the roof of the single-story ranch house. In the backyard, cypress trees lining the fence shot stiffly to the sky like a wall of cone-shaped sentries.

While he showered, Carolyn pulled herself slowly out of bed. She felt cool, not cold, in her nightgown, as her delicate feet touched the carpet. There was a charming simplicity to how her features aligned with acute angles around her cheekbones and nose.

She opened the bedroom door and walked into a hallway that led to the kitchen. Her petite figure moved so lightly that the hallway's hardwood floors muted her footsteps. *He'll be dressed in ten minutes and out the door in ten more*, she resigned as she turned on the coffeemaker.

They had to race to keep up with his schedule. She had grown accustomed to his absence. He left for work on Monday morning and didn't come home until Thursday evening. His back and forth made their life appear to others like a series of line segments: a long period of separation followed by a short reunion, repeated with disciplined regularity.

Carolyn knew another congressional wife who said her marriage would surely fail if it weren't for the weekly break she got from her husband while he was in DC. Carolyn never felt that way. But she didn't want to live in Washington. They had built a life in Ceres, from scratch. She had no interest in becoming a political "tagalong" wife in a big city. As a consequence of this distance, they had to race to keep up with his schedule.

It's always been this way. Nostalgia prompted a thin smile that underscored the fine blonde hair that fell around her hazel eyes.

They met in 1964, at Nathan Hale High School in Tulsa, Oklahoma. They were only sixteen, but she knew right away that she'd spend the rest of her life with him. She was on the pep squad and a good student and Catholic. And although she was shy, Carolyn was widely regarded as one of the prettiest and kindest girls in school.

He wasn't what she expected of the son of a hellfire Baptist preacher, particularly a preacher's son who had as a young boy traveled with his father from motel to motel on a revival circuit, where his father bellowed sermons at night on roadsides and under tents. Gary had even sung church songs on KROS's Revival Hour.

In high school, when friends asked Gary where he lived, he replied "next to the church, where my father works." Which was true—Gary grew up living in parsonages supported by his father's congregation. He had "just decided" to go a different direction than the ministry.

By the time Gary reached high school he drank beer and skipped class. He ran with a group of friends that, although characteristic for the time, naively thought of themselves as free thinkers who didn't believe that helping people required saving them. Still, in many ways, he *was* a preacher's son.

Gary paid attention to every detail of what Carolyn said to him, no matter the topic of conversation. He had always had the capacity to make her feel like the only person in the world. It had attracted her to him, and, she supposed, others as well.

She was known for possessing quiet kindness. People trusted her with their secrets. Perhaps they were drawn to confide in her because Carolyn had her own secret.

Shortly after she met Gary, doctors offered her two options. She could continue living with chronic pain pulsating from the back of her brain, and the pain would continue to get worse. Alternatively, she *might* relieve some of the pain by operating on the portion of the brain her doctors believed to be responsible for the condition that had plagued her from early childhood. The same doctors gave the invasive brain surgery a 50/50 chance of success and the certainty of collateral consequences to other human functions.

Carolyn chose to live with the pain she already knew.

It seems so long ago, she thought while pouring a cup of coffee.

Outside, the sky had transitioned from black to gray. Acorn Lane remained still, waiting for light to spill over the almond and apricot orchards stretching in every direction.

In the bathroom, steam had rolled up and covered the shower stall glass. Gary traced figures in the condensation, each disappearing quickly, and he thought about the past.

I'm in control now, he thought.

―

After graduating from high school, Gary worked for Carolyn's father at his chain of discount clothing stores. It was a steady job. Carolyn's father insisted that the best way to get ahead would be to go to college. Problem was, Gary didn't have the grades.

Oklahoma was on the tail end of an oil rush, and even at the tail, plenty of folks in and around Tulsa provided walking, talking proof that oil could make a man rich even without a college degree.

He spent the summer after high school graduation 330 miles from Tulsa, working in the oil fields on Oklahoma's panhandle. He was a kid working side by side with hard men. Sores on his hands morphed fast into a protective layer of rough calluses.

Fights broke out regularly, lit by a physical mishap or foolish words. They were grown men who relied on one another atop of rigs fitted with swinging parts. They were also grown boys who, when pushed to their limit, resolved problems by tearing at each other with their fists.

From sunup to sundown they worked. It was hard going. There wasn't much else to do. Even Guymon, the largest city in the Cimarron Territory, only had a few thousand residents. At night, there was empty space. It had been that way since the unforgiving land was taken from the Cherokee and opened to settlers.

Darkness is felt on that panhandle. Stars burn brighter because they are the only act on a heavy stage. Each night, Gary stretched his sinewy body under the silver moon and watched it transition from yellow to orange and then crumble off the earth's edge. His mind raced— thinking about what he was going to do next. Working the oil fields was a far cry from the life of the oil barons walking around Tulsa in hundred-dollar cowboy boots.

Mostly, he thought about Carolyn. Months of riding backhoes and cleaning debris-clogged cow catches under a blistering heat had increased his resolve to take control of his life so that he could start a new one with her. He just didn't know how.

When he returned from the oil fields, the blithe charm that made him popular in high school was reigned in and redirected. Gary went back to work for Carolyn's father, but he was biding his time for something else.

―

They married on January 18, 1967. Chad, their first child, was born six months later. Shortly after Chad was born, Adrian Condit, Gary's father, received an invitation to pastor the Ceres Free Will Baptist Church, a fledging congregation in Ceres, California. Carolyn didn't hesitate to say yes when Gary suggested they follow his family. California had junior colleges. From there, Gary could transfer to a four-year university.

They packed their '63 Chevy, bundled up the baby, and headed west. Gary enrolled in Modesto Junior College the week he arrived. A week later, he found a job working in the Tillie Lewis Cannery. A week after that, they rented a small white house with green shutters, on Kay Street. Gary went to school in the mornings, then worked all afternoon and night.

As Carolyn later reflected:

> Back then, he didn't even have time to stay and have a cup of coffee. It was all about us, you know. Not the college life. He just knew he needed to go to college and didn't have time to plan anything else. I didn't even have a car because Gar needed it for work. My means of transportation was a bicycle with a seat on the back for Chad. That's just how we were doing it.

―

From junior college Gary transferred to Stanislaus State College, where, like most other colleges across the country, the student body was caught in the throes of protests against the Vietnam War.

Gary worked day shifts at the Norris Industries munitions plant, helping to fabricate bullets that were then shipped off for war. He carpooled to work with an older man whose son was in the army and fighting in Vietnam. One evening, during their after-work drive, the man expressed his concern that if the war ended the munitions plant would likely close and they'd be out of jobs. For Gary, the man's comment brought into focus an idea he had been silently considering for some time.

Carolyn always assumed they'd return to Oklahoma after Gary earned a college degree. She was surprised when he told her he wanted to run in the upcoming election for the Ceres city council. He was only twenty-three, and they had no money. But she could sense a determination inside of him that was new. She told him to go for it.

Gary's father, Adrian, was a harder sell.

"Politics is a dirty business," Adrian had warned.

"Dad, church politics are the dirtiest," Gary replied.

In addition to his day shifts at the munitions plant, Gary worked night shifts in the paint department at Montgomery Ward. In between, Gary and his family walked door-to-door until he had knocked on the front door of every voter in Ceres.

Building a political base turned out to be no different than building a congregation. "Knocking on doors" had the same multiplier effect on Gary's nascent political career as it did for his father's ministry. The Central Valley was populated with transplants from Texas, Oklahoma, Kansas, Nebraska, and Missouri. There was a joke that you couldn't shake a Ceres tree without an Okie falling out. Gary was one of their own.

Gary surprised the local political establishment when he finished second in a seven-person race for three open seats on the city counsel. He'd done it with a campaign budget of $67. With his victory, Gary became one of the youngest elected officials in the nation. Stories about him were picked up in the national media. A telegram arrived from Carolyn's father that read, "Even Abe Lincoln didn't make it his first try."

In 1974, two years after his election to the city council, Gary became the mayor of Ceres. After serving as mayor for two years, he served six years on the Stanislaus County Board of Supervisors. After that, he served in the California legislature before being elected to the United States Congress in 1989, at the age of forty-one.

At each step along the way, he played high-stakes poker with the establishment, leaving a large wake of enemies, and skeletons, behind his rise.

Until Chandra Levy disappeared in 2001, Gary never lost an election.

~

They were more like each other now. Their sentences were shorter because so much could be communicated without words.

Gary's footsteps crossed the bedroom into the hallway.

He's a good man, she thought as she poured a second cup of coffee for herself, and a fresh one for him.

The house would be empty now when Gary left. They were a political family, and their two kids were all grown up.

Chad Condit was now married and lived with his wife and three kids nearby in Ceres. He was the governor's point man for the whole Central Valley. Chad had served in the navy before that. Tall and good looking, he had olive skin and, like his father, a natural ability to connect with people. Everyone assumed he would run for office soon.

Their daughter, Cadee Condit, was petite, fair skinned, and blonde. At twenty-three years old, she worked in the governor's private office in Sacramento.

Gary entered the kitchen and kissed Carolyn's cheek.

"Coffee?" she asked.

"Thanks," he answered.

There was a loud knock on the front door.

"Vince," Carolyn whispered, putting her coffee down on the kitchen table.

Gary picked up his small brown leather travel bag and left the house.

It'd become as regular as breathing. For a decade now, Gary had flown home every Thursday and returned to Washington, DC, every Sunday, except when Congress wasn't in session. He could count on both hands the number of times during that decade he did not come home to his family on the weekend.

VINCE

Outside, the fog had lifted.

"What took you so long?" Vince Flammini asked as Gary stepped onto the porch. "I'm fucking freezing."

"You could have honked and waited in the car," Gary replied.

The two men climbed into Gary's white Dodge Durango. The drive from Ceres to San Francisco International Airport took just under two hours.

Gary first met Flammini at a small gym on the outskirts of nearby Modesto. The gym was built beside a junkyard and known by locals as the "junkyard gym." Flammini ran the gym, and boasted to its patrons that he had arm-wrestled Sylvester Stallone and won, and had been a professional bodybuilder, and held the title of "Mr. Modesto." According to Flammini, before coming to California he had been "high up" in the Vegas mob.

Although he was an acquired taste, Gary enjoyed his company and thought he was harmless. Gary became a regular at the gym, and after a while, the two men began riding motorcycles together. They'd often stop near the Tuolumne River.

"When we get old, we're gonna go fishing without bait," Flammini often said, with a big grin. It made Gary smile too, as they visualized themselves as two old men standing near the river with empty fishing poles as a cover for enjoying the sight of the pretty women on the beach.

When Gary learned Flammini needed money, he offered his friend a job in his Modesto district office. Mike Lynch, Gary's chief of staff and closest political advisor for fifteen years, didn't want to hire Flammini. Lynch was always working, always on. In the morning, Lynch could be found at a local diner, drinking coffee and pouring over newspapers. He couldn't understand what Gary saw in Flammini.

Flammini's primary work responsibilities included driving Gary to and from the airport and escorting him to community events. Flammini told everyone that he had been hired to be the congressman's bodyguard.

Gary's older brother, Burl Condit, was a no-nonsense motorcycle cop. Although he and Gary had always been close, he didn't agree with all of his brother's decisions.

"The junkyard guy," Burl replied when he learned Gary had hired Flammini for his congressional staff. He knew exactly who Flammini was.

Burl called a detective and asked him to run Flammini's name through databases linked to organized crime. Flammini didn't show up on a single sheet from New Jersey to California.

This guy's phonier than a three-dollar bill, Burl thought, but also believing Flammini was harmless.

Gary became the only real friend Flammini ever had. The only thing he ever expected to receive in return was Flammini's loyalty.

CONSTITUENTS

Dr. Robert Levy opened the front door to his single-story ranch house in suburban Modesto, a stone's throw away from Ceres.

His wife, Susan Levy, was painting in the backyard. Their home's interior was filled with her original paintings and sculptures. Susan's art reflected an eclectic mix of Christian, Jewish, Buddhist, and nontraditional belief systems that was all her own.

Chandra Levy, their daughter, affectionately called her mother "flaky." She hadn't inherited her mother's taste for the eccentric. Any penchant for risk Chandra might have had was carefully guarded.

In high school, Chandra interned for the Modesto Police Department, and in college she majored in journalism and minored in criminal justice. She tried her hand at sports reporting but decided working in a newsroom was too cynical for her taste and refocused her ambition on a career in law enforcement.

Chandra was now twenty-four years old and working on her master's degree in public administration at the University of Southern California. She had completed internships in the office of the mayor of Los Angeles, and in the office of the governor of California, Gray Davis, where Chad and Cadee Condit worked as top aides.

After Chandra finished her internship with the governor, she started an internship at the Federal Bureau of Prisons, in Washington, DC.

In nearby Ceres, Adrian Condit drove his truck past the Ceres Free Will Baptist Church. He was no longer the pastor there. After four decades of preaching, he decided to enter semiretirement and became the chaplain at Memorial Hospital in nearby Modesto.

Adrian admired the resolve of the hospital staff who had to cope with a daily routine of sickness and death. He particularly respected one of the hospital's cancer physicians: Dr. Robert Levy.

PUBLIC AND PRIVATE TRUST

EASYRIDER

Gary was one of the "Gang of Five" who tried to topple then assembly leader Willie Brown . . . and has continued bucking the "status quo." He is now the leader of a group of conservative Democrats who call themselves the "Blue Dogs" . . . It's in this capacity that he now watches over the bikers and their causes, knowing that big government will always try to expand its reach, and we are prime targets . . . We welcome him into the *Easyriders'* Hall of Fame.

– *Easyriders* magazine, Oct. 1997 issue

GARY'S BLACK HARLEY-DAVIDSON HERITAGE SOFTAIL thundered underneath him. His legs were wrapped in black leather chaps.

Next to him, in the same lane, Vince Flammini rode on a white Harley-Davidson Fat Boy. His jet-black mustache had too much dye in it and his short-sleeve shirt gave way to a string of colorful tattoos and bulging veins running down his forearms.

The unlikely pair was a few miles outside of Laughlin, Nevada, on their way to the Laughlin River Run Motorcycle Rally, the largest motorcycle event on the West Coast.

As they entered town, the two friends passed a group of bikers wearing Hells Angels patches.

Gary wondered if Sonny Barger was with them. Barger, the founder of the Hells Angels Motorcycle Club, and Gary were long-time acquaintances. Gary didn't avoid Barger if the two men ran into one another at public events like motorcycle rallies.

The Hells Angels had been born in the Central Valley, and Barger's sister worked on Gary's campaigns. Barger and Gary also had a mutual friend in US Senator Ben "Nighthorse" Campbell from Colorado. Campbell, like Gary, was a registered Native American and a motorcycle enthusiast.

In 1994, Barger's parole ended for a conviction stemming from a conspiracy to blow up the clubhouse of a rival motorcycle gang. To celebrate, he threw a private party for seven hundred of his friends. Two politicians attended the Hells Angels bash: Gary and Campbell.

Gary suspected that the reason Hop Condit—the brother of a cop and a politician—always came out of prison unscathed had something to do with Barger and his Hells Angels looking out for him.

—

Hop was the youngest of the three Condit brothers.

His real name was Darrell Wayne Condit, but when he was born, his grandfather and brothers called him "Hop" after their favorite television cowboy, Hopalong Cassidy. Like Cassidy, the new baby had cotton-blond hair.

Hop was a straight-A student in high school and was accepted to the University of Oklahoma. He dropped out after his first semester. After that, Hop became a drifter. He spent time as a roadie for bands, and was in and out of prison.

On one occasion, Hop was caught smuggling a van full of marijuana across state lines into Arkansas. He led local police on a high-speed chase that ended when the van crashed.

Authorities in Arkansas didn't know Hop's real name—he was traveling under the alias "Stan Buchanan." As a result, news coverage detailed the exploits of Mr. Buchanan and the tale of Hop's wild ride didn't filter back to the political press in California.

Information wasn't ubiquitous—yet.

Sometimes, however, Hop's problems hit close to home. In the late 1980s, Hop took local Modesto police on a high-speed chase in a futile attempt to escape a drug bust. The story hit the front pages of local newspapers.

Strangers were shocked to read the headlines about the politician's brother. Locals, however, knew Hop was a sweet man with a bad problem that quietly plagued the Central Valley—methamphetamines. And they knew the saying about the Condit boys—"Gary writes the law, Hop breaks the law, and Burl enforces the law"—was not tongue in cheek.

Gary's last legislative initiative before leaving the state legislature for Congress was an overhaul of California's drug laws. When he left for Washington, he publicly promised to push to have money budgeted for the military moved to budgets to combat the war on drugs at home.

⁓

The road into town was gridlocked, packed from line to line with motorcycles and trailers carrying motorcycles. Women in tight jeans and cropped shirts clung loosely to the back of men in leather cuts.

Gary took two cigars from a bag, and he and Flammini relaxed, watching the feral parade of free people. They had pulled off the road to wait until the traffic let up in the evening.

A green Volkswagen minibus parked behind them. Two young women jumped out.

The women began unloading boxes. As they worked, Gary realized they were T-shirt vendors and climbed off his bike. "Need a hand?" he offered, approaching the van.

"Please," one of the women replied. "We've got a dozen more."

Gary and the women made small talk while he helped them unload their boxes. When they were finished, the brunette put a hand on Gary's forearm. "Can you do me another favor?" she asked.

"Sure," he replied.

"Take me for a ride, just up the road. I want to see how it feels."

"Of course, darling."

She followed Gary to his motorcycle. He got on, then she got on behind him, wrapping her arms around his waist. He pulled the motorcycle onto the road and they disappeared.

"What'd you do?" Flammini demanded when Gary returned a short while later.

"It's none of your fucking business."

STAY IN THE BOX

For almost a year, Ken Starr, the independent counsel, had dripped sordid details of the alleged affair between President Bill Clinton and Monica Lewinsky to the press while withholding the full results of his investigation from members of Congress.

Gary sat on the House Oversight and Government Reform Committee, which now devoted nearly all of its time to addressing the myriad of allegations and congressional investigations concerning the president's conduct. Gary and Congressman Henry Waxman, the chairman of the reform committee, held a joint press conference to draw the public's attention to the massive amounts of public resources being deployed by politicians to investigate other politicians.

"Tens of millions of hard-earned taxpayers' dollars have been squandered and Congress's preoccupation with partisan investigations has diverted us from addressing the real concerns of the American people," Waxman said as he stood behind a podium in a press room. "For years, my colleague Gary Condit has been a leader in the effort to try to bring federal spending under control . . . Earlier this year he asked a simple question: 'What are all these investigations costing the taxpayers?'"

When Waxman finished, he and Gary took questions from reporters.

"Mr. Condit, would you care to expound on how you see the impeachment inquiry?" a reporter asked.

"[W]e need to put some limits on ourselves. We need to put some timelines. We need to have a mission for each investigation. It cannot be just open-ended and go on forever and ever," Gary replied.

On October 8, 1998, Gary joined 31 other Democrats and 227 Republicans voting in favor of opening a formal congressional inquiry into whether the president committed perjury or obstructed justice. In Gary's view, opening a formal congressional inquiry was the only way to take control of the investigation away from Starr, partisan congressional committees, and the crisis-feeding cable news networks.

"The American people want us to bring this issue to closure," Gary explained, standing on the House floor. "There is no reason why every member of this House cannot have that information. We are not grade school kids. We understand it, and we know ultimately we need to make a decision. So my intent, Mr. Speaker, is simply to speed this process along so that we can make a decision and get back to the business of living our lives and running this country."

Gary went to see Congressman Dick Gephardt, the House minority leader, and told Gephardt he was going to resign from the government reform committee because he didn't come to Congress to talk about blowjobs. Gephardt asked him not to.

The resignation of a senior Democrat from the reform committee would be spun by Republican pundits as a negative reflection on the president at a time where it was unclear whether he had the votes in Congress to avoid actual impeachment.

Instead, Gephardt arranged for Gary to be reassigned to the House Permanent Select Committee on Intelligence.

Gary couldn't believe his luck. He'd long contemplated making a move into international issues.

His move to the intel committee didn't make any waves. He had voted in favor of the first Gulf War against Iraq in 1991. People assumed he'd be a hawk. Gary would soon prove that he wasn't, starting with Kosovo.

The Clinton administration was struggling to get a clear read on how the impeachment vote in the House would shake out within the president's own party.

On December 15, 1998, the *New York Times* published a list of "conservative" House Democrats who had stated they would vote in favor of impeachment, or who hadn't yet made up their mind. "Gary Condit" wasn't on that list. But many of the "unknowns" were fellow Blue Dog Democrats.

After hearing a report on the upstart Fox News network that ridiculed the president, Gary called the White House and let them know he was available to talk, "if the president wants to."

Fifteen minutes later, the White House called Gary's office.

Although Gary was moving off the government reform committee, he was still the leader of the Blue Dogs.

"How bad is it out there?" the president asked.

"It's bad, Mr. President."

"It feels really bad."

"It is. Don't get caught up in what is going on in Congress. Don't let anybody talk you into doing something you don't want to do. I just wanted to say I think you should stay in the box, Mr. President."

Many members of Congress and the political press expected Gary, the son of a Baptist preacher, would share their moral outrage and vote in favor of impeaching the president. They were taken aback when, instead, he told Congress the president's behavior was inexcusable and indefensible, but added "to overturn the electoral will of the American people requires a much higher threshold than personal misconduct."

On December 19, 1998, four articles of impeachment against President Clinton were brought to a vote in the United States House of Representatives.

As reported by the *Washington Post*, Gary voted as follows:

Article 1 Perjury Before the Grand Jury, Gary Condit (D-CA), NO.

Article 2 Perjury in a Civil Lawsuit, Gary Condit (D-CA), NO.

Article 3 Obstruction of Justice, Gary Condit (D-CA), NO.

Article 4 Abuse of Power, Gary Condit (D-CA), NO.

COLD CASE CAPITAL

The nation's capital had the highest homicide rate among major US cities, and the lowest rate of solving homicides, earning it the title "Cold Case Capital."

In 1998, Charles Ramsey was named the chief of the Washington, DC, Metropolitan Police Department. Ramsey vowed to clean up corruption in the police force. "I have never seen a place with so much wrong. You have to treat the bleeding, stop it first, before you can even address the cancer," Ramsey told reporters.

Ramsey hired Terrance Gainer as the department's deputy assistant police chief. Gainer had risen quickly through the ranks of the Chicago police. Once in Washington, he took to television cameras like a moth to light with a bigger-than-life personality.

✻

It snowed, and then it rained on January 9, 1999. Just around 8:20 p.m., Joyce Chiang exited the Starbucks coffee shop in Dupont Circle.

She wore a thigh-length green coat and a red velvet scarf. The coat looked too big on her petite figure. Shoulder-length black hair framed her brown eyes, and plastic grocery bags wrapped around her socks and tied at her ankles were hidden beneath her shoes. She learned this trick growing up in Chicago.

Joyce's friend had dropped her off in front of the Starbucks, at the intersection of Connecticut Avenue NW and R Street NW. She planned to walk the four city blocks from the Starbucks to the two-bedroom apartment she shared with her brother, Roger.

In the alleyway behind her, a message had been written in white on a red brick wall:

GOOD DAY J.C. MAY I NEVER MISS THE THRILL OF BEING NEAR YOU!!

✻

Joyce was twenty-eight years old and the second youngest of four siblings born to Taiwanese immigrants.

John, her older brother, was an elected official in California. Roger, her youngest brother, was the "advance man" for Andrew Cuomo, the secretary of the US Department of Housing and Urban Development.

She also had the political itch. Joyce had interned in California congressman Howard Berman's office on Capitol Hill while she attended night classes at Georgetown Law School.

Interning on Capitol Hill was the most common entry point into a career in national politics. She enjoyed the energy, an exciting mix of young, smart, and driven people competing to befriend the powerful men and women who ran the country.

After graduating from law school, she took a job at the US Immigration and Naturalization Service.

✻

Roger could tell that his sister wasn't home.

It's Saturday. She'll come home later or she's at a friend's place, he thought as he entered the apartment.

Later that night, Joyce's pager buzzed. She had left it in her bedroom, inside her briefcase. Roger didn't hear it. The number on the pager's screen belonged to a pay phone inside Dulles International Airport.

The next morning, a few miles from DuPont Circle, a couple jogging on a trail inside Anacostia Park found a black billfold resting on top of the white snow. It belonged to a stranger: Joyce Chiang. The couple turned the billfold over to the Park Police, the agency responsible for law-enforcement matters in the park and monument areas of DC.

On Monday morning Joyce's room was still empty.

Alarmed, Roger called Joyce's friends. The last time anyone had heard from her was Saturday evening before she was dropped off in front of the Starbucks in DuPont Circle.

Joyce's boss at the INS called his contact at the FBI. The FBI and the Metro Police opened an investigation into Joyce's disappearance.

—

Days passed without progress.

Joyce's family posted a $5,000 reward for information that would lead them to her. Weekly candlelight vigils were held for her at the Dupont Circle fountain.

Roger retraced Joyce's known steps on January 9—the day she was last seen—ending his search at the Starbucks on Connecticut Avenue.

After talking to the baristas inside, he searched under and around the newspaper stands out front. He then walked to the alley behind the building. There, a message was scribbled in white lettering on the dirty brick wall:

GOOD DAY J.C. MAY I NEVER MISS THE THRILL OF BEING NEAR YOU!!

Within an hour of getting Roger's call, an FBI agent arrived in the alley. The agent used his fingernail to scrape a small piece of the white paint from the red wall. After a brief inspection, the agent turned to Roger and told him that the paint had been on that wall long before Joyce's disappearance.

Nearby, Joyce's friends posted fliers with her picture on them. They approached a Metro Police car parked on Connecticut Avenue, near the Starbucks, and offered copies of the fliers to the two officers sitting inside.

"We haven't heard of Joyce Chiang," the officer in the driver's seat explained.

The Chiang family learned that the Metro Police Department had not listed Joyce's case as a missing person's investigation. There had been no coordination across law-enforcement agencies.

—

On January 17, a local Washington, DC, news station ran a feature on Joyce's disappearance. Other news outlets followed as her story matriculated into the national news cycles.

The Metro Police abruptly began wrestling the FBI for jurisdiction over case no. 020-963, and deputy assistant police chief Terrance Gainer made himself the press's point person in law enforcement for the investigation. From this point onward, the Chiang family found itself in a constant race to keep up with Gainer's comments to reporters, true and untrue.

The couple that discovered Joyce's billfold in Anacostia Park recognized Joyce's photo in media coverage and called the FBI. It was the first the FBI had heard of it.

The FBI organized a search of Anacostia Park, and on January 21 Joyce's oversized green coat, keys, grocery card, black gloves, and Blockbuster video card were discovered in a secluded grassy area, near the north gate of the Anacostia Naval Station. The location was not far from where her billfold had been picked up the day after she was last seen. The green coat was torn down its back.

Nearby, investigators found Joyce's government access card wrapped in pages from a newspaper dated January 12, three days after Joyce was last seen at the Starbucks in Dupont Circle.

Roger watched news coverage of helicopters hovering over Anacostia Park and lines of FBI agents marching through its open fields.

He couldn't stomach the coverage. He flipped through news programs. The major cable networks were slowly transitioning their attention away from the Monica Lewinsky scandal to the worsening situation in Kosovo.

The highly publicized search for Joyce lasted days, but ended without resolution. Shortly after the search ended, a local radio station, citing police sources, reported it was possible Joyce had committed suicide.

—✎—

Roger had a coil wrapped around his chest, and wires ran from his left arm and one of his index fingers to a polygraph box sitting on a table.

"Do you know what happened to your sister Joyce on January 9, 1999?" the polygraph examiner asked.

"No," Roger answered.

More questions followed.

"Mr. Chiang," the examiner said when he had finished. "These results are inconclusive. This means there isn't enough to conclude that you were telling the truth but there is enough to exclude you as a possible suspect."

Roger gathered his stuff and left. As he entered the main lobby an FBI agent marched aggressively toward him.

"I know you're providing information to the press," the agent warned.

"I'm hearing things from the press before I get them from you. Terrance Gainer is the problem, not me!" Roger responded.

Less than ten minutes later, Roger received a call from a reporter for the *Washington Post.* "What were the results of your polygraph exam?" the reporters asked.

Within two hours, CBS News reported Roger had taken a polygraph examination and that the results were not yet known. To many people, Roger was now a suspect in his sister's disappearance.

With nothing real coming out of the stalled investigation, news outlets unleashed a rash of wild theories. Some of them hurt more than others, like the well-publicized report that the FBI was investigating connections between Joyce and Asian prostitution rings.

—✎—

On April 1, a paddler pulled his canoe across the glass top of the Potomac River toward its shore in southern Fairfax County. As he neared the riverbank, an odd shape floating on the surface caught his eye.

The FBI called Roger to inform him there was a 50 percent chance the body belonged to Joyce. The corpse was so badly decomposed the medical examiner needed more time.

Several days later, the *Washington Post* reported Joyce's ATM card had been found inside a shoe attached to the body. A plastic bag wrapped around the foot had protected the debit card from the Potomac.

Congressman Berman paid tribute to Joyce on the floor of the US House of Representatives. "Mr. Speaker, I am truly heartbroken today to rise to say a final farewell to my friend and former staff member, Joyce Chiang . . . I cherished her friendship."

The medical examiner concluded that the cause of Joyce's death was "undetermined."

The FBI had no leads. The Metro Police had no interest in further pursuing case no. 020-963. The media's interest in the story had gone away.

WARNING SIGNS

POKING THE BEAR

LED BY THE UNITED STATES MILITARY, North Atlantic Treaty Organization (NATO) forces commenced aerial bombing against Serbian government infrastructure in Yugoslavia.

The Clinton administration was unable to obtain a formal war resolution from the United Nations or the United States Congress and, as a result, prosecuted the war through NATO. But without a resolution from Congress, funding for the NATO-led war would soon dry up.

The administration organized a congressional delegation, or CODEL, to visit Kosovo in an effort to gin up congressional support for ongoing operations. The list of attendees included influential members of Congress, including Gary, who, as the leader of the Blue Dogs, controlled critical swing votes in the House.

On Thursday, July 22, 1999, the CODEL members stepped off a US Air Force plane onto a runway at an airfield in Macedonia. At 10:45 a.m. local time, the group arrived at a military compound in Kosovo. They were first briefed by the commander of NATO's KFOR forces and then led to an airplane hangar, where Hashim Thaçi, the thirty-one-year-old head of the Kosovo Liberation Army (KLA), waited.

"Thaçi's been working with us," a State Department official informed Gary. "He's the head of the Albanian provincial government and the KLA."

"I'm aware," Gary replied.

The intel committee had been briefed on the CIA's program to arm and train the KLA, although many inside the US government considered the KLA a terrorist organization, and it had known ties to the al-Qaeda terrorist group.

"More men come every day. From all places. Men are training in Albania. But we need more help from America," Thaçi explained. "We need more weapons, and we need NATO to keep bombing the Serbian army."

Gary knew many of the KLA's fighters were mujahedeen flooding in from Afghanistan and Yemen, the aftermath of the US government's war against the Soviet Union.

When the meeting with Thaçi ended, CODEL members were taken to a village designated by NATO as a war crimes area.

The CODEL's caravan stopped in a cul-de-sac surrounded by homes riddled with bullet holes and mortar-round cavities. NATO soldiers secured the location.

A group of local men were huddled near one of the homes, smoking cigarettes. As the CODEL members approached, the group's leader waved his arms and pointed his fingers, as he explained in broken English the predicament faced by locals.

Gary followed the movement of the man's hands conducting a symphony of the surrounding violence, and gathered that the village men did not belong to the KLA. They had been driven into the mountains by Serbian government forces.

When the man was finished, he and his colleagues looked to the CODEL members for a response.

"Why don't you fight?" Gary asked them. He had just met the KLA and knew what they were. He felt that it was critical for him to know whether able-bodied men other than the KLA were willing to take up the fight for their country.

It appeared to Gary that his answer had perplexed the local men and upset the American officials who had brought him there.

—

After his trip to Kosovo, the House Permanent Select Committee on Intelligence, which now included Gary, was briefed on US intelligence and counterintelligence activities in and around Yugoslavia in the months leading up to the NATO-led campaign against the Serbian government. US spies, Gary learned, had made clandestine purchases of media outlets in Macedonia and deployed them to encourage instability in neighboring Yugoslavia.

Gary believed that the clandestine services were effectively dictating America's foreign policy in the dark, and that the precedent of allowing the intelligence community and executive branch to unilaterally start and fight wars abroad by grounding them in simple moral terms like "genocide" and "crimes against humanity" would turn Congress, and the American people, into the bankers of perpetual war.

Shortly after Gary returned from Kosovo, he and Rep. Tim Roemer wrote a joint letter to President Clinton formally stating their opposition to the continued use of US funds for counterintelligence efforts in Yugoslavia.

Gary, fresh to the intel committee, had just taken a shot across the bow of the most surreptitious people in the world.

—

Gary expected the intelligence report in front of him to conclude Slobodan Milošević would soon be taken to The Hague for trial on war crimes charges. But the report contained a slight hedge—a suggestion that the legal case against Milošević wasn't airtight.

"We're not going to prosecute him?" Gary asked, sitting behind a microphone inside the Intelligence Committee's hearing room.

"Congressman, that's not what we're suggesting. It's complicated—that's just a possibility based on a number of factors," an intelligence official responded.

"With all due respect, this isn't complicated. You don't just raise a flag and we all charge up the hill. If you're not sure we'll convict him, then I want to know why," Gary replied.

The next morning, at 8:00 a.m., Gary sat behind a table in a secured room with no windows and one door. Two intel committee staffers and a group of government attorneys had just finished walking him through the legal case against Milošević.

"Congressman, we can't be certain what will happen in a legal forum. We know he's guilty. But knowing that and proving it in court are different things."

The problem they faced was one of degrees. The evidence was two, or three, or fifty steps removed from the man they called the Devil. Milošević had taken great care to avoid leaving direct connections between acts on the ground by Serbian forces and his presidential office in Belgrade. As a result, they feared there might not be enough evidence to assure his conviction in court.

He won't be another Pinochet, Gary thought as he broke the vault's uncomfortable silence.

"We've got a guy responsible for killing innocent people. We told the world we had proof, and we acted militarily," Gary replied.

"Congressman . . ." one of the attorneys started.

Gary gently raised his right hand to signal he wasn't interested in a debate with lawyers. "Americans are sensitive to words like 'genocide.' We can't use those words, and charge uphill, and not be prepared to do what is necessary in public to show we were right. Even if that means we lose in court."

Gary feared there was another reason some in the US government didn't want Milošević to face a trial. An open international court proceeding might expose American clandestine activities in the region leading up to and during the NATO campaign, and it might expand to cover potential crimes committed by the Kosovo Liberation Army.

ENRON

In California, massive spikes in electricity rates and threats of blackouts were hammering residents. The press laid blame for the energy crisis on Gary's old friend, state senator Steve Peace, and Gary's closest political ally, California governor Gray Davis.

James J. Hoecker, chairman of the Federal Energy Regulatory Commission (FERC), met Peace at the US Grant Hotel in downtown San Diego.

"We're going to investigate," Hoecker assured Peace.

"Investigate?" Peace demanded. "You have the evidence to act now. Enron bet wrong and lost billions. Now they've doubled down through their own frigging trading floor. They're damn crooks." He was referring to the Houston-based energy company whose acts of accounting fraud led to one of the largest corporate bankruptcies in history.

Hoecker's poker face made it clear that he was not buying into Peace's extreme view of Enron. But, he conceded, "We underestimated the situation."

"Then do something."

"If I get pegged as anti-dereg, the entire industry will oppose me. Let me get past the election. I have a shot at being reappointed even if Gore loses to Bush, so long as I don't appear to be pro-regulation," Hoecker urged.

"I've got no choice," Peace acknowledged.

That evening, Peace called the only person in Washington, DC, he thought had the guts and, as the leader of the Blue Dogs, the clout to force the federal government to confront Enron: Rep. Gary Condit.

KHANDET

A large fist pounded on the front door of the Condits' home.

"Vince," Carolyn whispered, putting her coffee down on the kitchen table. Gary entered the kitchen and kissed her cheek.

As always, Gary picked up his small brown leather travel bag and left the house.

Flammini and Gary climbed into Gary's white Dodge Durango.

"Lynch called me last night," Gary said as the SUV pulled off the freeway into San Francisco International Airport. "He said you're not getting anything done."

"Lynch is out to get me," Flammini insisted.

"That's not true," Gary replied, although the truth was complicated.

In Lynch's view, Flammini was poisonous. And as much as Gary talked about compassion and loyalty, Lynch didn't think Flammini had the capacity for either. Lynch had "gotten rid of" Flammini two or three times, but each time Gary had convinced Lynch to bring him back, arguing, "Mike, have some compassion for him."

"Why didn't you call me if you had a problem?" Gary insisted when he discussed the matter with Lynch later.

"I can't get ahold of you."

"That's bullshit. You can always use the answering service."

Gary had a number that took callers directly to an answering service. When you called, you were greeted by soft music followed by a beep. Gary could check messages to this line from any phone, at any time. He gave this number out to constituents and friends. He gave his cell phone number only to his family and closest personal friends.

A flight attendant approached Gary's seat on the United Airlines flight bound from San Francisco to Washington, DC.

Gary hadn't met her before—which was strange. He had taken this Monday morning United flight nearly every week for the last decade.

"Anything to eat?" she asked.

"No thank you. I brought a granola bar," Gary replied as he sipped cranberry juice.

"Is it good?"

"Tastes like peanut butter," he said, pulling off a small piece and handing it to her. He guessed she was in her mid-thirties.

"Thanks," she answered, popping the morsel in her mouth. "I'm Anne Marie."

"That's a pretty name. I'm Gary."

"What do you do?"

"I work in government."

"What do you do in government, Gary?"

"I'm a congressman."

"I work in government—FBI," she teased.

"Let me know if you think anything suspicious is going on," he replied with a grin.

Anne Marie Smith asked about tours of Washington. Gary offered to help set some up for her, and gave her the phone number for his answering service.

—

A man with the screen-name "<Khandet>" sat behind his computer, deftly navigating his favorite Internet chat room.

Session Start: 8:00 PM

> **<maeri {MF}'>** squirms and wiggles
>
> **<Khandet>** d e a d, huh
>
> **<Khandet>** you are not the typical slut around here mary
>
> **<maeri {MF}'>** winds around your leg again, pressing in close and rubbing her face along your thigh
>
> **<Khandet>** no wait, I am supposed to use you like a slutty fuck toy
>
> **<maeri {MF}'>** wiggles, squirming at the thought, cunt juice running down her legs.
>
> **<Khandet>** what thought is that?
>
> **<maeri {MF}'>** being used like a slutty fuck toy, Master, coming by your place and letting you tie me up and have your way with me
>
> **<maeri {MF}'>** Master, this girl is very submissive in terms of relationships and sexuality although she would say she can hold her ground intellectually
>
> **<Khandet>** I have a surprise party for a retiring member . . .
>
> **<maeri {MF}'>** who's retiring
>
> **<Khandet>** Budget chairman
>
> * maeri giggles.
>
> **<Khandet>** Anyway . . . are we going to meet? It's a bit of an unequal yoke because you're so young . . .
>
> **<maeri {MF}'>** I have a friend in town . . .
>
> **<Khandet>** I don't have to be in love with you, but I do love women as a general rule—does that make sense
>
> **<maeri {MF}'>** it does Master
>
> * Khandet smiles.

Session Close: 8:53 PM

<Khandet> exited the chat room and turned off the computer.

The yellow eyes of a giant cardboard cutout of a blue dog followed him as he exited the office and entered the empty hall in the Rayburn House Office Building.

CHAPTER 4

INTERN

POLITICAL FIELD TRIP

OCTOBER WAS AT ITS END. Restless clouds refused to coalesce in the cool air and streaked the sky in faint brushstrokes that gave little resistance to fall's deceptive sunlight. Sirens, Washington, DC's fight song, wailed in all directions, and busy footsteps hit the pavement with thuds.

As he did most weekday mornings, Mike Dayton pulled a white Ford Explorer to the curb in front of the Lynshire building in Adams Morgan. It was a short drive from there to the Rayburn House Office Building.

A plain dark suit complimented Dayton's slim body. His hair was cut tight around his head, face clean-shaven, coat pressed, and shirt ironed. Black-rimmed glasses made him look younger than he really was, although he was only thirty years old. He had a polished yet boyish look that disarmed strangers.

Dayton was a local "boy" from Condit Country, born in Oakdale, which claimed to be "the Cowboy Capital of the World" and was fifteen minutes from Modesto. Chad Condit first met Dayton at a charity golf tournament when the two boys were in high school. Chad introduced Dayton to his father, and not long after Dayton graduated from high school, Gary hired him to work in his Modesto district office. He soon became an integral part of Gary's political operation, and of the Condit family. Gary asked Dayton to serve as his right-hand man on Capitol Hill.

Dayton managed the office, the Beltway press, and relationships with other congressional offices. Despite his youth, insiders respected Dayton's soft-spoken demeanor in an environment where most people were hyped on ego or ambition. His answers were thoughtful, and his conclusions were measured. He was, in large part, a reflection of Gary, content to operate behind the scenes.

Dayton chuckled at the sight of Gary skipping down the front steps of the Lynshire with a child's energy. Gary didn't carry a briefcase or have a cell phone strapped to his ear. Even by congressional standards, Gary was a Luddite. He didn't use e-mail, and could barely operate a computer. Dayton thought Gary was a bit of a roughneck with an itch of bohemian he had to scratch from time to time. In pieces, nothing about Gary made sense. But, somehow, for people who knew him well, they all fit.

⌒

Gary passed a wooden credenza as he entered his private office.

A giant cardboard cutout of a blue dog with yellow eyes was affixed to the wall above it. George Rodrigue, the Cajun artist, had given Gary the cutout.

His desk, which he had placed under a window, was a hulking piece of dark red wood that had been assigned to him on his first day in Congress. In its bottom drawer, Gary kept gifts he had received from visitors. In the top drawer he maintained a collection of gifts to hand out to visitors so that he was never caught empty handed.

Most of the gifts in the top drawer had been purchased by Carolyn. The current inventory included seven sets of silver cuff links and a half-dozen gold bracelets, purchased at a high-end gift store in San Francisco.

Near the front door Gary had two freestanding coat racks that he used to hang hats on. At any time he had anywhere from twenty to thirty hats on the racks, most all of them given to him as gifts associated with a political event. When kids visited, Gary often let them pick out a hat from the rack as a gift before they left.

—

"Two women from the district are here. Do you want to say hello?" Dayton said as he stepped inside Gary's private office.

"Sure," Gary replied.

Dayton led Jennifer Baker and Chandra Levy into his office. The two women, both graduate students from California, often met at lunch and walked "the Hill" in an effort to meet influential people. They called their walks "political field trips."

Jennifer had straight brown hair and wore a white turtleneck under a knit sweater. Chandra's hair was also brown, but full of unruly curls. She wore a necklace that sat on top of a soft sweater and had a small mouth with a pretty smile.

Chandra explained that she was from Modesto and had started an internship at the Bureau of Prisons. Jennifer, however, was still looking to land an internship.

Gary asked Dayton to check whether they had room to hire Jennifer as an intern or, if not, could help arrange one for her with another Blue Dog.

The young women asked if they could take a photo with Gary before parting.

Chandra handed her camera to one of Gary's staff members.

"Can I get another photo?" Chandra asked.

The staffer took a second photo on Chandra's camera.

This time only Gary and Chandra were in the picture.

CONGRESS

A buzzer went off overhead, and members filed out of the Democrats' cloakroom onto the blue-carpeted floor of the US House of Representatives.

Member seating in the House is arranged in a semicircle that is bifurcated by a wide center aisle. The more repulsed a member is by the political leanings of another group, the farther away from that group he or she sits.

The most liberal members of the Democratic Party sit out at one end of the semicircle's diameter just a short walk from their cloakroom, followed by less liberal members, and so on and so forth so that, ultimately, the Democrats are spread out from the most liberal to the moderate members, like a fan of paint colors moving from blue to green to yellow at the center aisle.

From the other side of the House floor, Republican members filed out of their cloakroom. Purist conservatives sit the farthest away from the stench of liberals, near the entrance to the Republicans' cloakroom, then fan their way toward the center aisle where the moderate party members sit, moving from red to orange to yellow.

Gary made his way to the center of the room.

At political roasts, Gary frequently brought the house down by telling guests, "You have to remember, guys, that no matter what you think, I'm the guy both sides have invited to switch parties, and I've declined them both."

For many Democrats, Gary's pragmatism undermined the party's purpose. In 1995, he authored a bill to prevent Congress from imposing unfunded mandates on state and local governments. Because of his experience, Gary understood what was happening at the ground level as a consequence of the race to make policy at the national level. His bill would have put an end to "blank check" legislating from Washington by requiring Congress to define how it would fund any new mandate as a condition to passing it into law.

The Democratic leadership "asked" Gary to drop the effort, but he refused to do so and a version of his bill was slated for conference committee. In response, Democratic minority leader Dick Gephardt took the unprecedented step of refusing to appoint Gary, the bill's author, to the committee.

Republican Speaker of the House Newt Gingrich made his own unprecedented move by appointing Gary, a Democrat, to the conference committee. Gingrich's move was a public statement that if the Democrats wanted to throw Gary out, the wolves would welcome him with open arms.

Still, Gary wasn't liked by all Republicans.

He was pro-choice, for starters. Worse, Gary had repeatedly opposed loosening Wall Street regulations, culminating with his opposition to the repeal of Glass-Steagall provisions that separated retail and investment banking operations. Many conservatives thought Gary was, at his core, a pro-regulation populist.

Gary's brand of nonpartisan politics was an existential threat to the powerful interests benefiting from a polarized body politic. If his enemies found an opening, they'd rush in from both sides of the center aisle and squeeze him out.

He survived because of Condit Country. Nobody, and no institution, could credibly threaten to unseat him. In an era in which the public felt increasingly alienated by politicians, Condit's simple brand of retail politics, stretched over three decades of service, had accomplished what few of his generation of politicians could approach—independence.

The Blue Dogs were now well positioned and established in Washington, DC, and Gary was intent on parlaying his experience into opportunities with international dimensions. The sky was the limit for Gary, Lynch, and Dayton. Gary would have to do something reckless to jeopardize what they had built.

⤚

The first vote of the day was the consent calendar—approving the action of the day before. Little else was discussed, because everyone was preoccupied with "hanging chads" in Florida. The results of the 2000 presidential election could hinge on how fragments of partially punched paper ballots were interpreted.

Gary walked off the floor.

Dayton met Gary in the cloakroom to brief him on messages that had been left for him with the office, and to go over his afternoon schedule.

"Anything else going on?" Gary asked.

"A woman came by looking for you; said you met on the plane. I think her last name was Smith." Dayton handed Gary a piece of paper with a phone number scribbled on it. "She said you could reach her at this number."

"Good looking?" Gary replied.

Dayton looked, reticently, at his boss.

—

When Gary got to his office he found Chandra Levy waiting for him in the reception area.

A month had passed since they first met. In that period, Chandra had visited his office a handful of times. She had asked him for career advice—more than anything, Chandra wanted to get a job with the FBI or CIA. She had also asked for help with a paper she had to write.

Gary motioned for her to follow him into his private office.

Chandra sat on the couch. "Just want to throw some more ideas at you about my paper."

"I have all kinds of books over there," he offered, pointing at a large cardboard box. "They're public policy books. Authors write something and they want us to read it."

Chandra walked to the box.

"I don't want to take these unless you want to give them to me," she explained.

"I leave them out like that so people can take them. I don't have time to read them. You'd be doing me a favor."

A staff member entered, handed him a letter, and left.

Chandra pulled a book from the box and turned to face him. He was still standing over his desk.

"Do you live here alone?" she asked.

"My family lives in Ceres."

"Is this your family?" she asked, moving to a glass cabinet that displayed framed photos of Carolyn, the kids, and the grandkids.

"Yes."

"I'll bring this back," she said, lifting the book.

"It's yours."

"Where does your name come from?" Gary asked as he walked to where she stood near the cabinet.

"It means 'moon' in Sanskrit."

"It's pretty."

"I'm glad you think so," she replied.

"Gary," a staffer interrupted, standing in the open doorway. "Your committee meeting."

"I'll be out in a second."

"Can I e-mail you?" Chandra asked.

"I don't use e-mail. But I check the answering service."

"I'll call."

Chandra stopped at the credenza near the entrance of his office. She picked up a framed photo of Gary with four other men.

"Is this the Gang of Five?" she asked.

"You know about that?"

"I worked in Sacramento. Everybody knows about Willie Brown vs. the Gang of Five. But, what's the real story?"

"It was never really about Willie. I'll have to tell that story later—I've got to run."

As Gary moved past the couch toward the door, he pointed at the cardboard cutout of the blue dog above the credenza and added: "Without that Gang of Five in Sacramento, there'd be no Blue Dogs on the Hill."

GANG OF FIVE
1989–1990

Gary quickly emerged out of the California state assembly class of 1982 as one of the most trusted and powerful members of Speaker Willie Brown's inner circle.

Privately, however, Gary grew frustrated by a policy drift that seemed increasingly out of sync with Condit Country. He wasn't the only moderate Democratic who felt the party leadership was moving far left of their constituents.

Gary joined with four other younger Democrats—Rusty Areias, Steve Peace, Jerry Eaves, and Charles Calderon—to press compromises on issues that had been stalled by politics. The first fight broke out when the five joined with moderate Republicans to pass no-fault auto insurance reform that was opposed by trial lawyers. Trial lawyers were the biggest campaign contributors to Democrats.

The schism leaked into public view when the five Democrats announced they would vote to confirm Senate minority leader Ken Maddy as state treasurer if the Republican governor made the nomination. Maddy was a moderate and universally respected Republican from the Central Valley—and a close friend of Speaker Brown.

The problem wasn't Maddy. It was math. The assembly had eighty members comprised of thirty-six Republicans and forty-four Democrats. When the five Democrats went public, they undercut the leadership of both parties. The Democrats couldn't bargain, and the right-wing Republicans couldn't hide.

Senior Democrats demanded that the Speaker punish the five rogue Democrats. Lobbyists delivered less than subtle messages to the five, making it clear they would pay a heavy political price if they didn't stop leveraging their ability to swing the vote in the assembly.

Convinced the Democrats were on a path to losing the majority, and that the brewing populist threat of a term limit initiative would be unstoppable unless Democrats reversed the trend toward increased partisanship, the five dug in. Soon press stories emerged branding them, collectively, as "the Gang of Five."

For more than a decade after the civil rights movement and the Vietnam War, Democrats held off legislation increasing criminal penalties by burying bills in committee where they would not be brought to a vote.

Republicans exploited the practice for political advantage by pushing unrealistically extreme language that Democrats could be counted upon to oppose. It was a purely political exercise designed to provide fodder for Republican attack ads at election time.

Technically, a majority of the full assembly could vote to extract a bill from committee for a floor vote. The unwritten rule was that such an act was in effect an act of sedition against the leaderships of both the majority and the minority. It was a divide-and-conquer strategy that diminished the influence of moderates from both sides.

The five Democrats began working with a group of moderate Republicans to force compromises, and to then cast their votes to bring that compromise legislation to the assembly floor for a vote.

In a short, frenzied period, the legislature passed wiretapping laws, streamlined the process for seizing and selling the assets of convicted drug traffickers, cracked down on the sale of chemicals used to make designer drugs, established the first statewide anti-gang task force, widened the legal definition of pornography, and required AIDS testing for arrested prostitutes and prisoners.

After a decade of relaxing criminal penalties and rising crime rates, the die had turned. "The police lobby appeared to win on almost every front," one reporter wrote under a headline stating that this was a banner year for law and order. Attribution for the sudden change wasn't given to either political party but rather to the Gang of Five.

The chairman of the Democratic Party publicly threatened all five, telling them they'd committed career suicide.

The only person capable of resolving the discord was the Speaker—Willie Brown Jr., the self-proclaimed "Ayatollah of the Assembly."

━

The Speaker controlled everything: political appointments, committee assignments, campaign contributions, and office assignments and budgets, right down to the carpet on which a member stood.

Willie wielded that power with a style wholly his own. His tastes included $6,000 Brioni suits, and he had a car collection rivaling those of his movie star friends. Born poor in segregated Texas, no one had given him anything.

Willie was a "members' Speaker." He doled out favors and protected rank-and-file legislators from both parties. In return, he expected loyalty, and his punishments were swift and severe for those who didn't show it.

During Gary's first six years in the legislature, Willie was his mentor. Gary reminded Willie of "his Texas folks in the way his cleverness was homespun and his smarts were genuine." They shared southern mannerisms, although neither man flouted their southern roots.

Like Willie, Gary wore the latest New York fashions and had an interest in world music. "A cat from Modesto—dressed like that. He wasn't an old-timer in any way . . . many members elected are already old-timers . . . he was not shopworn in any way. His enthusiasm, his demeanor all spoke of things to come rather than things that had been," Willie later recalled.

Willie introduced Gary to the decision makers. He made Gary the chairman of the Government Organization Committee, which had jurisdiction over industries including tobacco and gambling. It was the choicest of all committee posts because it put whoever was in charge in the position to be able to raise boatloads of campaign contributions.

In 1984, when Gary drew no opposition in his reelection campaign, Willie made Gary assistant majority leader.

This wasn't the way it was supposed to be. Gary represented a "marginal" Democratic district and lacked seniority. He should have been dependent on the Democratic caucus. But Willie and Gary had a special bond that was both political and personal.

In 1985, Willie celebrated his fifty-second birthday. He invited fifty-two friends to a party at George Hamilton's house in Beverly Hills. The invite list included Sammy Davis Jr., Joan Collins—and Gary Condit.

For many years, Willie and Gary could be found sitting together at nightspots in and around Sacramento, the two men talking politics and socializing with the political groupies common to capital towns.

Willie claimed he had never been drunk in his life. Gary did not drink at all.

They shared a different interest.

As soon they were seated, Willie would routinely ask, "Where are the good-looking women in the room?" And Gary would promptly answer, "Willie, there are three of them. Right there . . . right there . . . and over there."

Willie didn't believe in apologizing for extramarital affairs.

I can think of very few holders of major office in American life, including women, who have not had private relationships along the way. And yet invariably it seems that when these relationships are exposed, the politicians apologize. Enemies, schemers, the self-righteous are, of course, going to be looking for relationships they think are improper or out of which (quite foolishly) they think they can make political hay. When confronted, you just have to say it's nobody's business but your own. I think the public relishes the idea of having someone who's actually alive holding down public office . . . If you're going to have a reputation, have one for your dashing ways, not for your tears.

In this regard, Willie and Gary couldn't have been more different. Although rumors sometimes circulated that Gary, too, had girlfriends in Sacramento, proof was always absent.

One of those late nights, Willie decided to share with Gary his past as a shoeshine in Texas before bolting for California.

"Why don't you talk about that stuff? It's a great story. People can relate to that," Gary responded.

"Why the fuck would I let them picture me as a shoeshine?" Willie answered. He understood that the market for public discussion of private lives is limited almost exclusively to the exaggerated and the negative.

—z—

Despite the tight bond between Gary and Willie, the Gang of Five began pushing measures for political and government reform. Willie's inner circle fumed. "The boys are coming off the reservation!" Democratic assemblyman Phillip Isenberg warned him.

Willie tried to downplay the significance of the brewing fight. "I can't worry too terribly much about how doing my job as the insider's head guy looks to the rest of the world unless I am interested in some object other than being the insider's head guy," he told reporters.

Behind the scenes, however, he worked to put the fire out before it spread any further. Old foes within the Democratic Party known as "the Grizzlies" were watching closely to see whether Willie could control the situation or if the situation would make him vulnerable to a challenge from within. Willie needed to act.

He started with Gary, knowing he was the most seasoned politician of the bunch and, therefore, the most likely to appreciate the bind they had put him in.

The Speaker shook his head irritably and pointed his finger at Gary's chest. "You guys— you can't introduce no-fault auto insurance. You can't do death penalty legislation. You can't go out and do these things without discussing them internally. If you don't stop doing this, I'm going to remove you as chairman."

"I didn't get elected to the legislature to be threatened. We came here to do policy too," Gary replied.

"This can't be fixed overnight. You need to come back under the umbrella of the Democratic caucus and work from there," Willie counseled. "If you don't, I'll have no choice."

"It's simple, Willie. Don't fuck with me and I won't fuck with you," Gary answered, and walked out the door.

One by one the other members of the Gang of Five entered Willie's office. He worked each of them over, threatening to take their offices and their staff and to strip them of prestigious positions in the legislature. If he could get one body to drop, the informal separatist group would fizzle. Instead, the more Willie pushed, the stronger the bond between the five grew.

Years later, Willie reflected on this moment:

I can only surmise that in my pursuit of peace among the members sometimes my actions were quicker than they should have been . . . I thought that I really had more equity with some individual members of what became the Gang of Five—knowing how much respect I had for them and for their ability and how I viewed them as the future . . . I really operated under the theory that they would be more cooperative on the sacrifice side than I could expect from the Grizzly types—knowing that the Grizzly types had real reservations about me—period. I was not of their *ilk* so to speak. . . . Anytime anyone didn't give me the management room, then I had no alternative but to manage and in some cases manage poorly.

—z—

Inside information is the lifeblood of the political press, and they can't get timely inside information without close relationships with the insiders. Willie exploited the insider bias to counteract the good press the five dissenters generated in their home districts, where people applauded their efforts to take on Willie and "the establishment."

The *California Journal*, "the" capital insider political periodical, ran a story under the headline, **THE DECLINE AND FALL OF SPEAKER WILLIE BROWN JR.? A LEADER CAUGHT BETWEEN THE GANG, THE GRIZZLIES AND THE GOP.** The story profiled each of the Gang of Five members. Gary was a playboy who was uninterested in policy and came to Sacramento solely to have a good time. The caricatures of the other four were just as unflattering.

Twenty years later, Willie was asked whether the *California Journal* profile on the Gang of Five was a political hit piece. Willie responded, with a wide smile, "I don't think you get that kind of profile without it being orchestrated."

By March of 1988, the Gang of Five didn't have a single committee assignment among them. They had each been reassigned to closet-sized offices. Their staffs had been decimated. Willie's move, however, didn't have its planned effect.

All the titles, committee appointments, and gifts were nooses hung around my neck, Gary realized. He had discovered a political freedom he would never, voluntarily, give up again.

The Gang of Five responded to Willie's wrath by engaging parliamentary maneuvers to continue the parade of legislation coming to the assembly floor. Willie miscalculated how well he had taught his pupils.

—

The Gang of Five versus Willie Brown was the title card on the political docket for the next three months, dominating newspaper headlines. There was no turning back.

As Willie later reflected:

> It was a combination of the press and the outside world—of the political parties and the pundits; the experts; the analysts. There is no sex appeal in an issues fight . . . The idea that somebody may be deposed and dispossessed of their role is first-class award-winning journalism—and that more than anything else carried the day.

The fight played out across the front pages of California's largest newspapers. The Gang of Five accused Willie and the Democratic leadership of being out of touch with a new generation.

Willie punched back. "You understand that when you look through the crack in the door long enough, you're going to see the hearse taking every one of your enemies to the cemetery."

In Condit Country, Gary walked into restaurants and people patted him on the back. He showed up to Rotary Club meetings to standing ovations. When asked if the five would fold, Gary told reporters, "Anyone who thinks this is a show or a game, it's not. It's a real struggle. We're up against a gentleman who is as tough as they come and as clever as they come. It takes all five of us to be as clever as he is, but individually we are just as tough."

—

Willie went for the jugular in the 1988 primary election. The Democratic caucus put forward a candidate to run against Gang member Jerry Eaves. Spending Democratic money against a Democrat violated Willie's own rules. But he needed to send a message.

The dark money campaign to defeat Eaves would have succeeded had it not been for Rusty Areias's decision to call US senator Ted Kennedy and ask why he had agreed to send a telegram endorsing Eaves's opponent, Joe Baca. The answer was plastered across the headlines of the next morning's paper: **TED KENNEDY TELEGRAM A FAKE.**

Eaves won by the slimmest of margins.

The best way for a leader to lose his or her job is to publicly demonstrate an inability to win a high-profile fight. The Gang of Five was playing high-stakes politics with the Ayatollah, and they were winning.

Now they were prepared to commit the cardinal sin in Willie's house. The Gang of Five plus thirty-six Republicans could unseat Willie as Speaker—fundamentally altering the political structure of the entire state with one vote.

—

Media crushed the edges of the green floor of the state assembly like a Black Friday sale. In the rafters, politicos, staffers, and lobbyists elbowed one another to get a view of the circus starting below.

The experienced eyes were on Willie. Nobody was certain how many Republican votes Willie had tucked in the jacket pocket of his Brioni suit.

It was Texas Hold 'Em, and everyone was supposed to be all in.

But the vote wasn't being called.

It started near the members' entrance to the floor. Some faces turned white, others betrayed a bizarre mix of grief and relief.

The Gang of Five stood frozen until the whisper hit Gary's ears. *Richard Longshore is dead.* Assemblyman Longshore, a Republican, had died at 2:00 a.m. that morning.

It was simple math. Willie didn't even have to show his hand.

Longshore's was a natural death, but it would become part of the lore that Willie's luck was in the stars as much as in himself.

"Let me tell you, ladies and gentlemen, look out—I'm back!" Willie declared on the capitol steps.

—

Gary sat across from Willie at Frank Fat's restaurant, just the two of them. Instead of his office, he chose to meet Gary at a prominent hangout for insiders. It was high drama for onlookers.

Willie wore a striped suit.

Gary wore a plain coat, tailored close to his body. *Willie's brand of politics is modeled on* The Godfather. *I'm not at confession. I won't apologize*, he thought.

"I had to give away a lot of office furniture to keep other members from voting with you guys," Willie smiled, then took a sip of wine.

Gary didn't respond.

"You and I, we're two of only a handful of people that know how this place works," Willie said. Again, he paused.

We were in a policy fight, and you dangled a leadership fight. We took the bait, Gary recognized, appreciating Willie's skill.

"We need to bury the hatchet," Willie continued. "We need to be friends again. We need to work together and forget what just occurred. We should be seen together . . . it will be good for you to be seen with me again."

Gary leaned across the table, bringing his face close to Willie's. "We're not going to pal around together again. We're not going to be friends. I'm not going to apologize. I'm going to find the longest, sharpest stick I can and I'm gonna put it through your eye," Gary replied.

Willie didn't blink.

⚊

Fate threw Gary a lifeline, one far removed from Willie's iron fist.

A few weeks after Gary threatened to put a stick through the Ayatollah's eye, United States congressman Tony Coelho got caught up in a junk bond scandal. Coelho's district included Condit Country.

Rather than put his family through a drawn-out investigation into his personal affairs and the terrorizing scrutiny of the mainstream media, Coehlo resigned.

After discussing it with his family, Gary entered the race. Gary won the special election to replace Coehlo by a staggering margin.

Before his first trip to Washington, a reporter for the *Fresno Bee* asked Gary whether he'd change anything when he got to Congress.

"I'm not going to get caught up in the 'inside the Beltway' mentality. I'll still be Gary Condit from Ceres. I don't get impressed easily. I'm not the kind of person who gets swayed easily."

⚊

Less than a year after Willie Brown defeated the Gang of Five, the people of the state of California passed Proposition 140, setting term limits for California legislators, slashing their budgets, and stripping them of their pensions.

Willie went on to become the longest-serving Speaker in the history of the state. But it came at a heavy price. He watched, helplessly, as his legislature was pulled apart. Eventually, Willie was termed out of office. He would be the last real Speaker of the assembly, and the last true leader of the Golden State.

BLUE DOGS

Pete Geren, with his thick Texas drawl, made even the shortest sentences seem long. Like Gary, he had won a special election. Together they comprised the entirety of the two-member off-year freshman class in the House. It took no time for them to strike up a friendship. They were natural allies.

Gary and Geren joined the Conservative Democratic Forum, known by its initials CDF. Other members included senior conservative Democrats like Ralph Hall from Rockwall, Texas, and Sonny Montgomery from Mississippi. CDF served mostly as a debate society. While the Democrats comfortably controlled Congress during the '80s and early '90s, the party leadership had no use for the moderate or conservative elements of the caucus.

By 1994, CDF had a contingent of mostly junior Democrats itching to take on policy fights. Members like Gary, Geren, John Tanner from Tennessee, Jimmy Hayes and Billy Tauzin from Louisiana, and Mike Parker from Mississippi were tired of sitting back while the Democratic caucus leadership dictated national policy far left of their constituency and the Republic Party predictably promoted policies that were far right of their constituency.

They joked about their admission to the NLT, an affectionate moniker for "Not on the Leadership Track." They weren't aiming for committee appointments or titles; they were ready and willing to piss off the establishment on both sides of the aisle. "NLT" was their tongue-in-cheek acknowledgment that they would never have success in Congress playing by caucus rules.

Mike Parker, a bear of a man and a chain smoker, was Gary's closest friend in the NLT. Parker arrived in Congress with a strong business background. He owned and managed the largest funeral home chain in the greater Jackson, Mississippi, area. He was the only member of Congress with an embalmer's license, and insisted he had learned everything he needed to know about politics from dealing in death.

Gary's friendship with Parker and Sonny Montgomery made him one of the few members of California's congressional delegation who had significant personal relationships with members from southern states and on both sides of the aisle. As a result, Gary moved in and out of different circles with ease.

He was, by every measure and by design, in the middle. But being there had no tangible value. The Democrats had such a comfortable margin in the House that to be in "the middle" meant you weren't in the room. What Gary didn't anticipate was just how fast the middle would come to matter inside the United States Congress.

———

In the 1994 interim election, the Democrats lost control of the House for the first time since 1954. When the bloodletting was over, there had been a fifty-four-seat swing in the political makeup of the House of Representatives. Thirty-four incumbent Democrats had lost their reelection bids.

When Congress resumed, Gary found Parker inside his office pacing back and forth, and growling in a thick southern drawl, "You-u-u fuck with me, I'll fuck with you-u-u." Parker had been reelected by a razor-thin margin after a nasty campaign. The Democratic Party leadership had supported the candidate running against him in the primary.

The Democratic Party did the same thing to other incumbent Democrats. Going into the 1994 interim election, the party leadership made a conscious decision to try to rid itself of moderate and conservative Democrats.

Now, there was going to be hell to pay. Some Democrats simply switched to the Republican Party.

"Calm down," Gary advised, putting his hand on Parker's broad shoulder.

"My own party. The caucus was out there trying to kill its own members, whoever wouldn't vote with them. Well, they don't live where I live. They were so focused on control they lost the House!" Parker yelled.

Gary calmed Parker, but his own mind moved at a blistering pace. *I can control this.*

The purge of Democrats had an unintended consequence: the middle suddenly mattered. Gary, Parker, Hall, Geren, Tanner, Tauzin, Hayes, Blanche Lincoln from Arkansas, Collin Peterson from Minnesota, Pat Danner from Missouri, Sanford Bishop Jr. from Georgia, and a handful of other Democrats—they all had the same unspoken thought. And because of his experience with Willie Brown, Gary knew how to play their cards.

Assembled for the first time as a single group in Gary's office, the proposed policy coalition totaled twenty-three members.

Gary asked prospective members what they hoped to accomplish in Congress. If their goal was to obtain a key committee post, Gary dismissed them from consideration for membership in the group. Committee posts were handed out by party leadership.

They put in place a simple structure—three co-chairs: an administrative co-chair, a communications co-chair, and a policy co-chair. The group was further broken down into subcommittees that met with representatives from both parties to find a solution-oriented approach to policymaking.

The coalition didn't take money. It didn't get involved in campaigns, leadership fights, or caucus squabbles. The purpose of the coalition was to tackle critical policy issues facing the nation by putting forward solutions that worked and using their control position in the House to generate bipartisan support. Coalition members had to have the willpower to decline taking a position as a group on all other issues—setting aside their differences.

As soon as the coalition was formed, Gary called Dick Gephardt. The Democratic leader wasn't thrilled with the idea of a formal group of moderates formed inside his caucus. Gary, however, assured Gerphardt that the Blue Dogs would deliver their votes for the speakership.

At an early meeting, Jimmy Hayes handed out round blue-and-red pins with the face of a hound dog in the middle. Hayes figured if the coalition members all wore the lapel pins, they would stand out on the House floor. By the time they had left the floor later that day, the political press had picked up on the pins and labeled the coalition the "Blue Dog Democrats."

For the first two years, the Blue Dogs met in Gary's office for a members-only weekly meeting. There, they developed a unified position on some of the biggest policy issues facing the nation.

The Blue Dogs went after balancing the budget with the Republicans because the Democrats wouldn't budge. They offered an alternative to the Republican plan for welfare reform that ultimately gained tractions on boths sides of the aisle.

They rapidly gained momentum.

During President Bill Clinton's first two years in office, he led with his chin on both gays in the military and universal health care. After the '94 election, the president had to respond to a very different Congress. He needed moderate and conservative Democrats to bridge the gap between his party and the Republicans. Mostly, he needed the moderate Democrats to stand up to the party leadership so he could move to a more centrist position. Clinton invited the Blue Dogs to the White House for a one-on-one discussion.

Gary pulled Parker aside as the other twenty-one Blue Dogs filed onto a bus to take them from Capitol Hill to the White House.

"You good, Parker?" Gary asked.

"S-h-i-i-t," he let out deliberately. "What d-o-o I have to say to those s-h-i-i-t heads?"

The end of Parker's cigarette blinked red and his eyes twinkled with indignation.

"Stick with the plan. When we get to the end of the meeting, if you feel like it, slap him in the head and see if he can take a punch," Gary counseled.

When Gary and Parker walked into the meeting at the White House, everyone else was already seated at a long table. The seat to the right of the president's chair had been reserved for Gary. The only other open seat was the one to the left of the president, and Parker was the only man still standing.

"Gary, why don't you conduct the meeting," the president asked.

"Thank you, Mr. President."

Gary went point by point through the Blue Dogs' concerns with the policy positions taken by the Democratic leadership and their view of how to break the stalemate inside Congress between the two parties.

The Blue Dogs aggressively laid out the reasons, in their view, the president needed to move major policy positions to the middle. They wanted Clinton to push the Democrats in Congress to pursue reductions in the deficit and balanced budgets. They didn't threaten the president of the United States. But they left him with a clear message: if he didn't, the Blue Dogs were going to work with the Republicans to accomplish those things in Congress.

While Clinton's staff fidgeted like cats on a hot tin roof, the politician from Arkansas was comfortable with the Blue Dogs' bite.

Clinton stood and bid the Blue Dogs farewell. "You survived the tidal wave of Republicans. I am going to have you over again . . . and we are going to listen to your ideas."

Parker's eyes flashed like the lit end of a cigarette. "Mr. President," he said. "If you-u-u don't listen to us, and you-u-u don't take our advice, you-u-u better get yourself a nail apron 'cause you-u-u gonna be building houses with Jim-ay Cah-t-ehr down in Georgia."

Clinton laughed and put his arm on Parker's shoulder.

For the next four years, the Blue Dogs played pulling guard, clearing the path within the president's own party as Clinton moved Congress to middle ground.

CHAPTER 5

TURNING POINTS

CHANGE IN PLANS

Gary reached into his coat and grabbed a Davidoff, his last cigar, then struck a match. He was walking home from dinner at Pasta Mia, where he ate most nights. The restaurant was right around the corner from the Lynshire. The sidewalks were filled with college-age people. Gary preferred Adams Morgan to the stuffier places most members of Congress chose to live. Sandwiched between Dupont Circle and Rock Creek Park, it was hip and alive.

It was late when Gary entered his condo. He crossed into the small living room. Movement in the street below caught his attention. He adjusted the mini blinds to get a better look.

A woman emerged from the backseat of a parked four-door town car. It looked as though two men sat in the front seat. She crossed Adams Mill Road to the front steps of the Lynshire building.

Why is she here?

It was Anne Marie Smith, the flight attendant Gary had first met on a flight from San Francisco to Washington.

There was a knock at his door.

How'd she get up here?

She called his name.

He didn't answer.

A piece of paper rustled as it was slipped under Gary's front door. He picked the note off the floor. It read: "I really need to talk to you."

Congress adjourned on December 15. Like most of the other out-of-town congressional members, Gary went home to spend the holidays with his family.

On December 23, Chandra sent an e-mail to a friend in Modesto:

> My man will be coming back when Congress starts up again. I'm looking forward to seeing him.

She sent a second e-mail to another friend stating that she was headed back to Washington, DC, from California and that the man she was seeing had taken care of her plane ticket.

Chandra then called her landlord to inquire about breaking her apartment lease, telling him she had plans to move in with her unidentified boyfriend.

INAUGURATION

Gary returned to DC for the swearing in of the new Congress on January 3 but stayed less than a week because the House immediately recessed. When it did, Gary went home to Condit Country. He returned to DC again around January 18 when Congress came back into session. Cadee came to DC a day later, to attend an inaugural ball for President George W. Bush on January 20. Like she always did when she was in town, Cadee stayed with Gary.

"Dad, I'll see you later," Cadee called from the front entrance to the condo.

"Be safe. A lot of people will be out partying tonight," Gary answered from his bedroom.

Shortly after Cadee left, the phone rang.

"It's Chandra."

"I'll buzz you in."

Earlier in the week, she had asked him if he could get her tickets for one of the president's inaugural balls. Members of Congress receive an allotment, and because Gary's constituents lived clear across the country, he had quite a few extra tickets.

Gary opened the front door. Chandra was dressed in a flattering gown that hugged her body. Her hair was pulled back. Gary hadn't seen her this way before.

Chandra didn't stay long.

~

Ingmar Guandique stood on the banks of the Rio Grande, across the border from Texas. He had left El Salvador in January, leaving behind a girlfriend and a newborn child.

Nineteen years old, he had dark brown hair, black eyes, and an unusually flat forehead.

Guandique was raised on the front line of the Salvadorian civil war between the military-led government supported by the United States and the union of leftist guerrilla groups named the Farabundo Marti National Liberation Front. Guandique's father was a casualty of this war.

But there may have been another reason why Guandique had left his home country. He had been accused of sexually assaulting and almost killing a young woman there.

~

There was little anyone could do on Capitol Hill. Between the new Congress just getting started and the circus around the presidential election, the federal government was virtually shut down. Gary would have gone home as usual, except Rep. Howard Berman invited him to attend the World Economic Forum in Davos, Switzerland, scheduled for January 25 through January 30, and Gary had accepted the invite.

DAVOS

Snowflakes disappeared in brilliant flashbulbs as rings of financiers, executives, heads of state, policymakers, academics, and reporters gathered in front of the Congress Centre in Davos for the thirtieth annual meeting of the World Economic Forum.

Gary entered the grand hall, alone, wearing a black suit. He had agreed to be a table host for a dinner sponsored by big agriculture. Earlier that day, he participated in a roundtable discussion on international affairs. Gary and one of Egyptian president Hosni Mubarak's right-hand men had struck up a spirited discussion on US foreign aid, and the recent attack on the USS *Cole* in Yemen.

The Egyptian official knew Gary had voted against US foreign aid to Israel, and wanted to know Gary's reasons for doing so. He assumed, wrongly, that Gary's motivation must have been rooted in a particular view on the Palestinian crisis. Gary told him he didn't support US foreign aid being provided to Egypt, either. "The only aid we should be handing out is food," Gary explained.

"Congressman Condit," a voice behind him called. "Your table is over here."

One of the event organizers ushered Gary to his table decorated with silver centerpieces, where Gary introduced himself to the other guests, then sat.

"First time?" the woman sitting next to him asked.

It was impossible not to notice that she was very pretty. She had brown hair and fair skin that melted into her white dress. A thin gold necklace hung from her neck.

"Yes," he answered.

"Me too."

Gary and the woman engaged in small talk. He learned that she worked for a Russian company that sold heavy equipment. He told her he had recently visited Moscow as part of a CODEL. Because he was on the intel committee, the State Department warned him that his hotel room was likely bugged. "By you or by them?" Gary had responded, jokingly.

Their discussion was interrupted by a waiter pouring glasses of wine. Gary politely declined.

"You don't drink?" the woman asked.

"No, I don't."

"Did you know Gorbachev passed laws to stop abuse of alcohol? But they made Russians angry, so these laws failed."

"Well, he and Reagan succeeded in tearing down the wall," Gary said.

"They trusted each other."

"They weren't drinking."

⟋

Lighted heat lamps kept partygoers warm while they waited in front of the Congress Centre. A valet motioned Gary to a town car.

As Gary moved in that direction, he noticed the woman he had met at dinner was standing near the back of the line. She had put a heavy brown coat over her pretty white dress. He walked to where she stood and asked if she needed a ride to her hotel.

"I'm waiting for a taxi," she explained.

"I'll have the driver drop you off first," he offered.

She got out of line and followed him to the town car.

DOMESTIC PROBLEMS

Gary flew from Davos back to Washington, and then, almost immediately, he flew from Washington to California.

This trip home would be tough. Vince Flammini's latest transgression at work wasn't his worst, but it had to be the last because they were becoming more frequent and outrageous. His first morning back, Gary went to Flammini's house.

"I have to let you go," Gary explained as the two men stood near Gary's parked motorcycle.

Flammini insisted Lynch "had it out" for him and was lying. The conversation quickly turned bitter. There was nothing Gary could say that would make Flammini see and accept the truth.

"Vince, I can't fix it this time. I wish I could."

Gary kept Flammini on the payroll for a bit longer so that he could tell his friends he had retired as Gary's bodyguard and possibly qualify for retirement benefits. But the two friends never rode motorcycles together again.

Flammini felt Gary had betrayed him and left him destitute.

—

California's two largest energy utilities teetered on bankruptcy, and rolling blackouts had started in the northern and central parts of the state.

Just two days before George W. Bush's inauguration as president, FERC chairman James J. Hoecker—who had promised that he'd take action against Enron after getting reappointed—had unceremoniously resigned. Overnight, FERC went from being unresponsive to openly hostile toward California.

"Senator Peace," the pro tem acknowledged.

Peace stepped up to his microphone on the state senate floor. "Enron and FERC, Enron and FERC!" he bellowed, and then slammed his mic down. The dramatic declaration had become a near-daily ritual.

Peace left the senate floor and went to his office.

"Steve, you all right?" Gary asked from the other end of the line.

"We're at fucking war, Gar!" Peace started, without giving time to formality.

"What else can I do?"

"It's derivatives. It's unregulated criminal banking. It's not about electrons!" Peace shouted.

"I'm trying to help. But President Bush won't meet with anyone from the California delegation. He doesn't owe California anything after this election."

CHAPTER 6

EXCHANGES

TRYST

It was now March, and the weather in Washington, DC, had started to warm.

Ingmar Guandique had found work at a construction site near Dupont Circle. He also had a new girlfriend in Washington named Iris Portillo.

He lived with Iris and her mother at the Somerset apartment complex. A few months after his arrival, Guandique began spending time in Rock Creek Park, drinking and getting high with friends. He became violent. He bit Iris above her breast, and punched her in the face. Iris's mother kicked him out of her home.

He called his friend Antonio Flores and told him that he and Iris had gotten in a fight and he needed a place to stay. Flores and his girlfriend, Sheila Phillips, agreed to let Guandique crash at their apartment. He stayed only a few days. When Guandique left, they assumed he went back to living with Iris and her mother.

Guandique, however, had turned his attention to the gang Mara Salvatrucha, or MS-13.

MS-13 was founded in Los Angeles by young men fleeing civil war in El Salvador. Many of the gang's leaders were former guerrilla fighters and, as a result, MS-13 had adopted a para-military structure.

By 2000, MS-13 had established footholds in Washington, DC, Maryland, and Virginia. As a rite of passage, prospective male members were beaten nearly to death. To get the coveted symbol "MS-13" tattooed on their bodies, gang members first had to perpetrate a violent crime.

—

At 8:00 p.m., Chandra's unmistakable mass of curls bounced as she entered Tryst, a hip coffee shop in Adams Morgan just three blocks north of the Lynshire building. Gary was sitting at a small cafe table for two, waiting for her.

She had called him that afternoon to ask if they could meet to discuss her job search. He told her he would be tied up until the evening but would have an hour or so to meet for dinner if she wanted to meet at Tryst.

This was the first time they had met in a public place other than his office. Neither knew it at the time, but this would be the only time they would ever meet outside of his office or condo.

"My internship got extended," Chandra said, smiling as she set her backpack on the ground. "My boss said he can keep me on because someone hasn't come back from a leave. It's a bit of a break."

"That's good."

"I heard something interesting today from my boss," Chandra said, unable to hide her excitement. "He told me the FBI hid documents, from the defense, a lot of them, and it's coming out. The AG might delay McVeigh's execution."

Gary hadn't heard about the gaffe in the prosecution of the man who had bombed the Alfred P. Murrah Building in Oklahoma City, killing 168 people, and he was surprised that Chandra's boss would share this type of information with her.

"That's opening up a wound for a lot of good people," he responded.

"I know this hits home for you. I just thought it was strange the government brought this out six days before the execution date."

"Someone was going to blow the whistle. If not, they'd have buried it."

Chandra talked about her latest thinking on getting into a program with the FBI or CIA. She also mentioned she might apply for a special program at the Department of Justice. Gary advised her that she should get more language skills because it was something the FBI and CIA would put value in. He also offered to set up a meeting for her with someone at the FBI so she could get more particulars on what they might be looking for and the process for getting in.

When they had finished eating, she grabbed her backpack, and they disappeared into Adams Morgan.

GIFTS

Early April marked the start of peak tourist season, when tens of thousands of people flocked to the nation's capital to watch the cherry blossoms bloom like pastel fireworks along the Potomac's edge.

Chandra met Gary at his office.

"I don't think I'll get another extension at the bureau," she explained.

"Do you want to stay in DC?" he asked, throwing his jacket over the desk chair.

"I might apply for the special DOJ program. If it doesn't come through, and I don't get another extension, then I'll go home and figure things out."

"Your choices are all good. If you decide to stay in California, there are lots of opportunities," he assured her. "If you want me to set up that meeting with the FBI, let me know and I'll make it happen."

She reached into her backpack. "I know you like chocolate. It's a thank-you for all your help," she offered, reaching over the coffee table to hand him a small bag of chocolates.

He moved to his desk, opened the top drawer, and pulled out one of the gold bracelets Carolyn had purchased from Rumors in San Francisco. "Here's something for you. Getting your masters is a big deal."

"You're sweet," she beamed as she placed the bracelet on her wrist.

Dayton stepped through the open door. "Gary, you've got an intel meeting."

GOOD-BYE

On April 24, Gary worked a double Windsor with his favorite blue-and-green Jerry Garcia tie. The phone rang, and he picked it up.

"Buzz me up?" Chandra asked. Gary pressed a button on the phone that unlocked the door to the building.

With the exception of the dinner at Tryst, they had never met outside of his office or condo. The handful of times she came to his place it was often straight from the gym. He never visited her apartment.

Contact between them wasn't regular because they both had busy weekday schedules and Gary went home every weekend.

Gary had no idea if she was dating anybody, and never asked. When they did meet it was casual, and when they talked it was usually about Chandra's career.

Chandra walked through the front door of his apartment, wearing spandex leggings, a cotton workout shirt, and jogging shoes. Gary figured she had come from the Washington Sports Club, where she had a membership.

"Sorry to bother you so early. Thought you might have run out of chocolates," she said, handing him another small bag of candy. "Plus, we didn't celebrate your birthday."

"I don't need a birthday present. It's good just to see you."

"I know you don't like presents. But you like chocolate," she said, smiling.

"What's going on?" he asked, knowing from experience that she had stopped by his place for a reason.

"It's official. I can't stay any longer at the bureau. I'm surprised I made it this long."

"What about the DOJ program?"

"I missed the application deadline."

"Were you treated fairly?"

"I just missed the deadline. I applied for a few other things in DC, but I won't hear back for a while—when I get to California I'm going to look harder."

"When do you leave?"

"A week or so. Graduation is on the eighth. And I'm still thinking about taking a train home."

"You'd see a lot of the country."

"I came by to see about those interviews in California and with the FBI you said you could help set up for me. I've put some applications in. I know I should have gotten to this sooner."

"Give me dates that work and I'll make sure it gets taken care of."

"If I go back to California, then come back for an interview, I won't have a place to stay," Chandra said.

Gary caught the subtle request. "Don't you have friends or family you can stay with?"

"My friends aren't here, well, other than you."

"You won't have to stay too many days—you won't have to spend too much on a hotel," Gary answered.

"You've got to get ready for work?" she said, and stepped closer to him.

"I do."

"Right now?"

"Dayton's on his way."

"OK. I gotta run, too. I'll call the office with dates."

Gary returned to the task of knotting his Jerry Garcia.

On April 28, Chandra sent the following e-mail to her landlord:

I was just informed this week that my job appointment time is up, so I am out of work now. I am going back to California for my graduation during the week of May 8 and moving back there for good. I haven't heard from the other jobs that I applied for yet and I have a feeling that it will be at least a few weeks for me to hear back from any of them. I don't really think it would be worth it for me to stay in DC now since I have no job or school to keep me busy here. I would like to vacate the apartment on May 5 or 6 if possible . . . I really hate giving up the apartment but I think I need to be in California for a while to figure out what my next move is.

CHAPTER 7

FLOTUS AND POTUS

FIRST LADY

IT'S A TRADITION FOR CONGRESSIONAL wives to help prepare the First Lady's annual tea party. Friends convinced Carolyn to participate this year, which was a big deal for her and for Gary because she didn't make it to Washington often.

It was Sunday, April 29, and they hadn't made any plans so that Carolyn could rest. Gary borrowed Dayton's Ford Explorer and picked her up at Dulles International Airport the night before. Because of the time change, Carolyn didn't wake up until 9:00 a.m.

They ate breakfast at a diner near the Lynshire and then shopped for an hour in Adams Morgan. At 12:30 p.m., they drove the Explorer to the Rayburn Building.

They spent twenty minutes inside Gary's office, then left the building through the main entrance, leaving Dayton's SUV in the garage so he could collect it later that afternoon. It was a beautiful day. They decided to walk as far as she could along the National Mall and then hail a cab to take them the rest of the way to Adams Morgan.

Gary and Carolyn meandered for more than four hours, stopping periodically to enjoy an attraction on the Mall or to sit and rest in the shade as they made their way back to Adams Morgan.

It was early in the evening when they arrived at the Starbucks in Dupont Circle, at the intersection of Connecticut Avenue and R Street. Chandra Levy's apartment was close by. In the alley behind the Starbucks, a faintly sketched message was written on a brick wall:

GOOD DAY J.C. MAY I NEVER MISS THE THRILL OF BEING NEAR YOU!!

"You want to take a cab the rest of the way?" Gary asked, handing Carolyn an iced tea.

"Let's take a little rest here, then walk the rest of the way," she answered.

―⁄―

Carolyn stirred pasta in the kitchen. Gary moved to the bedroom and checked his answering service. It was a small condo. The television and phone were in the bedroom, which was adjacent to the open main area consisting of the living room, kitchen, and small dining area.

He had one message, from Chandra: "Call me back if you can."

Gary called Chandra. "It's me," he said. "Are you getting ready to leave?"

"I haven't finished making arrangements yet. I'm trying to schedule everything before I leave," Chandra replied.

"OK. I'll call you when it's a good time to talk."

Gary walked back to the kitchen, where Carolyn was finishing setting a small dining table.

He wondered what it would be like to have her there all the time. Whether he had missed out on things in the kids' lives, and whether they had missed out on anything as spouses.

"Gar, did you ever think we'd be here? I mean, you're having lunch with the president tomorrow." The next day, Monday, Gary was scheduled to attend President Bush's "First 100 Days Congressional Luncheon" at the White House. Many Democrats had declined the invitation, but Gary felt it was important to accept.

He put his fork down and looked at his wife.

The full day of sun had infused her skin with a youthful glow. She had always been beautiful. Here, in the world he typically inhabited alone, she looked radiant, her hazel eyes breaking the stale yellow light of his apartment into a million diamonds.

"I don't know if I'll see the president. There will be a lot of people."

"Chad said you might get appointed to work for the president?"

"There's been talk in the papers."

"Something new would be good."

"I feel that sometimes," he acknowledged.

~

Hop Condit walked along a highway, just outside of Key West, Florida. He was on his way home after a long night bussing tables at a local Denny's diner.

Cars zipped passed him at a steady pace until one veered out of the traffic lane and careened into him. Hop's body flung forward over his feet, then his feet over his head. His legs shattered.

The car sped away.

Blood poured onto the asphalt around Hop and down his face. *I'm gonna die*, he thought. He couldn't stand, and it was still a few hundred yards to his apartment. Hop put one arm out in front of him, then the next.

~

"Gar, what would you have done if we stayed in Oklahoma?" Carolyn asked, laying next to him in bed.

"Maybe running stores for your dad in Kansas. If it were up to Adrian, I'd be a preacher."

"They wouldn't have a problem with you marrying a Catholic girl," Carolyn teased.

He kissed her.

She pressed her body against him, with her back to his front. She couldn't see him, but she could feel his breathing brush against her cheek and sense the slight shifts of his body. She could anticipate almost everything he would do, and could trust those things she couldn't see.

PRESIDENT'S CABINET

On April 20, Chandra entered the Washington Sports Club near her apartment in DuPont Circle, dressed in sweatpants, a loose pink sweatshirt, and a fanny pack, and cancelled her gym membership. The attendant who helped Chandra with the cancellation thought she looked healthy and upbeat.

⤚

On the other side of town, Gary passed, unnoticed, through a crowd of reporters stationed near the entrance to the White House.

Senate Republican majority leader Trent Lott was already seated when Gary arrived at the table. He shook Lott's hand, and then the hand of House majority leader Republican Dick Armey.

Lott said something to Gary that Gary didn't hear, because his mind was preoccupied with the sudden realization of the significance of this event. *I'm the only Democrat at this table.*

Gary then realized the chair reserved for him was to the right of Lott, and to the left of the president. There was nothing subtle about the positioning.

The room staggered to attention, and festive camaraderie gave way to pomp and circumstance as President George W. Bush entered, then walked across the room, heading straight for the chasm next to Gary. The crowd focused on the president, applauding enthusiastically as he approached his seat.

When the applause ended, President Bush turned his attention to Gary. "I have heard a lot about you, most of it good," the president said with a smile as the men exchanged polished handshakes. "We're glad you're here."

"Mr. President, I'm honored. Though I didn't expect a front row seat," Gary replied.

"We've got him on your left," a member joked.

Laughter erupted. Each of the politicians at the table was seasoned enough to know that Gary had stumbled into an audition that was, by necessity, public.

Salads arrived under the controlled din unique to Republican gatherings. At some point, without fanfare, salads were exchanged for entrees and Gary sensed a pause on his side of the table.

He leaned to his right. "Mr. President, I've got an issue I'd like to run by you that I need help with."

President Bush leaned left. "What's that?"

Gary felt Peace's hot breath on his neck as though he were actually hovering over him. "It's the energy situation in California."

"What about it?" the president asked.

"We can't get a fair hearing out of FERC. Mr. President, I know your administration doesn't owe California anything, but I think it would show a lot of grace, and do a lot of long-term good, if you leaned on FERC to take up some of the issues we're raising."

"Dick is dealing with that."

"The vice president won't meet with California Democrats," Gary responded.

The president told Gary that the vice president would meet with him.

Gary rode back to the Capitol with a group of Republican congressmen, including John Doolittle and Dick Armey.

A MEETING WITH DICK

At 4:30 a.m. on May 1, Chandra Levy's neighbor called 911 and told the dispatcher she had been awakened by a woman's bloodcurdling screams.

That same day, Ingmar Guandique didn't show up for work.

Chandra's parents received an e-mail from her time-stamped 10:45 a.m. EST. The e-mail included a list of supersaver flights from Modesto, where the Levy family lived, to Los Angeles, where Chandra's graduation ceremony was scheduled for May 11.

At 11:00 a.m., Dayton picked up Gary in front of the Lynshire and drove him to the Rayburn Building.

At 12:30 p.m., Vice President Dick Cheney walked into a small conference room followed closely by a White House staffer. Gary and Dayton were waiting inside.

"Congressman," the vice president said, offering his hand.

Gary got right to the point. "We need some assistance in California with the energy crisis. The governor and others, they're trying to get FERC to take a look at some issues in the wholesale market."

"FERC," Cheney reacted tersely.

"Yes. It would be helpful if the administration could intervene and request FERC take a look at the actions of some companies in the market . . ." Gary started.

"California made its own decisions," the vice president interrupted.

Gary internalized the response. *Cheney has an active disinterest in this. There isn't the slightest hint of mercy. Derivatives and Ken Lay are off the table. I'm irritating the vice president and he's here to do me a favor.*

"I understand, Mr. Vice President—I'd appreciate it if you could have someone take a look . . . I do have one other matter I'd like to talk with you about."

Cheney nodded respectfully.

Gary and his chief of staff, Mike Lynch, could smell the finish line on a project that was important to them both: the creation of the University of California, Merced. It was part of a pact he had made with Governor Gray Davis that the Central Valley would be treated "equal to" the rest of California if Gary threw his weight behind Davis's election campaign. With Gary's support, Davis won, and Gary was cashing in.

"We're trying to build a new university in my district, and I'm concerned that the environmental issues holding up the project are out of touch with reality," Gary explained.

Cheney was interested in this part of their conversation.

—

At 2:00 p.m., Amber Fitzgerald walked briskly on the Western Ridge Trail in Rock Creek Park, near the historic Pierce Mill. She noticed a lone Hispanic man walking parallel to her, and she slowed to let him pass. The man disappeared into the woods.

Fitzgerald switched trails and began ascending a steep incline. Near the top, she turned and found the same man behind her. This time she ran, sprinting down the steep hillside. She didn't stop until she reached a road outside the park.

Fitzgerald didn't report the incident to the Park Police.

—

At 5:00 p.m., Gary left his office for a doctor's appointment to look at his aching shoulder. Dr. Morgan's office was located on Capitol Hill, just a short walk from the Rayburn Building.

After seeing the doctor, Gary went to the House floor, where he registered two votes, at 6:25 p.m. and 6:30 p.m. Shortly after 6:30, he reentered his office inside the Rayburn Building and sat behind his desk.

Gary picked up the phone. It was a call he didn't want to make.

"Did Cheney tell you he was going to nuke California?" Peace asked, before Gary could get a word in.

"He's not gonna help us. I know it's not what you want to hear."

"That's because the only thing Enron manipulates better than the market is the media. *Forbes* just named Enron the most admired company in America! We're fucked, Gary. We're fucking ourselves."

—

That evening, Sheila Phillips found Ingmar Guandique at her home. He had a large cut near his eye, a fat lip, and scratches across his neck. Guandique told Phillips that he had gotten into a fight with his girlfriend.

INFLUENCE

Gary grabbed almonds from a bowl on the coffee table. He had spent the morning in committee meetings, between which he went to the House floor to vote. He returned to the Rayburn Building around noon to meet with his staff and to check for messages on his answering service. He had a few, and one of them had been left by Chandra the prior morning, on May 1: "I'm leaving. Call when you can."

He took the phone from his desk and dialed Chandra's number. She didn't pick up. A strange buzzing sound—like static feedback—came through the receiver before his call was sent to Chandra's voice mail. "It's 11:45," he said. "Sorry, I've been tied up for the last few days. Sorry. Give me a call—give me a rundown on kinda what your schedule is. Things are looking pretty good for me today. Anyway—bye."

By mid-afternoon, Gary was back inside the Capitol Building attending meetings, including an Intelligence Committee Working Group briefing. He was tied up in those meetings until the early evening, then he had an appointment at Tryst in Adams Morgan to catch up with an old friend.

Carolyn spent the entire day across town, with other congressional wives at the First Lady's tea.

—

An attractive woman with wavy brown hair, athletic legs, and a pretty face entered the cafe.

"Hey darling," Gary said as she approached.

"Gary!" Rebecca Cooper responded as the two embraced.

"You look good," Gary said.

"So do you."

This wasn't the first time she and Gary had met at Tryst, the hip coffee shop in Adams Morgan not far from his condo at the Lynshire. It was convenient for both of them.

Rebecca was a political reporter for ABC News. She had called him earlier in the week to ask if he would consider helping her with a personal project.

Rebecca and Gary first met while she was a young producer at CNN. Her arrival on the Hill for CNN had coincided with Newt Gingrich's Republican takeover of the House after the 1994 election. One of the biggest stories that year in Washington was the budget showdown between Republicans, Democrats, and what at the time seemed like an emerging third caucus: the Blue Dogs.

When Rebecca asked insiders for information on the Blue Dogs, they passed her a name: Gary Condit. She sought him out. And when Gary learned she was from Oklahoma, he took an immediate interest in helping her career. She grew to trust him and contacted him regularly on stories, knowing he wasn't drawn to being on television like many of his colleagues but would always tell her off camera what was really going on behind closed doors.

In the summer of 1998, Cadee Condit worked as an intern for Rebecca at CNN. It was the third summer in a row Cadee worked in Washington, DC, and each time she lived with Gary at his apartment. In 1999, Rebecca left for New York to take a job as chief of staff for Bill Richardson, the US ambassador to the United Nations. After two years at the UN, she came back to Washington as a producer and reporter for ABC News. One of the first things she did when she returned was reconnect with Gary.

"How did the meeting go with Cheney?" she asked, pressing a mug of coffee to her lips.

"He's not going to help on the energy crisis, but he might help us out on some other things we have going in California."

"Don't you think it's a pretty big sign that he met with you?"

"Yes," he answered. "What about your project?"

"I want to write a book for regular people. *Fifty Ways to Influence Congress Even When You Have No Influence.* But I think it'd be more impactful if I had a member of Congress as a coauthor. You're perfect for it."

They talked for an hour, and then went their separate ways.

~

Back at the Lynshire, Gary and Carolyn were in bed by 8:00 p.m.

Carolyn left the next day, returning home to Ceres.

~

On May 4, Gary called Chandra, hoping to find out whether she had, in fact, left Washington and to check in on whether she wanted him to set up a meeting with the FBI. Again, she didn't pick up. Again, he heard strange static in the background before his call was directed to her voice mail. "It's 6:30. I haven't heard from you—so maybe you are out of the country or something. Anyway, give me a call if you pick up this message. Bye," he said.

MISSING IN DC

There were no clouds above Condit Country on May 6.

Carolyn propped open the patio door to let in the oncoming summer's warm wind. It had arrived early, and the cypress trees that lined the back fence moved, lethargically, with its welcoming current.

The phone rang, and she moved back to the kitchen to answer it.

"Is this Congressman Condit's house?" a man asked.

"This is his wife, Carolyn," she answered.

Gary kept his home phone number listed for the public, and it was not unusual for constituents to call.

"This is Robert Levy. Is the congressman home?"

"He's home, but he's out now." Gary had ridden his motorcycle to the Ceres Street Fair.

"Thank you. I'll call back."

Carolyn started dinner.

An hour later, the phone rang.

"Mrs. Condit, this is Robert Levy, MD."

"Dr. Levy, he's not home just yet. He should be home any minute," she replied.

"My daughter, Chandra—she's living in Washington and we haven't heard from her in a few days. We're very worried. We're hoping he can help."

"I will have Gary call you as soon as he gets home. What's your phone number?"

She made a note in the journal she kept next to the phone—*Dr. Levy called for Gary.* Carolyn didn't know the Levy family personally, but she had heard Dr. Levy's name before. She took care of an elderly friend in the neighborhood who was a patient of his, and she knew he worked in the hospital where Adrian ministered. But she had never met Dr. Levy's daughter or heard mention of the name Chandra before.

Gary's motorcycle growled as he pulled it into the garage.

"What's going on?" he asked as he entered the house. He could tell by the look on her face that something bad had happened.

"Gar, Dr. Levy called, he needs to talk with you. He said his daughter is missing. He's really shook."

"Do you have a number?"

"It's written down."

Gary picked up the phone and dialed.

A low voice answered. "Hello."

"Dr. Levy—Gary Condit, returning your call."

"Thank you for calling. Can you . . ."

Robert Levy stopped, abruptly, having been interrupted by his wife saying loudly in the background, "Tell him you're a doctor—make sure you tell him you're a doctor!"

"How can I help you?" Gary asked.

"Did you tell him you're a doctor," the woman's voice repeated in the background.

"Hold on a moment please," Dr. Levy replied.

The phone went quiet. When he returned to the phone, the voice in the background had gone quiet.

"Congressman, our daughter, Chandra, we can't get ahold of her. I know she comes by your office," he continued.

"Sure, I know Chandra. How long has she been out of contact?" Gary replied.

"We haven't been able to get ahold of her for a few days."

"Is she still in Washington?"

"We think so. Do you know where she might like to eat, or any of her friends?"

"I thought she was going back to California. I know Jennifer Baker. She works in my office. I don't know any of her other friends. Have you called the police?"

"Yes. The police said she is probably out with her friends. That's not like Chandra. They said she hasn't been gone long enough for them to do anything. We're very worried."

"I'll do everything I can. I will call some people tonight and make sure they talk to the police about making this a priority. When I get to Washington tomorrow, I will call the police myself. And I'll call you as soon as I hear anything."

Gary sat at the kitchen table.

"Gar, is everything OK?" Carolyn asked.

"He's worried about his daughter not being home. He's trying to get the police to take this seriously."

"Do you know her?"

"She's a friend. She's been by the office several times," he answered.

"How old is she?"

"Twenty-four or five."

He called Dayton and tasked him with calling the police, instructing him to stress to them that it wasn't an acceptable response to tell Chandra's parents, who lived clear across the country, that their daughter hadn't been missing long enough for law enforcement to take action.

Gary walked to the backyard and watched the cypress trees. He'd always been attracted to the manner in which the trees could bend into straight angles without breaking.

He sometimes took young politicians to his backyard, pointed at the wagging trees, and told them, "If you don't learn how to bend, they'll break you in half."

PART II
THE SEARCH

CHAPTER 8

FUMBLES

LACK OF EFFORT

THE NEXT MORNING, on the drive to San Francisco International Airport, Gary called Mike Lynch.

"A young woman from the district is missing. Her name's Chandra Levy. Dayton called the Metro Police to get them on it. Follow up with him. I want to make sure the police aren't sitting on their hands."

Lynch then called Dayton.

"I'm following up on the missing woman, Chandra Levy."

"The police are working on it," Dayton reported. "She's friends with Jennifer Baker. She comes by the office to see Gary."

"He knew her personally?" Lynch asked.

"Yeah," Dayton confirmed.

"Gary didn't mention that."

———

While Gary was in the air, Dr. Levy called Gary's Washington, DC, office.

"Doctor Levy, I've talked to the police, and so has Gary. They're looking for her," Dayton assured him.

"I think she might be held somewhere in a room," Dr. Levy said. "I've called this number that's on her phone bill a lot, and all I get is soft music."

To Dayton, the description given by Dr. Levy sounded like Gary's answering service.

The next day, Dr. Levy called Gary's Modesto office and asked if Gary could get the FBI involved.

Gary, now in Washington, called a contact at the FBI, and the FBI joined the search for Chandra Levy.

CRIME

On May 7, Tomasa Orellana came home from work early, arriving at the Somerset apartments in NW Dupont Circle.

As she entered her bedroom, she noticed a man wearing red construction gloves and a baseball cap crouched in one corner. Orellana screamed and the man fled, clutching screwdrivers in his hands.

She recognized the man, and within hours of receiving Orellana's 911 call, the Metro Police located and arrested Ingmar Guandique.

Metro Police officers found three screwdrivers on him, and a gold ring that belonged to Orellana. He was taken to the nearest police station, where they confirmed Guandique was in the country illegally.

A short while later, Guandique was released back into the public "on his own recognizance."

———

"Detective Durant?" Gary asked through the phone.

"Yes."

"This is Gary Condit returning your call. Detective Valvino left me a message as well."

"I don't know why Detective Valvino was calling you. This is my case," Ralph Durant replied.

"I assume he called about Chandra Levy. Do you have any news?"

"Do you know Chandra Levy?"

"She's a friend. I've had my office call your department a number of times," Gary answered.

"She's still missing."

"Is there anything I can do to help?" Gary asked.

"I'll be in touch. In the meantime, if you think of anything, call me at this number," Durant replied, then hung up.

What was the point of that call? Gary wondered.

Between his brothers Burl and Hop, Gary knew a lot about cops. *There's no urgency.*

Gary called Lynch to get Jennifer Baker's phone number, and then called Detective Durant back. Gary gave him Jennifer's contact details.

"Chandra works out at the Washington Sports Club. She likes to run," Gary informed Durant.

THE COWBOY WHO DOESN'T KNOW HIS BOOTS

On May 9, Chandra Levy had been missing for nine days.

"Mr. Condit?" a voice on the other end of the phone said. "This is Detective Durant. We'd like to talk with you in person. Do you think you could come down to the station?"

"I don't have a car but I can arrange transportation down there or you can come by my place if that's easier. I get home around eight tonight," Gary replied.

"We'll meet you at your place after eight."

———

Three knocks rattled the front door. Gary opened it and found two Metro Police detectives standing in the hallway.

"Gary Condit," he said, extending his right hand.

Detective Durant, about six feet three inches tall, was African American, wore parachute pants over dark leather cowboy boots, and had his hair pulled into a tight ponytail at the base of his skull.

Detective Ronald Wyatt was younger, white, and unassuming.

Gary led them into his living room. The detectives sat next to one another on a black leather couch.

Gary moved to the kitchen, poured two glasses of water, and then returned to the living room.

"Nice boots," Gary said, placing the glasses on the coffee table. "What kind?"

"Not sure," Durant replied. "Congressman, we have prepared a short list of questions."

Every cowboy knows the brand of boots he wears, Gary thought.

"Of course, go ahead," Gary answered.

"What is your relationship with Chandra Levy? How well do you know her?" Durant asked.

"We are friends," Gary answered.

"When did you first meet Chandra?"

"I've known her three or four months. I think I first met her in October or November, when she first came by my office with Jennifer Baker."

"How frequently did you see Chandra?"

"Several times—she would come by my office periodically."

"Did Chandra ever come by your apartment?"

"Yes."

"How many times did she come by?"

"Two or three maybe."

"Did Chandra ever come over to your apartment during the night?"

"Yes. She came over during the day and at night," Gary replied.

"What phone numbers did she have for you?"

"She had my voice service number and my office number."

"Did she have your home number or your cell number?"

"No. Only a few people have the number for my apartment. My voice service is the number I give out to people. She did not have my cell phone number. Even fewer people have that than my home number. My home number, in California, is listed in the phone book. She never called me there," Gary answered.

"What did you talk about?"

"She would call me periodically. She liked to do research on the Internet and would sometimes call me to tell me about an article that she had read or about some news at home."

"Do you know how she got around?"

"She had a metro pass."

"How did she get to your apartment?"

"I don't know if she took a cab, the metro, or walked. I always remember that I would tell her to be careful if she took the metro. She appeared to be physically fit. It wouldn't surprise me if she walked a lot of places. That's what I do."

"Did Chandra seem upset about anything?"

"No, she didn't."

"Did you find Chandra to be unstable? Was she overly emotional about anything?"

"No."

"Did you ever have dinner with her?"

"Yes, one time, she met me at Tryst for dinner."

"Did you ever go out with her to any clubs?"

"Clubs? No."

"Did you ever take a trip together?"

"No. It's possible that she may have been on the same plane with me on one of my trips home to California. I'm not sure, but no, we didn't take any trips together."

"Did you know any of her friends?"

"Nobody except Jennifer Baker."

"Who did she date?"

"I don't know," Gary replied.

"Did you ever take any pictures with Chandra?"

"Not that I recall."

"Did she have a key to your apartment?"

"No. She'd come to the front and I'd buzz her up; same as you."

"Have you ever seen her without jewelry?"

"No," Gary responded, wondering why Durant had asked such a specific question.

"Do you think that Chandra would leave her house without a wallet or ID?"

"It's unlikely, but I don't know."

"Chandra had all her bags packed and ready to go. When was the last time that you talked to her?"

"In late March, early April, a series of phone calls in which Chandra told me that she was planning on returning home for graduation and that she was considering taking the train. She tried to contact me towards the end of the week of April 23. She left a message saying that she was leaving, and asked me to call her back. I remember that there seemed to be some static in the message," Gary answered.

"Did you call her back?"

"Yes, I would always return her calls, but not always right away. I think I tried to call her during the middle or later part of the following week. I called and left a message, saying 'now would be a good time to call me.' She didn't get back, and I thought that was strange, because she was generally prompt about returning calls. Then I left a second message, maybe the next day, saying, 'Are you there? Apparently you have already left and have taken the train. I'll talk to you later.'"

"Did Chandra have any possessions in your house?"

"No."

"Did you ever e-mail Chandra?"

"No. I don't use e-mail."

"When was the last time that you had contact with her?" Durant continued.

"On the 23rd, the 24th, or the 25th I think. She gave me a bag of goodies and thanked me for helping her."

"What did you talk about?"

"She told me that in the past she was interested in staying on at the Department of Justice and that she was attempting to get hired through a special program for masters' students. On that day, she told me that she had missed the deadline for the program and, as a result, she wasn't going to be able to stay on with the DOJ."

"Did she seem upset?" Durant asked.

"Not overly upset. She seemed disappointed, but actually, I was impressed that she seemed to be taking it well. She seemed focused on getting back to California for her graduation. She also spoke about going back to Sacramento or LA, or coming back to DC to go to law school, I think. She had a real interest in getting a position in the FBI."

Detective Durant indicated that he was done asking questions.

Detective Wyatt then asked his first and only question. "Did you have sex with her?"

"If you can tell me the relevancy of that question I will answer it," Gary responded, without pause.

Wyatt sunk back.

These cops need an answer that allows them to move on with their search for her, Gary thought. "I don't think we need to go there, and you can infer what you need to from that for your investigation," Gary offered.

Durant fumbled with his notebook until a photo fell into his hand. He handed it to Gary. "Is this her?" Durant asked.

Gary let his fingers press into the photo's surface. "Yes," he confirmed, and handed it back.

"Thank you for your time and patience, Congressman."

"Anything I can do—you have my number."

He followed the detectives to the front door, where the men again shook hands, then parted.

Gary sat on the couch. As soon as he did, someone knocked on his door. He went back to the front of the apartment and opened the door. Detectives Durant and Wyatt stood in the hallway.

"Detectives, is there something you forgot to ask?"

"Congressman . . . I left my pen on the table," Wyatt explained.

"Come in."

The two detectives reentered the apartment.

Gary watched Wyatt. Durant watched Gary and Wyatt.

"Thank you again for your help," Durant said as the detectives left, again.

—~—

Back at the police station, Durant scribbled on a pad of paper: *Wyatt asked "Did you have an intimate relationship with Ms. Levy?" Congressman Condit stated, "I don't think we need to go there, and you can infer what u want with that."*

Metro Police detectives submit interview reports to the department's typing pool, internally referred to as "OASIS."

Durant typed up an official report of his and Wyatt's interview of Gary for submission to OASIS. In this official report, he did not include the information that he scribbled on the pad of paper concerning Wyatt's question as to whether the congressman had an intimate relationship with the subject, or the congressman's answer.

Gary dialed Dr. Levy's number.

"Hello?" a woman's voice answered.

"Mrs. Levy. This is Gary Condit."

"Mr. Condit."

"I know this must be terribly difficult. I told your husband that I would call if I had any news. I met with detectives this evening and they are looking for Chandra."

"I think she might be flying around with someone high up in the government," Susan Levy replied. "She doesn't have her passport or anything. I think she must be flying around with a high-level person."

"I don't think that is very likely, Mrs. Levy."

"I know she is having an affair with someone high up."

"Do you have any idea who that might be?"

"From what I know, it's Congressman Dreier, Congressman Miller, or Congressman Thompson."

"I am sure if she has a relationship with any of those men it's purely professional. They are all from California. I know she is not romantically involved with those men."

"I'm certain that she is having an affair with one of those men. She might be flying around with him now—she doesn't even have her passport."

"I will call you if I learn anything more. Please give my regards to your husband. Call my office if you think there is anything else we can do to help."

"Thank you," Susan replied.

She's gonna show up soon and this will pass, Gary thought.

LOSING EVIDENCE

Metro Police detectives Ralph Durant and Ronald Wyatt parked their unmarked police cruiser in front of Chandra's apartment building located in the 1200 block of Dupont Circle. They were less than two miles south of the Lynshire building in Adams Morgan and less than half a mile from the Starbucks coffee shop at the intersection of Connecticut Avenue NW and R Street NW where Joyce Chiang was last seen eighteen months earlier.

The building's surveillance cameras captured the detectives entering Chandra's apartment.

Once inside, Wyatt noticed Chandra's laptop computer was powered on and plugged into an outlet. He took a seat behind her computer and browsed its Internet search history while Durant looked around the apartment.

Detectives Wyatt and Durant searched Chandra's apartment for ten minutes. Before they left, Wyatt powered off her laptop.

The building's surveillance cameras captured footage of the detectives exiting the apartment.

It was the fourth time Metro Police officers or detectives had visited Chandra's apartment. Police officers had come on May 6 at the request of Susan Levy to confirm Chandra wasn't in need of medical attention. Officers and detectives returned the next day on May 7 and again the following day on May 8 to see if Chandra had come home and to interview her neighbors and the building manager.

Each time, Metro Police personnel left without asking for a copy of the building's surveillance tapes, even though it was a common practice in Washington, DC, for buildings to self-erase surveillance tapes every seven days.

On May 8, the building's surveillance footage from the week Chandra went missing self-erased.

CALLS TO HELP

Gary called the Levy home.

"Dr. Levy?"

"Yes," Dr. Levy's wrecked voice responded through the receiver.

Dr. Levy had spent the earlier part of the week calling every phone number he could think of that might lead to his daughter. He had left message after message on Chandra's answering machine until the automated voice indicated it was full and would not allow him to leave another.

Gary traced his finger across Mike Dayton's desk. "I know this is hard for your family. I'm praying for her," he replied.

"Thank you."

"I'd like to post a reward for information about Chandra, if you think that would be helpful." In the past, Gary had funded similar rewards for people who had gone missing in his district.

"We would appreciate that," Dr. Levy replied.

Gary's office immediately established the reward fund with the Carole Sund/Carrington Memorial Reward Foundation. The fund was seeded with $10,000 from Gary's campaign coffer. A press release from Gary's office announcing the reward described Chandra as a "great person and a good friend." Within a few days, the fund grew to $25,000.

The Levys were already working with the Sund/Carrington foundation, a Modesto-based victims' rights organization that specialized in helping victims' families navigate law enforcement and the media. The foundation's core piece of advice to the desperate Levys was to do whatever was necessary to keep Chandra's name and picture in the news. The Levys learned of the dark correlation between the amount of press a missing person receives and the likelihood he or she returns home unharmed.

⌒

"I heard something you should know," Rebecca Cooper pressed nearly as soon as Gary picked up his office phone. Her words were hurried, and her voice unusually serious.

"What's that?" Gary replied, with the phone's receiver stuck between his chin and shoulder.

"We were talking about this missing girl, the intern."

"Chandra Levy. It's awful."

"You do know her?" Cooper asked.

"She's from Modesto. She's a friend."

"I heard DC police are talking about putting a congressman in jail."

"OK."

"They're talking about you, Gary."

DESTROYING EVIDENCE

On May 10, Detectives Durant and Wyatt returned to Chandra's apartment. This time, they were accompanied by Charles Egan, a Metro Police Department crime scene forensics expert, two FBI agents, and Assistant United States Attorney Heidi Pasichow.

Egan, the forensics expert, snapped photographs. In Chandra's bedroom, he found packed suitcases. In the bathroom, he zeroed in on a comb, hoping it would provide hair samples for DNA testing. Inside Chandra's closet, he found a hamper full of dirty clothes. Egan didn't mark or remove any items of clothing because it was a missing person's case and not a homicide investigation.

The investigators located Chandra's telephone answering machine in the kitchen. It was full. The tape played back message after message from Dr. Levy begging her to call home. Her mother had left a message stating that she had sent Chandra five e-mails but hadn't received a response. Susan Levy's message ended with a plea: "Call your father. Bob's really upset and he's going to call the congressman."

The tape played back two messages from Gary.

[Tuesday, May 2] It's 11:45, uh. Sorry, I've been tied up for the last few days. Sorry. Give me a call—give me a rundown on kinda what your schedule is. Things are looking pretty good for me today. Anyway—bye. [End]

[Thursday, May 4] It's 6:30. I haven't heard from you—so maybe you are out of the country or something. Anyway, give me a call if you pick up this message. Bye. [End]

Although he had no training in computer forensics, Wyatt, for a second time, sat in front of Chandra's laptop computer and powered it on.

Something's wrong, he realized.

The computer was on but its screen was blank. Its operating system had been obliterated.

Chandra's laptop computer was so badly corrupted that it had to be shipped to a specialized FBI lab for repair, a job that would take months to complete.

CHAPTER 9

GOING NATIONAL

FIRST STORY

THE MAY 11 EDITION OF the *Washington Post* included a story on Chandra's disappearance with the headline NW WOMAN MISSING FOR A WEEK.

Later that day, Dayton received a call from a reporter.

"I'm calling to give you notice of a story we're going to run tomorrow about Congressman Condit," the reporter warned.

"What?" Dayton asked.

"Mr. Condit was dating Chandra Levy, the missing intern. Would you like to comment?"

Gary wouldn't "date" anyone, Dayton thought. "As far as I know, the report is false," he replied.

"Why then did the congressman describe Chandra Levy as a good friend in his press release?" the reporter pressed.

"Every constituent that comes in here is a good friend. That's how it works."

―

A news crew from KCRA TV, a local affiliate of NBC, entered Jennifer Baker's apartment in Sacramento, California. Baker recently finished her internship in Gary's Washington, DC, office, and had moved back to California.

On a desk in the apartment, Baker kept a framed photo of herself, Chandra, and Gary standing in front of the large cardboard cutout of the blue dog with the big yellow eyes.

A cameraman with the news crew loitered by the desk.

―

In Modesto, Stanislaus County Sheriff's Department officials met with members of the local press.

Sheriff Leslie Weidman assured reporters his department was checking all aspects of the investigation into Chandra's disappearance, including coordinating local efforts with investigators on the East Coast. Weidman had gone so far as to dispatch a sheriff's deputy to Washington to work directly with Metro Police detectives.

In Washington, Detective Durant met with local and national reporters.

"We don't know why she disappeared, and we don't know when she disappeared. We just know that she disappeared and we're investigating," Durant explained. His cowboy boots clicked clean against the concrete floor.

FOUNDATION

On May 15, Robert and Susan Levy arrived on the East Coast to kick off a media blitz organized by the Carole Sund/Carrington Memorial Reward Foundation.

Dr. Levy looked overwhelmed, and repeatedly burst into tears. Susan Levy clutched a giant yellow stuffed duck against her stomach. She looked determined.

Their first stop was ABC's *Good Morning America*.

The host, Diane Sawyer, asked Susan Levy about Chandra's alleged mysterious boyfriend in politics. Susan told Sawyer she was focused on finding Chandra and brushed the question off.

"Is there anything else you want to say?" Sawyer asked.

"We're going national with this," Susan replied, indicating that her appearance on *Good Morning America* was just the beginning of the campaign to keep Chandra at the front of the news cycle.

In Modesto, the Sund/Carrington foundation held a candlelight vigil. The foundation's director had mobilized a team of publicists stretching from California to DC. Quotes from Susan Levy and pictures of Chandra were delivered to news outlets with a promise that there would be a further steady stream of fresh material provided by the Levy family before the next deadline.

CNN, Fox, NBC, and CBS followed ABC into the story.

The *Washington Post* dove in headfirst.

MASHERBASHER

"They're going to say the two of you were dating," Mike Dayton explained.

"Based on what?" Gary demanded.

"She asked why you called her a good friend."

"What else should we have said?"

"How do you want to handle this?" Dayton asked.

"I'm not going to respond to that," Gary insisted. "I'll call you after my meeting."

Gary turned off his cell phone and entered California governor Gray Davis's office.

Cadee Condit, Gary's daughter, sat at her desk at the entrance to the governor's private office. She was barely five feet two inches tall, but her frame and demeanor projected strength that was punctuated by blonde hair, like her mother, and steel-blue eyes, like her father. She was a fixture, of sorts, inside the capitol. When she was a little girl and Gary was in the state legislature, he often brought her to work with him. He pinned his card on her shirt, and Cadee wandered the capitol making friends everywhere she went. She kept coming back, like a bug to a light.

How do I tell her this . . . she's been around politics, Gary thought as he processed his conversation with Dayton.

"Cadee, there's something we need to talk about," Gary said after they'd said hello. "There's a woman I know in Washington. She's missing. The papers are going to make a big deal out of me knowing her."

"What's her name?" Cadee asked.

"Chandra Levy. She's from Modesto," Gary replied.

"I don't know her."

"It's been about ten days since anyone has heard from her."

"Did you know her?"

"Yes."

"Rebecca Cooper called me this morning. She warned me that a 'shit storm' was coming in the press, and that it was about you."

Cadee gets it, Gary realized.

—⁊—

Gary ran into his friend Steve Peace in the crowded hallway outside of the governor's office.

Peace looked beaten. His face was gaunt. The energy crisis had taken a noticeable physical toll on him.

"Steve—you OK?"

"No," Peace laughed.

Gary had seen the press. For Peace and Governor Davis, it was brutal. The media blamed them for the energy crisis, while Enron and FERC got a pass. Worse, Gary knew that a conscious political decision had been made in DC by both major parties to avoid the political tar baby in California by simply letting the crisis play out.

"I ran into Bev. She told me you bet her that Enron would be bankrupt within three years," Gary told Peace, trying to lighten the mood.

Bev Hansen, Enron's lead Sacramento lobbyist, had served with Gary and Peace in the California legislature.

"They will. But it will be too late to unwind the damage to the country and the real money behind this doesn't care. They'll move on to the next industry and the next play, and leverage that until they've bled all the money out of it. Gary, I'm slow, but I'm not stupid. Took me a while. Sometimes the truth is just too damn boring to be the story."

Gary smiled and put his hand on Peace's shoulder. "You have a strong family. This shit doesn't matter as long as your boys are good."

"I know. Just pisses me off."

"Everything pisses you off. But the truth comes around, eventually," Gary replied.

"Not necessarily in this lifetime."

"It's the next one that counts anyway," Gary answered, his eyes cast toward the empty hallway.

Something is off, Peace thought. *It's the same smooth voice, the same quick banter. But Gary seems agitated, even hurried. Gary is never rushed. He always has time for everyone.*

"Something wrong?" Peace asked.

Gary looked at his old roommate. "Listen, I'm going to have to lay low for a while. Some stuff has come up in Washington. It'll blow over."

The two men spoke a while longer, then parted.

Peace walked to the floor of the state senate, picked up his mic, and exclaimed, "FERC, Enron! FERC, Enron!" He slammed the mic down and looked accusingly at the press standing at the back of the room.

The scene baffled tourists watching from the rafters.

—·—

It was evening when Gary arrived in Ceres. He found Carolyn in the kitchen, working on a list of people she wanted to send flowers. She had a habit of taking on the pain of others, adding to her own. It was a habit he wouldn't try to break because it was as natural to her as breathing.

He put his hands on her shoulders, and she put her right hand on top of his left, without turning to look at him.

"Gar?" she whispered.

"Yes."

"Did you hear anything else from the police?" Carolyn asked.

"No."

"I'm scared for her. Could you imagine, Cadee?"

"I can't think about it that way."

Carolyn turned her head so that her chin came flush with her thin shoulder blade, and her green eyes could search for answers in his. "I'd be out there looking for her, and wouldn't come home until I found her."

"I've done everything I can. Carolyn, they're going to try and connect me to this in the papers."

"Why?"

The last name on the list of people sitting in front of Carolyn read "Dr. and Mrs. Levy."

—·—

A few blocks from Acorn Lane, street lamps cast an orange glow on the sidewalk in front of Chad Condit's home. Inside, his wife, Helen, and their three young boys were getting ready for bed.

"How are the boys?"

The youngest, Gary Matthew Condit, named after his grandfather, was laying in her lap. The middle son, Couper Condit, was curled up next to her leg. Both were asleep. She was a pretty woman, part Mexican and part Italian. The end result of mixing her blood with the Cherokee in the Condit family's blood was three boys with olive skin and dark hair.

"They're fine."

"Where's Channce?" Chad asked, hoping his oldest son, who was twelve years old, was still awake.

"Taking a shower."

Chad walked to the bathroom. Channce was standing in the shower.

"How you doing, bubba?" Chad asked.

"I threw a touchdown."

"That's real good. Listen for a second, bubba. Turn around—you're going to get soap in your eyes."

Channce turned his body. Chad washed shampoo off the top of his son's head by pulling his hand tight from the forehead to the back of his skull.

"You're going to hear bad stuff about Chief and it's not all going to be true. I don't want you to pay any attention to it, all right? They're just lies."

"Is Chief hurt?"

"Chief's the toughest guy we know. He asked me to make sure you know everything will be fine."

FOLLOWERS

At 6:00 p.m. on May 14, Ingmar Guandique, shirtless, sat on a curb near the intersection of Broad Branch and Beach Roads in Rock Creek Park. A six-inch knife, wrapped in red cloth, was tucked in his front pants pocket.

Halle Shilling jogged from the Pierce Mill parking lot onto the Western Ridge Trail. Her blonde hair was pulled into a ponytail. Her headphones were attached to a yellow Walkman hanging at her side.

She noticed him as she passed.

When the trees stood closer together and the clouds blocked much of the day's remaining light, he drew closer to her.

She slowed, and picked up a stick.

He fell out of sight.

You're being paranoid, she thought.

She discarded the stick and continued jogging.

A few minutes later, the space around her suddenly collapsed.

Guandique jumped on Shilling's back, wrapping his gangly arms around her throat.

They fell, tumbling off the path behind the cover of tall trees. Rushing cars on a nearby road drowned out the sound of their bodies crashing through leaves and branches.

Swoosh. His knife passed her face.

She recognized her attacker. He was the young Hispanic man from the Pierce Mill parking lot.

She screamed.

He held onto her. She felt as afraid and as alone as she had ever felt in her life.

She shoved a hand in his face, trying to get her fingers into his eyes like she had practiced in self-defense class.

He fought it off.

She pushed him toward the canopy above them. "No! No! No!" she yelled.

"Shush. Shush!" he chided.

Again, she pressed her hand toward his face. She couldn't get to an eye, but this time she was able to jam her fingers into the man's mouth, far enough to dig a fingernail into his tongue's soft palate.

He bit down viciously on her fingers, breaking her skin.

She shoved her fingers harder into the soft portions of his mouth.

He fell off of her and ran away with his hands covering his mouth.

Bruised, Shilling ran in the opposite direction until she found two runners who helped get her to the Park Police station. There, she told officers that a young Hispanic man had tried to rape or kill her. She still had her Walkman, and he hadn't tried to steal her diamond engagement ring.

Park Police did not report Shilling's attack to the Metro Police.

––

On Adams Mill Road, spring's full trees cast solid shade over the cracked sidewalk in front of the Lynshire building.

"You want me to come up?" Dayton asked.

"No. I'll be quick . . . I'm gonna grab my gym clothes," Gary replied, and climbed out of the car. He walked quickly up the front steps and disappeared behind the building's gray exterior.

––

Bang. Dayton jumped.

Gary lifted his hand off the Explorer's hood. "You good?" he asked as he climbed back into the passenger seat.

"Look," Dayton said, pointing to the rearview mirror.

"I saw them from upstairs," Gary replied. "Stay alert."

Dayton pulled the Explorer back onto Adams Mill Road.

Two dark SUVs followed.

"She's not the type of person who would just run away," Gary said as he and Dayton discussed their dismay that Chandra was still missing.

"What else can we do?" Dayton replied.

"There's no playbook for this," Gary observed.

The Explorer moved left, merging into a faster lane.

"They're going to find her soon, and this will blow over," Gary insisted. "None of this matters. Finding her matters."

––

Jack Russ sat by his locker in the House gym.

Russ was once the sergeant at arms for the House of Representatives. He knew, as well as anyone, how law enforcement and the political press in the nation's capital worked together, and manipulated one another.

"Jack, you got a minute?" Gary asked.

"Sure," Russ replied, bending to tie the laces on his dress shoes.

"I was followed today from my apartment. Black SUVs. All the way here."

"You in trouble?"

"No. This woman that I know is missing. Some reporters are trying to tie me to her."

Russ stood. "You wouldn't have noticed law enforcement. It's the press."

Gary had undergone an intense background check before joining the intel committee. He knew he had been followed during that process, but he'd never noticed it. Russ had a point. The SUVs following him from his condo to the Rayburn Building made no effort to hide.

"Why?" Gary asked.

"Photos," Russ replied with a serious expression on his face. "The press following you, that's worse than the police. This is the start."

"I have rights."

Russ put his hand on Gary's shoulder. "Only people who have never had to deal with the press believe that. What you need to keep in mind is that the police also have to deal with the press."

—

At the Lynshire, detectives questioned Gary's neighbors about his lifestyle, and whether anyone had seen Chandra with him around the time she disappeared. The neighbors only had nice things to say about Gary, and nobody recalled seeing her in the building.

"We're treating this as a critical missing person's case," Detective Durant explained to beat reporters. "That means she disappeared under suspicious circumstances."

Fearful that local law enforcement in Condit Country was too close to the congressman, Metro Police brass called the Stanislaus County sheriff and demanded he halt his investigation into Chandra's disappearance. The move infuriated Susan Levy.

"What about the statement made by Susan Levy in the *Post*?" a reporter asked Durant.

"What statement?" Durant demanded.

"She said, quote, 'I'm not happy, we need a team effort. There's no reason there should be antagonism between the East Coast and the West Coast.'"

"I hadn't heard that," Durant responded.

—

"The Metro Police told us that if they need any help, they'll give us a call," Stanislaus County Sheriff's Department spokesman Kelly Huston explained to reporters gathered in front of the Levy's ranch home in Modesto.

"We had a difficult time initially establishing a relationship with the DC Metro Police," Huston added. "There are things we can do here in Modesto, and we're surprised they do not want to take advantage of this resource. It's unusual."

The local press issued a scathing opinion of the DC Metro Police:

Hotshot Durant acts like a big-city version of Barney Fife . . . Durant even asked our Sheriff's Department to stop gathering information . . . what sticks in our craw is this big-city Barney Fife saying this is our case and we've had plenty of experience in handling this kind of thing. We neither need nor want your help.

Washington's had experience all right. We seem to remember that at one time Washington had the greatest number of unsolved homicides in the nation . . .

Executive assistant chief of the Metro Police Terrance Gainer called a press conference to fend off the outcry in the press following Susan Levy's public attack.

"They're looking for answers, and we don't have them yet," Gainer exclaimed, his thin mustache not quite stretching to the corners of his mouth.

"Has the police department's inability to aggregate missing person's data across the metro area hampered the Levy investigation?" a reporter asked.

"I don't think it would hurt, but I don't think it has interfered," Gainer responded.

Before leaving the East Coast, the Levys met with representatives from the Metro Police, the FBI, and the US Attorney's Office to clear the air after Susan's public statements had sparked a bicoastal war of words between law-enforcement agencies.

SPECULATION

On May 16, Durant handed Egan a pair of white women's underwear.

"I took this out of Chandra Levy's clothes hamper," Durant explained, asking Egan to tag and file the underwear as evidence.

For his part, Egan didn't recall Durant or any of the other investigators going through the contents of Chandra's hamper during the May 11 search of her apartment.

It would be the start of a strange chain of evidence.

⌐

Citing "unnamed police sources," WRC-TV, Washington, DC's NBC affiliate, reported Gary had told Metro Police detectives Chandra had visited him at his apartment in Adams Morgan.

The *Modesto Bee*, Condit Country's major newspaper, then published quotes from an e-mail Chandra sent to a friend in which Chandra wrote that her "man" would return to Washington when Congress started up again. Other media reports leaked that Chandra told Jennifer Baker she was dating "someone high up in the FBI."

The stories went viral across the burgeoning Internet news world and blogosphere.

"There's always rumors out there," Susan answered. "Everybody wants to create juicy, scandalous stories. I don't care about those stories, I just want her home."

During an appearance on NBC's *Today* show, the host, Katie Couric, asked Susan about the speculation that Chandra was romantically involved with Gary. "I don't really know anything about it," she replied.

The May 17 edition of the *Washington Post* carried the following quote from Mike Lynch in response to a question from a reporter about the alleged affair: "To my knowledge, totally did not occur. It's really distressing that a lot of people are focusing on that issue when the focus should be on finding where Chandra is."

Lynch's response came from his gut. Gary hadn't shared with Lynch the details about the nature of his friendship with Chandra.

The media reacted immediately, and intensely, to the denial from the congressman's chief of staff.

Television and radio pundits demanded a public statement from the congressman clarifying "the nature of his relationship" with the missing woman.

⌐

Gary walked from his kitchen to a window at the back of the adjacent small living room area and peered through the mini blinds down onto Adams Mill Road.

SUVs and news vans lined both sides of the street. Two men were huddled and sipping coffee near the entrance to his building. A dozen reporters and photographers were gathered on the opposite side of the street. Some sat on lawn chairs behind tripods mounted with cameras pointed at the building. Others read books or were talking on their cell phones. They were all waiting for Gary to appear.

The prior morning, paparazzi had popped out from behind a car and snapped a photo of him as he exited the Lynshire. In the single shot, Gary looked like he was smirking. The photo had been widely distributed by the press with captions that read "Why is Condit smiling" and "What does he have to hide?"

Gary snapped shut the mini blinds and a few minutes later exited the front entrance of the Lynshire.

Reporters and photographers scurried from the median, then across the street, to the sidewalk below the main entrance.

"Congressman Condit!" they yelled as soon as he appeared on the front stoop.

"Do you know where Chandra Levy is?" a reporter demanded.

Gary pushed through the wall of people gathered on the sidewalk, climbed into Dayton's SUV, and shut the door.

"How you feeling?" Dayton asked.

"How the fuck you think?"

Gary's cell phone rang. It was Lynch.

"I've got messages from every news outlet in the country," Lynch explained.

"They're following me everywhere."

"I know—it's live on TV. What do we do?" Lynch asked.

"We don't respond to the press. Law enforcement is on this."

"Gary, the *New York Daily News* ran a story about you and Chandra," Lynch said.

"What'd they say?"

"That you and Chandra were seen together in Washington."

"What's wrong with that?"

"They have a photo of the two of you."

The *Daily News* had received the photo from NBC. NBC had received the photo from two separate sources: the Associated Press and NBC's local affiliate, KCRA TV. The AP had received the photo from the *Modesto Bee*.

The *Modesto Bee* had received the photo from Jennifer Baker, who is clearly in it alongside Gary and Chandra in Gary's office. Baker provided the photo to the *Bee* with the express request that the picture not be changed. When the newspaper provided the photo to the AP, it attached Baker's request. The AP in turn distributed the photo to NBC with an express caption attached to it that warned recipients not to make any alterations.

Either NBC or the *Daily News* had cropped the original photo to make it look as if only Gary and Chandra were present. Jennifer was cut completely out of the image.

By that afternoon, the cropped photo had been rebroadcast on news shows all over the globe. Within days, the cropped photo became the standard image—a branding—for the exploding scandal.

Ironically, the cropped photo would have been unnecessary if Chandra had shared all of her photos. For reasons only Chandra could explain, she never shared the second photo taken on her camera the day she and Jennifer first visited Gary's office—the one just of her and Gary.

—

Gary let his head fall back against the passenger seat's cloth headrest.

"I talked with Kadesh yesterday," Dayton said as the Ford Explorer descended from Adams Morgan into DuPont Circle.

Mark Kadesh was Senator Dianne Feinstein's chief of staff. Gary's office had helped arrange for the Levys to meet with California senators Feinstein and Barbara Boxer during their East Coast media trip.

"Did they meet yet?" Gary asked.

"I think they're meeting today."

"Are they coming by the office?"

"I get the sense they aren't going to ask to meet with us."

"I don't understand that."

"Kadesh said Feinstein's office thinks the reward made you look disingenuous. He sounded like people think you have something to hide."

"Is that our fucking MO? Members of Congress kill people? I'm a member of the intel committee. You don't think they know where I am?"

"I don't know," Dayton responded. "It's just not playing the same in DC."

"We aren't playing anything. She's missing," Gary replied, leaning forward as he finished and pointed his finger at the windshield. "What the fuck is that?"

Camera crews swarmed the entrance to the Rayburn Building garage as Dayton's vehicle approached.

—

Dayton and Gary stepped from the stairwell into the main hallway on the fourth floor of the Rayburn Building. They were immediately swarmed by a pack of reporters.

"Are you having an affair with Chandra Levy?" a reporter demanded.

"Did you have something to do with her disappearance?"

Gary and Dayton pushed their way through three dozen reporters camped in front of his office. More were waiting for him in his office lobby. Gary went into his private office and closed the door. Dayton cleared the office of reporters, then joined the rest of Gary's staff gathered around a television in an open workspace.

The scandal had exploded across the cable news networks, and both sides had been given their talking points. Democratic pundits described Gary as a "little-known conservative congressman from California's Central Valley." The story harped on the fact that Gary's father was a Baptist preacher. Republican pundits described Gary as a well-known Democrat with close ties to leaders in the Democratic Party, including the California governor. Their angle focused on drawing comparisons between Gary's behavior and the behavior of former president Bill Clinton.

"I've got to get to the floor," Gary interrupted.

"I'll come with you," Dayton insisted.

"Are you afraid I won't make it through?" Gary asked.

"Not talking is starting to piss them off."

Gary and Dayton fought their way from the Rayburn Building to the Capitol Building, where an even bigger mob of reporters waited.

"Did you have an affair with your intern!" a reporter demanded as Dayton and Gary approached Statuary Hall. Gary instinctively placed his left hand on the bronzed boot of Will Rogers, Oklahoma's favorite son. The left toe had faded to a dull gold from the touches of thousands of others over the years.

Inside, reporters and cameramen were spread across the black-and-white checkered floor. Statues lining the hall's perimeter looked like passive chess pieces readying themselves for an impending blitz on Gary, Dayton, and the scrum of media that had formed around them.

"When will you talk!"

⚊

After attending meetings, Gary slipped into a stairwell that led underground. Once below the Capitol Building, he weaved his way through its bowels until he found an entrance into the Rayburn Building and the protection of the House gym. He stopped at a row of small rectangular offices near the gym's entrance.

Each office was approximately ten feet long by eight feet wide and had a cot with a small side table. Members used the cot rooms to relax, oftentimes to get work done in an environment where they couldn't be bothered—even by their own staff.

Gary entered one of the office cells and pulled the door shut. He grabbed the phone on the side table and called Dayton.

"I've got to get out of here."

"You want to fly home?" Dayton asked.

"The flight schedule is too predictable. I don't want them following me home. Sam Farr said I might be able to borrow Rochelle's farmhouse in Virginia. I just need to get out of here for the weekend. They'll find her, and this will pass."

Sam Farr was a congressman from California. Rochelle was a member of Farr's staff who had worked with Gary during his time in the California legislature.

"The press will follow you there too," Dayton responded. "They've got people crawling all over the capital keeping tabs on you."

"I haven't missed a vote all year," Gary replied.

FUGITIVE BROTHERS

At 11:20 a.m. on May 17, members of Congress poured out of the cloakrooms and gathered on the House floor. In the gallery, press outlets had stationed stringers to watch over Gary. At each exit, reporters and camera crews waited to catch him.

At 11:26 a.m., House members placed votes. The spotters in the gallery called reporters waiting in the rotunda of the Capitol, informing them that they had not yet seen Gary.

At 12:32 p.m., House members returned to the floor for another vote.

"Condit didn't show again!"

At 2:09 p.m., House members made their last vote of the day.

"He snuck away!"

Many out-of-state congressional members head to the airport shortly after the final Thursday vote. It's a migration pattern as regular as that of birds.

Stringers were dispatched to Reagan and Dulles International Airports, San Francisco International Airport, Gary's district office in Modesto, and Gary's home in Ceres.

Reporters raced to the Lynshire building, where the press mob had grown so large that the Metro Police had to mark off areas on the sidewalk where the press couldn't stand so that pedestrians could pass.

The congressman was nowhere to be found.

Phone lines at Gary's offices lit up with reporters demanding to know his location.

—

Gary dropped a duffle bag on the floor of a small farmhouse in Luray, Virginia.

He had snuck away from the Rayburn Building in a staff member's red Ford Escort. When they were far from Capitol Hill, and sure they hadn't been followed, they linked up with Dayton in an empty parking lot. There, Gary got into Dayton's vehicle. On the passenger seat, Dayton had left a map with directions to Rochelle's farmhouse, and in the back, he had placed a duffle bag packed with clothes and toiletries, enough to get Gary through the weekend.

Gary stood at a window and watched the crooked mountaintops disappear into a jagged line that separated the shadow of the mountainsides and the lighter night sky. For the first time in more than a week, it was quiet and nobody was watching him. It was an eerie feeling to suddenly be alone, and under the circumstances, a disturbing one too.

He moved to the living room and switched on the television, watching news coverage of meetings earlier that afternoon between Chandra's parents and Senators Feinstein and Boxer. Feinstein's office had announced it would contribute $5,000 to Chandra's reward fund.

He turned the channel, to CNN's *The Point*, hosted by Greta Van Susteren.

VAN SUSTEREN: Chandra Levy is missing. And Capitol Hill is watching. Bob Franken has details of this disturbing case.

The picture dissolved to footage of the Levys' press conference held earlier that day at the Key Bridge Marriot. Dr. Levy had fallen into his wife arms, crying on her shoulder.

FRANKEN: Levy's parents have come to Washington to meet with law-enforcement officials. What police call "another missing person case" is getting unusual attention as investigators search for evidence of foul play.

The picture on television shifted to Metro Police Chief Charles Ramsey.

CHIEF RAMSEY: We've seen missing cases that have gone on for some time and the person has shown up. We've had others where we weren't quite that fortunate.

FRANKEN: The attention also focuses on Gary Condit, the congressman from Levy's hometown of Modesto, California. Levy, who was an intern in the Bureau of Prisons, frequently visited Condit's office. Following her disappearance, Condit issued a statement saying, "Chandra is a great person and a good friend." Repeatedly questioned about their relationship, a Condit spokesman denied that the congressman and the intern were romantically involved. Meanwhile Levy's parents met with the two US senators from California, but not with Condit.

VAN SUSTEREN: What about the relationship with the congressman? Is there any evidence that says anything more than a constituent-congressman relationship?

FRANKEN: It's really been very, very, very speculative questions asked about her relationships.

VAN SUSTEREN: Joining me now from Sacramento, California, is a friend of Chandra Levy, Jennifer Baker, who also did an internship in Washington this past fall. How did you two meet?

BAKER: We met in Sacramento before both of us went to Washington, DC. And we also took a class together in Washington, DC, and did quite a bit of touring.

VAN SUSTEREN: Did she date any men while she was here in Washington, as far as you know?

BAKER: As far as I know, she told me that she had a boyfriend in the FBI. And we didn't have any extensive conversations about it at all.

VAN SUSTEREN: What do you make of the discussion, and I don't want to draw any sort of wild conclusions, but it's been reported that she stopped in to see her congressman on a number of occasions. Did she ever talk about her congressman with you?

BAKER: Well, the reason that she stopped by the congressman's office is because I interned for the office and she would come to meet me for lunch. We both met him the same time together, and that's the only time that I know of that Chandra ever met Congressman Condit.

Gary checked his answering service. He had one message, from Anne Marie Smith, the flight attendant he had met about a year earlier on a flight from San Francisco to Washington: "It's me. I've got something important I need to talk with you about. Please call me back."

It was the second or third message he had received from her in as many days. Gary scribbled a phone number on the back of a receipt.

He put on a jacket and a baseball cap and drove to a strip mall off the main highway that cut through the center of Luray. He parked the car in a parking spot in front of a McDonald's, got out, and walked to a pay phone on the far end of the lot.

"What's wrong?" Gary asked.

"I want to sit down and talk. Can we talk?" Smith answered.

"There's nothing to discuss."

"Did you know Chandra Levy?"

"She is a friend."

"Where are you?"

"I'm at a friend's house."

"I want to meet with you, in person, to discuss things."

"I've got to lay low for a while."

"Can we still be friends?"

"Yes. I don't see why not," Gary answered.

"When are you coming back to San Francisco?"

"I don't know."

"Can we meet at the airport when you do?"

"I don't know my schedule."

"Well can you give me a date you think you might be here?"

"I've got to go. Take care."

Gary hung up, assuming the phone call had been recorded. He felt that Anne Marie's behavior over the prior weeks was strange, and their conversations awkward.

―――

Hop Condit lay in a hospital bed at a health clinic located just outside Jacksonville, Florida. He had a lengthy recovery ahead of him.

The car that hit him while he walked along the highway had left him for dead.

That night, Hop had mustered just enough strength to drag himself a few hundred yards to the front of the apartment he was staying in. At dawn the next morning, the man who rented him the apartment had found Hop covered in blood and passed out.

"Is there any family you want to call?" a nurse asked.

Hop's black hair was pulled into a long ponytail.

"No. I'm fine," he replied.

He wished he could call his brother but he knew he couldn't do that. He had been watching the television news, which seemed to be all about Gary. Now people on TV were talking about his "fugitive brother." It was torture.

Hop had an outstanding warrant for violating probation conditions related to a DUI arrest in 1997. He hadn't paid mandatory court costs and failed to submit a urine test. Investigators hadn't been actively chasing him given the nature of the violations, and Hop had been living under his favorite alias—Stan Buchanan.

Hop was sharp enough to know that was about to change.

"You need to rest, Mr. Buchanan," the nurse implored.

"I'm fine, darling," Hop lied.

―――

Federal investigators began coordinating with state and local law-enforcement agencies on a multistate search for Darrell "Hop" Condit. Wanted signs flooded areas of Florida and California.

"He had this warrant out for a really long time," one law-enforcement official opined. "It was not until members of the media wanted to know where he was that there was a manhunt."

STUPID THING TO DO

The Levys finished the day's media blitz on CNN's *Larry King Live*.

"Is Chandra a friend of Congressman Condit?" the host, Larry King, asked.

"I would say that professionally she was a friend. Basically, she probably had been down at his office a few times and would seek advice from Mr. Condit on the possibility about going into the FBI," Susan Levy answered.

"Were you hurt by stories that there was supposed to be some romance going on that the congressman . . ." King began.

"I'm not only hurt, I'm scared. And I just want my daughter home alive, and as far as the stories, there's going to be lots of stories floating around in the press. But I want my daughter home, and that's why I'm on TV right now."

On May 18, the *Washington Post* quoted a high-ranking Metro Police figure as saying that Chandra had visited Gary's apartment "more than a couple of times." The statement threw further fuel on a quickening media firestorm.

That same day, a task force of the Metro Police Department and the FBI created a list of suspect areas and persons. On that list were the initials "CM"—code name for "Congressman."

In San Francisco, Joleen McKay called the FBI's field office.

McKay had worked as a legislative aid in Gary's Modesto and Washington, DC, offices. She told the FBI that she and Gary had a three-year sexual affair beginning in 1993, and that she had given him a TAG Heuer watch as a gift. She also told the FBI Gary was never violent, but that he had strict rules for their relationship, including that she wear a baseball cap whenever they left his apartment so they wouldn't be spotted together in public.

Just south of San Francisco, in Condit Country, thirty-five thousand people attended the annual Hughson Fruit and Nut Festival. It was, by far, the largest turnout in the event's history, buttressed by an influx of national media hoping to catch the congressman after his mysterious disappearance from Washington.

With the media deposited at a celebration of fruits and nuts, and Gary safely secured for the weekend in Luray, Virginia, the two men closest to the embattled congressman found a brief pause to reflect on the brewing situation.

"What do you think he should do?" Dayton asked Lynch.

"I think he should make a public statement. Get it out there if there's something to it," Lynch replied.

"He's not going to give in to the press."

"He's got his family to think about and his career. He's going to make a decision with them in mind. I get that. But if he came forward publicly, people won't throw him out of office."

"He really doesn't think it's anybody's business," Dayton answered.

"That doesn't change the fact that if it's true, it was a stupid thing to do."

TRASH THURSDAY

It was a lottery day in the race for Levy-Condit content.

In Adams Morgan, Metro Police officers searched garbage cans and a Dumpster in the alley behind the Lynshire building. Paparazzi camped on Adams Mill Road snapped pictures of police cadets wading through Gary's garbage.

Elsewhere, investigators received, and leaked to the press, a tip that someone had spotted Chandra in Reno, Nevada. Nevada police, FBI agents, and a flock of reporters rushed to the scene. Television news pundits inundated the airwaves with speculative theories about the Nevada tip and Gary, as images of police officers sorting his garbage played in the background.

"He's been known to ride his motorcycle all around the Southwest," one pundit posited, claiming that Gary was familiar with the area.

Before sunrise the next morning, the Reno "tip" had proven to be a dead end. But Gary's office continued fielding reporters' questions about his rumored connections to Nevada for the next two weeks. It wasn't long before they also started asking about Gary's rumored connections to motorcycle gangs.

Carolyn looked through the peephole on the front door.

The mailman stood on the outside stoop, under the willow tree's shade.

"Good morning," he said.

She opened the door but did not step onto the stoop so that the photographers camped on the opposite side of Acorn Lane couldn't snap a photo of her.

"I wanted you to see this," the mailman explained, handing her a copy of a tabloid magazine with a cover story that touted Gary's alleged sexual exploits with men and women alike.

"I thought I'd let you know before you saw it somewhere else. I've got a few hundred of these on my route. People read it like the news. We call today 'trash Thursday.' You might want to avoid the supermarket on Thursdays."

Carolyn thanked him, closed the door, and walked back to the kitchen, where she called Gary.

"How do you feel?" he asked.

"An eight," referring to her level of physical pain that day.

"I'm sorry, Carolyn," Gary replied, knowing that probably meant her pain was really at ten, the worst it could be.

"Gar, there are vans on the street. People from the news are sitting in chairs on the sidewalk."

"They want pictures for their stories," Gary responded, clenching his fists and knowing that there was nothing he could do.

The mailman was right about trash Thursdays. They came as regular as the tides.

By the middle of summer, tabloid magazines had run dozens of stories about Gary, each more sordid and bizarre than the last. Topics ranged from "Intern died in congressman's bed—and her body was dumped; she was so distraught she went to Gary's apartment and committed suicide," to "Chandra killed in kinky sex game! Condit kept bondage gear under his bed and had a harem of eager beauties," to "I was Condit's sex slave—Torrie Hendley says she had 6-month fling with Condit; met in April 1996 in Laughlin; he liked spanking her," to "Chandra and the congressman's ruthless ex-con brother. Did he kill her?"

By late summer, tabloid headlines screamed that Gary participated in wild orgies with foreign diplomats, arranged Chandra's murder at the hands of the Hells Angels, and raped teenage girls.

A few blocks from Acorn Lane, Jean Condit, Gary's mother, spread a copy of the *Modesto Bee* across the breakfast table.

"Adrian," she called to her husband, pointing at the article as he entered the kitchen. "Look at that."

The headline on the newspaper's editorial page read, **A MISSING WOMAN AND A MEDIA CIRCUS, NATIONAL NEWS RUNS AMOK IN THE LEVY CASE**. Inside, the *Bee* accused the national media of fueling a frenzy through the use of anonymous and unreliable sources:

> We have been inundated with calls from other media. Our reporters have been invited to appear on talk shows, as if they are somehow experts . . . We talk to no one . . . It is more important to be right than to be first.

"It's about time somebody said it," Adrian said. "They've run amok."

PARANOIA

Word that Gary had reappeared spread quickly through the news and political worlds. Stringers stared at him from the gallery above the House floor. At every exit off the floor, news camera crews waited anxiously for the session to end.

Gary moved across the blue carpet, shaking hands with the members who made a point of talking to him and avoiding those who didn't.

"Gary, I've got a friend. I can set up an interview with Fox News if you want to come out and talk about this," a Republican member offered.

"No thanks," Gary replied.

"Hang in there," another member said.

"Thanks," Gary replied as he slogged toward the exit and the gauntlet of reporters and cameramen waiting on the other side.

Representative Bill Delahunt caught Gary by the arm. Delahunt's white hair was combed over to the left, and he wore a light gray suit. Before his election to Congress, he had served as a district attorney and, before that, as legal counsel to the Quincy Police Department in his home state of Massachusetts. He and Gary were political colleagues, but not close friends.

"How you doing, Bill?" Gary said, placing his hand on Delahunt's shoulder and expecting another friendly "hang in there."

Delahunt held onto Gary's arm. "I'm going to be your attorney for the next thirty seconds. You got that?"

Gary nodded.

"Don't talk to anybody here. Everyone likes you. But they all want to be 'in the know.' Anyone you talk to can be subpoenaed," Delahunt advised.

The advice solidified a thought that had disturbed Gary since he returned from Virginia. The shifty glances at him had grown quicker, the stares longer, and the whispers both softer and louder. *These people also think of me as a suspect whether they believe I did it or not.*

A stringer in the rafters called a reporter waiting outside the exit to the House. "Delahunt. Grab Delahunt. He and Congressman Blow-dry just had a private conversation," he exclaimed.

—

Inside the office of Representative John Conyers, books littered shelves and tabletops, and exotic musical instruments, it seemed, were everywhere.

Conyers had asked Gary to come by his office. Gary didn't know what it was about. A staffer led Gary into Conyers's private office and let him know that the congressman would arrive shortly. His prior meeting in the Capitol Building had run late.

Gary didn't mind the wait. His staff had helped him distract the reporters and plan a circuitous route to Conyers's office that successfully threw the media pack off his trail.

Conyers was from Michigan and represented big auto. Gary represented big agriculture. Their relationship was forged, largely, by their shared opposition to the North American Free Trade Agreement in the early '90s.

Conyers's arrival broke Gary's reflection.

"I assume you wanted to meet here to avoid the folks camped out at my office," Gary joked.

"It's amazing," Conyers answered.

"What's going on?"

"I talked with Dick Gregory this morning," Conyers replied. "He thinks you're getting set up."

It was the last thing Gary expected to hear. Dick Gregory was a legendary black comedian turned social activist who was well known within political circles for his conspiracy theories. But they had never involved Gary. *Conyers said it nonchalantly*, Gary thought. *He doesn't know whether it's real or not.*

"Anyone angry with you?" Conyers asked.

"We're in a business where we vote one way or another."

Gary's mind went back to the warning he received from Rebecca Cooper, and the advice he received from Delahunt. *The Judiciary Committee has oversight over federal law-enforcement authorities. Conyers and Delahunt are both on the committee.*

—

Adrian Condit answered the kitchen phone.

"How's everyone doing?" Gary asked.

"We're fine here. You worry about yourself. There's evil at work, son. God doesn't work to destroy a man's vocation and family. None of it makes sense."

"There's a lot going on that seems off," Gary acknowledged.

"People are saying terrible things. They don't add up. You need to say it like it is."

"Nothing I say will stop this. It will pass when they find her."

"Sins of the tongue are the worst because they don't ever stop. They destroy, and that's all they do," Adrian insisted. "You're strong, son. But this burden. It's only going to get worse."

ALLOCATING RESOURCES

On May 30, the *Washington Post* ran a story covering a meeting the prior day between President Bush and Governor Gray Davis regarding the continuing energy crisis in California. According to the *Post*:

> The governor's rhetoric, which in the past has demonized Texas energy companies, is unappealing . . . Unless both president and governor change their tune, California's economy may tank, possibly bringing the rest of the country down with it.

The governor's insistence that fraud was occurring in the wholesale energy market, led by Enron, didn't strike a chord with the paper. Instead, the *Post* assigned more resources to cover the Levy story.

In San Francisco, FBI agents interviewed flight attendant Anne Marie Smith. She informed the FBI about a yearlong relationship she alleged to have had with Gary. "He was a decent man," Smith explained to them.

After the interview, Smith left a message for Gary on his answering service.

Gary called her back. Smith told him that she had met with the FBI, and that she was being contacted by reporters. Gary, assuming that the call was being recorded and that it might be a press setup, listened. She wanted to discuss the allegations about Gary in the media, but Gary would not engage.

"I need to see you. I can meet you at the airport for coffee. I want to talk," she pressed.

"I don't think that's a good idea," Gary responded.

Smith would later claim that Gary told her she did not have to talk to the FBI. Gary maintains that this is not true, and that his only discussion with Smith around cooperation had to do with responding to reporters. Smith would also later claim that she was approached by the FBI. What is unclear is why the FBI, on June 1, would have reason to track down and interview Smith.

In Virginia, reports to the FBI and CIA suggested the threat of a terrorist attack against US interests had reached its highest level in more than two years. FBI counterterrorism agents requested additional resources to investigate potential domestic threats, including suggestions that terrorists had entered flight schools in the American Southwest. Those resources were not provided by the FBI brass.

Armed with Anne Marie Smith's story about her alleged relationship with Gary and allegations flying around the media about more women in his past, the FBI assigned additional resources to find and question all the "other women" in Gary's life.

—

Gary exited the back door and into the alley behind the Lynshire building.

"He's here!" a stringer screamed. "Out back!"

The mass of reporters and cameramen camped on Adams Mill Road made a mad dash around the building to the alley. Just as they arrived, Gary ducked inside Dayton's black Volkswagen Jetta. The Jetta belonged to Dayton's wife.

"Why won't you talk about Chandra Levy?" a reporter yelled as they drove away.

Gary and Dayton had planned the car switch the night before. They had both grown tired of Gary's ritual "walk of shame" every morning that was broadcast live around the globe.

"You sleep?" Dayton asked, concerned by the dark bags under Gary's eyes.

"I'm fine."

"The police acknowledged the leaks to the press."

"It's about fucking time. They ask us not to talk to the press but they can't get their people to follow their policy."

"Yeah, well, apparently the FBI is talking to all the women you've worked with. It'd be nice if they looked for Chandra instead of trying to figure out who you've slept with."

"Yes. It would be nice to know she is okay," Gary answered.

CHAPTER 10

TEMPEST

CHANGING STORY

MAY TURNED INTO JUNE, and Chandra was still missing.

The June 7 edition of the *Washington Post* landed on Dayton's desk with a thud. The byline listed Allan Lengel as its author. The story, citing "law enforcement sources," stated Gary had told police Chandra spent the night at his apartment. That, in and of itself, was enough to ratchet up the heat on Gary.

As Dayton read on, however, he realized the *Post's* latest story contained a bigger bombshell. The Levys had maintained, from the outset of the scandal, that they had no knowledge of a relationship between Gary and Chandra.

Now, suddenly, that changed.

> The missing intern told a close relative that she was romantically involved with the congressman . . .
>
> "We have nothing to hide" about Condit's relationship with Levy, said Mike Dayton, a spokesman at the congressman's office on Capitol Hill.
>
> But the Levy relative said, "Chandra has told me things that seem to contradict what the spokesmen for Congressman Condit have been saying."
>
> The relative, who spoke to the *Washington Post* on the condition of anonymity, said that she spent last Thanksgiving and Passover in April with Levy, 24, and that the intern told her about her romantic life in Washington . . .

The *Washington Post* would not release the identity of the relative right away. Instead, information would be dribbled to the public in bits and pieces, calculated to keep the world focused on the scandal.

—

Detective Durant prepared a supplement to his report on his and Detective Wyatt's interview with Gary on May 9 at Gary's condo in Adams Morgan.

The supplemental OASIS report (No. 2DDU01-185/19) read:

> On May 9, 2001, SUPPLEMENTAL REPORT NUMBER 2 WAS CREATED IN WACIIS. IN PARA-GRAPH 6 (CONVERSATION WITH CONGRESSMAN CONDIT), PARTS OF THE CONVERSATION WERE OMITTED FOR SECURITY REASONS. THE MISSING CONVERSATION IS AS FOLLOWS:

CONGRESSMAN CONDIT WAS ASKED ABOUT CHANDRA LEVY, STAYING AT HIS APARTMENT AND HE STATED THAT SHE HAD SPENT THE NIGHT THERE A COUPLE OF TIMES. HE FURTHER STATED THAT SHE HAD LEFT CLOTHING OVER THERE, BUT WHEN HIS FAMILY WOULD COME INTO TOWN, SHE WOULD HAVE TO TAKE THE CLOTHING OUT. SGT. WYATT ASKED, "DID YOU HAVE AN INTIMATE RELATIONSHIP WITH MS. LEVY?" CONGRESSMAN CONDIT STATED, "I DON'T THINK WE NEED TO GO THERE, AND YOU CAN INFER WHAT U WANT WITH THAT." HE FURTHER STATED THAT HIS FAMILY DID NOT KNOW ABOUT CHANDRA LEVY.

The supplemental OASIS report claims Gary told Durant and Wyatt that Chandra slept over at his condo and had left clothes there. Gary hadn't said either of those things in the May 9 discussion with Durant and Wyatt. Still, those alleged details were leaked to the *Post* by an unnamed police source.

Durant dated the supplemental report June 6, nearly a full month after the May 9 discussion with Gary and, perhaps not coincidentally, just one day before the June 7 *Post* story.

The internal inconsistency of the supplement is glaring. In one breath, the report acknowledges Gary's assertion that when the detectives asked him questions that got into the nature of his relationship with Chandra, he simply stated he didn't think they needed to go there, and they didn't press him any further. In the other breath, it attempts to document Gary discussing those very details they did not actually discuss.

The Metro Police would spend the next decade claiming that Gary had lied to them when they asked him on May 9 whether he had an "intimate relationship" with Chandra. The part of the unusual supplemental OASIS report dated June 6 that refutes this lie would be kept under wraps.

In retrospect, it appears the Metro Police had doctored records of their initial discussion with Gary so that they could have it both ways.

And for more than a decade, they got away with it.

─

Chandra's parents returned to the East Coast for the first leg of a second well-coordinated media blitz. During each interview, the Levys were pressed to comment on the report in the *Washington Post* that Chandra had slept over at Gary's apartment.

Susan Levy told reporters, "I don't care if she's been allegedly sleeping with somebody. That's irrelevant. All those things are just stories. Maybe they're true, maybe they're not."

Court TV's Nancy Grace, a former prosecutor, interviewed the Levys, pressing the distraught parents on the alleged sexual relationship between their daughter and the congressman.

"All we want is to get her back safely," Dr. Levy insisted. "Everything else is secondary."

Grace was a pioneer for the cable news networks as they plunged into the American justice system. "Cops only arrest the guilty, so why bother with a trial!" Grace told her entertained audience.

In 2001, Grace was still relatively unknown. Drama, however, was her ticket to the big time, and the Levy case oozed drama.

PERP WALK

On Adams Mill Road, reporters had leapfrogged one lane of traffic to the median, forming an island of bodies. They were gathered in circles, drinking coffee, smoking cigarettes, and sharing the latest rumors to come out of the exploding scandal.

On the far side of the street, cameramen remained camped behind their tripods with cameras pointed at the Lynshire building. They traded copies of the latest edition of the *Washington Post* as they waited.

In addition to the swelling media presence, a growing contingent of interested citizens was now planted on the sidewalks.

A man in a pink suit stared with unruly eyes at the fourth floor of the Lynshire. "NAZI!" he yelled. "Where did you put the body?"

Other spectators stationed on the perimeter of the press gaggle carried signs that read "RESIGN NOW COWARD!" and "MURDERER AND ADULTERER!"

Gary shut the blinds and went back to watching the Weather Channel while waiting for Dayton's call.

Lynch asked law-enforcement officials to monitor the escalating situation on Adams Mill Road citing a concern for Gary's safety. Gary had received a mountain of daily hate mail, including death threats.

In response, the Metro Police brass offered to send uniformed officers to the Lynshire every morning to escort Gary from his apartment to the Rayburn Building. Lynch declined the offer to arm the press each morning anew with the visual of Gary being led out the door by cops.

—

"Thirty seconds," Dayton said, and hung up.

It took Gary twenty seconds to get from his condo door to the front door of the Lynshire building. From there, it took twenty seconds to get to the street.

He emerged from the building entrance. *One-one thousand. Two-one thousand.*

"Is it true that Chandra slept in your bedroom?" a reporter shouted.

"Did you have sex with her!" another asked.

"Shame on you, Gary Condom!" the man in the pink suit screamed. "NAZI fucker!"

—

Dayton pulled the Explorer away from the curb and handed Gary a copy of Allan Lengel's story in the *Washington Post*.

"What's this quote from you about nothing to hide?" Gary asked.

"I wasn't interviewed by Lengel," Dayton answered. "I gave that quote to a different reporter a week ago. A woman called asking for our records—'everything,' she said. I asked if the *Post* could be more specific. But she demanded we hand over 'everything.' I told her that I'd give them everything I could, and we have nothing to hide."

Dayton whipped the car around a corner. Ahead, a press mob formed at the entrance to the Rayburn Building garage.

"It's worse inside the building," Dayton explained as they passed the mob.

Gary ran Delahunt's advice through his head. *"They can all be subpoenaed."* *The press is gonna start going after my guys. And the police will follow the press.*

"You need to stay alert," Gary warned. "They're going to try and pull you and Lynch into this."

TALKING

Gary sat in one of the small cell-like offices inside the House gym, going through a stack of phone messages.

He wasn't surprised that Rusty Areias had called twice in the last day. Areias, one of the Gang of Five, was also from the Central Valley, and they remained close friends.

Gary picked up the phone and dialed.

Areias didn't waste time on pleasantries, and he didn't need to. It was as though they were sitting, face-to-face, around the table at Paragary's in Sacramento talking about how to blunt Willie Brown's next move.

"You need a PR strategy. I know you don't want to talk with the press. But your silence is a liability," Areias insisted.

"We've sent press releases. I'm cooperating with police. What more do they want?" Gary responded.

"You need to give them something. Right now, because you're not talking, they're filling airtime with all this shit about you and other women."

"I'm not listening to it," Gary responded.

"You need to say something, even on your political record."

"This isn't a sex scandal. I know her. She's missing. If I say something, then I'm making it about me. I'm not going to feed that beast," Gary said.

"This has gotten so bad that people wouldn't care if you said you slept with her. They think you killed her."

"I don't understand why people think that way. I still hope she's fine."

"A lot of folks *hope* you killed her."

A pause in the conversation followed Areias's hard medicine.

"I've met with the consultants, some that advised Clinton," Gary explained. "Their advice was to apologize for 'something'—'anything' they said. You think I'll fucking cry on TV like some pussy-ass guy who resigns? I'm not gonna apologize for something that doesn't have anything to do with her being missing. Let them say whatever the fuck they want about me. I'm not going to insert myself into this by inventing some bullshit sob story. I'm not going to do that, Rusty."

"You don't need to go that far," Areias pushed. "Right now, it's just you and your guys getting your ass kicked. You need—"

"I asked one of the consultants who he last helped," Gary interrupted. "He told me 'Bob Kerrey.' I told him, 'That went really well.'" Gary was referring to Kerrey's dreary performance in his run for the presidency in 1992.

"Why don't you at least call Joe Cotchett? You need legal counsel. You've got a lot of people hoping you did this."

Joseph Cotchett was a well-known trial attorney in San Francisco.

—

It was past midnight, and Gary couldn't sleep. He pulled on a hooded sweatshirt and hat and slipped out the back of the building.

As he suspected, stringers camped on Acorn Lane were asleep or inattentive at this hour. He crossed Adams Mill Road and entered Walter Pierce Park, passing a colorful mural framing an asphalt basketball court.

He thought about Hop, praying that his brother, under whatever name he traveled by, was safe.

He found a place to sit. He thought about the lives he led. He was an Okie roughneck, and a member of Congress. He was a brother, and a preacher's son. He was a husband, and a father. He never considered not going home to Carolyn. Like most people, he was many things. He took great care to preserve them all, knowing that in each, he could not be the same.

He looked up.

Darkness never comes to the nation's capital. Its combative forces assault the sky with dramatic light and sound, preserving the value of what is gilded from the extraordinary depth of our common experience. It is very different than the humbling emptiness of Oklahoma's panhandle.

Gary thought about Delahunt's advice and about Conyers's message. *I've spent my entire career pissing off the establishment . . . all of them.*

PART III
THE CIRCUS

CHAPTER 11

SUSPECT CM

AFFIDAVIT

LYNCH, DAYTON, AND GARY SAT across from attorney Joe Cotchett, a gregarious man, inside his San Francisco law office. Cotchett's investigator was also in the room. Lynch gave Cotchett an overview of the latest allegations against Gary, and the correlated leaks springing from law-enforcement sources.

"We've received invitations from every news show offering Gary an opportunity to go public with the details of his relationship with Chandra Levy," Lynch explained. "We've turned down all of them."

Gary's refusal to speak publicly had gone on so long that many pundits suggested his silence was a proxy for guilt. At the very least, they argued, his silence was the absence of candor, which in the political world is a crime.

"He won't do it?" Cotchett responded.

"No, I won't," Gary said before Lynch could answer. "These women saying they've had an affair with me have nothing to do with Chandra. They don't know Chandra and they won't help find her. I'm drawing a line public officials should have drawn a long time ago."

"Politicians are public persons, like celebrities," Cotchett explained. "The press has a legal right to say anything they want about a public figure within the broad parameters of the 'truth'—they can do everything but extend that."

"They aren't always telling the truth," Gary argued.

"But you can't assert that unless you expose yourself totally, openly, and honestly. It's a waste of time to threaten them with the truth unless you are prepared to put it out there," Cotchett advised.

"What the fuck does that mean?"

"That means so long as they didn't know they were lies at the time they were printed, they're not liable. That creates a disincentive to check a source because they might lose their story. You have to create a public record of your version of the truth. The best way to do that is to take them up on their offer for you to tell your side of this."

"I have to give up my privacy to protect my privacy?" Gary asked sarcastically.

"You can look at it that way. From their perspective, they feel like they've offered you a chance to clarify these allegations, and they don't think they owe you any more than that."

"I have to defend myself openly but their sources can hide in the shadows?" Gary responded.

"To preserve your legal rights, you need to put them on notice of their mistakes and give them the opportunity to retract any false statements. If you don't, you might not be able to recover damages if and when your version of the truth is established."

"They're relying on unnamed police sources," Gary interjected. "And what the fuck do you mean by my 'version'? There aren't versions of the truth. I know what happened and didn't happen."

"Let's start with 'sources close to the police,'" Cotchett responded. "What does that mean? Is it someone inside the police department? Is it a detective's spouse? Is it somebody they interviewed standing on the sidewalk in front of the police station? Legally, any of those might be sufficient."

"You're saying I can't do anything about this unless I get on TV and spill my guts about shit that has nothing to do with finding her?"

"No. I'm saying unless you do that, this isn't going to stop. There are some lesser steps you can take, but they may not work."

The conversation with Cotchett turned to the latest crisis. Gary's office had received a legal letter from *Star*, the tabloid magazine, notifying him that it was going to run a story about an affair between Gary and Anne Marie Smith, the United Airlines flight attendant.

According to *Star*, she had been Gary's "lover" for nearly a year, during which time they met at least once a month for "nights of lovemaking" at hotels in the Bay Area or his condo in Adams Morgan.

"Can you call her?" Cotchett advised.

"Sure," Gary answered

Cotchett led Gary to a private conference room. "Let me know if you need anything," he offered before shutting the door and returning to the main room where Lynch and Dayton were still seated.

"Is there anything to this?" Cotchett asked Dayton.

"To what?"

"Was he sleeping with her?"

"Not to my knowledge," Dayton answered. "But I don't know."

Cotchett shook his head.

—

The phone rang three times before Anne Marie Smith answered.

"Hello?"

"It's Gary."

"Why haven't you returned my calls?" she demanded.

"I got your message," Gary responded, assuming that the conversation was being taped. "I'm sorry it took some time to get back."

"My roommate sold a story to *Star*."

"What kind of story?"

"A story about us. I tried to stop it," Smith replied.

"Is the story true?" Gary asked.

"No," Smith replied.

"There are certain people in this world you shouldn't trust. You better get yourself an attorney. You're going to be in the papers," Gary said.

"I have a family attorney."

"You should get a letter from your attorney to the *Star*, that's what I'm doing. You don't need to talk to them."

The door behind him opened and Cotchett stepped into the room.

"Ask her if she'll sign an affidavit," Cotchett instructed.

Gary turned back to his telephone conversation with Smith. "My attorney wants to know if you'll sign an affidavit. If you want to keep out of the papers, you might need to do that."

"Yes, I'd consider doing that. I don't want to be in the newspapers," Smith replied.

EDITORIALIZING

On Acorn Lane, Dick LeGrand and Mark Vasche stood stiffly on the stoop under the shade of Gary's willow tree. Gary met them there, and then led his guests through the plain ranch house and into the backyard, where they sat in white plastic patio chairs under the uneven shade of cypress trees.

Lynch had arranged the off-the-record meeting with the *Modesto Bee*'s top opinion writers.

LeGrand had been on the local political scene since Gary's first election to the county board of supervisors in 1976.

Vasche was taller and younger than LeGrand. He had a reputation for being straitlaced, and he wore his conservative Christian values on his sleeve.

LeGrand and Vasche asked for an update on the investigation. Gary told them he knew only what had been printed in the newspapers. They asked about his interview with Detectives Durant and Wyatt. Unnamed police sources had told reporters that during the interview Gary had denied any romantic relationship with Chandra. The allegation fed rumors that Gary wasn't cooperating with law enforcement.

"You didn't deny to detectives that you had a romantic relationship with her?" Vasche pressed.

"I did not lie to the police," Gary answered. "What was said in that interview is between me and the police, except of course the police are leaking bad information to the press."

The three men acknowledged that the media was turning into a circus. LeGrand and Vasche disagreed with Gary's characterization that the *Bee* had played a part in it, reminding him that their paper had published articles accusing the national media of "running amok."

The editorialists suggested Gary's popularity at home would insulate him against a potential political fallout with voters if Gary publicly acknowledged he had an extramarital affair with Chandra. They argued that because the investigation had strung out for more than five weeks, Gary now owed Central Valley citizens an explanation for what they were reading in the newspapers and hearing on TV.

"I'm cooperating with police," Gary insisted. "There is an active investigation to find a missing woman."

"If you address the rumor, people can move on," LeGrand responded. "Right now, it's a distraction."

"Do you really think that's true?" Gary asked, annoyed by the insinuation that he was the source of the distraction. "Do you really think if I answer that question the press will suddenly leave this alone and focus on finding her?"

"Yes," LeGrand answered.

"You owe it to the voters," Vasche added. "It's the best possible forum for you to do this."

The editorialists offered Gary an opportunity to break the truth of his relationship with Chandra to the *Bee*. In return, the paper would prominently publish, in full, a statement from Gary to the public.

"I'm not going to do that," Gary replied.

"You owe—"

"I don't owe anybody anything other than my cooperation with authorities."

LeGrand, Vasche, and Gary argued. Tension turned to outward anger.

"Did you have an affair with her or not?" Vasche demanded.

"I don't see how that's relevant," Gary responded.

"Of course it's relevant. It's a distraction!" LeGrand countered.

"That doesn't make it relevant. You're making it a distraction. Not me."

"Did you have anything to do with her disappearance?" LeGrand asked.

Gary's lips pulled tight. He focused on the cypress trees bending to the strong wind like pointed fingers. "No. Do you really think a sitting member of Congress would do something like that?" he asked.

⌐

Across town, the Levy's ranch home teemed with consultants from the Carole Sund/ Carrington Memorial Reward Foundation and law-enforcement representatives.

In the backyard, out-of-town reporters played in the Levy pool and sipped soda while sitting around patio tables, chatting about the scandal.

Inside, Susan Levy hung her latest painting on the wall.

According to reporters for the *Washington Post*, her latest work was a collage of pictures, paint, and paper. Gary's head sat at the center surrounded by missiles slamming into his skull. Blood gushed from his head. In the upper left corner of the painting, a shackled prisoner clad in an orange jumpsuit knelt beneath a decapitated head with a picture of Gary's face clipped from a magazine glued onto it. A photograph of Chandra, taken in Jerusalem, was set off to the other side, splattered with red paint representing Gary's blood.

RECORD KEEPING

Joe Cotchett's office contacted Anne Marie Smith to follow up on her discussion with Gary about the pending story with *Star*.

Smith stated the allegations made by *Star* were out of proportion, and reiterated that her roommate had been paid for the sensationalized story. She claimed to be embarrassed by the ordeal and provided Cotchett with the name and phone number of her family attorney: Jim Robinson.

Cotchett called Robinson, who was cordial and reiterated the point that his client, Smith, had no desire to become a public spectacle.

"Would she be willing to provide a statement about her relationship with the congressman in regards to the allegations?" Cotchett asked Robinson.

Robinson told Cotchett to send a draft over for his review, and that he'd make any needed changes.

Cotchett's office put together a short statement, to be signed under penalty of perjury, with the intention that Smith and her attorney, Robinson, would take the statement and make it their own.

Cotchett's office wrote at the top of the draft statement "Please edit, cut, suggest, etc." and sent it to Robinson via e-mail as a "draft." The body of the affidavit read, in part: "I do not and have not had a romantic relationship with Congressman Condit."

Shortly after the e-mail was sent, Robinson phoned Cotchett.

"Mr. Cotchett, my client is not inclined to sign anything at this moment regarding her relationship with the congressman. She doesn't want to get involved further, and this is a personal matter. She is upset with her roommate, and has already talked with the FBI and given the FBI details about the relationship. Any statement would have to reflect her conversation with the FBI."

After that, Robinson would not return Cotchett's calls.

─

Cotchett had demanded that the Metro Police make a public correction of misinformation leaked from police sources to the *Washington Post*.

Cotchett also asked that the Metro Police temper its interactions with the media. Chief Ramsey and his number two, Terrance Gainer, were holding press conferences and providing television interviews on a near daily basis, even when the only information they had to report was the lack of any new information.

Ramsey didn't respond.

POST POSITION

PETULA

On June 8, Petula Dvorak, a reporter for the *Washington Post*, stepped inside the terminal at San Francisco International Airport. Like Chandra, Dvorak was a graduate of the University of Southern California, and before coming to the *Post*, she worked as a reporter for the *Times-Picayune* in New Orleans, where she covered crime and the Yugoslav Wars. She held a list of Gary's current and former staffers and colleagues in her right hand. She didn't waste any time getting to work.

"Is this Walter Hughes?" Petula asked over her cell phone.

"Yes."

Gary and Hughes had worked together when Gary served in the California legislature.

"My name is Petula Dvorak. I'm a reporter for the *Washington Post*."

"What can I do for you?" Hughes answered.

"I'm in California on an assignment to get Gary Condit," she explained. "We're following up on rumors that he was a womanizer in the '80s during his time in the legislature. I've been told that you knew Mr. Condit back then and I'd like to ask you some questions."

— ✦ —

South of the airport, in Modesto, Mike Lynch slammed a copy of the *Modesto Bee* on his desk and opened it to the editorial page:

CONDIT MUST CLARIFY LEVY RELATIONSHIP

The latest came Thursday, with a story in the *Washington Post* headlined "Intern Spent Night, Condit Told Police." Condit's office denied the story, and the Congressman later in the day hired an attorney to demand a retraction . . .

He has a duty to publicly clarify his relationship with Levy, if for no other reason than to help focus the search for Chandra on fact, not rumor . . .

Five weeks of silence is enough. Condit would better serve his constituents by squarely facing the public and its questions.

Lynch sat behind his computer and typed a letter to Dick LeGrand, the editor of the *Modesto Bee*, that read, in part: "The mainstream press wants it both ways—it condemns the use of irrelevant rumors, unnamed sources, and distortions in the tabloids, and then demands the same rumors and distortions be 'clarified' in the public interest."

The true significance of the *Modesto Bee*'s editorial wasn't lost on Lynch. The local press had caved to the scandal's pressure and would no longer challenge the national media's narrative.

Gary would now be hammered from all sides.

On Monday, June 11, Petula Dvorak entered Simon's Chinese Restaurant and Bar, located a block east and a block south of California's state capitol.

Simon's was a well-known political watering hole—neutral territory for all factions. Dvorak had placed herself at the vortex of where Gary's long-time friends and enemies gathered. Somebody had sent her to the right place.

Inside, Gary was the principal topic of conversation. Legislators, staffers, lobbyists, and political consultants sat around square tables talking about the latest rumors. Television coverage of the Levy scandal provided a noisy backdrop.

She surveyed the long and narrow room, anchored by a horseshoe-shaped bar surrounded by cafe tables. Patrons hadn't noticed her arrival.

"I'm with the *Washington Post* and I'm here to get information on Congressman Condit. I'll be here if you want to talk," Dvorak declared, pointing to a corner table.

Patrons turned their heads.

Don Wilcox, a Sacramento insider, watched with bemusement as Dvorak asked people whether they had any information about Gary's alleged womanizing and infidelity.

The *Post* wasn't alone in the race to the next break in the scandal. *Star* had unleashed an army of its stringers on the state capitol, offering as much as $50,000 to any woman involved in Gary's life willing to come forward.

At 7:00 p.m. on June 13, Scarlett Parker's phone rang.

She was on a long list of former female staffers that members of the press had compiled.

"Hello?" Parker answered.

"Ms. Parker, my name is David Fahrenthold. I'm a reporter with the *Washington Post*."

"OK."

"Are you aware of what's going on with Chandra Levy?" he asked.

"Yes."

"I was wondering if I could ask you some questions about your time of employment with Congressman Condit."

"What is it you want to know?"

"How well do you know the congressman?" he asked, and then pressed forward.

"What do you think of the congressman?"

"Did the congressman ever display anger towards anyone, or get violent?"

"What do you think of the alleged affair with Chandra Levy?"

"Mr. Fahrenthold, Congressman Condit is one of the finest men I ever met," Parker replied, then hung up.

LEGAL ADVICE

California congresswoman Nancy Pelosi watched, with alarm, as the media swarmed Gary. The firestorm had grown to a proportion matched only by the Clinton-Lewinsky scandal and was crossing the point of becoming worse than that. The qualities she admired in Gary's political skill had turned on him in a PR crisis.

Hiring Cotchett was a good start, and a big step for Gary. But in her mind, he needed to engage counsel with experience handling the Beltway press. Pelosi and fellow California congressman Howard Berman approached Gary and suggested he call Abbe D. Lowell, a powerful DC attorney and friend of the Democratic Party.

Early in his career, Lowell represented Texas congressman Charlie Wilson during the Justice Department's investigation of billing irregularities during the US's clandestine operation to support the mujahedeen in Afghanistan. More recently, Lowell had represented House Democrats during the Clinton impeachment proceedings.

Dayton parked the Explorer outside the Democratic Club on Ivy Street.

The sound of music and clanging glasses escaped to the sidewalk.

Abbe Lowell, wearing a tightly tailored suit, exited the fund-raiser and walked toward the SUV. Dayton rolled down the passenger-side window.

"Congressman Condit," Lowell said.

"Let's go for a drive," Gary answered from the driver's seat.

Dayton got out of the Explorer, and Lowell replaced him in the passenger seat.

Lowell knew Gary's reputation was that of the strong, silent type.

"You already met with law enforcement without counsel. That was a mistake. You can't freelance this," Lowell said. He needed to know whether Gary understood his own limitations.

"I've cooperated," Gary answered.

"First and foremost, you need to regulate your response to law enforcement. You need to interpose counsel between yourself and investigators."

Lowell had been stunned to learn Gary had met with Metro Police detectives by himself. As a consequence, police were leaking to the press the suggestion that he had lied to them and Gary had no way, and nobody, to challenge the assertion. Although the decision reinforced Lowell's opinion that Gary had nothing to do with Chandra's disappearance, it also revealed the depth of Gary's refusal to play by conventional rules.

Only a stubborn man relies on his innocence alone, Lowell thought.

"You need to determine your priorities," the lawyer continued.

"I want them to find Chandra."

"We all do. This is about you and your family, too. I know you don't want it to be that way."

Gary nodded.

"There are considerations you need to prioritize," Lowell continued. "Avoiding a criminal investigation is number two. Avoiding criminal liability, preserving your political career, protecting your reputation; these all follow. We can hunker down or try to do more. It's up to you how you want to prioritize matters. But, understand that they're all in play."

"What does 'do more' mean?" Gary responded.

"Your best strategy is to embrace the Levys publicly. It may be hard, but it's the best thing you can do."

"I've tried. They chose not to see me."

"It's a two-way street. But you could do more to make clear to the public that you're trying to work with the Levys. It's up to them to decide if they want your help."

Gary steered the car down a one-way street. "I'm not going to go on television and make a scene," he replied.

"Perception is part of this. The Levys control that," Lowell explained. "You're not giving them anything to counter what's out there."

"She'll turn up soon."

"People rarely turn up alive after having been missing for six weeks."

Gary hadn't seriously thought about his decisions in the context of Chandra potentially not coming back. He believed and hoped that she was still alive.

"And a body isn't going to make this go away for you," Lowell added.

Gary internalized what was being said.

"I know you're not a big talker. That can work against you. Doing more means responding. Your silence is interpreted as a statement," Lowell continued.

"Doing more for who?" Gary responded, his eyes fixed on the windshield.

⟿

"How's Gary?" Chad Condit asked. It was peculiar, but both Chad and Cadee referred to their father by his first name. Being deeply involved in California politics, they didn't want to be talking about "Dad" in their professional circles.

"He's holding up," Dayton answered through his cell phone. "He's talking to the lawyer now."

"You got him?"

"I got him."

"He's probably telling Gary he needs to go on TV."

"Probably."

"You know he isn't going to talk."

"Yeah," Dayton agreed. "People keep trying though."

INFAMY

Dominick Dunne, the famous true crime writer for *Vanity Fair*, watched live coverage of Gary's exit from the Lynshire building.

Dunne's daughter had been murdered in 1982. After her death and the trial of her killer, he became a victims' rights advocate. Dunne started by penning an article for *Vanity Fair* titled, "A Father's Account of the Trial of his Daughter's Killer." With that, he became a regular contributor to the magazine, publishing true crime stories and commentary on celebrities in a monthly column titled Dominick Dunne's Diary. He penned several books and became a steady presence on cable news programs as an expert commentator on major scandals and trials.

Disgraceful! I don't like this congressman, Dunne thought, adjusting a pair of large round glasses resting on his pale button nose.

I don't like him at all. Dunne squirmed. *He waved! He casually exits.*

Dunne fumed as he watched Gary cross the sidewalk toward a white Ford Explorer. *His coat is thrown over his shoulder. He looks like he's smiling, and she's missing! He doesn't show the proper concern. He moves in a furtive manner. He's sneaky. I don't like Condit. I don't like him at all!*

Gary sat at a phone booth inside the Democrats' cloakroom. A pack of reporters had chased him into the room after he and Dayton were spotted emerging from the underground tram that runs between the Rayburn Building and the Capitol.

His attorney, Joseph Cotchett, explained to him that the press had not responded as he had hoped to the retraction demand letter.

"Gary, there's something else you need to get ready for," Cotchett said.

"What?"

"We got ahold of Ms. Smith's lawyer."

"What'd he say?"

"It's not good."

Jim Robinson, Anne Marie Smith's lawyer, hit the mainstream media circuit.

When asked whether *Star* magazine's report that Smith had a romantic relationship with Gary was true, Robinson answered, "My client would have no legal ground to sue *Star*."

On June 15, Cotchett received another letter from *Star*:

The story will say that Congressman Condit's affair with flight attendant Anne Marie Smith is still ongoing, and that Mr. Condit, through his attorneys, has recently had a number of conversations with Miss Smith about keeping the relationship a secret. Sources have told *Star Magazine* that for some time, Miss Smith has been complaining about always being broke, though in the last few days, she's suddenly appeared flush with cash. Sources say that they believe Congressman Condit has given Miss Smith money. The story will also say that law enforcement has the names of several other women with whom Mr. Condit has had extramarital affairs, and that is weighing heavily on their suspicions that Mr. Condit may be involved in the intern, Chandra Levy's, disappearance.

Cotchett decided that if his client, Gary, wasn't going to try and stop the bleeding, then, with Gary's blessing, he'd go out on the air to try and apply some type of tourniquet. He appeared on ABC's *Good Morning America*. When asked whether Chandra stayed over at Gary's condo during the time she disappeared, he replied, "She absolutely did not . . . if she did, she had to spend it on a couch because Congressman Condit's wife was in Washington the entire week she went missing."

Cotchett's statement had two immediate consequences.

First, investigators had worked on the assumption Gary was alone in his condo around the time Chandra disappeared. Within hours of Cotchett's interview, unnamed police sources leaked to the press that investigators wanted to talk with Gary a second time because he had withheld from them the fact that his wife was in DC.

Second, news reports stated Cotchett denied the earlier report by the *Washington Post* that Chandra had spent the night at Gary's condo. Reporters took Cotchett's comment that she could not have stayed at Gary's condo during the week she went missing and twisted it to appear as though Cotchett had claimed that Chandra had never stayed at Gary's condo.

—

"I think he could come out and share what he does know. We'd appreciate his help for having some questions answered," Susan Levy explained during an appearance on MSNBC.

When asked whether she knew of a relationship between Gary and Chandra, Susan replied, "There's been some conversation that we can't go into at this point."

When asked whether Gary knew where Chandra was, she answered, "It's a possibility."

Susan Levy's call for Gary to come forward spread rapidly through the media. On air and in print, everyone wondered aloud or demanded to know why the congressman wasn't cooperating with the investigation or the family—and what he knew about Chandra's disappearance.

Gary's office was caught off guard by the sudden shift from the Levy camp. "I don't know what Susan Levy is referring to. As far as I know, the police have said he's cooperated all along," Lynch said to reporters crammed into the lobby area of Gary's Modesto district office.

On or about June 16, Gary called the phone number he had been given for Susan Levy. He wanted to understand from her what it was she thought he knew, and to provide her with direct answers to the questions she had.

"This is Gary Condit."

"I can't talk to you without my attorney," Levy answered, and hung up.

Chad Condit had also tried many times to reach out to the Levy family and had gotten the same response.

—

Cotchett didn't know if Gary had an affair with Chandra—although he guessed it had happened. The media's assault on Cotchett and their twisting of his words after his few appearances on national television had cemented his view that the only way to stop the scandal from further unraveling was for Gary to publicly address the allegation that he had a sexual affair with her.

"We've tried letters. We've tried reasoning with the press about privacy and the fact that this is an open investigation. They're not working," Cotchett advised. "You need to go to the *Modesto Bee*—not the *Washington Post*—sit down with them and tell them the truth, the whole story about your relationship with Chandra. That's the only way you end this. Call the Levys and sit down with them and the *Modesto Bee* and end this."

"I'll meet with the Levys whenever and wherever they'd like. But it won't be a spectacle," Gary answered. "There is no reason the press needs to be there. They aren't entitled to that."

Cotchett and Gary liked one another, but their differences of opinion on how to move forward had become sharp and irreconcilable.

Gary was simply one of the most stubborn men Cotchett had ever met.

DRIP, DRIP

On June 15, Allan Lengel and Petula Dvorak teamed up to pen the *Washington Post*'s latest break in the scandal under the headline, **MISSING INTERN'S FAMILY ASKS CONDIT FOR HELP**.

The article detailed Susan Levy's plea on national television for Gary to break his silence, and also contained an extraordinary pivot.

Susan Levy said Chandra had spoken to her of a relationship in Washington without identifying the person. She said she learned the details from the relative and called her daughter in April and asked her if the man she had been seeing was Gary Condit.

"When I asked her that," according to Levy, "Chandra said, 'How did you know?'"

Susan Levy said that when she realized in early May that her daughter was not simply unreachable, but had gone missing, she called Condit, her hometown congressman, and asked him for help finding her. At one point, she said she asked him if he was having an affair with her daughter, an intern for the Bureau of Prisons. "He told me no, and their relationship was professional," Levy said . . .

Gary and Dayton sat in Dayton's backyard, just outside Alexandria, Virginia. Thick green bushes surrounded them.

"Susan Levy never called me," Gary said. "Dr. Levy did. Then I called her after the detectives interviewed me. She's making stuff up."

Dayton didn't respond. Nothing surprised him anymore, and Gary wasn't looking for comfort.

"The *Post* already printed what happened—do they print whatever Susan Levy says?" Gary continued, letting the light breeze carry away the smoke curling up from his cigar.

"I don't know," Dayton replied.

"She's entitled to some latitude. They need to target me to keep the media's attention. I get that. But this is getting too far out there. I've got the press reporting I lied to police and to her mother, and neither is true."

Smoke billowed from Gary's mouth. "How does this play out?" he asked between pulls. "One day the truth might matter but nobody will be able to find it."

"Jon Karl called me from CNN. He said a lot of people in the political press are getting tired of the story," Dayton replied.

"They should be."

"John Feehery and the White House can't control its weekly press agenda because all anyone wants to talk about is you," Dayton explained.

Feehery, the communications director for the Speaker of the House, described the situation he and other leaders on Capitol Hill faced during the Levy scandal as "the most intense media scrutiny I have ever seen. It was like a pack of wolves—a fevered pitch."

CBS Evening News was the only major network evening news program that hadn't covered the Levy story. For comparison, in a single week during the summer of 2001, Tom Brokaw and *NBC Nightly News* ran ten stories covering the scandal. Even other CBS shows were covering the story at a regular clip. But the anchor of *CBS Evening News*, Dan Rather, hadn't mentioned the names Chandra Levy or Gary Condit on air.

"It looks to me like this feeding frenzy of people who are excited that maybe he was involved in her murder. It feels like people are hoping, dreaming that it'll be a sensational story that will see them through the summer. I just find it beyond tasteless," *CBS Evening News* executive producer Jim Murphy explained in defense of Rather's decision.

MSNBC's president, Erik Sorenson, defended the nonstop coverage on his network: "Cable news channels dine on crisis, on major sustained stories. This is what we do. We find big stories, and interesting stories, and run with them."

The scandal was playing on the cable news networks *at least* every twelve minutes. At times over the summer, the story played on each network *at least* every five minutes. As reported by the *New York Times*:

For the month ended last Tuesday, the Fox News Channel's nightly schedule was watched, on average, by 683,000 people, more than twice as many as in the comparable period last year. CNN's prime-time audience increased 40 percent from the year before, to 662,000 people.

"It's a great story for some of the same reasons Monica was a great story, men in power and younger women," Fox News vice president John Moody stated. "Unfortunately, it has the added suspense factor of a missing young woman, in many quarters presumed dead . . . Some people say we shouldn't cover this, it's a slimy story. But people are fascinated by it."

CNN chairman Walter Isaacson told his reporters and producers to "hold their noses . . . [It's] a very interesting, fascinating story and we should be pursuing it—vigorously."

Tom Rosenstiel, executive director of the Project for Excellence in Journalism, summed up the ultimate consequence of the media's craze: "The real impact is not that there's no such thing as something that is private. It's that there's no such thing as public. What used to be private fills our public space. What used to be the subject of our public sphere is pushed out."

CHASING RATS

On June 20, Mike Lynch called the Metro Police.

"Mr. Lynch, what did this reporter say, exactly?" Sergeant Joseph Gentile, the Metro Police's public information officer, asked.

"The reporter said Mr. Lengel from the *Washington Post* was boasting to press colleagues that the Metro Police Department intended to charge Congressman Condit with complicity or obstruction of justice regarding the disappearance of Chandra Levy," Lynch explained. He had received calls from various friends in the press alerting him to this latest development.

The claim that Gary had lied to law enforcement about the nature of his relationship with Chandra had taken hold in the mainstream media. Believing that their reporting was true, reporters simply advanced that narrative to its next logical point.

Not everyone was ready to crucify Gary over an affair and his refusal to make a public confession while the woman was still missing. The *Modesto Bee* editorialists were right about one thing: Gary still had overwhelming support in Condit Country. As law enforcement in Washington, DC, blundered its way through the investigation, the narrative at home was turning to familiar territory for Gary—an us versus them storyline that had started to galvanize folks in his district. But even friends would abandon him if he was lying to authorities trying to find Chandra.

"That's not correct," Sergeant Gentile replied.

"In a prior conversation, Mr. Lengel indicated that he believed Chief Ramsey was susceptible to influence and pressure, presumably from Congressman Condit," Lynch continued.

Sergeant Gentile told Lynch the accusation had no basis in reality.

The conversation moved to the persistent leaks of information from police sources to the press.

"So there's nothing you can do about the leaks?" Lynch asked, incredulously.

"This place leaks like a sieve," Sergeant Gentile answered, honestly.

—

Chief Ramsey and Terrance Gainer listened as detectives assigned to the Levy case briefed them on its latest developments.

"Detectives," Gainer asked. "What is it we can do for you?"

"What you can do is you can leave me and my people alone and let us investigate this case. We will give you updates. But this daily update thing that is going on is not productive to the investigation," Detective Ronald Wyatt answered.

Gainer and Ramsey had started to receive some heat from the press over their daily briefings with the media. This was an assault from within.

Shortly after the briefing ended, Detective Wyatt received notice that he had been removed from the Levy case.

—

The *Washington Post*'s Petula Dvorak called Don Wilcox to follow up on their prior telephone discussion about Gary's time in Sacramento.

"I've spent a lot of time in Modesto lately, going to scuzz-bucket places to find people who knew Chandra," Dvorak told Wilcox. "I've got this theory about an FBI guy she was dating. I think he might have forged e-mail correspondence from Chandra to her friends."

Wilcox had nothing to add to Dvorak's view of the Central Valley or her theory about an FBI boyfriend.

"Does Carolyn Condit have thumbs?" Dvorak asked.

"Yes, she has thumbs," Wilcox replied.

Earlier that week, *New York Times* columnist Maureen Dowd's fact-checker had called Gary's office and asked whether Carolyn still had all five of her fingers. Somewhere in the behind-the-scenes press cycle, a rumor had taken hold that Carolyn was not only "sick" but also that she had some kind of abnormality. It was bizarre and completely unfounded.

"Is she a primate?" Dvorak asked.

⤝

Lynch called David Fahrenthold at the *Washington Post*.

"I object to some of the questions you asked Ms. Scarlett Parker. They were leading, inappropriate, and offensive," Lynch said.

Fahrenthold laughed. "I didn't call Ms. Parker. That sounds much more like the kind of call Allan Lengel would make."

"Mr. Fahrenthold, Ms. Parker singled you out by name," Lynch pressed.

Fahrenthold laughed harder. "Allan is a great imitator."

⤝

In a letter to Gary's representative, the *Washington Post*'s management would later challenge the legitimacy of the accounts of its reporters' behavior, including Dvorak, Langel, and Fahrenthold, claiming they had been misunderstood or misrepresented. Records, including sworn statements of persons with first-hand account of the incidents, suggest otherwise.

CHAPTER 13

ALBATROSS

CHANGING FACTS

DAYTON READ THE ARTICLE A second time to make sure he had read it correctly. The June 20 edition of the *Washington Post* included the latest story authored by Petula Dvorak and Allan Lengel, titled "Intern's Parents Return—with New Attorney."

In recent days, Levy's account of what may have happened between Condit and Chandra Levy has changed. Initially, the Levys said they knew nothing of a romance between their daughter and Condit . . .

But last week, the Levys said they had knowledge of an affair between the two, and they urged him, on national television, to break his public silence . . .

On Saturday, Condit called Robert and Susan Levy at their home. "We were praying when somebody called," Susan Levy said. "When I picked up the phone, he said, 'This is Gary Condit.'"

Although the Levys spent most of the previous week imploring Condit to talk, they told him they'd talk only with their attorney present, Susan Levy said.

She said that in early May, when she realized that her daughter was missing, she reviewed old cell phone records and dialed the area code 202 number that appeared again and again while Chandra lived in Washington.

Susan Levy said she dialed and, when prompted, punched in her own home number. Minutes later, she said, Condit called her.

The Levys and the Post *are using each other*, Dayton realized.

Dayton called Juliet Eilperin, a political correspondent for the *Washington Post*. "Your metro reporters, they're out of control," he insisted. Eilperin told Dayton she couldn't do anything to slow the *Post's* coverage.

THE REVEAL

June was quickly coming to its end. The Metro Police and the FBI scoured Chandra's recovered e-mails and interviewed more than one hundred people, but failed to turn up any clues about what might have happened to her.

"There's nothing very instructive in those interviews, or, frankly, in the e-mails . . . there's no smoking gun there," Terrance Gainer revealed to reporters. "Absent a dramatic development, we're considering whether to downgrade this case to a lower priority level."

Microphones were taped together into a mass of fuzzy balls, and news vans lined both sides of the street in downtown Washington, DC. Reporters crowded in front of the podium.

For days, the press had reported that the Levys had hired a new lawyer, and speculated about who he or she might be. The Levys chose to reveal the identity at a prescheduled press conference in Washington.

Susan Levy sobbed and turned her face into Dr. Levy's chest.

Billy Martin, wearing a crisp suit and yellow tie, comforted the Levys.

Stringers called in the big news: "It's Billy." The Levys had engaged one of Washington, DC's biggest hired guns.

Martin had cut his teeth as a prosecutor putting together the crack cocaine case against DC mayor Marion Barry. After moving to private practice, he represented the likes of boxer Riddick Bowe and basketball star Allen Iverson. More recently, he represented Monica Lewinsky's mother.

Martin was curt in his first public appearance. He made clear the Levys would not allow Gainer to downgrade the investigation. "We hope to have a team of investigators, and a full investigation," Martin told the crowd, explaining that, on his advice, the Levy family had hired two former DC homicide detectives to open a private investigation into Chandra's disappearance. He also revealed that the Levys had hired Porter Novelli, the powerful Washington public relations firm.

Martin finished by demanding that "the congressman meet with the DC police for as long as necessary to answer any and all questions relating to this investigation."

"What about the alleged relationship with Congressman Condit?" a reporter asked.

"We hope that during the investigation we can really find out the depth of that relationship. The parents know what the relationship was, but want to know more details," he responded.

When pressed, Martin added that he did "not want to jeopardize the police department investigation" and so would not elaborate publicly on "any details of what that relationship was."

On June 21, the Levy camp met with the FBI and Metro Police joint task force assigned to Chandra's case.

The Metro Police's chief of detectives, Jack Barrett, attended the meeting. A silver-haired veteran, Barrett had recently retired from the FBI. His twenty-nine-year career with the FBI ended as special agent in charge of the Washington, DC, Field Office's criminal division.

According to the *Washington Post*, Chief Ramsey convinced Barrett to come out of retirement to help him overhaul the Metro Police Department. Barrett was back on the job only a few weeks when Chandra's case came across his desk.

Barrett listened as Martin demanded law enforcement elevate the investigation from a missing person's case to a criminal investigation. Martin didn't have to spell out the consequences of not heeding this demand: his firm and Porter Novelli would turn their sights, and the media's attention, on the failure of law enforcement to find Chandra and other missing women.

Susan Levy expressed her belief that Gary was using his influence to obstruct the investigation into her daughter's disappearance.

Martin then demanded that investigators search Gary's condo, take a sample of his DNA, and force him to submit to a polygraph examination. The Levy camp also wanted other members of the Condit family, and Gary's staff, investigated.

—

Shortly after the Levy camp's meeting with the Metro Police brass, police sources leaked to the press that investigators would now beef up their focus on the congressman.

Terrance Gainer told the *Washington Post* the Metro Police planned to interview Gary a second time. "We want to try to get some clarity from him on his relationship to her. Was there something going on in her life that might have driven her to drastic action?"

It was the moment many in the media had eagerly anticipated: Gary's admission of a sexual relationship with Chandra, knowing that the details of his second conversation with law enforcement would be leaked to them within hours of its conclusion.

Gary's office immediately issued a press release stating his continued concern for the Levy family, and reiterating his commitment to provide whatever information he could to law enforcement.

JEFFERSON

Abbe Lowell called Billy Martin and offered the Levys the chance to ask Gary whatever they wanted in a face-to-face meeting, with no media present. In their daily press appearances, the Levys were verging on an outright accusation that Gary had something to do with Chandra's disappearance.

The attorneys agreed to a sit-down between the Levys and Gary later that evening, at the Jefferson Hotel.

Susan Levy and Martin entered the low-lit private dining room at the hotel.

Gary and Lowell were already waiting inside.

Why isn't Dr. Levy here? Gary wondered. *I want to look them both in the eye and tell them I didn't have anything to do with this.*

He extended his right hand to Susan Levy, but she lurched backwards, refusing to shake hands.

"Why don't we sit down?" Lowell offered.

Susan sat opposite Lowell, and Martin sat opposite Gary. The surface of the dining room table provided neutral territory.

Martin spoke first. "We've decided that we think it is best that we don't discuss certain matters related to the relationship between Chandra and Congressman Condit at this time."

Gary looked at Lowell, confused. Martin looked at Susan to indicate that she could begin. Susan then asked prepared questions.

How often did you see her?

When was the last time you saw her?

Gary answered each question.

Do you have any information about where she is now?

"Mrs. Levy, I don't know, I really don't," Gary answered.

"Will you cooperate with police officers?"

"Mrs. Levy, I believe I have, and I will continue to do so, fully," Gary answered.

Martin jumped in. "Will you cooperate with our investigators as well?"

Lowell responded quickly. He wasn't going to let private investigators hired by an emotional mother dictate an investigation that had already fallen off the tracks. *She's already made him the bad guy*, Lowell realized. *For Gary Condit to do this, to sit down and bare himself here, is huge. He's done that. But they don't care. This is a game.*

He and Martin exchanged a few terse words.

Gary had expected the meeting to go on for a long while, but Susan Levy's body language made it clear she was done asking questions. The meeting was over almost as soon as it began.

Neither Gary nor Lowell had placed any restrictions on the discussion. She could have asked him about anything. Instead, her own attorney came into the meeting and took those questions off the table.

"I appreciate the time we've had to talk," Lowell said, breaking an uncomfortable silence. "We are doing everything we can. I'm so sorry, Mrs. Levy."

They stood, momentarily, in a group near the door.

"Can I give you a hug?" Gary asked.

"Absolutely not," Susan replied.

After Levy and Martin had left, Gary turned to Lowell and vented his anger about Dr. Levy's absence from the meeting.

"What a chickenshit thing to do," he said. "The guy goes on television and says shit about me. And he sits in his hotel room while his wife asks me questions they know the answers to? The man that called me in May would have been here."

Later, when asked by reporters whether she and Gary discussed the nature of the relationship between her daughter and the congressman during the Jefferson meeting, Susan claimed that the lawyers had taken those questions off the table, implying that it was a mutual decision of the parties.

The next day, June 22, Gary's office issued the following statement to the press:

> I was very glad that I could finally meet with Mrs. Levy last evening. Dr. and Mrs. Levy and the Levy family are undergoing the most terrible and difficult circumstances that can face any family. My prayers, hopes, and sympathy are with them . . .

The Levys left Washington, scheduled to make an appearance at Sears Point Raceway, where race car drivers had agreed to put a picture of Chandra on the hoods of their cars.

CAROLYN

Carolyn stood in a narrow aisle inside the Sequoia Market, a small grocery store owned by the Chong family and located a few blocks from Acorn Lane.

She had stopped going to the supermarket because she felt as if everyone inside was looking at her and thinking the worst.

The tabloids now ran stories that suggested she was involved in Chandra's disappearance, and she had been told by many people that reporters were darting around town asking questions about her "mystery" illness.

Carolyn's pharmacist warned her that reporters brandishing business cards with national media brands had come to the Ceres Drug Store and asked, or in some cases demanded, to see a list of Carolyn's prescriptions. The pharmacy began secretly delivering her medications to the next-door neighbor's house. Carolyn's neighbor then passed the medications to her through two loose boards in the fence separating their backyards.

Packages delivered to the Condit home were intercepted. Carolyn was told to assume it was the paparazzi. The packages either never made it or showed up on the stoop after having been opened and hastily taped back together.

Carolyn had heard from multiple sources that reporters had gone so far as to state that she may not be able to perform sexually as an explanation for Gary's alleged infidelities. She knew it was just a matter of time before these whispers turned into tabloid headlines, and from there, matriculated, in some more polite form, into the mainstream press cycle.

Paparazzi camped on Acorn Lane swarmed her whenever she left the house. Because of this, Gary's parents had started doing her grocery shopping so that Carolyn didn't have to go outside. But there were times when she needed to get out. And, when those times came, she worked with her neighbors to sneak across backyards and into her neighbors' cars so that the press camped on her street wouldn't realize she had left.

She trusted the Chong family and the neighbors who shopped at the Sequoia Market. In fact, most members of the community tried their best to help Carolyn however they could. She was, perhaps, the most beloved person in Condit Country, even more liked than Gary. While the national media tried to cast her as a submissive housewife to a wretch of a husband, locals knew those characterizations to be false.

For three decades, she had been ever-present in their lives, quietly offering her support when families confronted crisis or tragedy. People who needed help from Gary often called Carolyn to ask for it.

She once hosted an event for women in California politics that was attended by a mix of homemakers, elected officials, and businesswomen. At the event, a newly elected California assemblywoman from Los Angeles asked Carolyn what it was she "did."

Carolyn answered, "I keep the fire going at home."

The women from Condit Country gave her a standing ovation, knowing what that meant—Carolyn worked full time helping Gary's constituents while he was away in Washington. She was at dinner tables, in classrooms and churches, and beside hospital beds. She planned community events, even if she didn't want to ride in the parades.

For locals, it hurt to watch someone as genuine and kind as Carolyn face something as artificial and hurtful as a media scandal. It didn't matter what Gary had done or not done, or even what ultimately happened to him. In Condit Country, Carolyn was her own person. Someone they cared deeply for.

Carolyn placed her groceries on the front counter, reluctantly bringing her gaze to the magazine stand near the counter. *It's Thursday, and they aren't here.*

The Chong family had removed the tabloids from the newspaper rack.

—

There was loud pounding at the front door.

"Mrs. Condit," a man's voice called. "It's the FBI."

Carolyn left the kitchen, where she had finished unpacking groceries, and went to the door. Through the peephole, she saw a woman and a man—both dressed in black suits—standing near the willow tree.

Carolyn didn't open the door. On more than one occasion, members of the press had pretended to be law enforcement in order to trick her into engaging with them.

Carolyn went back to the kitchen and called Lynch.

"Mike, there are people at the door. They say they are FBI," Carolyn whispered.

"Don't go to the door. I'm coming over. I'll have Abbe call you at the house."

"Mrs. Condit, did you just call Mike Lynch?" the woman outside asked loudly. "Can you please open the door?"

How'd she know that? Carolyn wondered, recalling the fact that she'd been told to assume someone was listening to her phone calls. She and Gary had been advised that law enforcement was certainly listening to their calls, whether or not they had a warrant, and to also assume members of the press were trying to tap their phone lines.

The next-door neighbors ran a cable between their homes so that Gary and Carolyn could make and take calls on their neighbors' phone line. They were told, if done right, this would likely throw the press off but to expect that the government would figure out the ruse and tap the neighbors' line as well.

The phone rang. Carolyn answered it.

"You don't need to talk to them," Abbe Lowell advised. "Even if it's the FBI. They came deliberately. They know Gary is in Washington preparing to meet with them tomorrow. Tell them they can contact me if they want to talk to you. They have my numbers."

Lynch arrived at the house and immediately escorted the FBI agents off the Condits' property. Carolyn opened the front door and walked confidently to where Lynch and the agents stood on the sidewalk, engaged in a heated argument over Carolyn's rights and their professional behavior.

Neighbors had exited their homes and stood on their porches or lawns watching the exchange.

"Did you call Mr. Lynch?" the female FBI agent demanded as soon as Carolyn was within shouting distance.

"Yes. I have that right if you are really the FBI," Carolyn answered.

Later that afternoon, Lowell called the FBI and scheduled an interview between the agency and Carolyn for the following week, in Gary's Modesto office.

Lowell set two conditions. First, the meeting was to be kept confidential. Second, investigators were not to badger Carolyn with questions about the other women alleged to have had sexual affairs with her husband.

—

That evening, Carolyn received a call from Chad Condit. He asked her if she could come to the grandkids' school the next day for a conference with school administrators.

Stringers and paparazzi had started camping in front of Chad's house, too. And reporters were now following the grandkids to and from school every day. Chad and his wife had to closely guard the kids whenever they left the house.

The school wanted to institute special security protocols to protect the children.

Everything suddenly seemed perverted.

Carolyn received daily letters from strangers imploring her to leave Gary, some even coming with instructions or how-to books on divorce. She had also received death threats aimed at her, reflecting the newest gossip on the Internet that she had something to do with Chandra's disappearance.

Even as the media tried to paint Carolyn as a virtual invalid and naïve, she had internalized all the abuse because no matter how upset she was, she knew she couldn't break. Her family was under siege.

Yet, today seemed as though it had more consequence than any before it. It was something Chad said.

In their discussion about the school and the two older boys, he mentioned that paparazzi had hounded his wife as she carried their youngest son, Gary Matthew Condit, who was only months old. They had managed to get off a number of photos, which in turn upset the baby. Carolyn didn't know why, but she feared that this would leave some form of permanent and negative mark on the younger Gary Condit.

A SECOND INTERVIEW

On Saturday, June 23, at 3:00 p.m., Detectives Ralph Durant and Lawrence Kennedy and Jack Barrett joined Gary and Lowell inside a friend's house in Georgetown.

They couldn't use Lowell's office because up to a dozen reporters were staking out the building on any given day.

Lowell's associate sat in a corner, charged with making a written record of the conversation. Dayton waited in the hallway.

"My only concern is doing whatever I can to help to locate Chandra Levy," Gary started.

Barrett spread his arms on the table. "One of the things the media and the Levys have suggested is that you may be getting special treatment, and we want to make it clear that there is no truth to this."

"It seems a bit the opposite, doesn't it?" Gary answered. "Have you been comparing this to any similar cases? Like the Joyce Chiang case?"

"When I was at the FBI, I headed a team investigating the Joyce Chiang case," Barrett replied. "She was missing and her body finally turned up in the river. I don't want to go too far into that because of privacy issues; she was under many pressures, including being under scrutiny by the INS, and she could have potentially hurt herself. This is not a good comparison to the Levy case."

"The department's public information officer told Mike Lynch that the police department is leaking like a sieve on this case. What are you going to do to prevent this in the future?" Gary asked.

"We are concerned about these issues as well. For one thing, we have 'locked down' the investigation," Barrett claimed. "We've limited access to the computer information system in the department so as to limit access to only those working directly on the case."

Barrett paused and looked squarely at Gary. "Even within the DC Police Department, we have the responsibility of briefing our own chief on this sensitive case."

Gary processed what he thought Barrett was trying to convey. *The problem is above his pay grade.*

Lowell spoke for the first time. "I want you to assume that Congressman Condit had a romantic affair with Chandra Levy, and to ask questions accordingly."

Knowing the likelihood that details of the interview would be leaked to the press, Lowell had determined to take this approach.

"We understand," Barrett responded, gesturing for Detective Durant to proceed accordingly.

Durant asked Gary a series of questions about the last time he saw Chandra. Gary answered each question, assuring the investigators that the last time he saw her she looked healthy and was her usual, happy self.

"Did you ever go out with her?" Durant asked.

"We went to dinner once," Gary replied. He and Durant then discussed the location, Tryst, and how he and Chandra had arrived there.

"How would you characterize your relationship with her?"

"She was a constituent who became a friend."

"How often did she visit you at your apartment?"

"Three or four times, maybe," Gary answered.

"You said in the last interview that she left clothes there," Durant pressed.

"No, I didn't say that."

"She never left anything at the apartment?" Durant prodded.

"No. And I didn't say that she did."

Barrett's attention was fixed on Gary. Much had been said in the media about what was or was not discussed on that day.

"Did she stay overnight?" Durant asked.

Gary knew Durant asked the question to try and pry a response that would corroborate the Metro Police's prior leaks.

Lowell interrupted the exchange to keep it from escalating. "The goal should be to avoid getting unnecessary things in the record which are not germane and which may get leaked out to the press. We fully understand the relevance of the question, but for the reasons we discussed, there is no need to get into the details of the relationship outside the relevant time period."

"The information we have received," Barrett responded, "indicates a difference between the frequency of contact the congressman has described and what we are hearing from others, and we do want and need to understand that. In particular, it would be relevant for us to understand whether what she was telling people was a fabrication to the extent that it stands in contrast with information which Congressman Condit has provided and could provide. We understand that there is a fine line between sins and crimes."

"I know that Detective Durant is trying to narrow the box," Lowell offered, "and I understand your interest in assessing candor and credibility. If people are saying something different about the frequency of contacts, perhaps they have lumped in the times Chandra came to the office as well." Lowell himself was starting to pick up on the fact that perhaps a key element in the disconnect between the "story" and the "truth" was the difference between the reality of a relatively short-lived and casual encounter and an intense romance the press and the Levy family were feeding the public and investigators.

Durant turned back to Gary. "How often did she come to the office?"

"Perhaps four or five times, but she came at times I wasn't there as well," Gary answered.

"How would you think she would describe her feelings for you?"

"I think she would say that she liked me as a person, and that I could be helpful to her career."

"Do you know why she might have or would tell people that she was pregnant by you?"

"I don't know why she would do that," Gary responded, surprised by the question and assuming its genesis was in a tabloid story.

"Did you ever give her gifts?"

"None that I can recall," Gary replied.

"Did she give you gifts?"

"Yes. Some candies."

"Did you have an argument or a fight with her around the period from the 23rd of April to the 1st of May?" Durant asked.

"No, sir," Gary answered.

"Did you ever see her in California?"

"No."

Detective Durant then asked Gary to try and account for his activities from April 28 through May 2. Gary pulled out a piece of paper on which he had reconstructed a timeline of all his activities and methodically walked the detectives through his alibi.

"Family members have said you may have given Chandra a gift—a bracelet," Durant asked.

"I don't recall this happening," Gary answered. Durant was referring to the bracelet Gary had given Chandra from the collection of small favors he kept in his office desk for constituents and visitors. He hadn't remembered the incident and later corrected himself in a subsequent interview.

When the interview ended, Barrett turned again to Lowell. "We'll need to confirm publicly that Congressman Condit participated in this second meeting. I'll be asked to characterize the meeting."

Gary interjected before Lowell could respond. "I would rather not 'characterize' the meeting in any way. I don't understand why the police feel it's necessary to give the press information."

"Detective Durant and I have not, and will not talk," Detective Kennedy offered.

"I apologize for getting worked up. I'm just venting a bit," Gary replied, sensing that Kennedy was being genuine about the fact that it wasn't the guys on the ground spilling information and misinformation to the press.

"Congressman, we understand that this is not a lot of fun for anyone," Barrett assured him.

The next day, Chief Ramsey appeared on ABC's *This Week*, telling the host that during his department's most recent interview of Gary, "We got some useful information but not a whole lot that would lead us to Chandra Levy, unfortunately."

Newsweek—an affiliate of the *Washington Post*—reported that the police were unable to use the surveillance camera footage from Chandra's apartment. When asked by reporters about the *Newsweek* revelation, Ramsey claimed "the footage was too poor in quality."

Two days later, Ramsey told reporters: "It was a week before we even knew about the missing person, so unfortunately some of the evidence that we would have had, had we known sooner, we won't have available to us."

Neither statement by Ramsey was accurate.

SPIN

On June 26, Dominick Dunne appeared on CNN's *Larry King Live* to promote his latest book titled *Justice: Crimes, Trials, and Punishments*. Below are portions of the interview:

DUNNE: . . . I had never been to a trial until I went to the trial of the man who killed my daughter. And I had never given justice a thought, if you want to know the truth. And, I was so horrified about what went on in that courtroom. I realized that I had the power to write about it, and the ability to go on TV and talk about it. And all the sort of sham that goes on at these trials.

KING: [D]id this warp Dominick Dunne enough? Because we kidded you, that every trial you have covered, the defendant is guilty?

DUNNE: Well, those are the trials I pick.

KING: You do have some people who have been incorrectly charged and convicted, as we have already seen guys that have gotten out on DNA.

DUNNE: But not any trial I have covered . . .

KING: What has to fascinate you in order to cover a trial, write about it? What's the trigger lock?

DUNNE: Well, I know this sounds so snobby to say, but I never write about street crime. I mean, I write about crime among the powerful, because it's different for them.

KING: What do you make of the missing intern?

DUNNE: What I wish in the missing intern is that the congressman had a better PR person. I mean, somebody really advising him, because he's not being well advised. I don't care what the police told him. He has got to make a public statement at some time.

KING: Even if it meant he had an affair with her? He's got to say that?

DUNNE: So what? You know, that doesn't mean he killed her. But the longer it goes on like this, the ickier it gets . . .

CALLER: Have you ever been sued? And what was the outcome? . . .

DUNNE: I haven't been.

KING: Really?

DUNNE: And I walk a very thin line.

"He's sort of breaking all the rules," one political strategist told Petula Dvorak and Allan Lengel. "We generally advise candidates to be open, and accessible, and to control the agenda, and he's doing just the opposite."

"While he's been criticized for not holding press conferences daily, to me that's vintage Gary Condit," Congresswoman Anna Eshoo told Dvorak and Lengel. "He's quiet; he's reserved. He always operated below a radar screen."

The latest coverage in the *Washington Post* detailed the respect Gary had built in the nation's capital. It was a description of him that stood in stark contrast to the portrayals in the mainstream press to date as a minor player who had little interest in policymaking.

Buried inside the *Post*'s story, however, was a serious and, perhaps, malicious error. Dvorak and Lengel wrote that Gary was "one of a handful of Democrats who voted in favor of the impeachment of President Bill Clinton" during the Monica Lewinsky scandal.

They, presumably, had failed to fact-check their story against the *Post*'s website dedicated to the Clinton impeachment proceedings, *Washingtonpost.com Special Report: Clinton Accused*, which was still live and still included an online spreadsheet showing the impeachment votes of each member of Congress.

On the right, Rush Limbaugh, the conservative radio talk show host, told his national audience that Gary was the ultimate result of "Clintonism" taking hold of Washington, DC.

On the left, Paul Begala, who had been a close adviser to and staunch defender of President Clinton, told his national audience that the difference between Condit and Clinton was that "Clinton was not a hypocrite."

Hypocrisy is a death sentence for an elected official, and in the wake of the *Post*'s exposé, the idea that Gary had voted to impeach the president over an extramarital affair took hold in the public square.

It just wasn't true. Gary had voted no on each count.

Maureen Dowd of the *New York Times* had also asserted Gary voted to impeach Clinton. The *Times* printed a correction to that story. But in the twenty-four-hour news cycle, nobody has time to care about yesterday's misreporting.

The *Washington Post* made its own correction: "We hereby refute all assertions that Gary Condit, the congressman at the center of the missing intern mystery, looks like Harrison Ford. He doesn't. But if a movie is ever made about the Chandra Levy affair, the California Democrat should be played by William H. Macy."

Newsweek reported investigators were looking at emotional distress suffered by Chandra from the sudden loss of her internship, and speculated that this distress may have led her to run away or kill herself. The *Newsweek* story cited "police sources" saying there was evidence that Chandra may have been upset by a recent breakup with Gary.

The same sources told *Newsweek* there was evidence Chandra "felt let down when someone in a position to help her keep her job didn't intervene" and that Gary might have been that person.

Friends had warned Gary that members of the press were quoting the private detectives hired by Billy Martin and the Levys as "unnamed police sources" and "sources close to the investigation," exploiting the private detectives' credentials as former Metro Police detectives to seed the public discourse with theories that pointed at Gary.

More recently, reporters were told by people close to the Levys that the relationship between Gary and Chandra was "heating up" around the time she disappeared, and that she had "flooded" Gary with desperate phone calls as the relationship reached a "boiling point."

Fox newswoman Rita Cosby reported that during Gary's second interview with the Metro Police, he revealed to investigators he had "broken off his close friendship" with Chandra just days before she disappeared.

"When Condit delicately broke things off with Levy with the explanation that she was moving back to California, she was extremely disappointed and distraught, refusing to take no for an answer and even becoming obsessed with him," Cosby told viewers, citing "Fox News Channel police sources."

According to Cosby, Chandra was so enraged, she left a barrage of desperate voice messages on Gary's answering machine.

Abbe Lowell and Mike Lynch called Rita Cosby to discuss her misreporting.

"Ms. Cosby, your facts aren't correct," Lowell began. "The law-enforcement officials in the interview confirmed that your report does not reflect what was said in the interview."

Lowell had written a letter to Chief of Detectives Jack Barrett that enclosed a copy of Cosby's reporting. Barrett had responded quickly, confirming in writing that Cosby's account simply wasn't true.

"We'll run a denial of the report while I recheck my sources," Cosby replied to Lowell.

The next day, Fox News reran Cosby's story about a heated breakup between Gary and Chandra in the days leading up to her disappearance without mentioning the denial of its truth by law enforcement.

The *New York Daily News* carried forward Cosby's story under the headline, **POL TOLD COPS HE REJECTED INTERN: REPORT.**

Rep. Gary Condit told police an "obsessed" Chandra Levy became distraught when he broke off their relationship two days before she vanished, Fox News reported last night . . .

Niles Latham and Andy Geller of the *New York Post* penned a story headlined **NEW CHANDRA TWIST: CONDIT DITCHED HER DAYS BEFORE SHE VANISHED.**

Rep. Gary Condit has admitted to cops he broke off all contact with Chandra Levy two days before the intern vanished, sending the dark-haired, hazel-eyed beauty into an emotional tailspin, police sources said yesterday . . . She refused to take no for an answer, he said . . .

His new dramatic account, first reported by Fox News Channel, bolsters a theory police are pursuing—that she became so despondent after being dumped by her lover that she killed herself or deliberately disappeared and is living under another name.

Cops are also seeking to interview Condit's wife, Carolyn, who was in Washington the week Chandra disappeared.

Susan Levy had made it known that she consulted a psychic to help find Chandra. She wasn't alone. Fox News's Paula Zahn interviewed "world-renowned psychic" Sylvia Browne.

BROWNE: I am sorry to tell you this, but this girl is not alive.
ZAHN: How do you know that, Sylvia?
BROWNE: Paula, you know, you can either be one place or the other. If you're not here, you've got to be there.
ZAHN: And why are you so convinced she's there?
BROWNE: Because I'm a psychic.

Zahn also interviewed "spiritual medium" James Van Praagh.

PRAAGH: She's dead. And she was strangled. Four of us psychics came up with that, as well, that she was strangled . . . And I think that she was called up by someone she knew in the office or the staff and came out to a car. And then I think that she believed she was going to Condit's—his office. And I don't think she made it there.

Zahn's national audience nearly tripled during her coverage of the Levy story.
And not without consequence.

A psychic perceived Chandra's throat was slashed and her body stuffed in the basement of the Smithsonian's storage building. The Metro Police promptly sent officers to check the building.

Another psychic had a vision of Chandra's body being dumped in the Potomac River near the Memorial Bridge. The Metro Police promptly sent divers into the river around the bridge.

A NEW SUSPECT

When asked by reporters what investigators hoped to get out of questioning Carolyn Condit, Gainer answered: "We want to get her impression of the congressman's 'friendly' relationship with Miss Levy."

The blinds inside Gary's Modesto district office were pulled shut. Out front, a news crew from NBC had used gaffer tape to mark a square piece of territory on the sidewalk, spelling N-B-C with black, sticky letters.

"How are you feeling?" Mike Lynch asked Carolyn as she entered through a back door.

"Why are they all worked up outside?" Carolyn asked.

"Someone leaked the interview to the press. Don't worry about it. They can't get in here."

Lynch's phone rang. It was Abbe Lowell. He stepped into another room to take the call.

"What the hell is going on?" Lynch said. "She is down here, and now there is a mob outside. But the FBI hasn't shown up."

"I got a call from the US Attorney's Office. They called off the interview at the last minute," Lowell explained. "The US Attorney's Office insisted that their people participate."

"They don't trust the FBI?" Lynch asked.

"Every law-enforcement agency is trying to get in on this case. Just get Carolyn home."

The US Attorney's Office requested that Carolyn's interview be rescheduled for July 5 in Washington, DC.

———

A random summer rain had finally let up. It was 7:30 p.m. on July 1.

Christy Wiegand jogged along the Western Ridge Trail in Rock Creek Park, near the Pierce Mill. She was tall, with blonde hair pulled into a ponytail. Her diamond engagement ring glittered.

Music from a Walkman radio attached to her arm kept her company while her feet carried her into an isolated and wooded area abutting a ravine.

Wiegand noticed a young Hispanic man in a white tank-top shirt staring at her from a park bench. A few minutes later, she noticed the same man jogging behind her, keeping pace with her strides.

Wiegand turned off the Walkman and jogged faster. The footsteps behind her drew closer, drowned momentarily by loud thunder.

Ingmar Guandique wrapped his arms around Wiegand's neck and pulled her off the trail, dragging her violently into a ravine.

He pulled a knife from his back pocket and held it against Wiegand's right cheek.

"Don't scream!" Guandique commanded.

He covered her mouth with his hand.

Wiegand stopped struggling.

He smiled, thinking she had surrendered.

When she felt the tension go from his arms, she kicked hard and screamed. He fell back off of her body, too light to keep her down.

She ran until she hit Beach Drive and walked into the middle of the road. A driver realized she was bruised and shaken and stopped her car.

Wiegand's description of her attacker matched a man the Park Police knew well. Within the hour, Park Police arrested Ingmar Guandique for a second time.

Wiegand identified him as her attacker.

At first, Guandique denied attacking Wiegand. A Park Police officer asked him if, perhaps, he had accidently bumped into a woman while he was in the park. Guandique bit and said he was bending down rubbing his leg when a woman ran into him and they fell off the trail. Guandique said he tried to help the woman but she screamed and ran away. It was all a misunderstanding.

Recalling the attack on Halle Shilling in early May, the officer asked if perhaps this had happened before. After some back and forth, Guandique said a few months earlier he was jogging behind a woman matching Shilling's description when she tripped and fell. He said when he tried to help the woman up, like Wiegand, she screamed and ran away. Again, it was all a misunderstanding.

According to the *Washington Post*, the Park Police officer then pulled out a photo of Chandra and asked Guandique if he had ever seen her in Rock Creek Park.

"Yes," Guandique replied. He said he had spotted Chandra while hanging out by the Pierce Mill.

"Did you think she was attractive?"

"Yes."

Guandique then claimed he never saw Chandra again.

According to the *Washington Post*, Guandique's admission to having seen Chandra in Rock Creek Park did not make it into the formal police report, and the Park Police didn't report this fact to other law-enforcement agencies.

MERCY

The morning's natural light was blocked out by the closed blinds.

"Cadee, the tabloids are going to say I'm into M and M, or M and S stuff," Gary said as he finished pouring a cup of coffee.

Cadee Condit didn't know whether to laugh or cry. "I think you mean S and M."

"They're talking to Vince and he's saying some crazy shit."

"Vince is a traitor."

"These media people are making him feel important. What do you expect?"

"I expect him to be loyal."

"You can't expect more from a person than they are capable of giving," Gary replied.

"Everyone can give loyalty. Even Vince," Cadee shot back, then left the kitchen to join her mother in the den down the hall.

Fox News's Rita Cosby had landed the first major "get" in the scandal—an exclusive television interview with Anne Marie Smith. Up to this point, Smith hadn't talked directly to the public. Her attorney, Jim Robinson, had done all the talking.

During the prime time interview, Smith told Cosby she had seen personal items in Gary's condo she assumed belonged to Chandra. While Smith and Cosby spoke, three FBI agents and five Seattle police officers stood guard in the news studio. Robinson had told reporters his client required protection from Gary's "powerful friends."

As the interview ended, Smith dropped a bombshell. "He told me, 'you don't have to talk to the media, you don't have to talk to anybody—you don't even have to talk to the FBI.'"

Robinson waved the draft affidavit prepared by Joseph Cotchett's office and declared, "The congressman asked her to commit perjury and obstruct justice!"

The FBI and the US Attorney's Office opened an investigation into whether Gary had obstructed justice and tampered with a witness.

↲

Carolyn rested her head against the back of the couch.

Cadee entered and sat next to her.

On the television, pundits discussed the latest allegations in the massive scandal that had engulfed the Condit family. There had been scattered reports that Gary told Anne Marie Smith he was separating from his wife. But the latest report was that Smith had told the FBI Gary wouldn't leave his chronically ill wife because "he didn't want to pull a Gingrich," referring to allegations that the then congressman had divorced his first wife while she was in the hospital recovering from cancer surgery.

Carolyn and Cadee heard Gary's footsteps stop in the hallway as he passed the den.

On the television a pundit asserted that up to five more women had come forward alleging to have had sexual affairs with "Congressman Condit."

Gary felt Carolyn's gaze fixed on the back of his head. He didn't know how his wife or daughter would react.

He turned and faced them.

For more than thirty years, Gary had been the one thing in Carolyn's life that never brought her pain. That had changed. The pain of the alleged affairs overwhelmed every other pain in her body.

She always accepted Gary for what he was. Neither person tried to change the other. But the allegations, if true, would be a betrayal of a relationship that began when they were sixteen years old.

But the pain of watching the world attack him was also real. *They're accusing him of murder*, she realized.

"They better be cute," Carolyn chided, lightening the mood.

She could have given him hell, and almost did. But in this moment, Carolyn decided to save that discussion for another day.

INDEPENDENCE DAY

"I think we should turn the sprinklers on them," Jean Condit, Gary's mother, insisted as the family ate dinner.

"That won't do anybody any good," Adrian Condit, Gary's father, responded. "It'll just draw more attention."

This wasn't the first time Jean had threatened to douse reporters camped in front of the home on Acorn Lane.

Gary cleared the table while Carolyn took a bag of trash to the backyard.

She stopped at the trash cans lined against the side of the house. Dogs barking didn't drown out an unfamiliar scratching sound. She looked up and saw a long black boom with a microphone taped to the end hanging just above her head. Someone on the other side of the fence was trying to maneuver the boom across the yard to the kitchen window, using the fence as a balance.

"Hello?" Carolyn called.

"Move. Run!" a voice whispered as the boom was pulled back.

⌁

At 5:00 a.m. on July 4, Gary and Carolyn walked across their backyard, each carrying a single carry-on bag.

The sky was still dark, and they had turned off all the lights in the house.

Gary pulled apart two loose boards in the fence. She went through first.

On the other side, neighbors escorted them across the yard and into the garage, where they got into the backseat of their neighbors' car.

"Lay this way," Gary said. He and Carolyn bent their bodies so that their heads fell below the line of the left rear passenger window.

⌁

Modesto's Fourth of July parade started while Gary and Carolyn were in the air. Throngs of people had flooded the city. It was the biggest crowd in the parade's long history.

Gary's detractors held signs demanding his resignation and calling him a murderer. Friends of the Levy family solemnly marched in the parade holding pictures of Chandra and long yellow ribbons.

A palpable anxiety hovered over the festivities. The press, the locals, the participants—they were all waiting for Gary to appear. When he didn't, reporters swarmed Gary's Modesto district office, demanding an explanation for his absence on Independence Day.

⌁

Cadee and two of her friends were lying out by the pool when a sudden and violent wind swept across the yard, whipping the water into a choppy sea.

Cadee's eyes flashed open. A helicopter hovered above her, close enough that she could make out the face of the cameraman staring down at them.

The girls retreated to the house, where Cadee called her brother, Chad. "There was a helicopter taking pictures of me in the pool," she explained.

"They'll probably get big bucks for that," Chad responded, only half-teasing. Paparazzi earned upwards of $5,000 per photo of Gary and his family.

"He needs to fight back," Cadee answered. "He needs to get into a campaign mode."

"What's he gonna say? I had to watch a special the other day about his ties looking like a penis," Chad replied.

"That's a joke?"

"Cable news."

Commentators on mainstream news networks questioned why Gary often held his coat in his arm or over his shoulder when he exited the Lynshire building in the morning. Psychologists paraded onto news shows suggested he did so in order to emphasize his neckties, because neckties are a prominent phallic symbol. Gary wore ties, they argued, to evoke sexuality even when he wasn't talking about his sexual affairs.

"I'm serious," Chad insisted. "That's what he's up against. I get what he thinks—that if he fights back, he'll just give them more ammunition. They've already turned his ties into dicks. What do you think they could do with his words?"

"If he can't be out there, then we should be."

"Abbe's advising him that because of the investigation we've got to stay out of the press."

"He didn't kill anyone."

MARITAL PRIVILEGE

At 8:30 a.m. on July 5, Carolyn Condit and Abbe Lowell arrived at the FBI's Northern Virginia Field Office and were promptly led into a room that Carolyn thought smelled like mothballs.

They were joined by assistant US attorneys Heidi Pasichow and Barbara Kittay, FBI special agents Robert Oxley and Tracy Fortin, and Metro Police detective Ralph Durant.

The interview lasted more than three hours.

"I'd like to note for the record that Mrs. Condit has thumbs on both her hands," Lowell began.

The investigators chuckled uncomfortably.

"Our interest in the alleged 'relationship' between Congressman Condit and Ms. Levy stems only from our desire to find Ms. Levy," AUSA Pasichow insisted. "We regret having to talk about the personal aspects of this, and we do not do so out of an idle curiosity about either you or your husband."

AUSA Kittay then leaned across the table to draw closer to Carolyn. "If you want to have an attorney who represents only your interests, and not the joint interests of the Condit family, you have that right, and provisions can be made for you to have counsel without regard to the issue of cost."

"I'm fine with Abbe representing our interests," Carolyn replied.

"While this discussion is for information purposes and is voluntary, since Agents Oxley and Fortin are federal law-enforcement agents, you will get yourself into trouble if you say anything to us that is not truthful. I want you to understand that," Kittay continued.

"Mrs. Condit, we understand that the media has been on a feeding frenzy in this case, with TV trucks parked everywhere. We want you to know that we are not in control of the media and can't do much to keep them quiet. They have their own agenda and techniques, which often include following people around," Pasichow said.

"The Condits have asked me to assist them in telling everything there is to tell falling within the relevant time period," Lowell offered, "but beyond this time period they are not interested in merely satisfying everyone's possible curiosity, or delving into things that are of mere prurient interest and are outside the relevant timeline."

After asking Carolyn a series of questions about the Condit family and her past, the investigators moved to questioning her about Gary's schedule and her trip to Washington in April.

"Was there ever a time where he had to travel and couldn't make it home on the weekend?" Pasichow asked.

"Sometimes during budget negotiations, but usually he came home every weekend," Carolyn answered.

"Does your husband like to spend time anywhere else on weekends?"

"No."

"For example, were there times he might have reason to go to Seattle or San Francisco or Palm Springs?" Pasichow pressed.

The tabloid magazine *Globe* had reported "the Harley Davidson riding congressman once attended gatherings of motorcycle gang members and hangers on and allegedly said that murder for hire could be both convenient and easy to arrange . . . He had a love nest in Palm Springs. He liked to take girlfriends and meet new conquests in towns like Reno and Laughlin in Nevada. He would take his mistresses away for wild weekends filled with raunchy sex." Federal investigators had scoured Palm Springs, Reno, and Laughlin to see if anyone had seen the motorcycle-riding congressman and Chandra Levy.

"No," Carolyn replied.

"Are there any health issues for either of you? In other words, is he in good health?"

"Yes."

"So there's nothing to all that in the media about you being sick?"

"No, it's just silly. Thanks for asking. I'm good to go," Carolyn answered. She had no intention of letting law enforcement leak to the press that she was "sick," which would be used to confirm the outrageous stories about her being an invalid. Carolyn's pain was chronic and to her it was neither a sickness nor a weakness.

"Who would you say your husband's closest friend would be?"

"Me, and his family."

The investigators then turned to questioning Carolyn about her knowledge of the events that had unfolded over the prior months.

"When I leave here today, do you want me to still think they were just good friends, or whether it was something more than that?" Kittay asked.

"I don't see how that is relevant," Carolyn answered.

"Did Mrs. Levy call you?" Pasichow asked.

"No. It was Dr. Levy," Carolyn replied.

Pasichow asked Carolyn a series of question about her phone call with Dr. Levy, trying to confirm whether Carolyn or Gary spoke with Susan Levy on that day. Someone had told federal investigators Susan had talked with Carolyn and Gary, and Pasichow was surprised by Carolyn's insistence that it wasn't true.

"After your husband's conversation with Dr. Levy, did you talk with him about the call?"

"I asked him what was going on. He said she had been in his office a few times and was a friend of an intern, Jennifer Baker, who worked in the office."

"Anything else?"

"I asked how old she was, because I was relating this to our daughter."

"Is there anything else you asked your husband after he had spoken with Dr. Levy?"

"I asked how he knew her."

"Did he say anything to you about her?"

"He said she was a friend of his, and that she had been into the office several times. It seemed she was just an acquaintance."

"Is the word 'acquaintance' your word or the congressman's word?" Pasichow asked.

"That would be my word," Carolyn replied.

"But your impression was that he knew her?"

"Yes. Gary is friendly, she was a young person, he had lots of friends . . . he was quite concerned that she was missing."

"So your impression was that she was like all of the other kids who came into the office or was she special in any way?"

"I don't know," Carolyn answered.

"Do you have the same impression now?"

Carolyn looked down at the tabletop, trying to submerge her gaze in it.

Pasichow stood. "You'll have to excuse me. I've got to get to the airport to catch a plane for a vacation I've had planned."

"Thank you for your time," Carolyn said as she shook Pasichow's hand. "I hope you enjoy your vacation." Carolyn was good at hiding her sarcasm.

After Pasichow had left, Kittay turned to Carolyn's schedule while she was in Washington, DC, starting with Sunday, April 29.

"So in terms of what we call alibi, you were in each other's company the whole time."

"We were in each other's company the whole time."

Carolyn then explained for investigators, step by step, the trek she and Gary had taken back to Adams Morgan from the Rayburn Building.

"Continuing with the timeline, what happened on Monday, April 30?"

"I did nothing. I stayed in the apartment," Carolyn answered.

"Did you talk to your husband?"

"Monday was a very busy day for him."

"So you knew where your husband was only because others told you where he would be?" Kittay asked.

"Yes. And I saw him on the news with the president of the United States," Carolyn answered.

"Now turning to Tuesday, May 1."

"This is the day before the luncheon, and I had to be there early because we had to start decorating. The committee of spouses did the decorating," Carolyn explained.

"You'd think that the Hilton could have done that for you," Kittay opined.

"It saves a lot of money to do it yourself. That's the way it works in campaigns, too."

"What did you do for dinner?"

"We had cereal, cinnamon toast, and hot tea."

"You're really getting down to the bottom of the barrel."

"That's all we had left."

Kittay concluded by asking Carolyn to walk her through her last two days in Washington: Wednesday, May 2 and Thursday, May 3. When they finished, Kittay turned back to asking Carolyn questions about the relationship between Gary and Chandra.

"Dr. Levy was asking questions which sound like he expected Gary to know more personal things about her habits than might have been expected under the circumstances."

"I think he was just asking questions," Carolyn replied.

"You didn't think they were too personal?"

"They were panicked. They hadn't heard from their daughter in days, and Gary was a link of some sort."

"Were you thinking, *Why are they calling Gary?*"

"Not at all. I just think they were panicked."

"Did you have a feeling that the congressman knew her better than just as a friend?"

"I think he told me everything," Carolyn replied.

"Are you now uncomfortable with the relationship he had with her?" Kittay pressed.

"I don't like the media treatment of this."

"But with the relationship itself—or does the media have it all wrong?"

"I don't want to go there."

"Again, this is irrelevant. Please move on," Lowell advised.

"You have said you want to be cooperative; this is the part that helps us," Kittay responded.

"I disagree," Lowell insisted. "I don't see how whether Mrs. Condit is comfortable with the congressman's relationship has anything to do with finding Chandra Levy."

"I don't like it when public statements are made about being cooperative, and yet certain questions are off limits!" Kittay yelled.

"I think you should be careful about characterizing Mr. Condit as anything but cooperative," Lowell warned. "They've gone out of their way to accommodate request after request from law-enforcement officials, even after having to watch investigators blunder their way through this thing."

"We understand," Kittay answered, then turned her attention back to Carolyn. "What do you understand the relationship to have been?"

"Friends," Carolyn replied.

"They were not having a 'romantic' relationship?" Kittay asked.

"No," Carolyn answered.

"On May 7 your husband goes back to DC. What happened then?"

"The next thing I remember is a media report drawing a relationship between Gary and Chandra."

"What do you remember reading?"

"As I recall, a Levy relative said that Gary was or might be the 'mystery boyfriend.'"

"What did you do with this report?"

"I threw it away," Carolyn responded.

"Did you ask, 'Why is this happening to me?'"

"Why is this happening to the two of us?"

"Does your husband wear a watch?"

"No."

"Does he own one?"

"He has several."

"Do you know the makes? Does he have a TAG Heuer?"

"I don't know. He has a box of watches, but he wears no jewelry."

"The luncheon with Laura Bush . . . that was the only reason you came to DC?"

"Yes."

"Not to confront your husband as some of the papers have said?"

"Over what?" Carolyn asked.

"That he had extramarital affairs."

"No."

"Did you ever have arguments with him over extramarital relationships?"

"No."

"Did you ever hear anything about the flight attendant?"

"No."

"Is it true that Gary posed for the Hunks of the House calendar?"

"I don't know. I read that in the paper recently. Other congressional members did too. It's an inside gag thing."

Within hours of Carolyn leaving the FBI's office, unnamed police sources leaked details of the interview to the press.

WHAT END?

On July 6, the *Washington Post* finally revealed the identity of the Levy family relative who, for nearly a month, had been cited but not named by the *Post* as it published the details of an alleged serious romance between Chandra and Gary.

The woman's name was Linda Zamsky, and the *Post* described her as Chandra's aunt, although not by blood.

> "It had to remain a secret. If anybody found out about this relationship, it was done, over, kaput . . ."

Zamsky's account places Condit at the center of Levy's life in Washington—a married man who gave her gifts, paid for a couple of plane trips to California, orchestrated their meetings and often spent weekends with her in his Adams Morgan apartment . . .

The picture painted by the aunt is of a woman who relished the attention of the older man, heeded his caution and treasured his gifts, which included a gold bracelet and Godiva chocolates. Levy hoped Condit would marry her and even envisioned a life with children, the aunt said.

Zamsky provided the press with a fifteen-page aide-mémoire packed with alleged details of her niece's alleged affair with a married congressman.

Zamsky claimed Chandra and Gary went out together for Thai food and that they had taken vacations together. Zamsky told reporters Gary took extreme measures to hide the relationship. "She would come out the door, grab the taxi, and then he would come out, baseball cap, jacket, kind of a little incognito, and he would get in the cab with her," Zamsky claimed.

She also alleged that Chandra and Gary had agreed on a "five-year plan" for Gary to leave Carolyn and start a family with Chandra. According to Zamsky, Chandra had left her a voice mail on April 29 stating, "I really have some big news or something important to tell, please call."

Theories as to what Chandra's "big news" must have been about exploded across the mainstream media.

Bringing Zamsky into the light was only one part of a multipronged attack on Gary orchestrated by the Levy camp. Stories about a bond between Anne Marie Smith and Susan Levy ran in newspapers on both coasts. When asked by reporters what she had said to Smith, Susan replied, "I thanked her for being brave and coming forward."

Lockstep, Anne Marie Smith and her attorney, Jim Robinson, appeared on CNN's *Larry King Live*.

KING: Did you say to him—"but you are married?"
SMITH: No, I never said that to him . . . I knew the fact that he was married.

. . .

KING: So he wanted you to sign an affidavit that it was not true?
SMITH: That's correct.

King turned to Robinson.

KING: Was that very smart that she didn't sign that, Jim?
ROBINSON: She could have gone to jail a long time if she would have signed that document, yes.

King turned his attention back to Smith.

KING: [W]ere you a prisoner of this relationship in a sense? I don't want to say under a spell, that seems trite.
SMITH: I know what you are saying. I really—he is very manipulative . . .
ROBINSON: [P]eople don't change their habits, who they date, how they try to control them, how they try to control the situation, how they react when a woman gets nervous, starts to get possessive . . .
KING: So if he did it with her . . . he has to be a controlling figure in Chandra Levy's life?

ROBINSON: Yes.

KING: Therefore it has to come under that veil of suspicion of something?

ROBINSON: Of something. She may have come—got to some point where she said enough is enough. I know about this, I know about this, I—this is all speculation—but pushed him to his limit . . .

KING: He never harmed you, did he?

SMITH: No.

KING: Ever come close to harming you?

SMITH: No.

. . .

KING: . . . Anne Marie did want to say something else tonight to other women who may have been involved. What?

SMITH: I just want to say that if there are other women that know anything about this and that are afraid to come forward, or have been threatened in any way, I encourage them from the bottom of my heart to come forward, because the longer you keep silent, the stronger you make these people, and just telling the truth will make you safe.

Robinson hit a number of cable news shows, alleging Smith had found what she believed to be Chandra's hair in Gary's bathroom, and that she had also found neckties tied together underneath Gary's bed. According to Robinson, Gary had sexual habits that were "not normal for a heterosexual male."

—

Billy Martin appeared on CBS's *Early Show*.

"Let me ask you about reports that Chandra told friends that she had a medical appointment just before she disappeared. Does her family consider the possibility, Mr. Martin, that she was pregnant?" the host asked.

"As the investigators looking into this, we've looked into all possibilities including all of her health and medical records and not—we don't want, in any way, to jeopardize the investigation that the authorities are conducting, and I don't think we want to answer that, but we do know the answer," Martin replied.

"You do know the answer?"

"We do know the answer," Martin confirmed.

Martin then fueled the angle that Gary's refusal to discuss the nature of his relationship with Chandra had severely hindered the investigation into her disappearance. Editorial pages across the country carried a new war cry: "Dance around the truth—about sex or anything else—and people wonder whether you have something else to hide!"

The *Washington Post* and *Newsweek* soon reported that investigators were demanding a third interview with Gary. This time, for the sole purpose of clarifying the nature of his relationship with Chandra.

—

Only an executive desk separated the two seasoned lawyers. Abbe Lowell had requested the meeting with his former law partner, Billy Martin.

"The Levys are not best served by focusing 100 percent of the police and media attention on Condit," Lowell insisted. "We accept that there is no way to de-link this investigation from the congressman. And we understand that there needs to be a certain amount of pounding on him to keep the media's interest, and he's willing to take that. But the onslaught, it's overwhelmed every other aspect of this. Billy, there's no hedge in your strategy. What if he didn't do it?" Lowell pressed.

"The Levys have no intention of scaling back their focus on Congressman Condit," Martin replied.

CNN's news program *Reliable Sources* debated the question: "Has the Media Declared Open Season on Gary Condit's Sex Life?"

BERNARD KALB (COHOST): Is the media being quote, unquote, "jerked around" to tell their story with respect to competing parties?

BOB FRANKEN (CNN REPORTER): Are we spun? You bet. As a matter of fact, it is very obvious that the reason that this aunt came forward was because she was being part—used as part of a coordinated media campaign, no doubt about it, nobody denies that—that is being conducted by Billy Martin.

HOWARD KURTZ (COHOST): I just wanted to turn to Rita Cosby. Isn't it possible that even if everything Anne Marie Smith told you on camera is true and Condit was trying to cover up, say, an embarrassing affair—then it could still be the case that Gary Condit had absolutely nothing to do with Chandra Levy's disappearance?

RITA COSBY (FOX NEWS): If she said, "Look, I had an affair with Gary Condit," we would have to decide whether or not that was a story.

KURTZ: If it was only a question of sex.

COSBY: Yes.

KURTZ: And there wasn't a question of a proposed affidavit?

COSBY: Right—and maybe information about Chandra.

KURTZ: You might not have gone with it?

COSBY: Possibly not. One thing that was interesting with her is she did also say that she saw dark hairs in the bathroom, some things that pointed to Chandra Levy.

KURTZ: She's a redhead, of course.

COSBY: Yes, she's a redhead. And said, "Look, these are not my hairs." And she said that Gary Condit said, "These are your hairs." And she said, "These are not my hairs."

Salon carried the following story in the newspaper's entertainment section:

[R]eporters have flocked to the story, hungry for dirt and detail. And the Levys have made sure their hunger has been duly fed.

Their inexperience has been apparent.

Susan Levy has now changed her own stories so often that her word has come to seem like a work in progress, as she denies a story about her daughter on TV one evening while a newspaper quotes her corroborating it the very next morning.

But the strategy has worked.

COOPERATION

"They want a third interview," Lowell advised, walking next to Gary in Mike Dayton's backyard as the two men smoked cigars.

"I've answered their questions."

"They need you to tell them directly that you had sex with Chandra."

"Do you really think they need that? I've never denied anything. If I answer that it's not for the police. It's for the press. And you know what, the next question they demand I answer will be about some other woman. You can't prove a negative, Abbe."

"The Levys are saying you have hindered the investigation by trying to hide your personal affairs. Billy Martin has the flight attendant on TV saying she's afraid of you. 'Why' doesn't matter at this point," Lowell replied.

"Abbe, it does matter. I'm drawing a line here. And I'm not going to cross it," Gary answered. "You need to make your advice on that basis."

Lowell was accustomed to dealing with clients who responded to political motivations. Gary's intransience was rooted in something more basic. He genuinely believed talking publicly meant not only talking about his personal life but also talking about Chandra's and Carolyn's personal lives.

"The aunt, Zamsky," Lowell continued. "She's feeding the idea that you had a motive to harm Chandra. That you promised her you'd start—"

Gary cut in before Lowell could finish the sentence. "I don't date, we are not boyfriend-girlfriend, and there is no fucking five-year plan. Women confide in friends, not distant relatives. That crazy woman doesn't have the first clue about what my relationship with Chandra is or isn't. She's making shit up about vacations and a five-year plan. This is the thing you have to understand. I know what's true and not true about me."

"That's what this third interview is going to be about. Answer for their record, and then they can move on."

"We all know whatever I say will end up on the front page of the *Post*—let's not pretend this isn't what it is really all about."

"The police are getting a lot of heat."

"If anyone's taking heat, it's me. And it's keeping the heat off of them. Tell me, explain that to me, sitting here, knowing I'm a suspect and everything is lined up against me no matter what I do, why I should continue cooperating with these guys?"

"If you don't, they'll compel you to," Lowell answered.

Gary shot Lowell an indignant stare. "They're the ones being compelled. I'll answer, but it won't stop anything. They're not interested in my innocence. Everything they're doing, and anything I do in response, it's just gonna pull the rope tighter and higher."

⌐

That afternoon, Lowell met Chief of Detectives Jack Barrett at a Starbucks in Chinatown.

"We need him to tell us the nature of his relationship with Chandra," Barrett said. "Directly."

"He'll do that tomorrow," Lowell replied. "But he's also—we're not convinced his providing that answer will allow people to move on."

"I can't control what other people will or won't do. But I'm sensitive to the congressman's concerns." Barrett paused briefly, but long enough for Lowell to conclude that he wasn't going to like what Barrett said next. "We also need to search the congressman's apartment."

"That's ridiculous. To search an apartment two and a half months after someone disappears? You haven't even established a crime has occurred," Lowell answered. "Where does it end?"

"A lot of demands are being made. We're not responding to all of them. But we're going to pursue searching his apartment."

"I'll have to talk with my client," Lowell replied, pressing a bitter cup of coffee to his lips.

"There's another thing. The prosecutors are asking for a DNA sample," Barrett said.

"Why, because a flight attendant says she thinks my client killed Chandra? Because Billy Martin demanded it?" Lowell asked, struggling to keep his voice to a level that wouldn't draw attention in the crowded coffee shop. "Just last week your office—Terrance Gainer—acknowledged my client's cooperation and stated he wasn't a suspect. What's changed?"

"It's not all in my control. We have a number of law-enforcement agencies involved."

"I've seen these prosecutors in action. They're out of control. Are they leading the investigation, or are you? Will the US Attorney's Office participate in the interview of the congressman?"

"They will. I'll keep the prosecutors on task, you have my word. But we're going to ask for the DNA," Barrett replied. "We'll get a subpoena."

According to Barrett, he told Lowell investigators had a pair of Chandra's underwear with semen stains and needed to know if the semen belonged to Gary or if there was someone else in her love life. Lowell recalls Barrett requesting Gary's DNA sample, but claims Barrett never mentioned a pair of underwear. Neither man ever told Gary investigators had Chandra's underwear and were going to test it for a DNA match.

"Let's not mix apples and oranges," Lowell replied. "Let's do the interview first. Let's not raise the request for his DNA now. It will be counterproductive. We'll decide after the interview whether it's still necessary."

"We can agree to that," Barrett confirmed.

Shortly after their meeting at Starbucks, the *Washington Post* reported Gary was going to meet with investigators for a third time.

WHAT SHOULD WE DO?

On July 6 at 8:30 p.m., Gary joined Abbe Lowell, Lowell's associate, AUSA Barbara Kittay, Chief of Detectives Jack Barrett, and Detective Ralph Durant in a conference room inside Lowell's law offices. The meeting had been arranged after work hours when the reporters who staked out Lowell's office wouldn't be there. Everyone had come in through the garage in case a stringer had been left out front.

Gary started before anyone else could get a word in. "In the past when I met with investigators I provided all information I thought would be meaningful or helpful while trying to carve out what I still believe is private and personal to me. The leaks themselves underscored my prior desire to keep personal things private. I know that when I leave this meeting, what I say in here will be in the papers. But I understand why you wish to talk about these very private things, and I am willing to do so."

Lowell asked Gary a series of questions about the nature of his relationship with Chandra, and Gary answered each one. Rather than Lowell telling law-enforcement officials to assume Gary had a sexual relationship with Chandra or to infer what they needed from Gary not denying the relationship was sexual, Lowell asked Gary whether the relationship had been sexual and Gary answered directly. Lowell decided he would ask the questions Barrett needed asked and answered in light of the prior behavior of AUSA Barbara Kittay.

Now, law enforcement "knew" what they already knew.

When Lowell finished questioning Gary, Barrett spoke before Kittay could crash in.

"It seemed that she had no friends here, and appeared that the only person she confided in was the aunt. So in this process we have to balance credibility. We are concerned, as you are, about the leaks, but frankly, I can't control it. I won't even apologize for it because it is simply something I can't control. We don't like it, and we want you to know that it isn't the people in this room who are the source of the leaks," Barrett stated.

"The relationship was not heating up as has been suggested in the press. Quite the opposite," Lowell offered.

"Can you describe her frame of mind the last time you saw her?" Durant asked Gary.

"May I interject something," Kittay said.

"You may not," Barrett replied.

Gary looked at Durant. "She was a happy person, focused on her career and her future plans. This was the same from the first time I saw her to the last."

"Did you talk about her not getting the job?" Durant asked.

"She said she missed the deadline for getting the job. I asked her if she thought she had been treated unfairly, but she said no, she just missed the deadline. I thought it was noble of her to fess up. Many young people would not have done so," Gary answered.

"On a scale of one to ten, how upset would you say she was?"

"Maybe a two."

"How had you left it with her?" Kittay asked.

"There was no discussion. I thought she would be back. There was no break in the friend-ship or the relationship. She thought that perhaps her best opportunities were in Sacramento, but I expected her to come back and get a job so she could get some experience and then go into the FBI," Gary replied.

"How did the arrangements work when she came to see you?" Durant asked.

"She would buzz at the front door; I'd pick up the phone and let her in."

"Did you exchange any gifts?"

"She gave me candies."

"What did you give her?" Lowell asked, making sure Gary corrected the prior record.

"I gave her a gold bracelet," Gary answered.

"How about for her birthday? Did you give her something?" Kittay asked.

"I don't think so. The relationship did not involve a lot of giving gifts and things like that."

"I'm trying to get into her head. This was an adult relationship; she was a young, impres-sionable girl, and she may have been sort of fantasizing. It takes a while to handle it in that way . . . to understand that it is not about romance and gifts, and the future and the kids and the kinds of things young girls might dream about," Kittay pressed.

"My impression was that she was very mature, and we didn't talk about things like that; the emotional things," Gary replied, aggravated by Kittay's apparent acceptance of the Levy camp's story and the false impression it gave, not just of him but of Chandra. *At least Barrett understands there might be a credibility issue on the other side. She's taking the position that if it wasn't true, then it was made up in Chandra's head. What if the Levy camp simply made this all up to stir the press? She's basing her whole investigation on a false assumption about the victim.*

"But perhaps she wanted to change you or the nature of the relationship, or fantasized about doing so. What do you think she understood the relationship to be?" Kittay continued.

"I think she liked me and thought that I could be helpful to her in her career. It wasn't this big, emotional, sappy relationship where you are going with these questions and comments," Gary answered.

"Don't you think she was hurt about not getting presents and the other things?" Kittay asked.

"Did you speak with her about a future with her—with you and you with her?" Durant interjected.

"The discussions were always about her future, not mine. My future was fairly clear, at least until recently," Gary replied.

"The papers and the tabloids are saying that she believed you would be together in the future."

"There was no discussion about any kind of permanent status."

"Were you seeing any other woman at the same time you were seeing Chandra?" Kittay asked.

"That's out of line, and you know it," Lowell intervened.

"It's not at all!" Kittay shouted.

Lowell stood and put his palms on the conference room table. "We can end this now if that's where she is going to go. We had an agreement—the congressman is here giving you everything you need about his personal life, and he doesn't have to do this."

"Let's settle down," Barrett interjected. "Can we limit the inquiry to a concern about whether Chandra knew or thought that he was seeing another woman? The issue is whether she knew you were seeing someone else."

"I encouraged her to make friends," Gary replied.

"That doesn't answer the question!" Kittay bellowed across the table, unable to stay in her seat.

Lowell leaned across the table so that he was eye level with Kittay. "The question is out of line. Do you think some other woman had something to do with this?"

"We need to figure that out," Kittay replied.

"This is a witch hunt. This is the second interview with you, and you've been out of line both times. Why don't you spend your time searching the parks instead of chasing every woman that has ever known the congressman?" Lowell responded.

"Abbe, don't tell us how to do our job," Kittay shouted.

"You're going down a path with no reason," Lowell shouted back.

"I don't need to explain my reasons to you."

Barrett again stepped in and stopped the two lawyers before they were at each other's throat.

"All right, in an attempt to guide the questioning to what we believe may be relevant information without treading on this one remaining area of the congressman's private life, but which Ms. Kittay in particular seems so energetically interested, Gary, in any way, did the subject of another woman come up when you were with Chandra?" Lowell offered.

"No," Gary answered.

"Without identifying who, there was no discussion of any other woman when you were with her?"

"No."

"We're actually trying to know two things. First, if Chandra knew of other women, and second, whether another woman knew he was seeing Chandra," Barrett calmly explained.

"Well, then do what you just did . . . ask the question like that, ask him if another woman discussed with him the fact that he was seeing Chandra," Lowell replied.

"She could have sat on a bench outside your house and found out that you were involved with another woman," Kittay interrupted. "This is an impressionable young person who was obviously fixated on you, and who knows what she did or what she found out."

"With all due respect, you appear to be going all over the country soliciting information about other relationships from everyone that has ever known me, just trying to dig up as much dirt on me as possible. All of this information immediately finds its way into the press," Gary replied.

"We are searching for people, friend or foe, to find out about the congressman, and if the people they talk to, or other people they haven't talked to, choose to go to the press, we can't stop that—they have a right to talk to whoever they want to talk to," Barrett explained.

"I think I have a right to know whether the people who are contacting you and your colleagues are people who know Chandra Levy, or know anything about Chandra Levy," Gary argued.

Barrett responded before Kittay could launch back into a tirade. "Often, they have no such knowledge. As soon as that fact is established we really have very little further to say to them," he assured Gary.

"The congressman's refusal to explain the true terms of the relationship with Chandra led to us asking about his relationship with other women so that we could reach our own conclusions based on sources other than him," Kittay shouted.

Barrett, again, tried to defuse the situation. "Once we establish that the people being interviewed don't know Chandra Levy, we try not to go into the intimacies of any other relationship. Nevertheless, it appears that Congressman Condit does not believe that is the case," he said.

Gary tried to digest the clear divergence in what he was hearing and seeing from Barrett and Kittay. *Barrett started the meeting by acknowledging the leaks without apologizing for something he couldn't stop. Why would the Metro Police brass and federal investigators continue tearing my private life open for the public when the lead investigators have ruled me out?*

"If I may, I would like to rephrase the question in a way that may satisfy everyone here. Did any other woman mention Chandra Levy to you?" Barrett continued.

"No," Gary answered.

"Did anyone see you with her and mention the fact to you?" Lowell asked.

"No."

Kittay stepped in again. "People learn things independent of you . . . people love to talk about these things. When I was a reporter I thought I would have to fight to get people to talk to me, but people love to talk. I never had to convince anyone to talk," she opined.

She was a reporter, that explains a lot, Lowell thought.

"Did you ever confide in any friend of yours any information about a relationship with Chandra Levy?" Lowell asked Gary.

Unbelievable, Gary thought. *They tried to put this on me. They tried to put it on Burl, on Hop, on Carolyn. Having exhausted my family, they're now going to try to find some jealous woman to put this on!* "No," he answered.

"She left you a message even after your wife got here. And you called her back on Sunday with your wife here?" Kittay asked him.

"I thought she was going to leave, but it turned out that she hadn't finalized her travel plans."

"Were you conscious of trying to separate yourself from your wife to make the call?" she asked.

"No," Gary replied.

"They weren't going to talk about anything kinky on the call, if that's what you are driving at," Lowell added.

Kittay shot Lowell a nasty look. "It seems sort of reckless to me to have this conversation on the phone with his wife right there."

"I asked you this before, but what do you think happened to her?" Durant asked.

"I have no idea," Gary responded.

"Do you think she harmed herself?"

"No, she just didn't seem like the kind of person who would do that."

"I know you don't want to talk to me again after this meeting, so let me just ask a few more questions," Kittay said. "One reason we have been asking people about your relationships with them is that we had to fill in the void that was created when you weren't talking about these things."

"Is there a question?" Lowell asked her.

"I have my own style of asking questions," Kittay insisted.

Lowell, Barrett, and Kittay argued loudly about who had been invited to the meeting, and who should be excluded from any future meetings. Gary sat calmly watching the circus. After a few minutes of screaming at one another, Lowell and Kittay took Barrett's advice and sat down. When calm was restored, Kittay resumed questioning Gary.

"Do you know why she would have lots and lots of your business cards?" she asked him.

"Did she? I didn't give her any," Gary answered.

Kittay asked why Chandra would have something on it with Chad Condit's address, and Gary answered that he did not know why.

"And you don't think Jennifer Baker would know if you two had a relationship? To me it makes more sense that she would know about it—two young people, friends, come here together, both come to see you, Jennifer starts working in the office, Chandra comes by there to see her. You'd think she would mention if she developed a relationship with you, you know. That's what young girls do," Kittay said.

"Jennifer Baker has said that she didn't know anything and I believe her. Why would she lie about that?" Gary replied.

"Mike Dayton didn't know about Chandra?" Kittay asked.

"No."

"But you trusted him. He picks you up and takes you where you need to go."

"I trust him, but I don't share my personal, private life with people. That's my business only," Gary explained.

"Do you think there are people who are being, or talking to us that are carving out areas, or trying to hold back anything in a protective way?"

"From what I've seen, no one is holding back anything."

"You have never asked anyone to hold back anything?" Kittay demanded.

"Never. That's not how I do things."

"What about Anne Marie Smith?" she pressed.

"I never told her not to cooperate or to withhold anything from the authorities. She left a message saying the press was hounding her. I told her she owed nothing to the press and had no obligation to talk to them."

"Just so you don't think we're sandbagging you when you hear about it, I want you to know that we already have an appointment set up to meet with her next week," Kittay said.

"The FBI has already talked to her and she told me about it immediately, so how could I have suggested to her that she not talk to the FBI? The discussion was about her talking to the press," Gary replied.

"Congressman, we will need you to submit to a saliva test, for your DNA," Kittay barked.

Lowell jumped out of his chair. "We agreed that this would not be raised as part of this interview!"

"They have no authority to make any decision like that. I'm tired of being fucking gone around," Kittay shouted back.

"What are you talking about?" Lowell asked.

"Don't be such an asshole!" Kittay demanded.

"Fuck you!"

"You're a motherfucking asshole!" Kittay yelled.

Barrett looked over at Gary.

Gary stared coldly at Barrett, and then Kittay.

"We're done!" Lowell roared.

"Come on, Barbara, let's go," Barrett said, realizing it was time for the meeting to end.

The investigators left.

According to Sari Horowitz and Scott Higham of the *Washington Post*, as soon as Kittay sat down in the passenger seat of Barrett's unmarked police cruiser, she lit into him. "Man up!" she shouted. When he arrived back at police headquarters, Barrett tracked down Chief Ramsey and cautioned him: "We have to replace these prosecutors."

According to unnamed souces inside the US Attorney's Office, around this time a message was delivered to the director of the Executive Office for US Attorneys, Ken Wainstein. The message stated that assistant US attorneys were pointing all roads to Condit and needed to be brought under control.

The source believes the message came from Jack Barrett. Like Barrett, Wainstein had previously been at the FBI.

According to this source, Wainstein responded by directing Kittay and Pasichow to stand down. The two AUSAs made multiple attempts to plead their case with Wainstein, including memos asking him, "What should we do?"

Kittay's and Pasichow's pleas were met with "deafening silence."

Detective Durant prepared his OASIS report (2DDU01-185/55). In his report, Durant wrote that in his third interview Gary told investigators he had ended his relationship with Chandra in March.

That simply wasn't true.

And its later leak to the press threw more fuel on the fire.

Moreover, the actual OASIS report was dated July 29, twenty-three days after the interview.

CREDIT

Outside the Starbucks on Connecticut Avenue, the square windows of newspaper stands carried the day's lead story in the *Washington Post*: CONDIT CONFIRMS AFFAIR TO POLICE, SOURCES SAY.

Terrance Gainer looked out at the familiar gaggle of reporters following the Levy investigation. He had called the press conference to discuss the prior day's interview between his detectives, the US Attorney's Office, and Gary.

GAINER: . . . I had been calling on behalf of the Metropolitan Police Department for the congressman to clarify his relationship with Chandra Levy . . . Late last night, from about 8:30 until 10:00,
the congressman met with our investigative team . . . And the congressman answered every question that we put to him. And we were comfortable with his answers . . .

REPORTER: Do you know the nature of the relationship now?

GAINER: We're comfortable with it. We understand the nature of the relationship and he answered
all our questions.

REPORTER: What was the relationship?

GAINER: I wouldn't go into specifics . . . It's unfair to him, unfair to the investigation process, and
probably unfair to the Levy family.

REPORTER: Did he say whether the relationship matched what the relatives described it as?

Reporters continued to press Gainer to reveal what, specifically, Gary had said about the nature of his relationship with Chandra. Gainer pushed back, insisting that he wasn't going to divulge those details. Reporters also pressed Gainer on whether Gary had obstructed the investigation and if the rumors that investigators were pursuing a grand jury charge against Gary were true. Gainer insisted that Gary had been cooperative, and that he hadn't obstructed the investigation in any way, and therefore, there was no need for a grand jury.

REPORTER: Chief Gainer, can you comment on the *Newsweek* magazine report that is about to come
where they say that Congressman Gary Condit apparently told DC police in this interview that he
did have an affair with Chandra Levy?

GAINER: I would have no comment on the substantive issues that we have discussed with him
or any other witness. Again, you all know very well that we're not going to get information from
people if I stand in front of police headquarters and blab who said what . . .

Gainer's assistant stepped in front of the microphone. Apparently, a reporter from the *Washington Post* was monopolizing the press conference.

ASSISTANT: Ladies and gentlemen, it's getting hot out here. The chief agreed to come out here, and I know this is not the *Washington Post* press conference. And we're going to take a few more questions.

REPORTER: Did his answers contradict any of the Levys'—the Levys' or the aunt's characterization?

GAINER: Allan—that would require me to discuss substantive issues and I won't. Again, it is really important to understand, yesterday, midday, we wanted more information. We wanted clarity. By yesterday evening, at shortly after 10:00, we had the information we wanted.

There was a strong possibility that "Allan" was Allan Lengel of the *Washington Post*.

—

Meanwhile, the Blue Dogs attempted a press conference on Capitol Hill to discuss California's continuing energy crisis. Gary didn't attend.

The *Fresno Bee* described the scene at the press conference: "The House television press gallery was packed, but after a perfunctory few questions about energy, the reporters zeroed in on their real target: What did members think of their coalition founder, Gary Condit?"

"What about the rumors she was pregnant?" a reporter asked.

"I want to stop this line of questions," Congressman Allen Boyd replied. "We're here to talk about the energy crisis."

"Will Condit talk?" a reporter demanded.

Boyd and the other Blue Dogs gave up and left the room.

Chandra had been missing for approximately seventy days.

UNRELIABLE SOURCES

FEMINISM

REBECCA COOPER WAS AT HOME with her husband on Friday night, July 6, when one of her bosses from ABC News called around 11:00 p.m.

He read to her an advance copy of the July 7 edition of the *New York Post*. Both Rebecca and her bosses had expected a story about her coffee with Gary at Tryst around the time Chandra disappeared.

But *Post* reporter Niles Latham had penned a far more sensational story alleging Rebecca had been Gary's mistress for several years. The newspaper was careful not to name Rebecca outright, but instead described her as a well-liked, attractive, and hardworking off-air reporter at ABC News.

ABC immediately placed Rebecca on leave and instructed her to not "under any condition, talk with the press."

ABC's management offered to hide Rebecca from reporters by relocating her and her family to a hotel. Camera crews had descended on her neighborhood, hoping to get footage of the latest "mistress." But Rebecca and her husband had recently moved into a different house, and she was determined not to be forced into hiding by the false story.

She turned down ABC's relocation offer. But she felt she had to accept ABC's decision for her to stay silent and away from work until the attention from the story died down.

After a week, Rebecca was able to return to work but only with the agreement that she stay inside the bureau and avoid answering her phone. Her bosses reasoned that "it would be impossible to let her go out to cover stories when she would be *the* story." Rebecca wanted to put out a statement repudiating the *Post* article, but management at ABC News felt that would only add to the press coverage.

The *New York Daily News*, the *Post*'s biggest competitor, threatened to report that Rebecca had dated *multiple* members of Congress. When the Washington publicist for ABC told Rebecca she was trying to fend off the story, Rebecca expressed both gratitude and outrage. She was grateful other colleagues at ABC News had proven largely supportive and sympathetic to her situation. But she was outraged that others in Washington were so eager to believe that a female reporter slept with her trusted source.

The *Daily News* responded by calling ABC's Washington publicist and demanding to know, "If Rebecca didn't date Gary Condit, then who did she date? We have talked to people around town, and here are some of the members of Congress she may have dated." They rattled off a long list, fresh from the DC rumor mill, among them John Boehner and Bill Richardson. Rebecca was horrified to hear the speculation. None of it was true. But she was quickly realizing that the truth was not going to matter.

Within twenty-four hours, Rebecca's private life was fodder for the media. The *National Enquirer* put out a front page story screaming **CONDIT'S HAREM**, with pictures of a half dozen different women on the cover, including Rebecca.

The *Daily News* defended its questioning of Rebecca's relationship with Gary, pointing to a fashion magazine story profiling Rebecca in the mid-1990s that revealed she dated a member of Congress while working as a Senate staff member handling international trade policy. The story did not mention the name of the congressman. *They assume it was Gary!* Rebecca realized. *Now that they're unsure, they're just throwing names out.*

Rebecca had, in fact, once dated a member of Congress when she worked in the Senate. But he was unmarried and so was she, and he certainly wasn't any of the men on the list being passed around by the *Daily News*.

The suggested affair with Bill Richardson, her former boss in the Clinton administration, deeply upset Rebecca. "That's so sexist," she responded when first hearing the allegation was swirling around the news world. "Jamie Rubin is young and one of Secretary Albright's closest advisors, but no one suggests he is sleeping with his boss. Bob Woodward gets credit for cultivating sources, for taking members out for coffee and staying in touch with them. I worked hard to cultivate a relationship with Condit. He was a great source, and someone other reporters missed. He generated his power behind the scenes. But because I'm a woman, I'm instantly a suspect for having slept with him!"

"Hello, this is ABC," a producer at ABC's assignment desk said as she picked up the phone.

"Hi, I'm a very close personal friend of Rebecca Cooper, and I'm having difficulty reaching her. Can you get me in touch with her?" Fox News's Rita Cosby explained.

Rebecca and Cosby weren't friends. While Rebecca was posted on Capitol Hill, Cosby was developing a reputation covering the White House as someone not to be trusted. Fellow reporters had relayed to Rebecca that Cosby was believed to embellish stories when calling in to her bosses.

When Cosby tried to reach Rebecca by conventional methods, she received a stern "no" from ABC's publicist.

The well-intentioned assignment desk producer, however, believed Cosby's claim and put her directly through to Rebecca's internal line.

"Hello?" Rebecca said.

"Rebecca, this is Rita Cosby."

Rebecca hung up.

Later that day, Cosby went on air and told her national audience that she had spoken to Rebecca. Cosby didn't mention that her conversation consisted solely of speaking to ABC's publicist and of Rebecca hanging up on her.

Robin Sproul, ABC's bureau chief and Rebecca's boss, called Kim Hume, bureau chief at Fox News and Rita Cosby's boss.

"That's not how it works," Sproul insisted, expressing her anger with Cosby's underhanded reporting.

"It's just a problem right now because Rita is doing such a great job on this story, and everyone is jealous of her," Hume answered.

—

Two cold case detectives met Rebecca and a lawyer from ABC News in a private conference room at the ABC Washington bureau.

The detectives made it clear they didn't think Gary had anything to do with Chandra's disappearance.

Although she felt Gary had completely mishandled the investigation, Rebecca didn't believe for a minute he was in any way involved in Chandra's disappearance. When Rebecca answered that she shared their view, the lead interviewer let out a frustrated sigh.

"We are busy here," one of the detectives acknowledged to Cooper—motioning with his hand to the left side of the table, "while the real killer is over here." The detective swept his hand to the far right side of the table.

But they had been sent to question Cooper.

We hate to ask you this, but, it's been said you had a sexual relationship with Congressman Condit?" the first detective asked, as politely as he could.

Rebecca let out a frustrated laugh that caught the investigators off guard. "Well, no, I didn't. Too bad my mother-in-law needs to hear about it every day on Larry King."

"Did you give him a watch?"

"No. Of course not."

She explained to them her relationship with Gary was purely professional. Not once had Condit ever made an inappropriate remark that Rebecca could recall.

"We're tired of the reporting, Ms. Cooper," the detective continued. "Rita Cosby at Fox News just keeps making stuff up. She just keeps throwing shit against the wall, hoping it sticks. I don't think she knows or cares about the fact that what she does creates problems for us."

They also shared problems they encountered trying to keep others from seeking out the spotlight.

"That stewardess—the one all over the news. We offered to get her off the plane in a way that she wouldn't get any publicity . . . the press was waiting inside the terminal. She refused. She insisted on getting taken off where she was in full view of the cameras," the second detective added.

"There's nothing anyone can do about that," Rebecca concurred. But she pressed further, wanting the answer to something that had been bothering her throughout the investigation. "Why aren't you all investigating the man who attacked other women in Rock Creek Park?"

As a reporter, Rebecca knew through media reports that the last thing Chandra had done on her computer before disappearing was to search online for jogging paths in Rock Creek Park. Rebecca also knew about the media reports of other women joggers in the park having been attacked around the same time Chandra disappeared.

"Chief Ramsey said we can't pursue him, because it doesn't fit the MO."

"Why not?" Cooper asked in surprise.

"Chief says the women he attacked are blondes, and Chandra's a brunette."

"You're kidding," Rebecca responded in disbelief. She knew how thoroughly they were examining every possible tie to Condit and couldn't believe this lead would be dismissed entirely—and on this basis.

"Look," the more senior detective said with a sigh. "Right now, every press conference Chief Ramsey and Chief Gainer have about this case is covered live by CNN and every other station. If we go from investigating a member of Congress for murder to some random guy attacking women in Rock Creek Park, all of you go away."

He leaned back in his chair, clearly frustrated.

Rebecca knew he was right. While she didn't believe anyone involved in the investigation would consciously avoid finding the truth about what happened to Chandra, too many people in Washington were now invested in keeping the focus on Gary.

—

Because *The New York Post*'s initial story about the "ABC reporter" hadn't mentioned Rebecca by name, a number of journalists and bloggers made wild guesses as to who the unnamed reporter might be.

Most Washington insiders knew, right away, that Niles Latham was suggesting Rebecca. But Jonah Goldberg, a conservative columnist, speculated that the unnamed reporter was ABC's assistant political director, Elizabeth Wilner. Rebecca walked to Wilner's office, intending to apologize for getting her caught up in the scandal.

"You've ruined the reputation of all the women at ABC News," Wilner lashed out as soon as Rebecca entered.

She thinks I slept with him!

Rebecca went back to her office.

She was exhausted.

Rebecca later reflected, "I had been convinced eventually the truth would win out and had kept my cool throughout the investigation. Besides, I knew the real victims weren't the people like me innocently caught in the chaotic coverage."

But the cutting comment from a female colleague struck a raw nerve.

This time, Rebecca closed her office door, sat behind the empty desk, and cried.

TRESPASS

Cadee Condit caught a man and a woman running across the front lawn of the Condit home. She called the Ceres police, and minutes later a police cruiser arrived on Acorn Lane.

The police officer joined the dozens of reporters sitting in lawn chairs or standing in small groups, chitchatting. Two reporters sitting on the curb opposite the Condit home matched the description of the trespassers given to him by the dispatcher.

He approached the reporters—Paul Schlindwein and Susan Richter of CNN.

"Did you see anyone enter the property?" the officer asked.

"A man and woman from a radio station. They knocked on the front door," Richter answered.

"We've got footage of it," Schlindwein offered.

Dispatch radioed to inform the officer that the two trespassers were attempting to climb over the backyard fence.

—

The officer found Mark Williams and Marna Davis, talk show hosts for KFBK radio, standing in an empty dirt lot behind the Condit home.

"Were you on the Condit property?" the officer asked.

"We knocked on the front door," Williams answered, turning his microphone toward the officer to make sure he got an audio recording of the exchange.

"You are not welcome on the Condit property," the officer warned. "If you return, you'll be arrested for trespass."

Williams and Davis turned off their recorders, letting the microphones fall to their sides.

"That was a great sound bite!" Davis said to Williams.

"Is there anyone else we should harass?" Williams asked the officer.

"You're not harassing me," the officer coldly replied. "You should stay off the Condit property."

"We really needed the sound of the knock at the door for the radio," Davis explained.

—

Mike Lynch stood inside Gary's Modesto district office staring through the window at a sea of media holding cameras and protestors holding signs with anti-Gary messages.

"Bob Franken from CNN is on the line for you," an aide interrupted.

Lynch walked to the phone on the edge of his desk.

Franken told Lynch that CNN had been approached by people peddling a story about a sexual affair between Gary and a woman named Jennifer Thomas.

"Who is selling the story?" Lynch demanded.

Franken couldn't say.

"I don't know anyone named Jennifer Thomas," Lynch said.

A short while later, a journalist at *Newsweek* called Lynch and gave him a similar warning.

Lynch stared through the window at the mass of reporters and paparazzi gathered in front of Gary's office. *Does the press even care about the truth anymore?*

—

At the front of the office, two women on Gary's staff did their best to politely respond to demands from reporters cramming the foyer.

"Did you have to sleep with the congressman to get this job?" a reporter asked of the staffers.

"I don't appreciate that question," one of them responded. "It's not called for."

"She's not his type. She's too fat," a second reporter cackled.

MR. MODESTO

"Gary's a predator like that . . . that's why he fired me," Vince Flammini insisted. Flammini had become a mini-celebrity, as Gary's former "bodyguard" acting as a source for salacious stories about Gary's alleged infidelities and making regular appearances on cable news programs.

"What do you mean?" a reporter for the *National Enquirer* sitting opposite him responded. "Did he hurt someone?"

"Gary, he wouldn't hurt a fly," Flammini answered. "I was his bodyguard and I drove him places. But I'm not going to talk."

"You're going to make big money. What do you mean when you say he's a predator?"

"I had a girlfriend. Gorgeous piece of ass. He just needed to have his hands on her. He couldn't help himself. I never saw nothing or anything. But we went to dinner, and he had her sit right between us, next to him. He arranged that. And then he used my phone to call her after. I had naked pictures of her."

"He slept with her?"

"That's what he wanted. I've ate with him. He eats like a bird. I've stayed in hotel rooms with him. He wouldn't hurt any girl. He just fired me because of that girl, and then we weren't friends. He rode off on his motorcycle and that was it."

"Anything else you want to tell me?"

"Don't print this until I say so. I'm not sure," Flammini answered.

―

An FBI agent rolled his shirtsleeves up to the bottom of his elbows. He was more than an hour into interviewing Vince Flammini.

"What kind of demeanor does the congressman have? Is he weird? Is he mean? Did he ever hit a woman?" the agent asked Flammini.

"Not in a million years. Gary would protect anyone, especially a woman. He may have had sex with women, but he would never hurt anyone," Flammini responded.

A large stack of paper sat near the agent's left arm. He had told Flammini the papers contained the names of women the federal government believed Gary had been sexually involved with at one time or another. Some media reports alleged Gary had affairs with at least twenty-seven different women during his time in elected office.

"What about Jennifer, or Jenny, Thomas—she was a college student at Stanislaus State University. Did Gary have an affair with her?" the agent continued.

"Never heard of her," Flammini answered.

"We have information that the congressman may have had a relationship with her. She's African American."

"That one's bullshit. I've never seen her. I've never heard of her," Flammini replied, bringing his tattooed arms across his chest.

"You never saw him with a black girl?" a second FBI agent followed.

"No. He'd tell me if there was."

"Do you know Otis Thomas?"

"I don't know him."

"You never picked up a black girl from Gary's house or a political function and drove her home?"

"There was no relationship with a black girl. Who told you that?" Flammini asked.

"Phil . . ." an agent started.

As the interview wore on it became apparent the FBI was taking its information from a variety of sources, including a man named Phil who lived and worked on a piece of land adjacent to a park on the Tuolumne River, just outside Modesto.

Phil's job was to turn mud inside large pits on the land, from which worms were harvested and sold as fresh bait to fishing shops in the Bay Area. Phil and Flammini went way back. If Gary and Flammini were going on a motorcycle ride that took them in the vicinity of the worm farm, they usually stopped to chat with Phil. He didn't know anything about Gary other than the bits and pieces picked up in casual conversations. But, apparently, Phil had become a source of information about Gary for the press and for law enforcement.

"The worm guy? Phil doesn't have it right," Flammini explained. "But he made a lot of cash for that one. *Star* and those other magazines, they've been after me. They've offered me a lot of money for what I know."

"Did you ever see Gary with young girls—sixteen or seventeen years old?" the FBI agents inquired.

"Gary's not stupid."

—

Flammini let his album of photos with Gary in them rest a fair distance from where he sat across from Petula Dvorak of the *Washington Post*.

"I arm-wrestled the guy in the movie *Over the Top*. The big guy who was in the movie with Stallone. I beat him," Flammini boasted.

"That's interesting," Dvorak answered.

"Gary and I worked out together. I met him at the gym I owned."

"Do you know anything about a former college student named Jennifer Thomas?" Dvorak asked.

"Thomas? Never happened—the black chick, it never happened. I told the FBI that. It sounds like a bullshit story."

"You never picked up a black girl and took her to his house?" Dvorak pressed.

"No. Whenever we got out of Cal State, we got out so fast. He'd never have a girl over at his house—impossible. I'd sign a paper to that effect," Flammini insisted.

"Jennifer Thomas, she told me that you gave her a ride," Petula lied.

"She's full of shit."

"What about teenage girls—was Gary ever involved with teenage girls?" Dvorak pressed.

"I told this to the FBI—Gary isn't stupid. I know a lot of stuff about Gary, but I'm not going to tell anyone."

Petula wasn't getting from Flammini what she had hoped for. He'd gone on and on about wild motorcycle rallies with Gary and having driven Gary to and from meetings with unnamed paramours. But Flammini wouldn't, or couldn't, confirm the story about an affair between Gary and the teenage daughter of an African American preacher.

This put Dvorak and the *Washington Post* in a pickle. Even Flammini wouldn't confirm the affair, and worse, he had vehemently denied the affair would even be possible, along with the suggestion that Gary would have her over to his house. But if the *Post* didn't proceed with the story it risked losing the biggest bombshell of the scandal.

"You said you have photos with Gary and nude women?"

"I said I have photos with half-naked women. Women in bikinis, at a motorcycle rally," Flammini clarified.

"Can I see them?" she asked.

"*Star* would pay top dollar for those."

"The *Post* doesn't pay for information," Dvorak conceded.

"Gary left me hanging here. I've got little. If you don't pay me money so I can survive, I'm not going to talk."

"I'm bored in Modesto," she offered, softening so as not to lose her source. "Do you want to go out and do something?"

"There's an Indian casino near here. We could go there?"

"Sure."

Flammini quickly recalculated. "Maybe we shouldn't. I don't have money for that."

"We can just go back to my hotel for drinks?" Dvorak replied.

—

On July 11, Dorene D'Adamo, legal counsel on Gary's congressional staff, interviewed Flammini. D'Adamo had informed Flammini and his attorney that the need for the discussion was prompted by a story the *Washington Post* was going to publish alleging an affair between Gary and a student at California State University, Stanislaus.

At times he expressed that he cared for Gary, and at times he expressed hatred for Gary. He claimed he was in hiding from Larry King, Geraldo Rivera, and their respective producers, who were chasing him relentlessly and threatening him.

In the process of bristling and bragging about the amount of dirt on Gary he claimed to possess, Flammini confirmed he had never actually seen Gary kiss a woman other than Carolyn or Cadee. He also confirmed he believed Gary had many girlfriends, and that he had driven Gary on two occasions to meet with an alleged paramour.

Flammini just couldn't prove anything.

In its most pertinent part, the interview went as follows:

FLAMMINI: [The FBI] asked about a woman at Cal State, and I said "that one's bullshit . . . I've never seen her." They asked me about a black woman, and I said that I had never heard of her. They asked me if I knew of her dad, and I said that I don't know him. The *Washington Post* asked me if I had ever picked up a black girl, and I told them "no." . . .

REPRESENTATIVE: Did you ever go to candidates' night or a political rally or for a speech not for graduation?

FLAMMINI: Yes, but I was with him every second. The *Washington Post* told me that she, the girl, had said that I gave her a ride. I told them that she was "full of shit."

REPRESENTATIVE: And "Charanda" is a different girl, and it's not Chandra?

FLAMMINI: Yes. She was doing Gary for many years. The person who is Charanda wouldn't give him up. I didn't tell the FBI about her, but the idiot in the park is the one who told the FBI. The *Star* gave him a few thousand bucks for that. Gary told me that he had a girlfriend in Washington. Said that she was black. He told me that she had breasts like melons, that she had a small waist, that she was always in the apartment building and would go down to the elevator, just like the papers reported. I told him, "Gary, you're gonna get caught, just like Clinton. Clinton's an idiot." He told me that she was black, and that her boyfriend was a police officer. She fit the description of Chandra Levy—he said that she was 107–110 pounds, that she was black, that she was crazy and totally in love with him, that she had long, black curly hair, that she had a light complexion.

REPRESENTATIVE: But Chandra isn't black. Why did you think that this was the same woman?

FLAMMINI: The rest of the description fit her.

REPRESENTATIVE: Did you tell the FBI this?

FLAMMINI: I didn't tell anyone. If it all goes out, Gary will go "bye, bye." The FBI already knows about a sixteen- or seventeen-year-old girl. The *Washington Post* asked about sixteen- to seventeen-year-old girls. But, this would never happen. Gary isn't that stupid. I know other stuff that I won't say to anyone.

REPRESENTATIVE: Would there be evidence of this "stuff"?

FLAMMINI: Yes. This would hang him. He broke my heart. He treated me like a brother, but still, I wouldn't say anything about this other stuff because he's been kicked enough. He wouldn't hang around with me while in Sturgis. Gary gave Burl money left and right, but wouldn't give me any, except finally he gave me a couple of hundred bucks, but then it was gone on food in a couple of days . . . We would go on Gary's schedule, and go to all of Burl's places—Yellowstone, Sturgis, Jackson Hole. I would have gone to Illinois to see my family if I had a choice. The way I figure it, he owes me ten years or nine years of vacation. Then, when we would drive and I'd say something like, "Isn't it pretty here?" Gary and Burl would just turn up the music. Then, Gary took a plane home, and I was stuck with Burl, who drinks beer and drives 100 miles per hour.

The written record of the interview between Gary's representative and Flammini was put in a file, where it sat untouched for ten years.

—

The *National Enquirer*'s coverage of the Levy scandal intensified.

HE'S A RUTHLESS, SEX CRAZED JEKYLL AND HYDE WHO WOOS THEM AND THEN USES TERROR TAC-TICS TO ENFORCE THEIR SILENCE! was the latest headline about Gary to grace the cover of the *Enquirer*. The issue carried the following quote attributed to Flammini, described as Gary's bodyguard: "Gary is a hunter and a predator!"

Inside, the story was peppered with more quotes from Flammini, including the following: "He was always curious about sex drugs and Viagra. He asked me about them all the time. It's possible he gave Chandra a potent sex drug that she never snapped out of, that's what I told the FBI. Gary's behavior is sociopathic."

The *National Enquirer*'s latest issue alleged Gary had sexually abused two fifteen-year-old girls: "One girl said she was raped. We've heard from sources close to the Levys that investigators think Chandra may have been hurt during rough kinky sex with Condit."

―

Meanwhile, on July 11 in Washington, DC, teams from the FBI, US Attorney's Office, and Metro Police met with Anne Marie Smith and her attorney, Jim Robinson.

According to court records, Smith repeated her claim that Gary was into bondage sex and she now alleged that Gary wanted to involve her in sex with other men, that she suspected he may have been seeing other women, and that she became afraid of him and last visited his condo in March 2001.

Robinson told reporters that his client had received "the standard gold bracelet" from Gary, in addition to a "leather motorcycle bracelet."

Federal investigators scoured Gary's campaign expenditures to see if he had misappropriated campaign funds to buy gifts for alleged paramours.

"He once told me he was going to attend an upcoming Hells Angels Bash . . . he told me he had to keep it secret from his brother because it was a birthday party for a cop killer," Smith told the *New York Daily News*.

The *Daily News* quoted sources "close to the Levy family investigation" to connect the dots: "Those are bad guys to be involved with . . . The big news might be what got her killed. Maybe she found out something . . . Investigators are also considering the possibility that Levy, 24, could have been pregnant."

Federal investigators looked into possible connections between Gary and the Hells Angels.

DEMANDS

Susan Levy stood on her driveway surrounded by law-enforcement officials.

The street had been cordoned off as a result of the massive media presence in front of the Levys' ranch home. Susan suddenly looked polished. She had a new haircut, clothes, and makeup.

"Mr. Condit has not been truthful to me up to this point," she announced to the gaggle in the street. "I want him to take a polygraph exam."

A Gallup poll found 83 percent of Americans believed Gary should submit to the polygraph demanded by Susan Levy. A local news reporter strapped himself to a polygraph machine to prove Gary wouldn't be able to "beat the box."

Metro Police chief Charles Ramsey acted swiftly to catch the current, telling reporters Gary should submit to the polygraph because the Levys had "the right to know the truth."

The Levys soon issued two additional demands. They wanted law enforcement to search Gary's condo and to take a sample of his DNA.

Major news outlets broke the story that federal investigators would issue a subpoena compelling Gary to do these things.

Chief Ramsey acted quickly again, calling a press conference where he told reporters the Metro Police would request an "immediate" search of Gary's condo, a sample of his DNA, and that he submit to a polygraph examination.

"Has Abbe Lowell agreed?" a reporter asked him.

"His response was he'll get back to us," Ramsey answered.

"Has the congressman refused any prior request to search his apartment?"

"Let's just say it's not the first time it's come up," Ramsey replied.

Gary sat in one of the small cells at the entrance to the House gym, holding the phone to his ear while Lowell walked him through his options. Lowell felt Gary's best strategy was to voluntarily allow investigators to search his condo and to provide them with a sample of his DNA.

"You're not going to submit to their polygraph. They know that. They know the polygraph most often yields inconclusive results, and that in your case, that'd result in a public hanging. But if you're not going to do that, we need to satisfy their other requests. You have nothing to hide. Give them concrete evidence that will exonerate you."

"We shouldn't fold every time we feel pressure," Gary answered.

"They'll go for a court order."

"That's bullshit."

"They'll get it. They've promised to keep the search quiet. They'll do it late at night. But we need to work under the assumption that everything will be leaked."

"If I've got no choice then why are we even having this conversation?"

CABLE NEWS

Billy Martin appeared on CNN's *Larry King Live.*

KING: [I]f you were his lawyer, would you tell him to take this lie detector test? . . .

MARTIN: I may have wanted to polygraph Congressman Condit just to know the answers. Would I take him in? There's a good chance I might. If he failed, I would never disclose it. But if he passed, I would have it on the front page of every newspaper that would accept it.

The show went to commercial. When it came back, Larry King had gathered his near nightly panel of former prosecutors and defense attorneys to discuss the latest developments in the case.

BARBARA OLSON, FORMER FEDERAL PROSECUTOR: There are two issues. Morally, you know, this man, what he did to their daughter—this is a girl who thought she was going to marry him and have his baby. And whether he's involved in her disappearance or not, he is involved in her life . . .

MARK GERAGOS, CRIMINAL DEFENSE ATTORNEY: What Billy has done has been magnificent for his clients. He's kept this story front and center.

. . .

LAURA INGRAHAM, REPORTER: If I didn't find him so repulsive right now, I would feel a little sorry for him, because he probably did have nothing to do with this. But he is now backed into this corner.

~

Lisa DePaulo, a writer for *Talk* magazine, stepped into an elevator inside CNN's offices. She was one of the half dozen "Chandra experts" driving the daily prosecution of Gary on cable news, along with the likes of Nancy Grace, Laura Ingraham, and Barbara Olson. It was difficult to tell them apart.

Susan Levy had given DePaulo details about other men Chandra had dated. DePaulo spent time in Modesto investigating those leads. Her much anticipated *Talk* exposé would soon hit newsstands: **SECRETS & LIES**—"In all the frenzied coverage of Chandra Levy, little has emerged about the vulnerable nature of the intern herself. Independent, discrete, and romantic with a taste for older men, she seemed like a perfect girlfriend for a married congressman—one with plenty of secrets of his own."

"Chandra would have been very happy if she had become pregnant by Condit—but it would have been a disaster for Gary," DePaulo crowed on television, in advance of her big break.

Jeff Greenfield, a senior analyst at CNN, entered the elevator. He turned to DePaulo. "So, if a serial killer did this, will you apologize to Gary Condit?"

"If Condit did this, will you apologize to all the serial killers?" DePaulo replied, laughing. Greenfield was not amused.

After DePaulo's article on Chandra's private life was published, the Levys appeared on *Larry King Live*.

KING: Lisa DePaulo's *Talk* magazine story came out last week. Were you surprised?

S. LEVY: No, we knew her story was going to come out.

KING: Were you surprised at what it contained, Bob?

B. LEVY: Not really. I mean, she is a good reporter and took a lot of history. I think some of the facts weren't completely accurate.

KING: Like?

B. LEVY: Like saying that Chandra was going out with married men. Well, the policeman that she dated for a long time was unmarried. And other people were divorced. So as far as we knew, she didn't go out with married men.

KING: Were you surprised at that, that she wrote those things about Chandra?

S. LEVY: Oh, yes, but I'm not surprised how things get twisted with the media . . .

KING: So you think Lisa had it wrong? The only married man she dated to your knowledge is the congressman?

S. LEVY: To our knowledge. Well, as far as the police officer, whom we knew, he was not married. And another one was divorced, but you know, things get twisted sometimes.

KING: Of course, it certainly questions her morality as well, right?

B. LEVY: Yes.

. . .

KING: Did it pain you to read it?

B. LEVY: . . . You know, our daughter is so private, to see everything in the news magazines and TV, which are good honest reporting, and some of the other magazines, the exposé magazines, I hope she's really embarrassed by it—we hope she's alive.

S. LEVY: She's a very private person.

B. LEVY: But she would never like to see anything like that. It's just not her at all.

. . .

KING: But did you also say to her, "Don't be a Monica Lewinsky?"

S. LEVY: I apologized to Ms. Lewinsky . . .

FATHERLY ADVICE

"Cadee," California governor Gray Davis said warmly as she entered his office in Sacramento. "We'll get through this. Everyone here is behind Gary," he assured her.

"That means a lot to our family. A lot of politicians have taken advantage of the situation and are trashing my dad."

"Tell your dad to hang in there."

―⁊―

The next day, Cadee met Jennifer Baker in a park outside the state capitol building.

"Mrs. Levy wants me to move into her house. She offered to pay my bills—to take care of me if I help her bring your father down. 'Help finish him.' I don't want any part of it," Baker explained. "I don't want any part of any of this."

―⁊―

In Ceres, Adrian Condit picked up his kitchen phone.

Memorial Hospital's CEO had offered Adrian time off from his duties as chaplain. Reporters had showed no qualms about trying to corner Adrian inside the hospital. Adrian insisted on continuing to work, telling the hospital CEO he had no interest in "letting the Devil win this."

"Carolyn says they're going to search your apartment?" Adrian asked Gary.

"I'm gonna give them my DNA too."

"Don't give them something they can hurt you with. They've done enough," Adrian pleaded.

"They'll find a way to make me do it."

Adrian clenched his hands into hard fists. "I'm asking you, son, don't you give them your DNA. They have no right to do this to a man."

"There's no use getting angry," Gary replied.

"It's not a sin to get angry. You've never backed down in nothing. Don't do it now."

"There's nothing I can say that will stop this."

"We're humped up in a corner. We're taking the attorney's advice. But this isn't about the law," Adrian replied.

"I know how you feel but this is baiting me. They want me to go public. Not to defend myself but to feed this. We won't do that."

"I think it's someone high up going after you."

"Nothing like that's going on."

"They made her disappear."

"Well, if they find me floating in the Potomac or with a bullet in my head, you know I didn't do it."

CORRUPTED

The FBI received Chandra's computer files back from its specialized lab. This information provided the first clues about what she may have been doing on the day she disappeared.

On May 1, someone logged onto Chandra's computer around 10:30 a.m. The user searched a number of websites, including Southwest Airlines and Amtrak. The user looked up train fares from Washington, DC, to Stockton, California.

The user also searched for information about Gary, Carolyn, Chad, and Cadee Condit, and viewed the web pages for Baskin Robbins, the *Los Angeles Times*, the *Modesto Bee*, the House Agricultural Committee, the *Drudge Report, USA Today*, and *National Geographic*.

At 10:45 a.m., an e-mail was sent from the computer to Chandra's mother listing airfares.

At 11:30 a.m., the user clicked on a link to the *Washington Post*'s website and, once inside, checked the weather forecast. It was going to be a nice day.

The user clicked on the *Post*'s entertainment guide for Rock Creek Park. The guide listed the address for the Pierce-Klingle Mansion, which serves as a headquarters for the park's superintendent and is perched on a hill where a number of popular jogging trails come together, including the Western Ridge Trail.

The user clicked on a map that provided an overview of the park's trails, including popular jogging trails near the Pierce Mill.

The last time someone logged off of Chandra's computer was May 1 at 12:24 p.m.

Police officers and cadets searched the jogging trails and wooded areas in and around the mansion. They didn't turn up any new clues.

Chandra's computer, it seemed, was another dead end. According to reporters for the *Washington Post*, investigators had misinterpreted Chandra's Internet searches. The main URL for the website Chandra pulled up to search Rock Creek Park listed the address for the Klingle Mansion. "The investigators focused on that URL and the mansion, but they failed to focus on the searches Chandra conducted minutes later, when she went deeper into the site and clicked on links for a map of the park and its hiking trails."

CHAPTER 15

OPEN SEASON

DNA

GARY OPENED HIS MOUTH AND looked up at the ceiling while a man wearing a lab coat and rubber gloves pushed a swab under Gary's tongue. When he finished, the technician inserted the swab into a pre-labeled plastic tube.

"Again, please," the technician asked.

Gary opened his mouth. When the technician finished, he put this second swab into a second pre-labeled plastic tube.

Lowell informed Barrett that Gary had provided a DNA sample to the same lab that performed DNA analysis for the FBI, and that the lab would deliver Gary's DNA sample directly to the Metro Police.

Barrett told Lowell he would confer with Terrance Gainer.

A short while later, Barrett called Lowell to inform him that the Metro Police would not accept the DNA sample and instead demanded they take their own.

―

Gary stepped out of the car into a dimly lit school parking lot on Wisconsin Avenue. Lowell had chosen a place where he knew it would not be filmed.

Detective Durant stepped out of an unmarked cruiser and motioned for Gary to get into the front passenger seat he had just vacated.

"This is the first time I've done this," Durant remarked as he crawled onto the bench seat in the back of the cruiser.

"This is my second time," Gary replied.

Durant didn't respond.

"Why do you need my DNA?" Gary pressed.

"So that we can rule you out if we find her body. You're not the only person we're asking."

At Durant's request, Gary turned so that he faced the car's rear window, with his knees digging into the back of the front seat.

"Open your mouth," Durant directed.

Gary stuck his head over the back of the seat and obliged.

Durant reached into a brown paper bag, pulled out a single long Q-tip, and jammed it into Gary's right cheek, twice. He then pulled the Q-tip out and put it back into the bag.

"That's it," Durant explained.

The Metro Police now had three samples of Gary's DNA.

WATCH BOX

When the scandal entered the middle of July, reporters began to question whether the city's top cops could fight crime in the nation's most dangerous city when they spent all their time talking publicly about the Levy case.

Investigators warned that the unending leak of information and the frequent press appearances by Ramsey and Gainer may have compromised the investigation. "It's unusual to have daily briefings," one federal official said. "It goes beyond everything that we've been taught."

Gainer went on the defensive. On WTOP radio, he stated: "We want to scale back the use of everybody in dealing with the media. It seems of late, we've spent too much time dealing with rumors . . . and all sorts of malarkey."

As the *Fresno Bee* reported:

More information will now be filtered through the department's public information office, instead of having the chief or his deputy go before the cameras on a daily basis. Gainer, in particular, has been an almost daily presence on radio and television as the national and Washington media pursue the Levy story. He's been quoted in more than half of the stories that have appeared to date.

Dayton handed two bags of food to Gary, who sat in the passenger seat. He had waited inside the car while Dayton went into the Five Guys hamburger joint near the border between DC and Alexandria, Virginia.

Gary consolidated the hamburgers and french fries into a single bag. As Dayton pulled the Ford Explorer onto the road, Gary took out a bag of items he had removed from his office and transferred them into the now empty bag from Five Guys.

By the end of June, dozens of items had been stolen from Gary's office, including personal letters and photos. Even his business cards could be purchased on eBay. His staff had to assume anything thrown in an office trash can underwent a screening process by the press before its ultimate removal from the building.

Gary started cataloguing items and finding secure places to store or toss them. Earlier that evening, he had emptied his desk drawers and placed the items he wanted to keep in one trash bag and the items he intended on throwing out in another. Items in this second group included an empty box that once contained a TAG Heuer watch.

"Pull off here. I want to throw this stuff away," Gary said.

Dayton stopped the car beside an open field. Gary got out, walked to a public trash can nearby, and tossed the Five Guys bag containing the items from his office desk into the bin.

Just as Gary got back inside the car, a red Ford Mustang came to an abrupt stop behind them.

A man hopped out of the Mustang and ran for the trash can Gary had just left.

"I ought to get out and kick his ass," Gary said.

"Let it go," Dayton laughed, having no clue what it was Gary had thrown away.

BROWN BOX

Law enforcement had to shut down Adams Mill Road. Hundreds of people had gathered for the big event. Floodlights were aimed at the fourth floor of the Lynshire building. Satellite dishes on top of news vans dotted the street like staggered mushrooms. Gary's neighbors sat on the front steps of the building, staring angrily at the mob. Millions of people worldwide sat in front of their televisions, watching live coverage.

A reporter asked Gainer about the looming search of Gary's condo, and Gainer replied, "What you're looking for could involve blood, hair, telltale signs of a struggle."

At 11:20 p.m. on July 10, investigators carrying heavy bags of equipment passed the raucous crowd.

A trail of forensic investigators poured into the condo like worker ants. Detective Durant followed. His leather cowboy boots tapped cleanly on the wood floor. Carolyn watched from the living room couch, holding onto Dayton's arm. Two investigators inventoried the front hallway closet, pulling out a Cuban baseball hat.

"Congressman, do you know what that is?" an investigator asked Gary while pointing at a spot on the hat's bill.

"It's blood. I have psoriasis on my thumb."

Gary showed investigators the worn skin at the end of his finger.

An investigator sprayed luminal solution on the walls and fixtures in the front bathroom. Another investigator turned off the lights and ran a black light over the bathroom's surfaces.

"How's it going in there," an investigator in the living room called.

"Couple of places. I'll show you in a minute," the men in the bathroom replied.

"I'm looking for anything—stains."

Investigators moved into the living room and kitchen.

An investigator turned over a potted plant.

"No bugs," he announced.

Men emptied the kitchen cabinets.

They turned the couch over.

"Now," an investigator instructed.

The mob on Adams Mill Road gasped as the fourth floor windows turned black . . . then fluorescent purple.

Investigators found brown spots on mini blinds' blades. They cut out six discolored portions of the mini blinds and placed them in a bag.

"Gar, they promised it would be private," Carolyn whispered.

"It will be over soon," Gary answered.

"Mrs. Condit, I'm sorry you have to go through this," a uniformed Metro Police officer offered.

"It's not your fault," Carolyn replied, unable to keep her voice even.

"You are the only tantalizing summer story," he answered kindheartedly.

When investigators finished ransacking the front of the apartment, they moved to Gary's master bedroom.

They affixed a tank onto the master bathroom toilet and a suction glass over the drain in the adjacent sink. A tube ran between them. One of the men referred to the contraption as a "vacuum box."

Suddenly, a loud sucking noise filled the room. The tube, in turn, filled the tank above the toilet with brown water and large chunks of what Carolyn assumed were human feces. She looked away.

Near Gary's closet, investigators took photos of the bottoms of his shoes.

"We only have one more thing to check, then we'll get out of here," the man in charge explained.

Investigators lined up on both long sides of Gary's bed.

"Tip it this way," the man in charge directed.

The bed turned over.

They're disappointed, Carolyn realized. *They thought they'd find ropes and sex stuff.*

Outside, investigators exited the Lynshire building carrying black trash bags. Reporters rushed to meet them.

Inside, there was a loud knock on the front door.

Dayton opened it.

A middle-aged woman stood in the doorway. "Mr. Dayton, right?" she asked.

"Yes."

"I'm with the Associated Press. I was wondering if Mr. or Mrs. Condit would like to make a statement."

"It's three in the fucking morning!" Dayton yelled and slammed the door shut.

Before sunrise, "sources close to the investigation" leaked to the press that investigators found what appeared to be spots of blood in Gary's apartment.

BAD URGE

Executives inside CBS's Black Rock Studio watched the live news footage of forensic investigators exiting the home of a sitting member of Congress. It was unprecedented.

Still, Dan Rather, the anchor of the *CBS Evening News*, maintained his refusal to cover the story, telling colleagues he didn't feel it was newsworthy. Few of his colleagues agreed with his assessment.

Sixty-three percent of Americans now followed the scandal, which meant more than half of all viewers had a reason to tune out the *CBS Evening News* in favor of its competitors.

Many felt the late-night search of Gary's apartment would be the breaking point for Rather. "Even the *New York Times* had put the story on its front page," they pointed out. Rather, however, made no mention of the search during the next edition of the *CBS Evening News*.

The *Washington Post*'s Howard Kurtz interviewed Jim Murphy, executive producer of the *CBS Evening News*, to get Murphy's take on the stance taken by Rather and his program.

Murphy told Kurtz he thought the enormous amount of publicity given to the Levy story made him "sick to his stomach." When asked why the *CBS Evening News* didn't cover the search of Gary's apartment, Murphy answered: "By the end of the day, I felt like I'd been swamped with information, but didn't see any outstanding headline that I thought forced it into my broadcast."

With no leads in the investigation, Chandra missing, and Gary not talking, the press began feeding on its own.

Michael Isikoff of *Newsweek* said of the *CBS Evening News*'s decision to ignore the Levy story: "They have lousy news judgment."

Newsday columnist Paul Vitello, who had described Gary as the "blow-dried California congressman," added, "CBS deserves a missing person's file of its own if it believes this is not a story."

"I think the only person across America who doesn't think Gary Condit is a suspect in this case is probably Dan Rather," Laura Ingraham opined on CNN's *Larry King Live*.

Lowell was feeling better about where his client stood. It hadn't been easy for Gary to do the things demanded of him by the Levys and, in turn, investigators. But he had done them. Lowell thought the narrative would now start to change. At the very least, the drumbeat in the press that Gary had somehow impeded the investigation would have to die down. And with that, Gary would be able to finally move forward.

His optimism was short lived.

"The *Post* is going to run the story about an alleged affair with the black teenage daughter of the Levys' gardener," Lynch explained.

Lowell called an editor at the *Washington Post*. "Give us time to disprove this," he pleaded. "It's both outrageous and disprovable. The FBI will have the answer on this soon. Give us twenty-four hours."

The editor couldn't do anything to stop or slow the story.

"This is where you cross the line into actual malice," Lowell warned. "This is beneath the dignity of the *Post*!"

MORE SPIN

Dayton stared at the July 12 edition of the *Washington Post* sitting on his desk. The major headline read: **CONDIT IS LINKED TO A NEW AFFAIR.**

A photograph of investigators taking boxes of evidence from Gary's apartment sat squarely above the bolded headline. The caption under the image read: "Rep. Gary Condit is alleged to have had a relationship with a woman who was 18 at the time."

The body of the *Post*'s latest article read, in part:

FBI agents have approached and interviewed a Pentecostal minister who described an affair between his then-18-year-old daughter and Rep. Gary Condit . . .

Four law enforcement sources confirmed that the father, Otis Thomas, has been questioned by the FBI . . .

Thomas'[s] account of his daughter's affair with Condit has been known to the Levy family since mid-April, before Chandra disappeared. By then, the Levy family knew Chandra was having a relationship with the congressman . . .

Thomas, who has parlayed his weekend grounds keeping at his Modesto church into a weekday freelance gardening business, had done work at the Levy home for about four years.

He had a conversation with Chandra's mother, Susan Levy, in April while he was tending roses in the backyard. The conversation continued by the pool, where Susan Levy brought him a cold drink. The two often talked about their children, and Thomas said he asked Susan Levy how Chandra was doing in Washington.

Susan Levy replied that Chandra was doing well and that she had befriended a congressman, Gary Condit.

Thomas said he remembered that his daughter had asked him for advice about seven years ago, when she wanted to break off a bad relationship. He said he had been shocked when she told him the man she was seeing was Condit, whom she said she met at a political rally at California State University, Stanislaus . . .

At the Levy house that day, Thomas said he and Susan Levy talked about Condit, gingerly at first . . .

The two eventually confessed to each other that both their daughters had relationships with Condit. "I told Mrs. Levy that with my daughter, it ended badly, that I think her daughter should end the relationship with him right away," Thomas said.

He says Susan Levy then got on the phone and called Chandra in Washington . . .

"Mrs. Levy talked to Chandra about it, but Chandra told her mother to mind her own business, that she was a grown woman who could deal with it," Thomas said.

Susan Levy confirmed she had the conversation with Thomas and said she had sparred with her daughter about the relationship with Condit over the phone.

In mid-April, when the Levys were in the Washington area to celebrate their daughter's birthday, Chandra Levy told her mother that she had talked to Condit about the affair described by Thomas and that the congressman had "explained it all" to her, Susan Levy said . . .

The article also alleged Jennifer Thomas was in hiding because she feared Gary.

Six people contributed to the *Post*'s explosive story, including Petula Dvorak, Allan Lengel, and a name Dayton hadn't seen before: Sari Horwitz.

〜

In California, Lynch sat in his chair with a copy of the *Modesto Bee* and a cup of coffee.

The headline read: **MINISTER: DAUGHTER HAD AFFAIR WITH CONDIT. MODESTAN ALLEGES TWO-YEAR RELATIONSHIP STARTED IN THE '90S.**

The byline in the *Bee*'s article was shared among Petula Dvorak and Allan Lengel of the *Post* and Jeff Jardine of the *Bee*.

The content of the *Bee*'s article mirrored the article published in the *Post*, except the following details were included in the *Bee*'s publication but not the *Post*'s version of the same story:

1. Jennifer Thomas had visited Gary's home in Ceres during the relationship.
2. Otis Thomas had received an anonymous call instructing him to "shut up and listen" and warning him not to talk to anyone about Gary.

Fear of backlash would have kept Gary's fiercest political opponents from fabricating a story so outrageous, Lynch thought. He grabbed the newspaper and drove to the *Bee*'s headquarters.

When he arrived, Lynch honed in on Mark Vasche. The two men exchanged heated words.

"We didn't have a chance to refute it!" Lynch exclaimed.

"The *Washington Post* reached out to your office in DC," Vasche argued, in reference to the call between Lowell and an editor at the *Post* that occurred less than twenty-four hours before the story hit the front page of both newspapers.

"And Abbe told the *Post*'s people this is not true. Not to publish it until we could respond. Nobody from the *Bee* called. Nobody! How can you publish damaging information without corroborating material?" Lynch responded. "What link is there to Gary Condit? There's no relationship there. What link?"

"What about his relationship with Chandra Levy? What about his relationship with the flight attendant Anne Marie Smith? Will the congressman admit publicly to those affairs?" Vasche responded.

"So because he will not answer those questions publicly, to the press, that justifies the *Bee* not even giving him the benefit of providing facts to refute this story about a teenage girl? Justifies the *Bee* blindly following the *Post*?" Lynch yelled.

Representatives of the *Washington Post* had called and chastised the *Modesto Bee* for adding its writer, Jeff Jardine, to the story's byline, and for including details in the *Bee*'s version of the story that had not been included in the *Post*'s. The *Post*'s lawyers had vetted its story for potential liability for libel. The *Bee*'s changes potentially exposed both newspapers.

In the moment, Lynch didn't see the significance in the discord between the newspapers and the slight differences in their respective publications of the same story with the same reporters in the byline.

The *Post* had not interviewed Jennifer Thomas. Dvorak lied to Flammini to try and get him to confirm what she wanted to write. Even with that, Flammini wasn't willing to corroborate the relationship or the idea that Thomas would have visited Gary's home, to which Flammini said, "I'd sign a paper to that effect."

The *Post* then proceeded to publish the story as though Dvorak's discussion with Flammini had never occurred. Except the *Post* didn't include the allegation that Thomas had visited

Gary's home. That detail still made it into the *Bee*'s publication of the story with the *Post*'s reporters in the byline.

The only sources for the far-fetched story were Otis Thomas and Susan Levy.

Just when Gary had done everything asked of him, the *Post* reported something so salacious that it turned everything back onto him.

━

The next morning, the following note was pinned to the front door of Otis Thomas's house:

> . . . I will tell you I never knew Mrs. Levy's daughter. Never met that congressman who's involved in all of this . . . I never met Mrs. Levy until she showed up at my father's house looking for me. I don't even know how both me and my father got mixed up in this. We don't know anything so stop calling us and showing up at our door.
>
> SIGNED: Jennifer Thomas

The Prayer Mission Church of God in Christ in Modesto was besieged by the camera-wielding horde. But Otis Thomas wasn't there.

The FBI initiated a manhunt to find him and his daughter.

Nobody wanted to talk about the fact that Gary had voluntarily given law enforcement access to his home and his DNA. Instead, Gary faced wall-to-wall coverage and commentary of his alleged affair with an eighteen-year-old college student who happened to be the daughter of an African American minister.

A number of news outlets rehashed a play from the Clinton-Lewinsky scandal, reporting Jennifer Thomas had a mixed-race son who didn't have a father listed on his birth certificate.

BACKING AWAY

The morning after the FBI tracked down Otis Thomas, news organizations tried to step away from the story they'd bit hard on. Word had leaked that it didn't take the FBI long to determine Thomas's story was a total fabrication.

The *Modesto Bee* led the charge in the other direction: Its July 13 edition carried the following front page headline: **CONDIT DENIES AFFAIR WITH TEEN:**

Condit's former driver, Vince Flammini of Ceres, echoed Lynch's assertions, saying Thursday that he had never heard of Jennifer Thomas. "That's a bull —— story," Flammini said. "I worked for him all through that time. I was his driver. I never seen that girl in my life . . . Gary would never do that . . . There's no way I ever took girls to Gary's house. I don't know how it could have gotten by me . . ."

Some readers may have been confused by an article on Page A-1 Thursday that carried the credit lines of reporters Jeff Jardine of The Modesto Bee and Petula Dvorak and Allan Lengel of The Washington Post. The article contained the reporting done independently by the two newspapers. For separate accounts by the two papers, see www.Modbee.com.

The bold disclaimer of collaboration on the story between the two newspapers was unusual.

On the day the original story ran, Vasche told Lynch that the *Post* had called the *Bee* and chastised the local paper for *adding* Jeff Jardine, a reporter for the *Bee*, to the byline in the *Bee*'s publication. Now the newspapers were trying to pretend the opposite; that the *Bee*'s story was done independently of the *Post*.

The idea that there had not been cooperation between the two newspapers in publishing the same story made no sense. The truth was, there was a lack of coordination at the eleventh hour that left both newspapers exposed to potential liability rooted in Petula Dvorak's interview with Vince Flammini's prior to publication of the original story, and they immediately collaborated to clean up the mess before a third party put the pieces together.

The *Bee*'s follow-up story on July 13 not only quoted Flammini, but time-stamped its interview with Flammini for July 12 after the original story had gone to publication that morning.

Together, the claims that the *Bee* had independently reported the original story, and that the *Bee*'s reporters hadn't talked to Flammini until July 12, provided cover for the *Bee* to run the detail about Jennifer Thomas visiting Gary's home in its July 12 story. So long as nobody knew Dvorak had interviewed Flammini prior to July 12, it also provided cover for the *Post*'s decision to make no mention of the fact that Dvorak had interviewed Flammini or what Flammini had said to her when she pressed him on that issue.

Lynch would later compile notes of his discussions with representative of the *Bee* and send them to one file, and the record of the interview between Gary's representative and Flammini revealing what Flammini had told Dvorak prior to July 12 was sent to a separate file.

In the chaos of the moment, nobody on Gary's side put all the malicious pieces together. Lowell was right—the *Post*, it appeared, had crossed into actual malice.

DETECTING LIES

On July 12, Lowell and Gary entered a nondescript house belonging to Lowell's friend.

"Mr. Lowell," Barry Colvert said, extending his hand.

Colvert had recently retired from the FBI after thirty-five years of service. For seventeen of those years, he served as the FBI's lead polygraph examiner and primary interrogator in the DC field office. He was also the FBI's designated examiner for counterterrorism and espionage cases in most regions of the world.

A small silver box sat on a table, and wires ran from the box to a chair.

A blood pressure cuff was put around Gary's right arm and galvanometers were placed on his fingers. Around his waist and chest, Colvert strapped pneumographs. Each of the sensors measured different physiological responses: breathing rate, pulse, blood pressure, perspiration.

Colvert ran Gary through a serious of initital test questions covering basic biographical and medical information before turning to the issue at hand.

"Were you involved in any way in the disappearance of Chandra Levy?"

"No."

"Did you physically harm or have someone physically harm or injure Chandra Levy?"

"No."

"Do you know where Chandra Levy can be found?"

"No."

Colvert helped Gary out of the chair. "You passed. You would pass anybody's lie detector test."

The two men found Abbe Lowell sitting just below the stairwell.

"Not deceptive in any way," Colvert informed him. "It's not even close."

Colvert summarized the results in a short report. The charts and other information law-enforcement officials would need to verify the parameters and results of the examination were compiled and shipped to the FBI and the Metro Police.

—

A large presentation board sat on an easel behind Abbe Lowell. On it, he had listed each of Gary's and Carolyn's interviews with investigators, Gary's production of records, the search of Gary's apartment, Gary providing his DNA, Gary arranging for law enforcement to interview his staff, and Gary taking and passing a polygraph examination administered by the FBI's own expert examiner.

"With regards to the lie detector test, the congressman was not deceptive in any way. Congressman Condit has exhausted the information that he can provide, and the spotlight should be turned elsewhere," Lowell told assembled reporters.

Terrance Gainer caught footage of the press conference. As soon as it ended, he called Lowell.

"What do you mean he's taken a polygraph!" Gainer demanded.

"He passed," Lowell responded.

"He can't do that!" Gainer screamed. "He can't do that!"

"He has submitted to a polygraph examination by former FBI specialist Barry Colvert, the best in the business."

"You went around me!" Gainer screamed. "We had a deal!"

Lowell had no idea what "deal" Gainer was talking about.

"With all due respect, the congressman has done everything you've asked."

"It doesn't mean anything. Nothing!" Gainer continued. "The test doesn't mean anything."

"Run the raw results by one hundred people and see what they can come up with."

"The exam is not valid!"

"How dare you besmirch this man's credentials," Lowell fired back. "You haven't even looked at the results. You have no basis."

"You guys are bordering on obstructing justice!" Gainer screamed.

"When you calm down and recognize we have had three interviews, a DNA test, had Mrs. Condit come to be interviewed, allowed the congressman's place to be searched, and have subjected him to the world's best polygrapher, it is the strangest definition of obstruction of justice."

"Goddamn it!" Gainer screamed, and hung up.

—

Gainer's public reaction to the polygraph examination was fast and furious. In an interview with the *Washington Post* he declared, "I can tell you, in my homicide days, I had people who passed who were the murderers and I had people who failed the polygraph and in fact were not the murderers. It is not infallible."

On Fox News's *The Edge with Paula Zahn*, Gainer said: "I talked to Abbe as recently as yesterday when we talked about this—our own polygraph, and this never came up. Obviously, they had their own game plan, and I emphasize 'game.' Frankly we're getting a little tired of it."

Gainer further characterized Lowell's decision to have Gary take a private examination as "theatrics" and "disingenuous."

"How much of what he has told you so far can you believe based on what happened tonight?" Zahn asked.

Gainer mentioned that Gary had answered law enforcement's questions, made his apartment available, and had given a DNA sample. "You know, it is hard dealing with someone when you can't take people at their word. It's just frustrating, and we probably shouldn't—I shouldn't be making decisions when I'm a little bit taken aback, angry, or frustrated," Gainer admitted.

On another Fox News program, the host asked, "Do you still want Gary Condit to take a polygraph test under your supervision?"

"Yes, I do think there are other questions that we can explore that will help us satisfy ourselves and, I think, maybe even the Levy family," Gainer replied.

On NBC's *Today* show, Chief Ramsey characterized Colvert's polygraph examination of Gary as "meaningless," "not credible," "useless," and "a slippery PR ploy."

Ramsey used his fury over the polygraph examination as a springboard to publicly question Gary's alibi, which had been cleared by Ramsey's own investigators and the FBI. In doing so, he gave credence to rumors that Gary may have hired someone, perhaps one of his brothers—the cop or the con—to "do the job." As Ramsey explained to reporters, "It's not just whether there was any direct involvement, but what about indirect involvement?"

The Levy camp moved quickly to head off any traction Gary might gain from the polygraph examination.

On NBC's *Today*, Billy Martin made the following statement: "I've never seen a situation where an attorney in the middle of those negotiations would go out and get their own polygraph, so the family believes it's highly suspect, and I know the police department does also."

Martin's comment about the polygraph directly contradicted the advice he had given days earlier on CNN's *Larry King Live*, where he acknowledged that if he was Gary's attorney he would administer a private polygraph and if the results were positive he would "have it on the front page of every newspaper that would accept it."

Lowell received a letter from Billy Martin with a list of requests from the Levy family's private detectives. He tried calling to discuss the requests, but Martin wouldn't take his calls or return his messages.

Lowell sent Martin a letter that read in part:

> Since there is so much misinformation reported in the media about what the congressman has said and not said, I fully understand your view that there are questions to be answered. With this in mind, the congressman has authorized me to answer the questions in your letter that could assist you and your investigation. Call me when you want, and I will provide the information as best I can.

Martin never responded to Lowell's letter. Instead, he appeared on NBC's *Meet the Press* and made the following statement: "For some reason, Chandra appears to have been lured, called, or brought out of the apartment expecting to return, and lured, brought out with no identification taken with her, and it's suspect."

Martin told reporters Chandra commonly didn't carry identification when she met her secret lover: "Chandra instructed friends and family that that was the procedure used . . . There appears to have been some concern that if stopped, he did not want her to be identified."

As Fox News's Juan Williams reported: "I've read where one columnist suggests there are only two places a woman doesn't take her purse, and that would be to the gym or on a motorcycle. And we know that Congressman Condit has a motorcycle."

CONTRADICTIONS AND MISSES

ORGANS

ON JULY 15, BILLY MARTIN appeared on NBC's *Meet the Press* with the show's host, Tim Russert.

RUSSERT: A lot of discussion as to whether or not Chandra Levy was pregnant. What can you tell us?
MARTIN: That's something that we're looking into. As part of our investigation, we're looking into all of her past medical records and the fact that if she was pregnant, what that would mean. But we do not yet have a final answer on that.

Martin's answer to the question about whether Chandra was pregnant directly contradicted the answer he gave five days earlier on CBS's *The Early Show* when he declared "we do know the answer." He then appeared on CNN and declared the issue of whether Chandra was pregnant was "a crucial piece of this investigation."

The media bit hard on the pregnancy bait.

Vince Flammini appeared on MSNBC news with host Geraldo Rivera, each sporting a carefully groomed mustache.

Flammini told Rivera that Chandra had "melons" for breasts and the greatest body Gary had ever seen. When the nationally televised conversation moved deeper into Gary's alleged sexual exploits, Flammini added, "Gary Condit has been cut for many, many years. If he didn't have a vasectomy, he would have an awful lot of children running around."

Flammini's revelation spread quickly through the news world. Pundits and news reporters halted further reporting on the rumor Chandra may be pregnant and that the pregnancy was the "big news" she had planned to tell her aunt, Linda Zamsky, just before she disappeared.

The *New York Daily News* put two and two together: "If true, the revelation would clear Condit of siring the son of a minister's daughter in Modesto, Calif."

The Levy camp moved immediately to get in front of the story.

Susan Levy gave an interview for *Vanity Fair* in which she acknowledged Chandra was not pregnant when she went missing. *Vanity Fair* writer Judy Bachrach explained the revelation to Ann Curry on NBC's *Today* show:

One of the things the Levys told me is that Chandra was not pregnant at the time of her disappearance, which is very important, because a lot of news articles have suggested that that might be a motivation for somebody to make her disappear; that she was pregnant and demanding of a longer, more serious relationship . . . She had recently had her period right before her disappearance. So that would not be a motivation in Gary Condit making her disappear.

The Levys used the press to break the rumor, and then as a scapegoat when cornered.

Truth was, however, Flammini had no idea what he was talking about when he told Rivera that Gary had been "cut." Gary hadn't had a vasectomy. The revelation on Rivera's show was as empty as Al Capone's tomb.

Rivera departed from further discussion of Gary's penis, telling his national audience a trusted former FBI agent had confided in him that Chandra menstruated in late April.

The *Washington Post* had reported extensively on accounts by Linda Zamsky and others about the alleged relationship between Chandra and Gary heating up in the months before she disappeared and their "five-year plan" during which Gary would leave Carolyn.

The *Post* carried more than a half dozen articles covering some aspect of the Levy scandal in its July 16 and 17 editions. Not one of those stories mentioned the conflict in the Levy camp's public representations about whether or not Chandra may have been pregnant.

FORCE

On July 15, Terrance Gainer revealed to reporters that on the day Chandra disappeared she had searched on the Internet for information about the Pierce-Klingle Mansion.

The Metro Police began an intensive two-week grid search for her across the metro DC area. As reported by the *Washington Post*:

The DC police, apparently stymied, are staging the full media show with nearly daily events for our excitement. Police officers are paraded around town, riding horses through Rock Creek, following snapping dogs into abandoned houses, walking through random stretches of park land.

Much of the latest search again concentrated on the area around the Pierce-Klingle Mansion in Rock Creek Park. Terrance Gainer told the *Post* police were now looking for a body or a fresh burial spot in "areas where people picnic, park, or have romantic liaisons."

Piggybacking on the quote from Gainer, the *Post* reported the Klingle Mansion was "conveniently" located two miles from DuPont Circle and one mile from Adams Morgan "where [Chandra] was known to visit restaurants and Condit's apartment."

News vans clogged streets in and around the mansion and members of the press fanned out across the surrounding area, ignoring police instructions and requests from homeowners to stay out of their yards.

Officers on mounted horses pushed slowly across the ground while lines of police recruits waded through tall grass. The search didn't turn up any new clues.

The next day, the Metro Police released renderings of Chandra, showing how she might look with different hairstyles. The depictions of Chandra were so cartoon-like and absurd that it caused many people, including the Levy family, to question the competence of the Metro Police (see photo in center color section).

That afternoon, California congresswoman Jane Harman issued the following press release:

The feeding frenzy over the Condit matter is spreading recklessly throughout Washington. Because my DC home is located near the Klingle Mansion, my family has been besieged with camera crews trespassing on my driveway and making outrageous claims about my relationship to Gary Condit or Chandra Levy. Gary Condit has never visited my home as a personal guest . . . To protect the privacy of my family, I have asked the Sergeant at Arms to alert the DC police about possible unlawful efforts to enter my property.

Susan Levy made the following observation about the latest efforts of the Metro Police while appearing on CNN's *Larry King Live*: "I sometimes think that they nonchalantly walk the grid and really, not really, looking—I mean, that's kind of how I feel."

—

On the eighth day of the citywide search for Chandra, twenty-eight police cadets and three sergeants gathered at a picnic area in Rock Creek Park.

According to the *Washington Post*, Jack Barrett had issued an order for the cadets to search "one hundred yards from all roads" that crisscrossed the park. The cadets formed a long line facing the park's wooded innards. Cadaver-seeking dogs walked ahead of them. The thick canopy above cast shadows like dark lakes over the uneven terrain. When the cadets had walked one hundred yards from Grover Road, they stopped.

Not far from where they stopped, the Western Ridge Trail, a popular jogging route, ran above a ravine. The bottom of the ravine was less than a hundred yards from the trail, which was a short distance from the Pierce Mill parking lot and the locations where a number of women had been attacked by Ingmar Guandique around the time Chandra disappeared.

But, the bottom of the ravine was more than one hundred yards from the "nearest road."

The cadets and dogs turned back before reaching the bottom of the ravine.

They had been instructed to measure their search against roads and not trails, even though investigators knew Chandra was an avid runner.

The Pierce Mill was easy to reach via the metro's Red Line from DuPont Circle.

—

Terrance Gainer told ABC's Charles Gibson, "Clearly, the theories are that she is dead or hopefully alive. Following up on the theory that she may be dead, that something may have happened to her criminally, we are going to look at a lot of landfills in the area."

The waste management firm overseeing city landfills publicly informed Gainer that his bold plan would cost the city between $6 million and $8 million *per* landfill, and that to sift through seventy feet of compacted trash at each of the sites would take up to one year.

The Metro Police quickly backtracked from Gainer's ambitious plan.

The sister of a woman murdered in early July held a press conference in an attempt to focus investigators on her sister's death and the hundreds of other unsolved homicides in Washington, DC. "Everyone is working on the Chandra Levy investigation. But a murderer is here, on the loose. In the shadow of Chandra Levy, we must give the police the resources they need to do the job," the woman pleaded.

City leaders echoed her concern.

"They are pulling homicide detectives away from their districts," the Metro Police union's president explained to reporters. "We need investigators on unsolved homicides. People are complaining in the community. They believe all of this is media driven," the union's secretary added.

Chief Ramsey gave a glib response: "We can walk and chew gum at the same time."

BREAKING NEWS

On July 18, FBI special agent Brad Garrett and Barry Colvert, the polygraph examiner, met inside an FBI field office.

Garrett, a former marine with a PhD, had recently been assigned to the Levy case. The *Washington Post* described him as a legend in the counterterrorism world. He was the person most responsible for tracking and capturing Mir Aimal Kasi, the terrorist who had opened fire at CIA headquarters in Langley, Virginia, in 1993. Garrett had also forced the confession of Ramzi Yousef, the mastermind of the 1993 bombing of the World Trade Center in New York City.

His friends called him "Dr. Death."

Garrett and Colvert were joined in the meeting by FBI special agent Melissa Thomas, a victim profiler, and Metro Police detectives Ralph Durant and Lawrence Kennedy.

Colvert explained to the group how he had been retained by Lowell and then administered Gary's polygraph examination. He walked Garrett through his process of formulating the questions used in the examination. For Durant and Kennedy, Colvert provided a short "101" overview of psycho-physiological responses.

Colvert then walked investigators through the results of the exam. He concluded by explaining the scoring algorithm he used to determine that Gary was telling the truth.

"I deliberately biased the test towards me as the examiner," Colvert explained. "It's possible, because the relevant questions were worded so broadly, that Condit could have had a false positive." Colvert looked squarely at the two Metro Police detectives. "That means an innocent person deemed deceptive."

"We understand," Durant responded.

"I don't feel like Condit is the man based on my interview and observation of his demeanor," Colvert concluded. "He'd never go to the extent of killing or hurting someone because of his ego and arrogance. He would just let any disclosures of their relationship be a congressman's word against an intern's word."

"Condit is an asshole," Durant blurted.

"You might be right—he's an asshole—but I don't think he killed anyone, is hiding anyone, or had anything to do with Levy's disappearance," Colvert answered.

—

When CBS correspondent Jim Stewart first came to Dan Rather with what he learned from sources inside the FBI, Rather still wasn't convinced the Levy story warranted attention.

Although there was still no evidence in the Levy case, Jim Murphy, the executive producer for the *CBS Evening News*, disagreed with Rather. He thought Stewart's story validated the position taken by Rather all along.

At Murphy's urging, Rather reconsidered, and that evening, July 18, on the *CBS Evening News*, Rather spoke about the Levy investigation for the first time on air:

> There is news tonight worthy of national note in the case of missing person twenty-four-year-old Chandra Levy. The young woman disappeared in Washington more than eleven weeks ago and became one of tens of thousands of missing persons across the country. CBS News correspondent Jim Stewart reports that now both the status and the nature of this widely publicized investigation have changed.

The newscast turned to Stewart:

> Earlier this week the FBI officially transferred the Chandra Levy investigation to its cold case unit . . . Law enforcement sources say the shift in responsibility coincides with the belief that local police have put an inappropriate emphasis on the role of Congressman Gary Condit in the case . . . Prosecutors are said to be particularly unhappy over the multiple press appearances local police make each day with essentially nothing to report.

Rather closed the story:

> You may want to keep in mind that the case remains officially a missing person case. No crime has been established. No one has been accused by lawmen of anything, much less formally charged.

Chief Ramsey hit the airwaves, claiming the reason the FBI was taking a more active role in the investigation was "because of a connection to a member of Congress."

When asked about the alleged charge by the FBI that too much focus had been put on Gary, Ramsey blamed the press: "The media's coverage has been beyond anything that I would consider reasonable."

―

On July 20, Park Police informed the Metro Police that, in late May, twenty-nine-year-old Karen Mosley had been walking her dog near the Pierce Mill when a young Hispanic man exposed himself to her. She got away.

According to the *Washington Post*, four days later, Detectives Durant and Kennedy contacted Park Police to follow up on the Mosley lead. Park Police informed the detectives they had arrested a man who matched Mosely's description—Ingmar Guandique—and believed he had attacked at least two other women in the same area of Rock Creek Park, Halle Shilling and Christy Wiegand.

Guandique was being held in a local DC jail. Still, neither the Metro Police nor the FBI came to question him about Chandra Levy until September 21. Moreover, Durant and Kennedy didn't file a report on what they had learned about Guandique until three days later, on September 24. As a result, information about any potential link between Chandra's disappearance and Guandique wasn't leaked to the press.

The world's focus remained on Gary until September 11.

RED HANDS

By now, we've all been thoroughly debased in this Chandra orgy, led, as usual, by our insatiable bottom-feeding media tastemakers—CNN, MSNBC, Fox News, the *National Enquirer/Globe/ Star*, the New York tabloids, and, remarkably enough, the *Washington Post*.

— Washingtoncitypaper.com, July 2001

"I'm calling to give you a heads-up on a story the press is going to break about a watch box Gary gave a woman," a reporter warned Mike Dayton over the phone.

"Why is that a story?" Dayton asked.

"They caught Condit throwing the box in the garbage in Virginia."

Dayton's mind flew back to the night investigators searched Gary's apartment. Dayton didn't know what Gary had thrown in the trash when they stopped in Virginia on the way back from the Five Guys.

"They traced the watch to a woman who used to work for the congressman."

Dayton didn't protest.

On July 20, the FBI released the following perfunctory statement: "After what we believe to be a thorough investigation of allegations previously made by O.C. Thomas regarding Congressman Gary Condit, we believe these allegations to be unfounded."

Lynch eagerly read the July 21 edition of the *Washington Post*. He liked the headline, and expected an apology would follow.

MINISTER RECANTS STORY ABOUT CONDIT
Allan Lengel and Petula Dvorak

A Pentecostal minister who told the FBI of an affair between his then-18-year-old daughter and Rep. Gary A. Condit informed investigators this week that he had fabricated the story, a law enforcement source said today . . .

In six lengthy interviews, Thomas, a part-time gardener at the Levys' California home, told the *Post* that his daughter had broken off the relationship with Condit and that Condit had warned her at the time not to tell anyone of the affair.

A spokesman for the Levys said today that the family did not understand why Thomas would fabricate a story in mid-April, weeks before their daughter disappeared.

Lynch expected the *Post* to be fair when it became apparent its sources had lied. Instead, the paper concocted a complicated scenario that gave legal cover to its reporters by pointing all roads back to Susan Levy, while avoiding any direct suggestion that she may have fabricated the story.

The Levy camp moved to head off the risk that the mainstream press might turn its glare on Susan's credibility.

On CNN's *Larry King Live*, Linda Zamsky, Chandra's "aunt," told host Larry King that Otis Thomas had told the truth and only recanted his story because his daughter was afraid to come forward. Later, also appearing on CNN, Susan Levy stated: "I believe that his story was real even though he says it wasn't. It's my gut feeling—even though the FBI says that it's a story."

The *Post* then carried a number of additional stories about Otis Thomas and his whopper, continuing to make news out of a lie.

—

Dayton's phone rang again. It was Lynch.

Perfect timing, Dayton thought.

"Otis Thomas recanted his story to the FBI. This will be *the* story tomorrow—that the story in the *Post* was complete bullshit. Maybe we can turn this around," Lynch said with unmasked enthusiasm.

"Don't get too excited," Dayton warned, his voice soaked in dejection. "There's gonna be another story."

That evening, Fox News's Rita Cosby reported that Gary had "dumped" a watch box only hours before police searched his apartment. According to Cosby, a man walking his dog in Alexandria had seen Gary "acting suspiciously" and notified police, and police then located the watch box and traced it to Joleen McKay. She told law-enforcement officials that she had a sexual relationship with Gary while she worked in his DC office in the mid-1990s, and that the watch was a gift she had given him. According to Cosby, the US Attorney's Office was probing "this latest possible case of the congressman obstructing justice."

WUSA TV 9 in Washington carried a symptomatic account: "Detectives are now wondering what other items, if any, had been removed from the congressman's apartment in the time between Ms. Levy's disappearance and the pre-arranged police search of the apartment . . . A detective says while the disposal of the case may not have a direct bearing on the Levy investigation . . . 'it shows a pattern of deceit.'"

LOYALTY

The *Washington Post* reported "similarities" between Anne Marie Smith's allegation that Gary asked the flight attendant not to cooperate with the FBI and an assertion allegedly made by Joleen McKay to the FBI that Dayton had called her and asked her not to talk with investigators.

Time magazine's coverage was characteristic of the shift in the story, which had been forewarned by Congressman Delahunt:

UNDER THE HOT LIGHTS: GARY CONDIT'S COWBOYS.
NOW IT'S HIS TOP AIDES WHO ARE IN THE CROSS FIRE.

. . . Authorities want to know whether Dayton's duties went beyond that. First, they want to know what happened the night he reportedly drove Condit to a Virginia suburb to dispose of a case that once contained a watch that had been given to the Congressman by a former staff member . . .

Second, they want to hear more about Dayton's recent conversations with McKay . . . According to McKay, Dayton urged her to remain quiet, saying, "Leave it in the past, or it will ruin you." That could amount to obstruction of justice . . .

The Metro Police called Abbe Lowell to request interviews with Gary's staff and to search their cars.

"Let me get this straight: You think a US congressman murdered a woman and then drafted members of his staff to help dispose of her body? You think those professionals then helped him put a dead body in their car and move it to a secret location? Rather than continuing to harass my client, why don't you search the alleys and parks!" Lowell responded.

—

Dayton and his attorney sat in a blank room inside a federal courthouse.

Assistant US attorneys Barbara Kittay and Heidi Pasichow, along with Metro Police detectives Ralph Durant and Lawrence Kennedy, sat opposite them across a laminate-top table.

So far, Dayton's answers hadn't satisfied Kittay's curiosity.

"If you don't answer, we'll go to the grand jury," Kittay threatened. "Tell me. What did you tell Joleen McKay?"

"I told her, 'Why would you want to be part of this story, the tabloids will have a field day with you. It will ruin you,' or something to that effect," Dayton responded. "And look, that's exactly what happened."

"We can make you take a polygraph exam," Kittay insisted.

The maniacal look in her eyes didn't bother Dayton. He wouldn't give an inch.

"Listen, we're taking him down. You can either go down with him or help us out," Kittay warned.

"You're taking him down for what?" Dayton asked with an incredulous grin.

Kittay read from a long list of women's names. After each name, Kittay asked: "Did Gary have an affair with this woman?"

Each time, Dayton answered, "I don't know."

"You don't know anything about him seeing other women?" she insisted.

"No."

"Did you ever socialize with him?"

"Yes."

"With women?" she demanded.

"Yes—with women and men."

"Well, when you go home at night, is there anything that bothers you, or anything that keeps you up at night that you'd like to tell us about?"

"No," Dayton responded.

"He's yours," Kittay announced, looking to Durant and Kennedy.

Durant shot up in his chair. He pulled his hands over his head and down his ponytail. He blinked hard, and looked up.

"How often did, umm, how often, umm, did she, ummm, did . . ." Durant mumbled.

"Chandra?" Dayton asked.

"Chandra, come by the office?" Durant finished.

When they were done with their questions, Durant and Kennedy asked Dayton for permission to search his cars and home.

Similar interviews were held with Gary's other staffers.

A few days after Dayton's interview with Kittay, a forensics team dismantled a staff member's red Ford Escort in a garage on Capitol Hill. The car was stripped apart, piece by piece. Investigators found car parts. Nothing else.

Propelled by the news that authorities were dismantling cars belonging to Gary's staff, reporters stood in the middle of Adams Mill Road and stopped cars as they passed in front of the Lynshire building. Motorists assumed the reporters were law enforcement and let them search the backseats and trunks of their vehicles.

JOURNALISTS

John LeBoutillier, a former congressman and political commentator tied into the mainstream media, crafted the following e-mail:

Subject line: Condit: GAYS, BISEXUALS AND MURDER.

Yesterday I spoke to "RJ"—an inside-the-Beltway source who, over the years, has never steered me wrong.

RJ said, "John, do you know the true story of Gary Condit?" RJ then proceeded to outline a scenario for what happened in this case: "Condit has been known inside the gay community in D.C. for being a big, big user of gay male prostitutes—especially blacks from the Caribbean who ride motorcycles and love to wear black leather.

"Condit lives in Adams Morgan—a terrible commute to and from the Hill— and it is a notorious neighborhood for gays and bisexuals.

"Now, here is the dirty little secret behind the disappearance of Chandra Levy: Condit goes both ways. He likes to get sodomized by male prostitutes before having sex with women. The gay sex turns him on and he can then 'perform' with women.

"Condit had one particular Caribbean male prostitute he frequented. When it was determined that Chandra had to go, this guy was given the assignment.

He picked her up on his motorcycle, took off somewhere, killed her, and dumped her body. Then, on orders from Condit and with money from Condit, he headed back to Haiti or wherever he came from—far, far away from investigators and the Feds."

The media has heard all of this—but has yet to report it. The other night both Michael Isikoff of *Newsweek* and Tom Squitieri of *USA TODAY* referred to "dark aspects of this story that we can't report yet."

Other media players are aware of this—and more: Apparently Condit liked three-ways and even four-ways with himself, the gay male prostitute and two women.

Some of his girlfriends obviously knew of this over the years; some participated in the three-way sex. This explains his absolute paranoia over any of the girls ever talking about their relationship with him. And explains the fear we are now hearing about from not just the flight attendant, Anne Marie Smith, but others, too . . .

As for Chandra leaving her apartment with only her keys? As RJ put it, "Perhaps the only time a woman would leave her purse behind would be to ride on the back of a motorcycle." . . .

If RJ's scenario is accurate, then poor Chandra—and other Condit girlfriends—have fallen into the sickest group of perverts imaginable.

No wonder Condit, representing a conservative district, went bananas every time one of his girlfriends talked.

Buckle your seatbelts: Things are going to explode soon.

LeBoutillier fired his tasty e-mail off to a number of friends at the major news networks and other media outlets. Within hours, the e-mail was the toast of the town. The list of people receiving, sending, and commenting on the story constituted a who's who of the news-making world. Below is a sample:

Michael Isikoff, *Newsweek*
Maureen Dowd, *New York Times*
Jill Abramson, *New York Times*
Sidney Blumenthal
Tony Snow
Isaacson@aol.com (presumably Walter
   Isaacson, chairman and CEO of CNN)
Ann Coulter
Craig Turk
Jonathan Weisman, *New York Times*
Eleanor Randolph, *New York Times*
Jodie Allen, *US News*
Margo Howard, *Slate*
Andrew, *Drudge Report*

Joe Conason
Gene Lyons
B Comstock, RNC HQ
Jane Mayer, *New Yorker*
Lucianneg@aol.com
Jay Tolson, *US News*
B Olson, BGRDC
Sidney Goldberg, *United Media*
Jeannette Walls, MSNBC
John Fund, *Wall Street Journal*
Nick Schulz, Fox News
John Podhoretz, *New York Post*
Joan Mower, *Freedom Forum*

Adrian and Jean Condit, Burl, Gary on Adrian's lap, and Hop on Jean's lap.

Burl and Gary Condit.

Couper Condit and Chief in the backyard.

Gary and Cadee fishing.

Gary and Carolyn.

Gary and Carolyn at the prom.

Chad, Gary, Cadee, and Carolyn in 1975.

Gary Condit and Gary Condit.

Gary and Chad Condit.

Gary and his parents.

Gary on congressional trip to Australia.

Gary and Carolyn, Adrian and Jean, Chad and Helen, Channce, Couper, Gary, and Cadee

Carolyn and Gary Condit.

The Gang of Five reunion, c. 2010 (left to right): Rusty Areias, Charles Calderon, Gary Condit, Gerald Eaves, and Steve Peace.

"Channce, Thanks for being my buddy. Love, Chief"

Channce and Gary on the Capitol steps.

Chad and Cadee, the day they resigned from the governor's office.

Early Condit campaign.

Gary Condit, mayor of Ceres.

Carolyn and Gary Condit.

From left to right: Carolyn Condit, George H. Bush, Barbara Bush, and Gary Condit.

Condit Country photo for annual event promotion.

Condit Country photo for annual event promotion.

Gary Condit and Mike Lynch.

Gary at a concert in Washington, DC with friends. Back row (right to left): Gary, Rep. John Kasich, Rep. Pete Geren. Front row (right to left): Rep. Collin Peterson, Rep. Mike Parker.

Gore 2000 presidential campaign stop in Condit Country. From left to right: Gary, Chad Condit, Gov. Gray Davis, Cadee Condit, Vice President Al Gore.

Israeli Prime Minister Ehud Barak, Gary Condit, and Rep. Howard Berman.

Egyptian President Hosni Mubarak and Gary Condit.

Gary Condit and Gloria Molina ride in the Mexican Independence Day Parade in East Los Angeles, September 16, 1984.

Photo provided by US military to CODEL members from trip to Kosovo in July 1999. Taken when UN forces were leading Gary and other CODEL members to speak with local men in front of war-torn homes.

Blue Dogs meet with President Bill Clinton at the White House following the 1994 election and turnover of Congress. Front row (left to right): Gary, President Clinton, Rep. Mike Parker. Middle row (left to right): Rep. Pete Geren, Rep. Nathan Deal (current Gov. of Georgia), Rep. Jimmy Hayes. Back row (left to right): Rep. Greg Laughlin and Rep. Ralph Hall from Rockwall.

Gary leaving the front of the Lynshire building in the morning.

Gary leaving the front of the Lynshire building in the morning, immediately surrounded by the gaggle of reporters camped outside on Adams Mill Road as he moves down the stairs toward the street where Mike Dayton is waiting to pick him up.

Joyce Chiang.

Joyce Chiang c. 1997 while working as an attorney for the U.S. Immigration and Naturalization Services.

Courtesy of Roger Chiang

Actual composite prepared and distributed by the DC Metropolitan Police Department in mid-July 2001 depicting Chandra Levy with different hairstyles.

The original photo of Chandra Levy, Jennifer Baker, and Gary taken in his Washington, DC, office.

The same photo as cropped by the media to depict only Gary and Chandra.

This photo of Chandra Levy and Gary was never distributed and was developed from Chandra's camera by federal investigators after her disappearance.

Gary at a motorcycle rally in Sturgis, South Dakota.

Ingmar Guandique at his 2010 trial. Images on right show devil tattoos on his head and neck.

Gary Condit testifying at Ingmar Guandique's 2010 trial.

Gary Condit testifying at the 2010 trial. Susan Levy, wearing black hat, in gallery (bottom).

Dominick Dunne took the contents of the e-mail as further proof of his low opinion of the congressman. Wanting more, Dunne tracked down Vince Flammini's phone number and called him.

"Gary bragged about fucking more than one thousand women," Flammini explained to Dunne.

"He's so busy, and people must be watching him," Dunne replied.

"Yeah, the people in Modesto call him Gary Condom," Flammini answered.

"Is he mean?"

"We went to motorcycle rallies together. He knows those kind of guys. We went to a rally and the top guy at the Hells Angels wanted to talk only to Gary."

"Wow, wow."

Flammini asked if Dunne would send him an autograph.

The two men talked many times, and for many minutes. Dunne "heard a lot of things from Vince."

"What is this?" Gary asked Dayton, slamming a copy of LeBoutillier's e-mail on the desk.

"An e-mail flying around Capitol Hill," Dayton explained. "The news site that hosted it only had it up for an hour. But the damage is done. It's all over the Internet."

"You know where this is coming from?" Gary asked, rhetorically. "That Khandet bullshit in the computer chat rooms."

Just before Chandra had disappeared, Dayton discovered one of Gary's staff members used a work computer to enter sex chat rooms under the alias "Khandet." The computer logs were compiled by Congress's information technology team and delivered to Dayton so he had the proof needed to fire the employee, which he intended to do. But Gary insisted the employee not be fired and instead be warned to "keep that shit in his private life and out of the office."

"You think someone inside the building would leak those Khandet files?" Dayton replied.

"I do. The press got ahold of those records and they think I'm 'Khandet.' They already think I'm on a sex club circuit." Gary couldn't help but laugh as the words came out.

"I heard they're going to give a national interview to Monica Lewinsky," Dayton said, smiling.

"She going to say I slept with her, too?"

Dunne moved with purpose to where John LeBoutillier stood at the back of the church. They were attending the funeral of a mutual acquaintance.

"I'm stunned. I'm stunned," Dunne exclaimed. "Haitian male prostitutes and motorcycle gangs!"

The two men discussed the latest allegations about Gary's sex life. Dunne was gripped by LeBoutillier's claim that the FBI was actively investigating whether Gary was also into men.

"He's a pervert. His constituents even refer to him as Gary Condom," Dunne remarked.

Days later, two hundred people gathered inside Café Milano, a swank DC restaurant, to celebrate Dominick Dunne's latest book, *Justice*. The gathering included many members of the mainstream literati.

"It's been fascinating," Dunne said, when asked about the Levy scandal. "I love the frenzy and excitement when we all get caught up in the same thing."

Heads nodded affirmatively.

"They call him Congressman Condom."

Mouths laughed, and wine poured.

When the party at Café Milano ended, friends invited Dunne to a dinner party hosted by Jim Hoagland, a writer-editor for the *Washington Post*. The distinguished group spent the evening discussing rumors about the missing intern and the motorcycle-riding congressman with an insatiable appetite for kinky sex.

Dunne searched for an opportunity to add something to the delicious conversation.

But he had nothing fresh of his own.

He felt like he was on the outside.

POLITICIANS

Republican senator Trent Lott told Fox News's Rita Cosby: "Infidelity is always unacceptable, but particularly when you have an elected official involved in a position of trust with a young girl, an intern . . . If these allegations are true, obviously he should resign."

Republican congressman Christopher Shays came to Gary's defense: "If infidelity is the test, there'd be a number of members of Congress that should resign."

Democratic congressman Bill Delahunt added: "If that's the new standard for service in the US Senate or House, he could have spoken out on many occasions previously and sought resignations from Senate colleagues . . . The bottom line is, if hypocrisy was a virtue, this place would be heaven and Senator Lott would be the Archangel Michael."

Democratic congressman Charlie Stenholm—a Blue Dog—issued a stinging press release: "Through his actions and behaviors, Congressman Condit has brought controversy and discredit to his family, his district and the Congress."

Republican congressman Bob Barr wrote to the chairman of the House Committee on Standards of Official Conduct demanding the committee begin an inquiry into Gary's conduct.

Judicial Watch, a conservative public interest law group, submitted a letter dated July 10 to the committee alleging Gary had violated federal laws and should therefore be forcibly removed from office. Judicial Watch's complaint included a total of eight citations to support its positions. Seven of the eight citations used by the ultraconservative organization were to articles published by the *Washington Post*. The only non-*Post* citation in the entire complaint was a reference to the official rules of conduct for the House.

Barr and Judicial Watch needed a majority of the ten-person ethics panel to institute an investigation. The panel was made up of five Republicans and five Democrats.

The committee took little time to dismiss the complaint.

Members of the Congressional Black Caucus listened respectfully as Gary talked. The group had vocally defended President Clinton during the Monica Lewinsky scandal.

"I realize you can second-guess me. But I haven't done anything illegal and there isn't anyone with any clout over the media or the police coming to my defense," Gary summarized at the close of his request that they take a more active role in protecting his civil liberties.

Although some members of the caucus were sympathetic, it was clear to Gary that the group wasn't going to get out front on sex issues for a second time.

After the meeting, some members of the caucus went public.

Congressman John Conyers told reporters, "We're not a bunch of scalawags that go around condoning adulterous conduct. Condit's not up for impeachment or even censure. Guess what? People don't care anymore what happens in people's private lives. Every time congressmen start waxing pious, then you find out their closet is full of skeletons."

"Monica Lewinsky was still a warm body," declared Congressman Bennie Thompson.

"I've always taken the position that the media has more ink than we do, so I don't get in an argument with the media. It's not that we don't believe that his rights may have been trampled on, but he hasn't been accused of anything. The difference here is there is no special prosecutor investigating Mr. Condit and leaking information the way Mr. Starr did," Congressman John Lewis explained.

In addition to the members of the Black Caucus, other elected officials at last broke their silence on the scandal.

"When someone hits a rough spot, do you throw him overboard? I don't think so," California congresswoman Anna Eshoo told reporters.

Florida congressman Mark Foley echoed Eshoo's remarks: "None of us is here wishing him ill. It's almost a Shakespearean tragedy—you wish the water torture would stop."

Gary walked into the hearing room for the House Committee on Agriculture.

The purpose of the hearing was to discuss the new farm bill, the most critical piece of federal legislation for Condit Country. Gary's office was fighting to have more federal monies delivered directly to state governments. Doing so would ensure California got a larger share—its fair share—of federal farm subsidies.

A low murmur preceded a loud rumble.

Television cameras followed him.

He took his seat behind the dais and focused on the baby blue walls enclosing the packed hearing room.

The American flag hung weakly behind him. The chairs on either side of him were empty. The members assigned to those seats had moved before his arrival. They didn't want the pressure of sitting through the hearing with cameras locked onto them and television pundits analyzing their every move.

On television screens across the country it appeared Gary sat alone.

Committee chairman Larry Combest called the hearing to order.

For more than three hours Gary tried not to look uncomfortable or to inadvertently smile. When he took a bathroom break, the image of his empty chair played live on television under the banner REP. CONDIT ATTENDS AGRICULTURAL COMMITTEE HEARING.

When the session ended, Congressman Saxby Chambliss leaned into his microphone. "Mr. Chairman, I'd like to compliment you and Mr. Stenholm for crafting a heck of a farm bill. When we get this kind of national media attention for a farm bill, I think it really says something. I can't imagine why else they are here!"

Committee and audience members laughed.

It's like I'm not even here, Gary thought. *We're a nation of drama queens.*

A mob of reporters waited to catch Gary in the hallway outside the hearing room.

"How do you keep working with all this scrutiny and attention," a reporter asked when he appeared.

"What attention?" Gary answered.

<hr>

Dayton and Gary met in the House gym.

"Members are calling for your resignation," Dayton explained as he handed Gary a stack of letters.

"Then watch how fast the rest of these people turn on me," Gary replied. "I'm a suspect. I resign and all of DC will come out against me. Some people are still hedging their bets."

Dayton handed Gary a copy of comments made by Congressman David Dreier that had been quoted in *Newsweek* magazine.

I was told early on that his wife was ill, and that he went out. I'd heard she'd been ill for 30 years. This is a guy who's active, and if his wife can't do much of anything with him that's sad and unfortunate, and if he ends up seeing other women, it wouldn't come as a humongous shock.

"I'm in front of an ethics panel because I won't talk to the press and he's out there making statements about another member's wife?" Gary shouted.

Gary had faced the barrage of comments made about him with a poker face. His lack of response to attacks in the press confused and, in many respects, enraged reporters accustomed to driving content through the simple game of action and reaction.

This was different. Dayton knew, without having to be told, that Gary needed to be alone.

"One of those letters is from Ralph Hall. He marked it personal," Dayton said, then left.

Gary sat in one of the small cells near the front of the gym and opened the letter from the fellow Blue Dog congressman. The letter held a copy of a short story titled "Old Drum, A Monument to Man's Best Friend Is Also a Memorial to the Men That Defend a Dog's Honor."

It was a true story about dogs caught in the grudges that plagued western Missouri after the end of the Civil War. A man's hunting dog, named Old Drum, was shot by his neighbor. The neighbor claimed he confused Old Drum for a wild dog. The dog owner and the neighbor knew that wasn't true. Still, rather than seek revenge, Old Drum's owner sought redress in court.

In thick black ink, Hall had circled the plaintiff's closing argument:

Gentlemen of the jury, a man's dog stands by him in prosperity and in poverty, in health and in sickness . . . When all other friends desert he remains. When riches take wings and reputation falls to pieces, he is as constant in his love as the sun in its journey through the heavens. If fortune drives the master forth an outcast in the world, friendless and homeless, the faithful dog asks no higher privilege than that of accompanying him to guard against danger, to fight against his enemies.

Gary turned out the light, lay on the cot, and closed his eyes. Ralph Hall from Rockwall had impeccable timing, and a grace fleeting from this world.

HOP

At 3:30 a.m., Hop parked a silver minivan in front of the Red Carpet Inn, on State Road 84 near Fort Lauderdale, Florida.

An off-duty police officer recognized him from the wanted posters that had flooded the area. He approached the van. The front windows were down.

"Sir, can I see some identification?" the officer asked, flashing a badge as he approached the open window.

Hop reached into his pocket, pulled out a Florida driver's license, and handed it through the window.

"Stanley Buchanan?" the officer asked.

"Yep."

The officer pulled Hop from the van and handcuffed him.

A local police spokesperson was asked by reporters whether the press could characterize Hop as a fugitive. The spokesman replied: "I suppose you can call him that. He does have an outstanding warrant."

Headlines the next day read: **CONDIT'S FUGITIVE BROTHER CAUGHT!**

It was the "Summer of Chandra" inside prisons, too. For his own protection, Hop was moved to solitary confinement.

Federal investigators flew to Florida to interrogate Hop. They quickly discovered that it was not possible for him to have been involved in Chandra's disappearance, and that he knew nothing about Chandra.

News that Gary's younger brother had been cleared didn't deter pundits. On *Larry King Live*, Barbara Olson asked Hop's attorney if his client knew any people that might do criminal acts for hire.

DEMANDS

The US Attorney's Office called Abbe Lowell and requested another interview with Gary. Shortly after, the FBI called and requested an interview between its agents and Gary. Within hours of the press reporting federal investigators had requested further interviews of Gary, the Metro Police called Lowell and demanded its own.

Predictably, Terrance Gainer called a press conference to discuss the reasons why *he* had called for a fourth interview.

These uncoordinated requests had nothing to do with Chandra Levy or his client and had everything to do with jockeying between law-enforcement agencies for the public square.

Lowell called for a face-to-face meeting to sort out the mess.

Dan Friedman of the US Attorney's Office, Metro Police detectives Ralph Durant and Lawrence Kennedy, and FBI agents Brad Garrett and Melissa Thomas waited in a conference room. Lowell had conditioned the meeting on the US Attorney's Office agreeing to exclude AUSAs Barbara Kittay and Heidi Pasichow.

Lowell found an open chair and started. "Leaks from the first interview made it seem as if he was not helpful at all, when in fact he had provided significant investigative information. The congressman has made some mistakes. And I think he's been candid in his interviews in addressing them. But he has not in any way tried to obstruct justice."

Lowell stopped, looking at Friedman, then added, "His acts are better understood as the acts of someone who is struggling to reconcile his roles as husband, father, and public figure."

Before Friedman could respond, Lowell turned his attention to the Metro Police detectives. "The information getting leaked is information that only people in this room and their immediate superiors would know. Chief Ramsey and Terrance Gainer have even gone as far as making personal attacks in the press against me, against my client, and even against Barry Colvert. How dare they besmirch that man's reputation!"

Lowell paused, knowing Colvert and Brad Garrett had worked together at the FBI.

"Police sources are telling reporters that the watch box was taken from the congressman's apartment to ratchet up pressure on Gary. We all know that watch box was taken from his office, and it has nothing to do with Chandra Levy . . . This week Chief Gainer made multiple comments to the press about your desire for a fourth interview with the congressman; he even told one reporter that the congressman 'owed' him an explanation about the watch box . . . It's unfair for the police to consistently leak information in an effort to damage the congressman, but never to leak information that would exculpate him. Why haven't they leaked the results of the apartment search to the press? Chief Ramsey has never met my client!"

He turned to Friedman. "Why should I allow a fourth interview when the US Attorney's Office is trying to build an obstruction case?"

Lowell swung his focus to Durant. "Why should I allow another polygraph when the MPD has trashed Barry Colvert and polygraphs in general? The police have undermined good faith dealings in this area."

Lowell looked to Garrett. "Agent Garrett, is it true that Gary could register a false positive?"

"Yes," Garrett answered without condition.

"How could I possibly allow a false positive result to turn the congressman into a suspect when he isn't one now?" Lowell asked the group. "It's off the table."

Having set his parameters, Lowell asked the group to explain to him what the purpose of a fourth interview would be.

Friedman stated the US Attorney's Office wanted to ask questions related to the watch box. Garrett stated the FBI wanted to ask questions about Chandra to help build a victim profile. Durant and Kennedy couldn't articulate a true purpose behind the Metro Police request.

"With respect to the watch box," Lowell answered, "the police leaks on this subject have eroded the congressman's faith in the process and made additional questioning impossible. You have my attorney proffer on that subject. The government will have to live with that."

"Abbe, if you came to say no, no, no to all of our requests, you could have done so more quickly," Friedman objected.

"You have my proffer," Lowell replied. "Agents Garrett and Thomas, it would be helpful if you could explain in greater detail the questions you'd like to ask my client."

"The critical question is: What was Chandra likely to have been going to do when she left her apartment with just her key?" Thomas answered. "We'd like to know if the congressman ever discussed jogging with Chandra. I'd like to stress that we're not interested in the intimate details of Gary's relationship with Chandra."

The discussion returned to Lowell's frustration with the amount of information leaked to the press.

"I think the leaks come when the detectives' notes are submitted to OASIS," Detective Durant offered.

Unbelievable, Lowell thought. *He just admitted the leaks are coming from the Metro Police brass.*

After further discussion, the parties unanimously agreed to a proposal made by Garrett. Detectives Durant and Kennedy agreed to take limited notes of the fourth interview, but only for their personal use, and not for submission to OASIS. The FBI had cut Chief Ramsey and Terrance Gainer out of the investigation, and the Metro Police's own detectives supported the decision.

Shortly after the meeting ended, reporters broke the story that the FBI wanted the fourth interview of Gary to be conducted solely by its profilers.

Chief Ramsey acted quickly, telling reporters, "We're the lead investigators on this case. We've been working with the FBI on this, and there's just no way that would happen. They're trying to play us off against each other, and that's not going to happen."

A July 25 press release issued by the Metro Police literally underscored Ramsey's chief concern:

> The department receives and is grateful for the assistance provided by the Federal Bureau of Investigation. The F.B.I. is not doing anything unilaterally and continues to provide assistance with information gathering and forensic matters.

FOURTH INTERVIEW

At 7:00 p.m. on July 26, Gary stood and walked to the nearest exit behind the dais of the Agriculture Committee hearing room.

News cameras followed his distinct gait. The media gaggle assumed he had taken a bathroom break, but Gary never reappeared.

At 7:45 p.m., he arrived at Abbe Lowell's law offices and was directed to a conference room where FBI agents Brad Garrett and Jennifer Thomas, Metro Police detectives Ralph Durant and Lawrence Kennedy, and Dan Friedman of the US Attorney's Office were seated.

Garrett wore black tailored jeans and a black long-sleeved shirt.

"Why do you look so much better than me?" Gary joked, noting Garrett's dapper attire.

"I haven't been through what you have," Garrett answered, then continued: "Imagine the water bottle is a wagon wheel with spokes coming out of it," he explained, setting an empy water bottle on its side at the center of the table. "We're trying to understand all of the spokes in Chandra's life."

Gary knew they were also profiling him.

"Is there something we should know about you?" Garrett asked.

Gary put the tip of his index finger on the table. "You see this circle? Inside I've got me, my wife, and my kids. Nobody else gets in."

Garrett nodded.

"Did she talk about her family?" Agent Thomas asked.

"She did not dwell on those things. I know her father is a cancer doctor and her grandmother lives in Florida. I know she has an uncle. She said her mother had asked her to stay away from her uncle who lives on the eastern shore," Gary answered.

Thomas turned to personal questions about Gary's relationship with Chandra. They didn't get into any new areas. Just greater detail.

Gary answered all of them.

Thomas then asked Gary about Chandra's alleged previous relationships with men. Gary couldn't provide any information about the alleged relationships disclosed to the public by Lisa DePaulo and Susan Levy.

"Is Chandra in awe of you?" Thomas asked.

"She's not. She was mature for a twenty-four-year-old and knew the deal. It was not a sappy deal," Gary replied.

"Did Chandra ever make demands?"

"No."

"Did she get jealous?"

"No."

"Did she ever talk about group sex or gay sex?"

"No."

The questions kept coming, and Gary answered each one.

"Can you provide any more information," Thomas asked.

"I really can't. I purposefully limited my involvement in her life," Gary answered.

Durant and Kennedy were given an opportunity to ask questions.

"Did she want to have kids?" Durant asked.

"I have no idea."

"Have you had a vasectomy?" Kennedy asked.

"No, I have not."

Agent Garrett took out a personality profile checklist and ran Gary through questions about Chandra in the form of "would you say she was more this kind of person or that kind of person." Garrett's questions and Gary's responses were as follows:

Personality Traits	Gary's Response
Alright being alone vs. needs to be with people	Alright being alone
Self-interested vs. concern for others	She was balanced
Aggressive vs. passive	Aggressive about her career
Emotional vs. rational	Rational
Responsible vs. irresponsible	Responsible
Risk-taker vs. conformist	As evidenced by her coming to DC, she had some risk-taker in her

The parties exchanged thank-yous and pleasantries as the meeting ended.

But something about it puzzled Gary. *Why would the FBI assign Garrett to me—he's one of our top terrorist experts?*

⟿

According to Sari Horwitz and Scott Higham of the *Washington Post*, shortly after the meeting Barrett received a call from Terrance Gainer wanting to know details about the interview with Gary.

According to the reporters, Barrett told them that Gainer's call pushed him past his limit, and that he told Gainer he no longer trusted him because everytime he gave Gainer details about the investigation they were given to the media. Barrett further stated that he told Gainer if he worked for the FBI he would have been fired.

Barrett told Horwitz and Higham that Gainer again demanded details of the interview and told him, "That's an order." Gainer claims the discussion did not occur.

Gainer was likely ignorant of the depth of the mutiny against him and Chief Ramsey within their own department. There were no detailed notes from the meeting to be shared.

The next morning, the FBI issued the following press release:

Rep. Gary Condit met with DC Metropolitan Police detectives and FBI agents last night and provided additional information to investigators concerning the investigation into the disappearance of Chandra Levy.

As a result of the plug in the information leaked by the Metro Police to reporters, only mundane details of Gary's fourth interview showed up in the press, such as "the interview focused strictly on Levy" and "the FBI asked 99.9 percent of the questions." The fourth interview, however, was the least mundane of all.

⟿

In Modesto, Susan Levy stood outside her ranch home and told the horde of reporters camped on the street: "As far as I know, her last phone calls seemed to be coming from Condit. If he's a good friend, he'll come forward and care that a constituent is missing."

PERSPECTIVE

CNN's Larry King convened his regular panel of pundits and attorney Mark Geragos to discuss the latest scuttlebutt on the Condit-Levy scandal.

GERAGOS: Why don't you listen to what the police say which is, we are satisfied, we don't have him as a suspect, and nothing to do with him.

GRACE: When you talk to a guy four times, you want a polygraph . . . when you search his apartment, he is a target . . .

GERAGOS: Nancy, the problem is that the police don't want to talk to him anymore . . . He cooperated. They got four interviews. He took the polygraph, he gave DNA and records. What more is he supposed to do?

. . .

GRACE: Do you really think that the police will tell you everything about their investigation?

JULIEN EPSTEIN (LEGAL COMMENTATOR): Unfortunately, if you were paying attention to the case you would realize that nearly everything that goes into the police department seems to be coming out in simulcast . . .

GRACE: If you were watching the case you would note that two weeks ago he was throwing out evidence in the Dumpster.

GERAGOS: Nancy, Nancy . . . the police chief, Gainer, this week himself said . . . that he not a suspect . . .

GRACE: Everybody's a suspect until the suspect is found.

EPSTEIN: The death by a thousand cuts . . .

GRACE: No, I want to find Chandra Levy, and he hasn't told all.

For months the media had reported that the relationship between Chandra and Gary was "heating up" the week she disappeared, citing a "barrage" of frantic calls made by Chandra to Gary's answering service.

Although the Levy camp and police had obtained Chandra's phone records at the outset of the investigation, the records weren't leaked and the allegation had run unchecked, used by muckrakers as motive for either Gary or Carolyn to harm Chandra.

The lead article in the July 23 edition of *Newsweek* was titled **CONDIT'S SECRET LIFE**. The story was anchored by statements allegedly made by Gary to law-enforcement officials during his closed interviews. For example, according to *Newsweek*, "As Condit portrayed it, no matter what she decided to do, their secret romance would continue."

The *Newsweek* story also acknowledged what many inside the press had known for some time:

From the beginning, the Levy family, aided by Washington lawyer Billy Martin and PR giant Porter Novelli, had kept Condit and Lowell on the defensive, launching a carefully timed barrage of allegations about the congressman's personal life. The PR team promoted the claims of flight attendant Anne Marie Smith . . . Then the Levy team brought out Chandra's aunt Linda Zamsky . . . when "we felt we needed to ratchet up the pressure," says the source . . . The certainly sad, possibly tragic, story of a young woman gone missing is being played out in a uniquely—some would say depressingly—American way, a media frenzy with witnesses testifying on *Larry King Live*, police officials walking the 24-hour cable news beat.

The latest edition of *Newsweek* included nine full pages dedicated to the Condit-Levy scandal.

On page 34 was a story discussing the difficulties faced by government attorneys in the prosecution of Slobodan Milošević for war crimes.

A few weeks later, *Newsweek* carried the following headline: **NONEXISTENT PHONE CALLS (AND OTHER FALSE TALES)**. The story read, in part:

Was Chandra Levy frantically trying to reach Rep. Gary Condit in the days before she disappeared? A flurry of last-minute calls has been widely reported—but it didn't happen . . .

[T]he available evidence points to no emotional crisis between Condit and Levy before she disappeared. Other widely circulated accounts are also inaccurate. The police have found no evidence that Levy was pregnant. Media speculation that a substance found in Condit's apartment might have been Levy's blood turns out to be entirely false . . .

None of this means Condit is off the hook.

↗

The Center for Media and Public Affairs broke down the scale of the "feeding frenzy" for Chandra content within different news mediums. The center's report showed that the story had simply overwhelmed the national dialogue.

During the two-week period following Anne Marie Smith's first interview with Rita Cosby, NBC's *Today*, ABC's *Good Morning America*, and CBS's *Early Show* together averaged more than seven stories *per day* covering some aspect of the scandal. The evening network news shows and cable news programs showed a similar insatiability.

Not surprisingly, the *Washington Post* led the charge within print media. Between May 16 and August 8 the *Post* ran approximately three articles *per day* covering the story, nearly doubling the coverage of every other major newspaper.

Number of Stories

	Total May 16 - Aug. 8	Peak Period July 2 - July 16
Print	**332**	**108**
Washington Post	157	48
New York Times	39	17
Los Angeles Times	79	23
USA Today	57	30

Excerpt from *Media Monitor*, vol. XV, no. 4, July/August 2001.

The center's analysis of the media content concluded: "It's about sex" and "the Condit/ Chandra story got more coverage last month than the G-8 summit and the stem-cell debate combined."

FISH BOWL

"Mr. Condit?" a stewardess asked for a third time.

Gary opened his eyes.

The plane had landed at San Francisco International Airport.

He had come home to spend Congress's August recess with his family.

"The captain asked if you want to deplane first," she said. "Inside the gate there's an exit down below that doesn't go into the terminal. It's for the maintenance crew but the pilot thought you might want to use that."

More than one hundred reporters lined the terminal windows facing the tarmac, with cameras pressed against the glass as they waited to confront Gary when he came through the gate.

Gary nodded. He grabbed his brown leather bag from under the seat and walked to the front of the airplane. The awkwardness of the moment was absorbed by sympathetic words of support from other passengers who remained seated as the most despised man in America exited.

Gary was taken down a small stairwell. At the bottom of the stairs he was escorted to an unmarked police cruiser. Gary got in and was whisked off the tarmac.

The press mob in the air-conditioned terminal snapped photos and shouted complaints at United Airlines employees.

Neon signs in hotel windows read NO VACANCY.

The Stanislaus County Library struggled to manage the volume of visitors requesting to photocopy portions of Chandra Levy's high school yearbooks.

Modesto's mayor thanked the national press for their presence. Local businesses reported a 10 percent increase in sales over the prior year.

National journalists moved in and out of the Levy ranch home and the porta-potties that lined the street out front.

Gary spent most of August inside his house. When he and Carolyn did leave, they coordinated with neighbors so that the press camped on Acorn Lane didn't notice.

His apparent absence led to speculation.

WABC radio in New York reported the Condit family was hiding at a luxury inn on Catalina Island located just off the coast of Long Beach, California.

The State of California, through the University of Southern California, owns an inn . . . Well, that's where Condit is . . . He is staying there so Gray Davis can say, "the congressman needs privacy. He's there with his two grown children, who are on my staff . . ." Your tax dollars are going to hide Gary Condit from the truth.

The Catalina story was picked up by other media outlets, which acted quickly on the opportunity to drag a high-profile governor into the scandal.

The WABC report is the first evidence that Gov. Davis has taken an active role in helping Condit survive the political maelstrom that threatens to sink his career . . . While on his taxpayer funded getaway, Condit is staying in a room now known as "The Grand Suite," which rents for $625 per night, has a bedroom, full bath, and harbor views.

Governor Gray Davis's office was inundated with media requests for an official statement about the Catalina hideaway. The idea that a governor was hiding a congressman on a little-known island was award-winning journalism.

But Gary wasn't on, and had never been to, Catalina Island.

Moreover, USC has always been a private university. The state of California had no stake in the Inn on Mt. Ada, and the governor had no control over its operations.

The Catalina rumor was symptomatic of the dozens of bizarre and untrue stories now circulating within various press circles.

A profile of the Levy family in *Time* magazine named each prominent politician from California who had publicly supported the search for Chandra: "Interestingly, Susan Levy noted that California's Governor Gray Davis has yet to call her family."

Susan then demanded that the governor deploy the National Guard and Civil Air Patrol to search for her daughter.

For many months, as California spiraled into an energy crisis impacting tens of millions of people, Governor Davis had tried, without success, to get the media to take a closer look at Enron and price irregularities in the wholesale energy market.

The governor finally had the media's attention, and all reporters wanted to talk about was the alleged use of taxpayer dollars to hide Gary in an island hotel the state didn't actually own and the reasons why the governor would not deploy critical emergency resources to find a woman who had gone missing in Washington, DC.

CHAPTER 17

FIGHTING BACK

FAMILY DECISION

ADRIAN AND JEAN CONDIT GRABBED trays of food from the floor of the truck's cab and walked toward Acorn Lane.

"Look," Adrian said as he and his wife came into view of their son's besieged home.

Parked in an unbroken line along the side of Acorn Lane closest to the home were four large motor homes. For safety reasons, the police had forced the media to camp on the opposite sidewalk. As a consequence, the motor homes created a wall that blocked the media's view of the Condit home.

Adrian and Jean entered the house and joined the rest of the family in the living room.

"We need to get out there and set this straight," Chad argued.

"I should go on TV and tell people I'm not a murderer?" Gary replied.

"If this was just about sex it'd be one thing. You're not the president. But we can't survive a missing woman unless you let people see what kind of person you really are."

"I've done more than a person normally would do," Gary answered.

"Live coverage of the FBI searching your home in the middle of the night—that makes you look guilty. Publicly it doesn't look like you're cooperating."

"How can I get out there when she's missing?"

"Someone has to defend you, and it's not Abbe."

"I don't think you should," Gary responded. "You don't want to become public people. This isn't your fight."

"There's no sin in fighting back. I don't want any Washington lawyers telling us what to do," Adrian insisted. "I'm with Chad and Cadee. We should have come out fighting earlier."

"Dad, don't do that. They'll take something serious you say and make it into something silly. The press will ridicule the way you talk."

"Let them," Adrian replied. "I'm gonna go tell it like it is."

Gary looked at his wife, expecting her to side with him.

"I'm for it," Carolyn said.

Everything Gary had done up to that point had boomeranged back on him. For the first time, he questioned his instinct to remain quiet. *They can't go out there while I stay quiet. This isn't their fight*, he concluded.

Outside, the motor home at the front of the line lurched forward. The second motor home followed, then the third, and then the fourth. Behind the fourth a new set of four motor homes lined bumper-to-bumper followed, so that in total the eight motor homes moved in tandem, like train cars pulling by the Condit house.

The enterprising press had complained to the police department that the vehicles violated a local ordinance that prohibited parking motor homes on the street for long periods of time. In response, Gary's neighbors organized a rotation, so that when the press wasn't expecting it, a new line of motor homes came down the street to replace the prior line, restarting the time period under the local ordinance.

Gary was the summer's biggest "get."

The nation's most high-profile media personalities called or wrote to Abbe Lowell to make their pitch for Gary's interview, often providing callous and unsolicited opinions on their competition.

The finalists were ABC's Connie Chung and CBS's Ed Bradley.

Chung hadn't been a big name in prime time media for many years. Gary's interview was the type of "get" that could bring her back from the dead. Her pitch to Gary in a handwritten note to him was built around a single word—trust.

Dear Honorable Gary Condit —
I know this is a difficult time for you but I am hoping that you might feel you can trust me for a time in the future when you might want to do an interview.
If there also comes a time when you would feel comfortable having an off-the record meeting to establish trust — I'd be thrilled to come to be at anytime.
Washington happens to be my home-town and I've spent many years covering the Hill in the 60's + 70's. It would be a pleasure to meet you to pay a courtesy call. (212) [redacted] (office)
(917) [redacted] (cell.) Best wishes —
Connie Chung

Connie Chung • ABC News • 147 Columbus Ave • New York, New York • 10023

Although Chad and Cadee expressed reservations about Chung given her need for a career springboard and her record of railroading interviewees (including former First Lady Barbara Bush), the group ultimately decided she would be the better choice.

As soon as word leaked out that Gary was going to give an exclusive interview and the *Modesto Bee* hadn't landed it, the newspaper formally called for his resignation:

His self-absorption has been a lapse not only of judgment, but of human decency. With Levy's life at stake, Condit knowingly hindered—if not obstructed—the police investigation into her disappearance, letting the trail grow cold . . .

We sometimes disagreed with him on policy issues, but we always believed his independent brand of politics served his San Joaquin Valley district well.

But a good record does not guarantee indefinite tenure in office . . . Condit can restore some of his honor and dignity. He can set aside his own ambitions now and do what is in the public interest: resign.

WHO DECIDES

More than one hundred of Gary's supporters gathered at the Assyrian Reception Hall in Turlock.

Gary, a lifetime politician, did not attend the rally.

Adrian Condit stood on the raised stage at the front of the hall.

"Thank you," Adrian said, then cleared his throat. "I'm here this evening to speak to you on behalf of my son and the Condit family. Gary and Carolyn are doing just fine. I believe the people of this valley know Gary and Carolyn Condit better than the news media."

The crowd applauded.

Adrian looked defiantly at the mass of reporters lined against the back wall. "I want you to know that no amount of news media rhetoric, implications, or accusation—sources known or unknown—will ever divide the Condit family!"

The crowd erupted with approval, chanting "WE DECIDE, NOT THE MEDIA!"

"The Condit ties are unbreakable!" Adrian shouted, his voice tearing through the air like thunder.

He took a small step forward and looked gently over the familiar folks in front of him. "Before we go, I'd like to pray for Chandra Levy and her parents Susan and Doctor Bob Levy."

The crowd bowed their heads.

"Lord, I pray that you put your arms around them and love them and comfort them . . . and may in some miraculous way, you bring that precious daughter of theirs home."

—

It took all of her willpower for Jean Condit to walk into the headquarters of the *Ceres Courier.*

She and Adrian had agreed to an interview with the paper's editor, Jeff Benziger.

"Sure, Satan had a role in this. Gary's just about destroyed . . . People are destroying him, not only in reputation, but him," Jean explained, wiping away tears.

"I know he would not withhold one thing if he thought it would help find that girl. He hurts because she's gone," Adrian added.

"Why won't he talk to the public?" Benziger pressed.

"Why should he have to come before the news media and make any type of confession? He's confessed to God what he's done wrong . . . I have prayed with him several times. In all this stuff, there's not any sense of forgiveness. It's all judgmental," Adrian said, perplexed by the media's inability to appreciate the simple lesson that no good comes from compounding sins, and that a man does not save himself by further punishing his wife.

"That's all people want to hear?" Jean interjected. "We had sex."

"His relationship with Chandra Levy was a great mistake. He's never said this to nobody about how he's taking this beating, partly because he doesn't want to say anything derogatory in any manner toward Chandra Levy, or even toward Dr. and Mrs. Levy," Adrian continued.

The interview was placed on the *Courier*'s front page under the headline: GARY CONDIT'S PARENTS BELIEVE SATAN HAD A "BIG TIME ROLE" IN SCANDAL.

PREPARATION

Gary, Cadee Condit, Chad Condit, Mike Lynch, Mike Dayton, and Abbe Lowell sat at a conference table in a Los Angeles, California, law office.

"Before Connie Chung can get to her first question you need to tell her that you'd like to offer a few words. You need to get your message out before she takes control," Lowell advised.

"You need to apologize for the affairs," Lynch insisted.

"What's he got to apologize for?" Chad demanded. "He didn't commit any crime."

"My private life is nobody's business," Gary added.

Lynch fell back in his chair, dumbfounded by the disconnect between what he felt needed to be done and the response he received from Chad and Gary.

"People know what happened. They need to hear it, and hear an apology," Lynch fired back.

"That's bullshit, Lynch," Chad yelled.

"I know you think that," Lynch responded. "If he had the affair it was wrong. We all agree on that. So why not tell people you're sorry?"

"Mike," Gary broke in. "I'm going to do this. That doesn't mean I'm going to talk about sex or apologize to people I haven't hurt."

"You can't control this, Gary. You can't. If you can't go out there and apologize for having an affair, then you are better off doing nothing."

"You're the one who said he needs to get out there!" Chad responded.

"I'm not going to give some mea culpa," Gary added. "If that means we know how this will end, then that's how it'll end."

Abbe Lowell received a call from a producer for *People* magazine. The producer wanted an interview with Gary and Carolyn, and offered the cover of the magazine's next issue.

Gary had finally decided to make a public statement, and the team thought a story on Gary and Carolyn, together, would make a particularly strong one to counteract the persistent, and widespread, rumors about their marriage falling apart.

The two-story Beverly Hills home was set back from the street and enclosed by a cyclone fence.

"Gar, cats," Carolyn whispered, her nose and throat swelling as they stood in the musty kitchen.

Cadee, Chad, Lowell, Lynch, and Gary were led into the living room. The magazine's staff had asked Carolyn to wait in the kitchen. Dayton stayed with Carolyn.

"I'm allergic to cats," she explained. "Can I go outside?"

"We need to prep you for the photo. We'll open a window, is that OK?"

"I'll try. Can I get some water?"

Two women began applying makeup to Carolyn's face.

"No thank you," Carolyn protested. "I don't need any more makeup."

"We're just going to do a few things," a third woman insisted while ratting Carolyn's blonde hair.

"How does it feel to be in the place you are in your life?" a fourth woman asked, handing Carolyn a glass of water.

"Bet you never thought you'd be here?" the woman ratting her hair offered.

Why did they separate us? Carolyn wondered, trying her best to remain polite.

"Are you upset with your husband? It must be tough to read about all these women," one of the women applying makeup opined.

"No," Carolyn replied, feeling that her eyes were starting to swell. "Where's Gary?"

"You can't see him now."

"Are you sick?" a woman asked.

"I'm having an allergic reaction, that's all. Can I . . ."

"No, I mean like sick. We've read that you are sick."

"That's not true," Carolyn insisted.

"She's crying," someone suggested.

"I'm allergic to cats."

Dayton noticed Carolyn didn't look well and walked over to where she sat.

"You OK?" he asked.

"I need to get out of here," Carolyn whispered.

The makeup woman kept padding her face.

"We're going to go outside," Dayton said, and helped Carolyn out of her seat, ending the assault.

⟶

Gary sat on a couch, in a parlor room protected from daylight by heavy purple drapes. Champ Clark, a reporter for *People* magazine, sat across from him. Abbe Lowell sat near Gary, and Cadee and Chad stood at the back of the room.

"We should have done this on the beach," Cadee said to Chad. "This place is depressing."

"They want to bring us down," he agreed.

Clark started questioning Gary. Not long into it, Gary figured out Clark had no interest in writing a story about the strength of his wife and their marriage. He wanted to corroborate the rumors of the Condit's marriage falling apart.

"Are rumors about a divorce true?" Clark asked.

"No. Move off of it," Gary answered.

They sparred until Clark finally moved to another topic.

"On *Rivera Live*, Billy Martin told Geraldo that his clients are, quote, 'very angry with Gary Condit right now.'"

"I don't understand that," Gary answered.

"Martin said, quote, 'even if he by chance had nothing to do with her disappearance, he's hurt their daughter,' referring to statements made by her aunt that you promised to marry her and start a family," Clark continued. "That you had a five-year plan."

"We never discussed things like love or marriage. It didn't happen," Gary answered. "I would never do that to my wife. I've been married for thirty-four years. I love Carolyn very much. I'll stay with her as long as she'll have me. It's about forgiveness. My wife and children know I'm not a perfect man."

The interview lasted nearly three hours, and with every minute the tension in the musty room tightened. Gary was answering all of Clark's questions; just not in the way Clark wanted.

"Your timeline for the day she went missing shows that you had a doctor's appointment. Where was that appointment?" Clark asked.

"In the Capitol."

"What's your doctor's name?"

"I don't remember. My regular doctor wasn't available. I saw whoever else was there."

"You don't remember?" Clark pressed.

"I just said, I don't remember."

"You're sure?" Clark asked.

"Yes, I'm sure. Move off of it," Gary replied,

"Is there a number we can call to confirm the doctor's name?"

"Move off of it."

The interview ended without resolving the doctor's name. Gary was led to the front lawn, where Carolyn was waiting.

"How'd it go?" she whispered.

"These people are hostile for some reason," Gary answered.

"Stand over there and face this way," the producer directed.

"Don't smile," the cameraman instructed.

"I think we should smile," Carolyn replied, reaching to hold Gary's hand.

When Clark's article hit newsstands it contained the following description of the exchange: "Carolyn appeared frail and uneasy, smiling tentatively at her husband as he placed his arm around her."

Clark peppered Gary's office with requests for the name of Gary's doctor. Gary's office refused to give Clark the name on the basis of medical privacy.

Chad walked across the backyard of his parents' house. It had been a long drive from Los Angeles back to Ceres, and it was after midnight.

"Freddy!" he shouted. "Come here."

Gary's dog had run to Chad as soon as he entered the backyard, and was whimpering. But Chad's dog, Freddy, was nowhere to be found.

Gary, Cadee, and Carolyn joined Chad near the pool.

A shadow at the bottom of the pool caught Chad's eye.

"What's . . ." Cadee started to ask.

As the words came out, Chad dove into the pool.

Gary dropped to his knees.

A moment later, Chad resurfaced, holding a rolled-up patio rug. Gary grabbed one end of the rug and pulled it out of the pool. As the rug unraveled, the dog's corpse rolled onto the cold concrete.

PREGAME

Abbe Lowell sent a letter to Bill Martin reiterating his offer to provide information to the Levy family and its private investigators. He wrote the letter because Martin still would not return his phone calls.

Martin, again, did not respond.

On August 15 Susan Levy appeared on CNN's *Larry King Live.*

KING: The other night you said, if Gary Condit were not in your daughter's life, she'd be here today.

S. LEVY: I feel like that for some reason internally that, as a mother, that it's possible that my daughter would have graduated and she would be here with us for the summer.

KING: Therefore, you have to have a scenario that thinks he's responsible?

S. LEVY: The only thing that I can say is that he mentioned he's a good friend of my daughter, and he never mentioned to me personally that there was any kind of relationship going on. But I called a specific number and asked him a specific question, and it was not told to me in a truthful manner.

KING: So you're saying he lied to you?

S. LEVY: Yes . . .

KING: You think he knows more than he said?

B. LEVY: We believe so.

KING: Did you know that she was having an affair?

B. LEVY: Yes.

KING: What did you know then?

B. LEVY: Well, we knew that she was seeing a congressman, that he had arranged for her to do certain things, such as go to the inauguration, and she would not tell us who. She would absolutely keep it secret.

KING: So then you had to know she was dating?

S. LEVY: Somebody.

B. LEVY: We didn't know who.

The Levys' comments on CNN directly contradicted the *Washington Post*'s story that Susan and her gardener, Otis Thomas, had discussed their daughters' affairs with Gary and that she then confronted Chandra about the relationship.

From the archives of the *Post*:

Susan Levy confirmed she had the conversation with [Otis] Thomas and said she had sparred with her daughter about the relationship with Condit over the phone.

Susan Levy's latest account also called into question the widespread allegation, first carried by the *Post*, that days after Chandra disappeared Susan had asked Gary, directly, whether he had an affair with her daughter, and that Gary had lied to her.

As the Levys kept talking, they blew more holes in the *Post*'s reporting.

Billy Martin made a guest appearance on CNN with host Wolf Blitzer to discuss Gary's upcoming interview with Connie Chung.

BLITZER: What does the Levy family want to hear from Gary Condit Thursday night?

MARTIN: The only thing the family wants to hear, and I spoke with Dr. Levy and Mrs. Levy today, they just want to hear information that could lead to information on Chandra's whereabouts or what happened to her. They don't really want to hear anything about the relationship . . . They don't want to know how he felt about Chandra. They don't want to know how Chandra felt about him.

Discussion on the Fox News network's political talk show *Hannity & Colmes* was characteristic of what the nation heard in the days leading up to the much anticipated Chung interview.

SEAN HANNITY (HOST): Until now, Condit has avoided the media and was less than forthcoming with the DC police. Will tonight really be any different?

TED WILLIAMS (ATTORNEY/FORMER DC DETECTIVE): What you are actually witnessing and what we're going to witness tonight is the self-destruction of a congressman. It's a fraud on the American people. He will not tell anything about whether he had a physical relationship with Chandra Levy.

ELEANOR CLIFT (*NEWSWEEK* CONTRIBUTING EDITOR): The sad part here is that there is no evidence. There is no evidence at all connecting him.

WILLIAMS: I beg to disagree with you. Look, the big question is "why isn't the United States Attorney taking a more focused look at this?" This man attempted to obstruct justice.

HANNITY: Absolutely.

WILLIAMS: He hid a box, a watch box!

HANNITY: Absolutely.

WILLIAMS: He asked Anne Marie Smith to lie. This man is supposed to be a representative of the Congress of the United States, and he's an embarrassment!

ALAN COLMES (HOST): Don't go anywhere. Coming up, *Talk* magazine's Lisa DePaulo joins the debate.

Gary was dead on arrival.

MORNING OF

On August 23, a letter from Gary was delivered to every mailbox in Condit Country. In it, he offered his sympathy for the Levy family, reaffirmed he had cooperated with the investigation, and acknowledged he had made mistakes and was "not a perfect man." The letter did not specify what those mistakes were, and ended as follows:

> Before speaking to the media, I wanted to write to you. I have known so many of you for a long time. You know me to be hard working, committed to our issues and dedicated to my community and my family. I hope you also will understand that I am not perfect and have made my share of mistakes. I hope our relationship is strong enough to endure all of this.

Todd Fahey's Internet blog *Disinformation* dissected the letter and discovered in it proof that Gary had also killed Joyce Chiang.

—

A helicopter churned overhead. Gary and Connie Chung stood at the edge of the lawn in front of a large ranch house, at the point where it bled into an almond orchard.

"What kind of trees are those?" Chung asked.

"On the trees, they're 'all-monds' and on the ground they're '*ah-monds*'—because we love the 'L' out of them," Gary explained.

After posing for pictures outside, they returned to the ranch house.

Gary was led to a chair at the center of the great room.

In her left hand, Chung held a yellow pad of paper on which she had written six pages' worth of questions for the thirty-minute interview.

INTERVIEW

President George Bush's chief adviser, Karen Hughes, and his national security adviser, Condoleezza Rice, sat in front of a television inside a home on the president's family ranch in Crawford, Texas.

Like tens of millions of other people worldwide, including twenty-four million Americans, they turned the channel to ABC to watch the most anticipated prime time interview in many years.

CONNIE CHUNG: Congressman Condit, do you know what happened to Chandra Levy?

CONDIT: No, I do not.

CHUNG: Did you have anything to do with her disappearance?

CONDIT: No, I didn't.

CHUNG: Did you say anything or do anything that could have caused her to drop out of sight?

CONDIT: You know, Chandra and I never had a cross word . . .

CHUNG: Did you cause anyone to harm her?

CONDIT: No.

CHUNG: Did you kill Chandra Levy?

Gary's eyes turned gray. *You're talking about a missing woman. That's a question you ask a man on death row*, he thought. In that moment, "Chung became Putin to me," he later admitted.

CONDIT: I did not . . .

CHUNG: What exactly was your relationship with Chandra Levy?

CONDIT: We had a close relationship. I liked her very much.

CHUNG: May I ask you, was it a sexual relationship?

CONDIT: Well, Connie, I've been married for thirty-four years, and I've not been a—a perfect man, and I've made my share of mistakes. But out of respect for my family, and out of a specific request from the Levy family, I think it's best that I not get into those details about Chandra Levy.

CHUNG: What we're talking about is whether or not you will come forward to lift this veil of suspicion that seems to have clouded you. Did you have a romantic relationship with Chandra Levy?

Gary repeated his answer.

CHUNG: Did she want to marry you and have your child?

CONDIT: I only knew Chandra Levy for five months. And in that five-month period, we never had a discussion about a future, about children, about marriage. Any of those items never came up in that five-month period.

CHUNG: Did you ever make promises to her?

CONDIT: Never.

CHUNG: Did she want you to leave your wife?

CONDIT: No. I mean, I've been married for thirty-four years, and I intend to stay married to that woman as long as she'll have me . . .

CHUNG: [D]on't you realize that part of the reason why you're in the situation that you're in is because that there have been ambiguous or evasive answers to specific questions? . . .

CONDIT: Well, no, there have not been. I have talked to the people who are responsible for finding Chandra Levy. I've been very specific. I've told them every detail in every interview about my relationship with Chandra Levy . . .

Chung then pressed Gary, three more times, on the allegation that he wasn't truthful with law enforcement during his interviews. Each time, Gary insisted that wasn't the case.

CHUNG: Did they specifically ask you if you had a romantic relationship with Chandra Levy?

CONDIT: They asked every question they wanted to ask. And I answered.

CHUNG: And you, did you tell them that you did have a romantic relationship with her?

CONDIT: I told them everything they asked. Answered every question. And I did nothing to slow down the investigation.

CHUNG: Now when Mrs. Levy called you and said that her daughter was missing, and she asked you point-blank, she says, at a critical time in the investigation, as to whether or not you had an affair with her daughter, you answered, according to her, matter-of-factly, "No." Were you telling the truth?

CONDIT: I never lied to Mrs. Levy. Fact of the matter is that whole week I had several conversations with the Levys. Dr. Levy and Mrs. Levy . . .

CHUNG: So when you said, "No," you were telling the truth?

CONDIT: [W]hat Mrs. Levy asked me was a series of questions about a lot of things. And I'm sorry if she misunderstood those conversations. But in those conversations, she made a lot of statements. My job was to console and do what I could do to be helpful. But I never lied to Mrs. Levy at all . . .

CHUNG: So are you saying that she misunderstood you.

CONDIT: Yes.

Chung took three more stabs at the allegation by Susan Levy that Gary had lied to her. Each time Gary gingerly tried to move the discussion forward, as it was an impossible question for him to answer.

Chung looked at the timer under the camera. The clock read fifteen minutes. *Oh my God,* she thought. *I'm halfway through and I have four pages to go.*

She was in a bit of shock.

The standard political advice to her interviewee would have been to confess to the relationship and provide a heartfelt apology, then move the discussion on.

But, true to his word, Gary refused to follow the formula. She and Gary continued to go back and forth, Chung asking questions designed to get Gary to admit on television to a sexual affair with Chandra or that he lied to her mother, and Gary refusing to make those admissions.

CHUNG: But aren't you here to set the record straight?

CONDIT: I think I am setting the record straight.

CHUNG: Would you like to tell the truth about the relationship with her?

Gary refused to take the bait.

Chung then asked Gary to explain the "frantic" phone calls he allegedly received from Chandra around the day she disappeared.

CHUNG: She had called you repeatedly on that date. Correct?

CONDIT: Well, no, that's not true.

CHUNG: Her phone records show that . . .

CONDIT: [T]he news media reported that she made all these frantic calls. And that's just not correct.

CHUNG: But her phone records show that she called you repeatedly.

CONDIT: . . . [S]he didn't make frantic phone calls to people . . .

ABC was behind the curve on the allegation about the heated telephone calls.

CHUNG: [T]here has been talk about a possibility that Chandra Levy was pregnant. Do you know if she was pregnant?

CONDIT: I have no reason to think that.

ABC was also behind the curve on the pregnancy rumor. Gary wanted to jump out of his seat but knew he couldn't. *Millions of Americans watching have no idea she's asking me about allegations that have already been proven false!*

Chung moved to Anne Marie Smith, and the allegation that Gary had asked her to lie to law enforcement. Gary refuted the allegation, stating that he had told her she didn't have to deal with the press. Chung read from the draft affidavit attorney Joe Cotchett's office had sent to Smith's lawyer, Jim Robinson.

CHUNG: I mean, why would you want her to say that she didn't have a relationship with you?

CONDIT: Because she didn't.

CHUNG: Why—why would she make it up?

CONDIT: You know, Connie, I'm—I'm puzzled by people who take advantage of tragedy. A missing person that they don't even know . . .

CHUNG: Hours before DC police searched your apartment, you were seen throwing away a watch box in a dumpster. Why did you do that?

CONDIT: Well, the watch box had nothing to do with Chandra Levy and the police know that . . .

CHUNG: But were you trying to cover up a relationship with yet another woman? . . .

CONDIT: It was a gift . . .

CHUNG: A woman who worked in your office?

CONDIT: Years ago.

CHUNG: And did you have a relationship with her?

CONDIT: I did not . . .

CHUNG: Do you fear that the public out there may be very disappointed that you didn't come forward and reveal details today, as we sit here tonight?

CONDIT: Well, I think I have revealed details. The details that I've been fully cooperative with law enforcement . . .

CHUNG: You don't think you're stonewalling?

CONDIT: No, I don't think I'm stonewalling at all. I think that people expect that you can maintain some of your privacy. I think the Levys expect to maintain some of their daughter's privacy. And I'm trying to honor that. I'm trying to do that with dignity. I, I'm trying to retain some privacy for my family and for their family. And I think your viewers out there will understand that.

CHUNG: I would think that many people would want you to maintain your privacy. However, you have constituents out there, something like 680,000. Do they deserve the truth?

CONDIT: They deserve the truth. And the truth is that I have done everything asked of me by the people who are responsible to find Chandra Levy . . . I have not been part of the media circus if that's your point. But it's not the news media's responsibility to find Chandra Levy . . .

CHUNG: But isn't much of what has happened partly your doing?

CONDIT: In what respect, Connie?

CHUNG: You said yourself, to your constituents, in a letter, that you've made mistakes, and you said that to me earlier.

CONDIT: Right . . .

CHUNG: But what mistakes are you talking about? Are you talking about moral mistakes?

CONDIT: Well, there's a variety of mistakes. I mean, I've made all kinds of mistakes in my life, but I'm not going to go into details on this program about the mistakes that I've made in my life . . . I acknowledge them. And I'm sorry for them.

CHUNG: Do you think you're a moral man?

CONDIT: I think I am a moral man. Yes.

CHUNG: Okay. I think we are out of time, Gary. Thank you so much, Congressman Condit.

CONDIT: Thank you.

Gary removed the mic from his coat and looked at the stunned faces lining the edge of the great room.

The people in the room felt as though they had just witnessed the torture of both the interviewer and the interviewee. Lynch's face looked as though it had frozen in a knot, while Lowell's chin was drawn under a listless frown.

"They just saw the toughest, hardest guy I know," Chad said to Cadee.

Every major television news network ran special post-interview programming where pundits and "experts" derided Gary's performance.

In a post-interview Gallup poll, 62 percent of Americans polled said that it was "very likely" or "likely" that Gary was directly involved in Chandra's disappearance.

A classified memorandum titled "Bin Laden Determined to Strike in US" was delivered to President Bush at his Crawford ranch. The intelligence community had determined that al-Qaeda was in the final stages of planning "something very, very, very big."

Later, Karen Hughes and Condoleezza Rice briefed President Bush on the Condit-Chung interview the prior night. Afterward, the president addressed reporters: "I'm not worried about the gossip or the Washington whispers. This isn't about a congressman or a network. This is about a family that lost a daughter."

Nobody told the public that the intelligence community's warning system was "blinking red."

FALLOUT

Minority leader Dick Gephardt had stuck by Gary through three months of intense media pressure. His support held most of the balance of the Democratic Party in check.

The day after Gary's interview with Connie Chung, that changed.

Gephardt started the drumbeat. "I was disappointed," he told reporters.

"What about his future in the party?" a reporter asked.

"I need to talk to my colleagues. I didn't hear candor. I didn't hear an apology. What he said last night was disturbing and wrong. I think it fell way short. It adds to the general perception that politics are no good and politicians are a bunch of bums," Gephardt answered.

A barrage of negative statements about Gary from prominent Democrats followed Gephardt's appearance. Each statement was grounded in a message that had been crafted by the party leadership: Gary hadn't been "forthcoming" to law enforcement or to the public.

Comedian Jay Leno summed up where Gary now found himself: "It looks like Condit is being abandoned by the Democratic Party. Imagine that. You are being abandoned by the party who stood behind the Kennedys, Gary Hart, Dan Rostenkowski, Jesse Jackson, and Bill Clinton! This is like getting kicked out of Sodom and Gomorrah."

⟶

No Democrat of national prominence was under more pressure to turn on Gary than California governor Gray Davis. Despite the energy crisis, Davis was still on the short list of potential Democratic candidates to challenge George W. Bush in the next presidential election.

On August 25, Davis and his top advisers attended a retreat with political consultants for the national party.

On August 26, Cadee Condit received a call from the governor's chief of staff, Lynn Schenk, informing her that the governor was going to make a few remarks about Gary.

"He needs to say something at this point."

"OK," Cadee replied.

"You'll always have a place here," Schenk assured her.

On August 27, Governor Davis met with representatives of the California State Sheriffs' Association in Woodland, California. Uniformed peace officers stood behind the governor as he signed legislation that provided funding for rural law-enforcement programs. The crowd applauded as the governor handed the last pen to his staffer, then opened the floor to questions.

"Do you have anything to say about Congressman Condit?" was the first question.

"I'm disheartened that Congressman Condit did not speak out more quickly or more fully. While I get no joy out of this whatsoever, I just think it is important that Gary Condit be as forthcoming as possible, do everything humanly possible to help law enforcement identify the location of Chandra Levy," Davis replied.

The next morning the following headline splashed across the *Los Angeles Times*: TOO LITTLE, TOO LATE FROM CONDIT, DAVIS SAYS.

⟶

Gary sat, alone, in his backyard.

Neither the house nor the breeze drowned out the voices of reporters shouting and laughing on Acorn Lane. He closed his eyes, and looked around the next corner.

There was no high-paying lobbying gig or cushy appointment waiting for him when he left office. Nobody would touch him. Gary didn't have a 401(k), and he didn't own stocks or bonds. He didn't have a family business. He owned two houses in Ceres, two cars, and a Harley-Davidson.

He had given his entire adult life to public service, and his rise from the city, to the county, to the state and, finally, to Washington had been timed so he never vested for a full retirement with any employer. That meant he and Carolyn would have no health coverage after he left Congress unless he found an employer willing to hire the most reviled man in America.

His thoughts were broken by Chad's voice. "I'm going on Larry King."

"My opinion hasn't changed. I don't think it's a good idea for you to put yourself in this," Gary replied.

"It's not your choice," Chad answered, with a defiant look in his eye that Gary knew well. "Everyone's got their trigger point."

"Well, Governor Davis did."

"We're in the politics business," Gary responded.

"After everything you did for him? You think the governor's statement was fair? You think he needed to do that surrounded by cops?"

"I'd hoped he might take issue with Connie asking me if I murdered somebody. I get that he had to say something. Maybe he should have picked up the phone and called me so I was ready for it. I wouldn't have talked him out of it. We've been through a lot. I thought on that basis he'd extend me that courtesy. But I guess he couldn't."

Within days of Gary's interview with Connie Chung the national and local Democratic Parties, including some of his closest friends, had forcefully and publicly abandoned him.

DUNNE

Dominick Dunne joined a panel of guests on CNN's *Larry King Live* convened to discuss Gary's interview with Connie Chung.

During his appearance, Dunne stated: "There is just something sneaky about this guy! I still think that we cannot overlook the thing about motorcycles in this story. He is a big motorcyclist, and he rides with the Hells Angels, and I think that that is how she disappeared, on the back of a motorcycle."

When taping of the show ended, the guests and producers gathered in the green room to, as Dunne later explained, sip water and "talk dirt" about Gary. Green rooms, where the likes of Dunne, Nancy Grace, and Barbara Olson assembled on a near nightly basis, are the breeding grounds for novel theories and salacious rumors in the mainstream press.

"What a disaster he was on Connie Chung. I mean, I find it so false how he kept bringing up his thirty-four-year marriage as if they are Bess and Harry Truman when it's just a false impression of a bizarre marriage," Dunne told his colleagues. "And he threw that watch box away!"

As Dunne later admitted, Gary was "not looked on favorably" in the green rooms.

The next day, Dunne received the following voice mail from Susan Levy: "This is Susan Levy. I am the mother of the missing girl. I heard you on Larry King last night. My husband, Dr. Levy, and I would like to talk to you."

Dunne left a message on Dr. Levy's office phone. A few hours later, the Levys rang him back.

As Dunne later recalled, "I said little to them and they said much to me." Susan Levy did all the talking. Although Dr. Levy was on the line, he only cried. It was one of many telephone discussions Dunne would have with the Levys over the following few months.

"I am very interested in this motorcycle theory. Will you meet with our investigator?" she asked. "Well, he is not our investigator. He is the investigator working with our lawyer, Billy Martin, in Washington. He is FBI. His name is Jerry Gruner."

"Sure," Dunne replied.

Susan provided him with Gruner's contact information.

"Mr. Dunne, do you ever get over it?" she asked.

"You never do. But you go on."

Dunne immediately called Jerry Gruner.

"Mrs. Levy and I spoke about your motorcycle theory," Gruner explained.

"Probably a Haitian man. Someone from a Haitian motorcycle gang the congressman associates with. I mean, she left her wallet. She left her ID. That is an unusual thing for a woman to do," Dunne responded.

"Uh-huh."

"Motorcycles played a big part in Mr. Condit's life. He had friends with motorcycles. And some of those friends are bad people. I just think, and a lot of people think, that she went off on the back of a motorcycle," Dunne insisted.

Gruner told Dunne they'd check it out.

Dunne took Gruner's reply to mean the FBI was now actively investigating Gary's potential connection to a DC-area Haitian motorcycle gang and its role in Chandra's disappearance.

SUE

The August 26 edition of the *Washington Post* published Petula Dvorak's most innocuous and curious story to date: **THE WAIT OF THEIR LIVES; BOB AND SUSAN LEVY FILL TIME WITH WORK AND STUDY WHILE THEY WAIT FOR THEIR CHANDRA TO COME HOME.**

. . . [Susan Levy] is, by her own definition, "a little nutsy" . . .

Her greatest talent is playing herself . . .

She is the Mother of the Missing Intern, the worn-looking woman who first came to Washington clutching a fuzzy yellow duck, wearing a floppy purple hat, pleading for her daughter's safe return . . .

Chandra's mother studied mysticism and worked for years on an autobiography she titled "Life Is Illusion, or Is It?" She copied poems about God into her paintings . . .

Sue Levy says, "Chandra always thought I'm a little flaky."

Why was Chandra drawn to Rep. Gary Condit, a married, much older politician? Her parents say they're mystified. "He's a smooth talker," Bob offers, "and obviously seduced a lot of other—you know, it's not secret."

She found men her own age too immature, her parents say. In her teens she dated a Modesto police officer.

The Levys knew for months that their daughter was dating a politician. But Chandra never named him. She told them the congressman was divorced and in his "late forties," Bob says . . .

Throughout the summer, the Levys vent their anger. At themselves. At Chandra and her secrecy. At the best target they have, the man whose name they speak with contempt and disgust. Gary Condit. It doesn't matter that the police have never called him a suspect. They accuse Condit of being a predator . . .

The Levys don't mind the media stakeout on their lawn. It's actually reassuring. They don't want the story to die.

Sue struggled with a learning disability to become an art teacher. She says she suffers from auditory dyslexia: sometimes words and conversations get mixed up in her mind. This appears to contribute to her disjointed manner of speaking. She flits from topic to topic, her ideas connecting at right angles instead of in straight lines.

Her mind is open to signs; she heeds the vibrations of intuition.

The close relationship between Sue and the *Post* lasted another decade.

CHILDREN

On August 27 Chad Condit appeared on CNN's *Larry King Live*.

LARRY KING: You were going to run for the assembly, right?

CHAD CONDIT: I was thinking about running for the assembly. I was really torn, because I enjoyed my job with the governor so much. But this has, you know; if this is what public service is about, I don't—I don't know that I would want any part of it.

. . .

KING: What has it been like for the—for the family?

CHAD: [I]t's been real tough. It's been hard on mom, dad, Cadee and I, and the entire family. But the Levy family's pain and grief and suffering, we just can't imagine that. So from that standpoint, our pain doesn't measure . . . When folks start calling my dad a murderer or suggesting my mom and dad had something to do with the disappearance, that's too much, too far, unfair, and it's wrong. And somebody has got to say enough is enough.

. . .

KING: But I mean, how did you feel about the relationship aspect, when you heard about that?

CHAD: . . . I didn't feel one way or the other . . . [T]he family knows the details of the relationship. We have chosen not to go on the national news or the Connie Chung show and discuss those details. Out of respect for Gary's family, he's chosen to do that. And I think that's fair and that's the right thing to do. And by the way, it's the gentlemanly thing to do . . .

KING: [C]ertainly he contributed to his dilemma. Whether that's right or not, whether it's PR or not, or whether that's what media is, it is what it is. And the media, once they became hounds on this . . .

CHAD: I don't think that until you go through something like this you really know. But when the media points a finger at you, boy; God bless the folks that have to go through it. And I'm learning and our family is learning about that now. So—maybe we could have picked a different PR strategy. I don't know. Is this is what this is about, a PR strategy? We're convicting Gary Condit over a PR strategy?

. . .

KING: [H]e played a part in it though, didn't he?

CHAD: In what?

KING: In the way this has been handled, by not coming forward. He came forward to the authorities by not coming forward to the public . . .

CHAD: To the media?

KING: Yes.

CHAD: So the media has a role in it?

KING: Sure, don't they?

CHAD: Well, if that's where we're at in American history, I have to come here and talk to you, that the media needs to be involved in every part our life if they want to be, when they want to be, then maybe we ought to, you know, analyze where we are at.

KING: This is a puzzling case, you will agree. Police all over America say that they never can remember a case that has apparently no leads.

CHAD: Right. And every time the police catch heat, all they have to do, because of the environment the media has created, is point the finger at Gary Condit.

⌐

The next morning, Chad and Cadee Condit entered Governor Gray Davis's office in Sacramento.

"I have something for you," Cadee said, handing the governor a letter.

> Dear Governor,
>
> The Condits are a very proud and loyal family—not only in the good times, but also during the darkest hours. You may remember our father's strong public support, endorsement and organizational efforts for you during the bleakest moments of your 1998 primary campaign. It is that kind of loyalty to friends that has been the hallmark of his career and is a standard we strive to live up to . . . Therefore, we respectfully submit our resignation effective immediately.

That night, Governor Davis called Cadee.

"If you ever want to come back, you're welcome here," he said.

"I'm completely disheartened. He's always been loyal to you," she responded.

"If you ever want to come back you have a place," Governor Davis reiterated.

"I'll never work for you again."

⌐

On September 5, one week after she resigned from the governor's office, Cadee Condit appeared on *Larry King Live*.

KING: When you first learned of all this, were you curious about Chandra?

. . .

CADEE: [W]e sat down as a family and talked about it . . . [A]nd I'm OK with my dad. My dad and I have been good friends and we're going to remain that way. With the twenty-four-year-old thing, you know, people have said that we're close in age. I'm a grown woman, and anyone close to my age can make decisions for herself.

. . .

KING: How has your mom done?

CADEE: She is an amazing woman.

. . .

KING: And if anything, she forgave?

CADEE: If anything, she's standing right by him, yes.

KING: That's an awful lot of credit to a person, to be able to do that in the face of what has become public humil—your dad has been . . .

CADEE: Humiliated.

. . .

KING: Do you date?

CADEE: I'm not here to talk about my personal life.

. . .

KING: So, your mother doesn't have a violent temper, and didn't throw things.

CADEE: My mom can calm me with her voice or with her touch. There's nothing violent about Carolyn Condit.

. . .

KING: You know, there are all those stories, there's a million . . . stories about your father, and they all regard women. And that, that rolls off you?

CADEE: Well, it pretty much rolls off of me, but I'm ashamed of a man or a woman that would sell stories, true or not true, to tabloids, in the time of a crisis.

. . .

KING: How is your father doing? We got no indication of that in the Connie Chung interview as to how he's doing.

CADEE: Totally different guy. He's heartbroken.

KING: Lines coming where they weren't there before?

CADEE: Uh-huh. And I'm really sad that my kids might not get to meet the Gary Condit that raised me.

KING: How do you mean?

CADEE: You know, I don't know if we'll ever get the twinkle back.

KING: Oh, really?

CADEE: It's just unbelievable how much this has changed him.

KING: Yeah, that's—there was a twinkle?

CADEE: That's right.

KING: But this is something new to us, we didn't see this.

CADEE: My dad loves life. He loves to go to my nephew, his grandkids' Little League games. He loves to work out in the backyard, your regular stuff, and that's just been sucked out of him. And he can't go to Little League games anymore because he'd be followed.

. . .

KING: Well, what we don't know is the real Gary Condit that you've described.

CADEE: He's a great guy.

. . .

KING: We don't know.

CADEE: Unfortunately.

KING: And that point, don't you think we should?

CADEE: I think that people shouldn't believe everything they read and they see on the news.

SUICIDE

Roger Chiang ascended the stairway at the front of the Metro Police headquarters building.

"What are you going to say to Chief Gainer today?" a reporter asked as he passed. Terrance Gainer had deflected assertions that there might be a connection between Joyce Chiang's disappearance and Chandra's disappearance by suggesting Joyce committed suicide.

Roger had met with Chief Ramsey twice over the summer to discuss Gainer's statements. Both times Ramsey assured Roger that Joyce's case was still an open homicide investigation. And shortly after each meeting, Gainer publicly suggested Joyce had committed suicide.

Roger didn't want the suicide angle to become the final verdict on his sister's life. But Gainer refused to meet with him. He felt his only option was to file a formal complaint with the inspector general alleging misconduct by Gainer. Less than twenty-four hours after Roger filed that complaint, Gainer requested a meeting to discuss their "differences."

"I'm going to ask him to review the evidence the FBI has in my sister's murder case," Roger replied as he entered the building.

The meeting between Roger and Gainer was short, but Roger felt good about its outcome. Gainer promised that the Metro Police would reexamine the evidence in Joyce's disappearance, and would refrain from further statements suggesting she killed herself.

Roger exited the building just as Chief Ramsey finished up a press conference on DUI crackdowns. Gainer joined Ramsey as Roger passed.

"Chief Ramsey, what was discussed with Roger Chiang?" a reporter asked.

Gainer intercepted the question. "It is difficult to hear, and I'm sure the family doesn't like to hear the truth, but as I explained to the brother, at this juncture, we have to conclude that his sister committed suicide. It's the position we've maintained all along."

Reporters scrambled to where Roger stood.

"How was your meeting with Gainer?"

"What did Chief Gainer tell you?" Roger replied.

"He said your sister committed suicide and you need to learn to accept that."

"This morning I met with Chief Gainer, and I shared with him some of the evidence I know the FBI has in my sister's murder case. The FBI maintains that my sister was murdered."

Roger then ran through the litany of facts that pointed to Joyce being murdered instead of killing herself, including her torn jacket, DNA evidence, and the anonymous message written on the brick wall behind the Starbucks in Dupont Circle where she was last seen.

WORST DAY

The September 11 edition of the *Washington Post* declared: **GRAND JURY RULES OUT INVESTIGATION OF CONDIT.**

With the support of Judicial Watch, Anne Marie Smith and her attorney, Jim Robinson, had filed a citizen's complaint against Gary, Mike Lynch, and Don Thornton alleging they were guilty of criminal conspiracy and subornation of perjury. A grand jury in Stanislaus County needed little time with the actual evidence to conclude the allegations that had been pursued by Smith and the US Attorney's Office and debated by the media for more than two months had no merit.

At 7:59 a.m., American Airlines Flight 11 left Logan International Airport bound for Los Angeles.

The September 11 edition of the *National Enquirer* announced: "Former mistress drops bombshell: Condit's plan to get rid of body. She'll tell all to the FBI—that Condit had a step by step operation in place to remove and hide his own corpse if he were to die while having sex in hotel room!"

At 8:14 a.m., United Airlines Flight 175 left Logan International Airport bound for Los Angeles.

The September 11 edition of *Star* screamed: "Condit Wife's Agony—she trashes home and destroys their family photos—her suicide threat over Chandra—how he brainwashed her for 34 years!"

At 8:20 a.m., American Airline Flight 77 departed from Dulles International Airport bound for Los Angeles. Barbara Olson was one of fifty-eight passengers on board.

The September 11 edition of the *Globe* proclaimed: "Condit's Lies Exposed—now he faces arrest. Body language betrays cold, scary robot. Voice stress test nails Congressman!"

At 8:42 a.m., United Airlines Flight 93 departed Newark International Airport, bound for San Francisco.

Gary sat on his black leather couch, eating cereal. The smell of cigarettes generated by reporters camped on Adams Mill Road snuck in through the open window.

At 8:46 a.m., American Airlines Flight 11 raced low across New York City's skyline and slammed into the north tower of the World Trade Center. Flames engulfed the top portion of the building.

At 8:49 a.m., CNN replaced headlines about Gary and Chandra with "World Trade Center disaster."

The phone rang.

Gary walked to the kitchen and answered it.

"You got on the TV?" Dayton said.

"You know I don't watch TV," Gary replied.

"You need to. We're under attack."

Gary moved back to the living room and flipped on the television.

At 9:41 a.m., a man jumped from near the top of the north tower of the World Trade Center into smoke billowing upward in a black mushroom cloud.

Gary ran back to the kitchen and called Carolyn.

"Carolyn, the kids, they're in New York." Chad and Cadee were in the city to conduct interviews on morning news shows.

"They're OK," Carolyn assured him.

By 11:00 a.m., Gary felt trapped in the small apartment. He took the stairs to the bottom floor of the Lynshire, opened the front door, and stepped outside.

Fall had knocked leaves onto the sidewalk.

There were no voices.

There were no cameras or news vans.

Even the reporters had vanished; the only evidence of their prior persistent presence was the trash that littered Adams Mill Road.

PART IV
JUDGMENT

CHAPTER 18

HORSE WHISPERER

CRIMES

On September 17, Halle Shilling selected a photo of Ingmar Guandique from an array and told investigators she believed he was the man who attacked her four months earlier in Rock Creek Park.

The lawyer for Ramon Alvarez, a prison-mate of Guandique's, called the US Attorney's Office and told them Guandique had confessed to his client that he murdered Chandra Levy.

On September 21, US Marshals transported Guandique from his prison cell to the US Attorney's Office. After months of ignoring the lead given to them by the Park Police in July, investigators interviewed Guandique, for the first time, in connection with the investigation into Chandra Levy's disappearance.

Detectives Ralph Durant and Lawrence Kennedy and an assistant US attorney put a picture of Chandra in front of Guandique.

Guandique insisted he had only seen Chandra before on television.

He was sent back to jail.

HAMBURG

September turned to October.

On October 2, *Vanity Fair* published Dominick Dunne's latest "diary" on high society. In it, Dunne described Gary as a pervert, hypocrite, and liar. Dunne's diary also referenced LeBoutillier's e-mail, described as follows: "The [LeBoutillier] letter depicted a sexual lifestyle so unsavory that I could not embarrass this magazine by repeating it. The only thing I actually believed in the story was the description of how Chandra disappeared because I had arrived at a similar theory myself."

Dominick Dunne received a telephone call from a literary agent he knew well.

The agent had received "the damnedest" call from a guy in Hamburg, Germany.

The man in Hamburg had just visited the Middle East, where he learned information concerning Chandra Levy that he desperately wanted to pass to Dunne.

"Get him on the line!" Dunne told the agent.

Ten minutes later, Dunne received a call from Germany.

"Mr. Dunne," the man on the other end said. "I'd like to discuss the missing intern."

"Who are you?"

"I'm a horse whisperer. My name is Monty Roberts."

Roberts explained that he broke in horses for high-net-worth owners.

"Like the Robert Redford movie?" Dunne replied.

"Well, yes. But that is my story. Not the romantic part of the story. But what happened between Redford and the wounded horse was my story and I told it to the author of the book."

"Where are you calling from?" Dunne asked.

"Hamburg."

"Germany?"

"Yes. But I'm originally from Salinas, California. I'm American."

"That's Gary Condit's district?"

"No, but it's the same area," Roberts explained. "Can you take this in confidence?"

"Yes," Dunne confirmed.

"And I want you to promise you won't give anyone my name."

"I promise."

"All right."

"But can I refer to you as the horse whisperer?"

"Of course."

"What do you want to discuss?"

"I work in the Middle East. The sheikhs are big on horses. I work for the Sheikh Mohammed of Dubai. He has the largest racing stable in the world, on par with the Queen of England. Right now I'm in Germany because I'm at the horse farm of a rich German. But I was just in Dubai, three days ago. And I ran into a man who is a procurer of women."

"What?"

"He procures young women for the nocturnal pleasures of high-ranking men in the Middle East," the horse whisperer explained. "This concerns Congressman Condit."

"How so?"

"This procurer of women, well, he's a big man. His German isn't good, but he speaks English without an accent. Well, the point is, he procures women for powerful men. He does this in the Middle East, but also at embassies, including in Washington, DC."

"How could he get prostitutes into the United States?" Dunne asked.

"They don't get checked. These are young women mostly from the Philippines. Late teen-agers and so forth. When they come into Washington, DC, they come in diplomatically, so they just come into the country like that. The procurer, he has a commercial-sized private jet."

"Well yeah, he's very powerful," Dunne answered.

"Exactly," the horse whisperer concurred. "This procurer, he only runs in the highest circles. His clients pay a premium to keep this quiet."

"Condit uses this procurer?"

"He goes to Middle Eastern embassies in Washington, DC. The procurer has these late teenage girls, who are sex slaves, flown in for him. The procurer told me Mike Dayton goes with him."

"They treat him like a chauffeur," Dunne cut in.

"Well, yeah, but he also gets to partake in the young pussy, too."

"Do you know Gary Condit?"

"I don't personally know Mr. Condit. But we all knew who he was before Condit went to Washington," the horse whisperer answered.

"How did Condit get mixed up with Middle Eastern embassies?"

"I'm not sure. But he's on the Intelligence Committee. A lot of people don't realize how powerful Condit is. That's how he's gotten away with having this double existence."

"How did you meet the procurer of women?" Dunne asked.

"At a party in Dubai. The procurer, he's an Arab, I'd been brushing by him for the last three or four years in the Middle East. We'd see each other. I knew who he was and he knew who I was. He's an upper-class Arab around forty years old. Everyone knew he was a procurer."

"What was he wearing?"

"He wears Savile Row clothes. Occasionally, he wears a dishdasha. That's the Arab thing with the veil on the head. This is a sophisticated man, who moves in powerful circles."

This man has incredible detail about the procurer! Dunne thought. "Why did the procurer bring this to you?"

"He came up to me at the party and said, 'Where are you from, are you from Salinas, California?'" the horse whisperer continued. "And I said, 'Yeah, I am.' And he said, 'Do you know Dominick Dunne?' And I said, 'No, but I know who he is.'"

"What do I have to do with this?" Dunne interjected.

"The procurer, he said you had a theory about how Chandra disappeared on the back of a motorcycle."

"That's right!"

"He said he videotaped you on the Larry King show saying that you thought she had gone off on the back of a motorcycle driven by the Hells Angels or something and been taken elsewhere and taken care of," the horse whisperer explained. "He said, 'Dominick Dunne is wrong. That's not how it happened. I know how it happened.'"

"Did the procurer tell you what he thinks happened to her?" Dunne inquired.

"He told me that Condit let it be known to his Arab friends that his relationship with Chandra was over. But she was a clinger."

"I heard that from Lisa DePaulo," Dunne said. "Apparently Chandra was into older men and had some older boyfriends before Condit. And she was a bit of a clinger."

"That's right. But here, she's dealing with a powerful man who is surrounded by these young women and powerful Arabs. He told them he couldn't get rid of Chandra, and that he made promises to her he couldn't keep."

"That's what the aunt is saying."

"Who?"

"Chandra's aunt. She told the *Washington Post* the same thing; that Condit promised to run off with her and so on and so forth."

"The procurer, he said Condit told his friends that she knew things about him, and threatened to go public. And at one point, while he's in this embassy, you know, in these sex parties, Condit told them that Chandra was driving him crazy or words to that effect."

Dunne wrote furiously, trying to take down everything he was hearing from the horse whisperer in Hamburg.

"Condit, you see," the horse whisperer continued, "he created the environment that led to her disappearance. Shortly after he said all this to his Arab friends, she vanished. It is very easy for them to make people disappear."

"How did she disappear?" Dunne asked, mesmerized.

"The procurer told me that she was put in a limousine, and that he saw her being put on a private plane, on one of those big commercialized private planes that the Arabs have, rich princes, and those people."

"A limousine?"

"That's where you were wrong, he said. He said, 'Dominick Dunne's theory about the motorcycles and Hells Angels isn't correct. It was a limousine and rich Arabs.'"

"Where did they take her?"

"Let me put it this way: she wasn't walking."

"Not walking! Was she on a stretcher?" Dunne responded.

"No, no, no. He said she was upright; but she was surrounded by five men. There were two in front of her, two on each side of her, and they were moving her along. But her feet weren't actually touching the ground. The procurer, well, he thought she had been drugged. She was not dead. But, that's what he could see."

"He actually saw this happen?"

"Yes."

"What do you think happened to her?"

"She was dropped at sea. Over the Atlantic."

THE PROCURER

On October 7, Dunne wrote a letter to Graydon Carter, the editor of *Vanity Fair*, in which Dunne relayed the story he had heard from the horse whisperer.

The letter read, in part: "Girls were provided for him as well as for his assistant Mike Dayton who was the one who drove Condit to Virginia to throw away the watch box. Apparently Condit was in pig heaven with all the fresh young pussy."

Dunne tried calling the FBI, but he could only get through to an automated message machine. The FBI was busy investigating the 9/11 attacks.

Still, Dunne felt the significance of the horse whisperer's story warranted talking directly with a warm body. He called *Vanity Fair*'s lawyers, and they gave him two phone numbers for the FBI. Dunne called both numbers but he still couldn't get through.

He next called US senator Chris Dodd. Dodd passed Dunne to an aide in his DC office.

"Mr. Dunne, how do you know this story is true?" Dodd's aide asked.

"Well, I am not sure it is true. But I think it bears investigation."

"Mr. Dunne, we're not in a position to get involved with this."

"Somebody in the FBI ought to hear this!" Dunne demanded, "pissed" at Dodd's aide for blowing him off.

Dunne next called Maureen Orth, an investigative journalist for *Vanity Fair*. Dunne told her the horse whisperer's story and asked whether Orth or her husband, NBC newsman Tim Russert, could help.

"Oh yeah," Orth replied. "Tim's got contacts there."

Her contacts at the FBI also proved to be a dead end.

In his frustration, Dunne recalled his earlier conversations with Susan Levy and the man Dunne believed was investigating the Levy disappearance for the FBI—Jerry Gruner.

On October 14, Dunne called Gruner and relayed the horse whisperer's story.

"Mr. Dunne, we are very interested in this story. We have no idea what happened to Chandra. We'd like to talk to this horse whisperer."

"I promised the horse whisperer that I would not use his name," Dunne answered.

"Can we use you to find out more information?" Gruner replied.

"Well, yeah. I don't see why not."

Gruner sent Dunne a list of eleven questions he wanted him to ask the horse whisperer.

Dunne contacted the horse whisperer the same day. He answered most of the questions, but he would not answer the most important one. As Dunne later explained, "He would not tell me the name of the procurer. And, you know, I got all the languages he speaks. I got how his beard is only one-eighth of an inch. I got all this stuff. He dresses in English clothes and speaks better English without an accent."

Dunne called Gruner to report back on the outcome of his mission.

"Mr. Dunne, will you come to Washington, DC, and meet with me and the legal team?" Gruner asked.

"Absolutely."

"Can you come tomorrow?"

"Yes."

"You understand that our discussions are to be kept confidential."

"Of course."

"Don't fly. I want you to take a train," Gruner instructed.

On October 15, at 8:00 a.m., Dunne stepped off the train and onto a platform at DC's Union Station.

Jerry Gruner waited for him in the main hall.

Gruner, dressed in plain clothes, led Dunne outside, and the two men got into Gruner's Jaguar sedan.

"This is a very nice car," Dunne said.

"After two years, the company sells the cars," Gruner explained. "The agents buy them."

Dunne assumed he meant the FBI had a fleet of luxury Jaguar cars and allowed its agents to purchase them at the end of their two-year service life.

Gruner drove Dunne to Rock Creek Park. The two men walked through the park, with Dunne speaking candidly and casually about his views on Gary and Chandra. Gruner asked Dunne a lot of questions but said little about himself.

According to Dunne, Gruner confirmed for him that people they called "strap hangers" fly into the United States on planes and enter the country without actually going through customs. Dunne believed it confirmed the horse whisperer's story that Arab diplomats were sneaking young prostitutes into DC embassies.

That afternoon the two men joined partners from Bill Martin's law office in a room at the Watergate complex. Martin was in another city, but called in to hear Dunne's story.

"Mr. Dunne, if you could walk us through what you've learned," one of the lawyers asked. Dunne walked them through his contact with the horse whisperer.

Gruner asked Dunne if he'd go to England to check the story out.

"When?" Dunne replied.

"Right away. The Dewhurst Stakes horse race is in just a few days. The race is sponsored by Dubai. The fifth race is called the Dubai Stakes."

"Do you think the procurer will be there?" Dunne asked.

"Yes," Gruner answered. "He has a liking for eleven-year-old girls. The procurer will be there."

"How do you know all of that? I mean, this is like overnight?" Dunne inquired.

"We have people everywhere," Gruner replied. "And my wife, she's CIA."

"Oh, wow," Dunne replied.

Dunne continued assuming Gruner was an active FBI agent. It's what Susan Levy had told him, and everything he saw and heard during his one-day trip to Washington seemed to confirm it.

It didn't surprise Dunne when Gruner let slip that his wife was in the CIA. It was also true; she was a career intelligence officer.

Mr. Gruner, however, had not been forthright about his own background. Based on public records, Gruner wasn't with the FBI. If Jerry Gruner is the same "JK Gruner" of "JK Gruner & Associates" then, like his wife, Anne, he was a career CIA agent.

Jerry "Jay K" Gruner spent thirty-three years in foreign intelligence operations for the CIA, rising to the top ranks of the clandestine services. He had served as the CIA's station chief for key countries in Latin America, Western Europe, and Eastern Europe. His time with the CIA in Latin American coincided with the Iran-Contra affair.

In 1991, Gruner's identity was leaked to the public by a member of the Senate Intelligence Committee. The *New York Times* covered the matter with a story dated July 18, 1991, and titled **SENATOR'S SLIP COSTS CLOAK-AND-DAGGER AGENT THE REST OF HIS CLOAK.** It read:

. . . Mr. Boren's widely quoted remark would curtail, if not end, the overseas career of the officer, Jay K. Gruner, a former Latin America division chief who has been chief of the C.I.A. station in a European capital for about two years . . .

After retiring from the CIA, Gruner became a member of the Surveys and Investigations Staff of the House Committee on Appropriations. After that, he went into private practice.

"Mr. Dunne, are you up for it?" Gruner asked.

"Absolutely. I'll book a flight for London right away," Dunne answered. "But how will I get in touch with the procurer?"

"He'll find you."

Gruner stood and walked to the phone. "I'm also going to put a call into a friend in London named Simon Stokes. I've worked with him on cases before. He's with MI6."

As soon as the meeting ended, Dunne called *Vanity Fair*'s management to confirm the magazine would cover the expenses of his trip to England to try and lure the procurer of young women into speaking with him.

According to Dunne, *Vanity Fair* was "thrilled to do so."

D. DUNNE'S "WAD"

Dunne's first order of business when he arrived in London was to contact Simon Stokes. According to Dunne, Stokes arranged for "someone from MI6" to accompany Dunne on his trip to Newmarket.

Dunne arrived in Newmarket before the start of the Dubai Stakes race. He had dressed "nattily" so that he would stand out. He didn't want the procurer to miss him.

When he arrived at the Rowley Mile racetrack, Dunne started looking for groups of rich Arabs. He floundered about the promenade, asking people, in particular Arab-looking people, if they knew of "the procurer." Nobody knew what he was talking about.

Perhaps I've been hoodwinked, he thought.

Dunne tried calling the horse whisperer, many times. Based on their prior telephone discussions, he believed the man would be at the race and was staying at the Rutland Arms Hotel. Each time Dunne called the hotel, the receptionist informed him that Monty Roberts was not in.

At 5:00 a.m., the telephone in his hotel room rang.

"What are you calling me for?" Roberts spat into the receiver.

"The procurer wasn't at the race!" Dunne shouted.

"What race?" the horse whisperer replied.

"I went to the Dubai Stakes, to find the procurer."

"Why are you in London? You'll be murdered!"

"Listen, all I want from you is the name of the procurer. That is all I need."

"I don't know his name," the horse whisperer admitted.

"I don't believe you. You've told me too many facts about him. You know too much about him."

"I met him once. I met him on a plane."

"You said you met him at a party in Dubai," Dunne responded.

"I'll get murdered."

"Look, Monty, I'm going to the FBI and I'm going to give them your name and I'm going to let them come after you because you know somebody who has information about this woman."

"Keep me out of this. You agreed to keep me out of this!"

"Just give me the name of the procurer of women!" Dunne demanded.

"I don't know the name!"

"You're a fucking liar!" Dunne screamed.

—

Later that morning, Dunne called Simon Stokes and told him about his early morning discussion with the horse whisperer.

"What time did you say he called you?" Stokes asked.

"5:00 a.m.," Dunne replied.

"No, it was at 4:48 a.m."

"How do you know that?"

"We've got the records at the Rutland Arms. At 5:00 a.m. the horse whisperer had a call from a driver, who was waiting to take him to Heathrow. You must have really scared him because he went back and made ten calls from the hotel after he spoke with you."

Dunne left the discussion believing MI6, working with the FBI, was wiretapping his exchanges with a horse whisperer from Hamburg Germany about a procurer of women from the Middle East.

—

As soon as Dunne returned from London he called Jerry Gruner and informed him that he had failed to find the procurer.

Gruner asked for the horse whisperer's phone number, and Dunne gave it to him.

"I'm not sure what I'll write about this story," Dunne explained.

"Be very careful what you write," Gruner warned.

A few days later, Dunne followed up, eager to find out what Gruner learned from the horse whisperer.

Gruner was guarded.

"Mr. Dunne, Monty Roberts is very upset with you. He is very annoyed that you tried to call him twenty times while you were in England."

"He's a liar. I only tried to call him eight times."

"Well, he doesn't like you."

"What did he say?" Dunne asked.

Gruner refused to talk with Dunne about the horse whisperer.

"Mr. Gruner, this is my story. I brought it to you," Dunne insisted.

"We are very grateful. But I have no obligation to you."

The call was curt.

Dunne felt "frozen out" by a man he still believed was with the FBI, and who had actually been one of the country's top CIA spies.

As Dunne later reflected, "Once Jerry Gruner talked to the horse whisperer he distanced himself from me . . . I mean, I had given him my wad, and he had nothing else to get from me."

CHAPTER 19

SENTENCING

RUNNING

MIKE LYNCH DIDN'T THINK GARY should run for reelection. It'd be difficult to fund-raise and impossible to get endorsements. After settling legal bills, Gary's campaign funds had shrunk from $315,000 to $72,000.

The polls were also bad, like nothing insiders had ever seen.

Gary's approval rating was still nearly 70 percent, yet nearly 60 percent of voters felt it would be a "bad idea" for Gary to run.

On October 23, Democratic state assemblyman Dennis Cardoza formally announced his candidacy for Gary's congressional seat. Gary had given Cardoza his start in politics, first as a driver on one of Gary's campaigns and then as a staff member in his office.

"I don't believe Congressman Condit is electable at this point. I have nothing but the best regard for the Condit family," Cardoza told reporters when announcing that he'd challenge Gary in the Democratic primary.

When asked by a *Los Angeles Times* reporter about Cardoza's decision to run, an unnamed top Democratic Party strategist answered: "It's a big, fat hint to Condit: don't run."

—

On November 6, the US Attorney's Office—led by AUSAs Roscoe Howard and Roderick Thomas—issued a formal grand jury subpoena to Gary demanding his telephone message slips, calendars, and other office-related documents.

Grand juries conduct investigations in secret. For most Americans, that means the subpoena remains private until the grand jury determines whether it will move forward with criminal charges.

For members of Congress, this is not the case.

House Rule VII states that congressional members who receive a properly served subpoena "shall promptly notify the Speaker of its receipt in writing. Such notification shall promptly be laid before the House by the Speaker."

As required, Gary sent a letter to Speaker of the House Dennis Hastert notifying him that his office had received a subpoena for Gary's records.

On November 15, the House clerk rose and read Gary's statement out loud, into the public record.

The next morning, Allan Lengel's latest article in the *Washington Post* flew off the presses: CONDIT RECEIVES FEDERAL SUBPOENA.

The scandal had nearly bankrupted Gary. Abbe Lowell would have represented him in any event, but was in the middle of a trial in New York. As a favor to the family, defense attorney Mark Geragos agreed to represent Gary in connection with the grand jury request.

Geragos advised Gary that the subpoena was not necessary because Gary had already given the federal government the records demanded under the subpoena.

Gary disagreed. *This isn't about the law. This is about finishing me off.*

As reported by the Capitol Hill newspaper, *Roll Call*: "Just three weeks before he must decide whether to seek reelection, Condit was forced to publicly link himself to a word dreaded by every elected politician: subpoena."

DECISIONS

Ingmar Guandique sat in a chair with wires attached to his body.

"Were you involved in Chandra Levy's disappearance?" the polygraph examiner asked.

"No," Guandique answered.

The raw data produced by the polygraph examination were deemed "INCONCLU-SIVE." The polygraph examiner, however, interpreted the inconclusive results based on his impression of Guandique. The official result of the polygraph examination was then deemed "NOT DECEPTIVE."

Years later, reporters for the *Washington Post* defended the polygraph examiner's use of discretion to clear Guandique by pointing to the inadequacies of polygraph examinations, generally: "Polygraphs can be a useful law enforcement tool, but the results are not admissible in court because they are considered too unreliable."

It was a consideration the *Post* extended to Guandique that it had not extended to Gary, a member of Congress.

———

DC Superior Court judge Noel Kramer presided over Guandique's sentencing for his attacks on Shilling and Wiegand. The judge reviewed a copy of the presenting report, which read, in part:

> [I]t is quite clear that he is becoming more psychopathic in his behavior. The defendant appears to be targeting victims that can be overpowered, as well as carefully selecting the location of his crime to minimize the possibility of witnesses and his chances of getting caught . . . the defendant appears to be drawing some kind of satisfaction in attacking helpless victims.

Assistant US Attorney Kristina Ament proceeded with the prosecution's recommendation that Guandique be given a light sentence, notwithstanding the conclusions drawn in the presentencing report.

"Your honor, there is a matter we need to disclose before formally sentencing Mr. Guandique."

"What is it, counselor?" Judge Kramer asked.

"He has been a cooperative defendant," AUSA Ament replied. "He has been interviewed by detectives investigating the Chandra Levy case."

The Metro Police and the US Attorney's Office had taken great pains to hide from the public the fact that they had, finally, looked at Guandique in connection with the Levy investigation.

Guandique and the US Attorney's Office had made a deal. If Guandique cooperated and agreed to plead guilty to two counts of assault with intent to commit robbery, the government would take attempted murder charges off the table.

"He also passed a polygraph examination."

"In other words, there's no suggestion that he is involved in the Chandra Levy case?" Judge Kramer responded.

"There is no suggestion at this point, now, that he is involved," Ament answered. "And his polygraph went a long way in defusing the suggestion. He should receive credit for the fact he voluntarily did come in and submit to a polygraph examination in that case."

Guandique faced a maximum sentence of twenty-six years—thirteen years for each of the assaults on Shilling and Wiegand.

"I want to tell you something both candidly, on the record," Judge Kramer replied. "This is such a satellite issue. This is a serious case. I never for a moment thought that he had anything to do with Chandra Levy. Just to me it doesn't have anything to do with this case."

Shilling and Wiegand were given the opportunity to make victim statements.

Shilling went first. "I reject the notion that he intended to simply rob me. This attack was a physical one, pure and simple. He stalked me for a mile. He attacked me with a knife. He left my valuables on the path when he fled. I do not doubt for a second that, given the chance, he would repeat his crime against another woman. I would request that this person be given the harshest possible sentence for his crime and that he lose the privilege of living in this country."

Wiegand followed. "I don't think that he should be given the opportunity to do this to someone else or to do it to me again or do it to the other victim. So, I too, would ask that you award him the maximum sentence."

Judge Kramer then explained her view of the case. "There appears to be absolutely none of the indicia of a sexual assault . . . He went out of his way to struggle, to have a physical encounter with each of these women . . . So, I'm left to wonder, as we all wonder, what was really going on here?"

The US Attorney's Office had described Guandique as a predator, and yet had downgraded his crimes to assault with intent to rob and asked for lenient sentencing.

Judge Kramer acknowledged that the bare facts of the case showed Guandique had gone out of his way to physically assault each victim.

Yet, Kramer sentenced Guandique, an illegal immigrant, to a total of ten years in federal prison, well less than half the maximum twenty-six-year sentence requested by the two women he had brutally attacked.

In the process, the US Attorney's Office and Judge Kramer accepted Guandique's "INCONCLUSIVE" polygraph results to clear him of any involvement in Chandra Levy's disappearance. According to the *Washington Post*, AUSA Ament even apologized to Guandique for having to put him through the polygraph examination in order to clear him from the Levy case.

ANNOUNCEMENT

On December 7, 2001, at 4:00 p.m. Gary, Chad, and Cadee arrived at the courthouse, where a mob of reporters waited. The deadline for Gary to file for reelection was in an hour—at 5:00 p.m.

Gary woke up that morning still not sure if he was going to run. After some debate among the Condit family members, Gary concluded he had to do it even though he knew he'd likely lose. *As a private person I'm accountable to my wife and family. As a public person I'm accountable to my constituents. I have to face both of those judgments.*

The national press had returned to Condit Country to cover Gary's final act.

"I'm running," Gary announced.

"What about Chandra Levy?"

"You guys will have to decide if you're going to be fair to me or not and whether that's your main issue. I'm going to dwell on my record and what I've done for the valley and what I'm going to do for the future," Gary snapped back.

On December 12, the latest episode of the adult animated series *South Park* aired. In the episode, Gary Condit joins John and Patricia Ramsey and O.J. Simpson in the search for "some Puerto Rican guy" responsible for Chandra Levy's death.

Gary Condit—the cartoon character—is called a liar and a murderer.

—

Six candidates qualified to run in the Democratic primary. In addition to Gary and Dennis Cardoza, the field included a gas station manager from San Jose, a record producer from Los Angeles, a Sikh leader from the Central Valley, and a city councilman from Stockton.

Joseph Martin, the gas station manager, told reporters he decided to run because "the only requirement is that you live somewhere in the state."

Elvis Pringle, the record producer, hailed from Inglewood by way of Jamaica. He asked that people call him by his familiar name—Jah Elvis. His platform was built on two pillars. The first, running against "the Man's racism." The second, building a space flight center in the Central Valley. When asked why he hadn't run for Congress in Los Angeles, Jah Elvis answered: "They don't have room for a space center."

Jah Elvis had competition for control of the future space caucus. Republican candidate Park Yonker ran on his own intergalactic platform calling for the colonization of the moon and the removal of Gary Condit from earth.

Dr. Sukhmander "Sukhi" Singh had lived in the Central Valley for three decades. Dr. Singh was the former president of the Sikh Council of North America.

Ralph White had been involved in Stockton politics for over thirty years. He spent sixteen of those years on the Stockton City Council.

The primary election was shaping up to be a big spectacle. As described by the *San Francisco Chronicle*:

Condit karma has brought the quiet Central Valley unwanted attention, embarrassment and a strange cast of intertwined characters worthy of a Robert Altman film. First came Fox News and all the rest with their beach chairs and North Face jackets lined up on the sidewalk. Then came the interlopers, the sweet-sounding San Jose gas station manager and the Los Angeles record producer turned space station dreamer challenging Condit for reelection. Even the Klu Klux Klan showed up in the valley again.

THEORIES

On December 20, Dominick Dunne was a guest on the *Laura Ingraham Show*—a syndicated radio talk show billed as "Your Healthy Radio Addiction."

DUNNE: I publicly wrote and said on both of Geraldo's shows and on the Larry King show that I had
a theory . . . that as Condit rode with motorcycle gangs and so forth, that it was perfectly possible
that she vanished from Washington on the back of a motorcycle.

LAURA INGRAHAM (HOST): A Hells Angels situation.

DUNNE: This guy calls me . . . He said, "I am a horse whisperer." And I said, oh. And he said,
"I spend most of my life in the Middle East or may deal with my life in the Middle East." He said
that he works for the Sheikh Mohammad of Dubai, who indeed has the largest racing stable in
the world, you know, on a par with the Queen of England.

INGRAHAM: A horse situation.

DUNNE: Now the man was an upper-class Arab, forty years old, approx, and moved in high circles,
but he was a *procurer*.

INGRAHAM: What do you mean?

DUNNE: He provided women for the nocturnal pleasures of high-ranking people in the Middle East as
well as the Middle Eastern embassy in Washington . . .

INGRAHAM: The pimp had a videotape of you on Larry King?

DUNNE: That's right.

INGRAHAM: I call him a pimp. You call him a procurer . . .

DUNNE: Hooker booker is another one.

INGRAHAM: Exactly. That's a good one.

DUNNE: He apparently says Dominick Dunne is wrong. That's not how it happened. I know how it
happened. Now, some of this I can't explain and I don't want to get [in] any trouble saying.

INGRAHAM: Right.

Dunne then proceeded to rehash all the details of his horse whisperer story.

INGRAHAM: It was always my view, Dominick, that Condit himself wasn't the person who took her
out, but that he knew a lot of people. Whether it was the Hells Angels or another individual that he
just happened to make an offhand remark to, that that individual decided to take matters into his
own hands and get the job done.

DUNNE: Into his own hands, and therefore he can pass any lie detector test because he specifically
does not—I mean he does not know what specifically happened . . . I mean, I've always remembered the line of the procurer. He said he created the environment that led to her disappearance.

INGRAHAM: Yes. That just makes such beautiful sense.

Federal investigators chased Dunne's tip. The FBI obtained flight records of all private planes leaving Dulles airport, and agents were sent to interview employees of a company that flew from the DC area to the Middle East. After spending weeks investigating Dunne's story about the horse whisperer and a "hooker booker," federal authorities concluded it was false.

In Dunne's next *Vanity Fair* column, he wrote that he had accepted the invitation to appear on Laura Ingraham's show because he "felt like creating some trouble for Gary."

—

Dunne received a call from Champ Clark of *People* magazine.

Clark wanted to ask Dunne questions about Monty Roberts, the horse whisperer. Clark had managed to track down Roberts by posing as the horse whisperer online.

"I was hoodwinked," Dunne explained. "I just, he was so clear about meeting the procurer at the party in Dubai. And he had all these details."

"No. That's not where it happened," Clark interrupted.

"No, Champ, that's—what he has told you in his second version in which he said he met the procurer on a plane to Phoenix. The horse whisperer was just trying to distance himself from Dubai because it was the main source of his income . . . The Sheikh doesn't want Dubai tied up in a tacky story," Dunne responded.

"Condit still hasn't given over a name for the chiropractor he claims he visited on the day Chandra disappeared," Clark offered.

"Why aren't authorities all over that?"

The two men began speaking regularly.

—

On December 30, Dunne attended a dinner hosted by Wendy Stark at Trader Vic's in Los Angeles. Stark was the daughter of producer Ray Stark and a contributing editor of *Vanity Fair*.

Twenty-four other guests were in attendance, including actress Anjelica Huston and writer Gore Vidal.

Vidal gave an impassioned defense of Timothy McVeigh, calling him a patriot. The defense earned a mild if not cold response from the crowd of socialites.

Stark then asked Dunne to speak. Everyone wanted to hear more about the story Dunne had conveyed to Laura Ingraham about the horse whisperer and Gary "Condom."

Dunne recounted what the horse whisperer had told him, as well as his trip to England to try and locate the procurer.

Not a fork lifted.

When he was done storytelling, Dunne sat. Gore issued an Irish Catholic slur in Dunne's direction. Dunne took exception, and the longtime friends began hurling nasty words at one another.

After the party, Dunne and Gore engaged in a public exchange of barbs. Dunne wrote that Vidal's defense of McVeigh had been a colossal flop, whereas Dunne had held the room with his latest juicy scoop.

Chandra had been missing for approximately 244 days.

ENDORSEMENTS

As expected, the *Modesto Bee* not only endorsed Dennis Cardoza, it lashed out at Gary.

Lynch received calls from a number of elected officials stating they couldn't give Gary a formal endorsement for fear of retribution from the press.

Not everyone was afraid. California congresswoman Nancy Pelosi endorsed Gary. She and the handful of other prominent politicians who publicly backed Gary were criticized for doing so.

The *San Francisco Chronicle*—Pelosi's hometown newspaper—reported: "Pelosi's move could become an embarrassment to the Democrats—who want to play down Condit and his relationship with Levy."

As soon as he learned of Pelosi's endorsement, Gary went to see her, handing her a letter that read, in part: "I am grateful for the support of my colleagues in Congress over the last several months. Because I don't want debates of endorsements to distract from my ongoing discussions between my constituents and me, I am releasing those members who have endorsed me from their commitments. This election is about my 30 years of service to the voters of California's Central Valley and is a matter between my constituents and me."

"I'm putting this letter out to everybody asking them not to endorse me. Including you," he explained.

"I've never had so much pressure in all my life in politics," Pelosi answered.

It was an ominous statement coming from her. She was elected to Congress in 1987 and, before that, had served on the Democratic National Committee and as the chairwoman of the California Democratic Party. Pelosi also came from a political family. She understood, as well as anybody, the pressures of elected office.

"I'm sorry for that," Gary replied.

"My brother told me that if I don't hang with you, there will be a day I regret that I didn't."

The mainstream media reported that members of Congress had "pulled" their endorsement of Gary.

Within its narrow worldview, the press had won.

In the world of real people, loyalty had carried the day.

—

Lynn Dickerson, the publisher of the *Modesto Bee*, was expecting Chad Condit's visit. Her son had interned in Gary's DC office. Gary had given her son the phone number for his answering service and instructed the young man to call if he had any problems. When the internship was over, Dickerson sent Gary a letter thanking him for treating her son so well.

"Lynn, I'm not asking you to endorse him. All I'm asking is that you leave him and his supporters alone. It's not fair to attack people for endorsing Gary," Chad explained.

"That's not what we're doing," Dickerson replied.

"It's not news. He had nothing to do with it. People want to move on," Chad pressed.

"We disagree. People want to follow it," Dickerson replied. "Financially, the *Bee* is having its best year."

Chad got up to leave. He paused in the doorway, and turned to face Dickerson. "There's a hell for newspaper publishers. You'll be there."

⟿

Heaps of metal occupied the areas that once served as the bases for the World Trade Center's twin towers. It was mid-January, and a united resolve to answer our enemies now reigned over the wreckage of the worst attack on US soil ever.

Gary joined other members of the House Intelligence Committee standing in front of the wreckage.

"We need a photo," a staffer announced.

The members gathered in a line. California congresswoman Jane Harman took the center position, while Gary stood on the far right.

Shortly after the intel committee's visit to New York, Harman's office posted the photograph on her web page. Dayton brought a copy of it to Gary.

"They cut me out," Gary said.

Harman's office had cropped Gary from the photo of the intel committee members at ground zero.

She had her own reelection campaign to worry about.

SPACE CAUCUS

Yard signs in Condit Country read "We Decide! Not the Media! Re-Elect Gary Condit."

Gary stepped out of an SUV into a Starbuck's parking lot. As soon as he did, a tape recorder was shoved at his face, followed by television cameras and a volley of questions.

"I'm here to discuss issues that are important to California's Eighteenth Congressional District with the people who live here."

"One issue that is definitely important to voters is your credibility," a reporter replied.

Gary put a hand up and pushed past the press gaggle toward the entrance to the Starbucks.

"A lot of people think you lied to the Washington police," the reporter continued.

Gary looked for a friendly face. A bearded man smiled from underneath a ten-gallon cowboy hat. Gary moved in his direction.

"I have one question," the man in the ten-gallon hat said as he stepped toward Gary. "Where did you bury the body?"

Gary immediately recognized the thick brows and protruding eyes underneath the cowboy hat.

The man had aged. He had a beard, and had gained weight.

But Gary would never forget his evil eyes. *It's the Klansman.*

In the 1970s, the Ku Klux Klan announced its intention to burn a cross in Ceres as part of its ramped-up recruiting efforts in the Central Valley. Gary fought ferociously to keep them out. He met with the head of the KKK in the area and made it clear that "the KKK and its shit weren't wanted in Ceres."

Gary and the local Klansman had remained enemies for three decades.

"You're a joke," Gary fired back.

"No," the Klansman replied. "You're a joke."

Chad pulled Gary away from the Klansman before a punch was thrown in front of a dozen reporters.

That night, video footage of Gary arguing with the Klansman appeared on news telecasts, except the Klansman was described simply as a constituent in Gary's district.

—

Gary met supporters at a local restaurant. At the front of the restaurant, a group of eight protestors, including the Klansman, carried signs that read "Fire the Liar" and "Gary's Scary."

"We have not forgotten! Gary Condit's rotten!" the group chanted as he passed.

Just as Gary entered the restaurant a couple exited with their young daughter in tow.

"Oh my God—they brought children to this!" a protestor screamed.

The couple and the child hurried to their car.

"Gary might appreciate that!" a second protestor erupted.

The crowd howled.

While Gary met with constituents inside, a local reporter interviewed the Klansman and his brood.

"We've been demanding his resignation or expulsion from Congress," the Klansman said. "He's a liar—he knows where Chandra's body is at. I asked him this morning. I asked him where he buried the body."

The national news media picked up the interview with the Klansman. Neither the local nor national broadcasts of the interview made any mention of the man's affiliation with the KKK, even though it was well known in Condit Country who he was.

DEBATE

Gary, Carolyn, Chad, and Cadee Condit walked into the blue-and-white castle-like Assyrian Hall in Ceres. Gary took a seat on stage, followed by Dr. Sukhi Singh, Joseph Martin, and Ralph White. The candidates looked at one another, then at the empty seats on both ends of the long table. Dennis Cardoza and Jah Elvis were no-shows even though the debate had been scheduled weeks in advance.

"Cardoza is not gonna show," White said. "He's not going to debate you."

"Yeah, well, he knows I'd kick his ass. But what about Elvis?" Gary joked. "Anybody seen Elvis in here?"

Members of the press lined the back wall, with their cameras sitting on pedestals or shouldered. Audience members carried signs, many of which expressed angry views of Gary captured in cunning phrases.

The murmur of the packed room grew to a grumble as the clock sped past the scheduled start time.

"He talks about helping people—then where is he for the parents of Chandra Levy?" a man yelled, standing on his chair.

A woman stood in protest. "You don't know what you're talking about. You're just coming here to get on TV!"

"It took him four times to talk to the police!" the man screamed.

The crowd became angry and volatile.

"People, please calm down," the moderator implored.

Police officers moved from the back of the room into the crowd to prevent the situation from escalating into a physical confrontation between Gary's detractors and supporters.

Once calm was restored the moderator started the proceedings. Each candidate was given an opportunity to make a statement.

Martin, the gas station manager, went first. "Some people are up here—some people are down here. What about the lower people?"

As soon as the moderator announced Gary's name, raucous applause and rancorous booing erupted. It took the moderator many attempts to calm the crowd.

"This Eighteenth Congressional District will decide who they want to represent them. Not the East Coast pundits—not these cameras and all these news people," Gary began, pointing at the back wall. "But you folks—you decide if Gary Condit has worked hard for you—that's the mission—and I want to tell you I need your help. I will know who sends me to Congress. I will know it will be the people out in the streets—the people that live in these houses . . . A nation is watching this election."

~

On January 24, Casey Ribicoff, the widow of Connecticut politician Abraham Ribicoff and the doyenne of New York's high society, hosted an opulent dinner party for ten distinguished guests.

Dominick Dunne was on the list.

Joining him were advertising executive Peter Rogers, ABC news correspondent Cynthia McFadden, clothing designer Adolfo, fashion executive Helen O'Hagan, television producer Tommy Corcoran, fashion news editor Ellin Saltzman, media columnists Liz Smith and David Patrick Columbia, and a former United States senator and governor of Connecticut.

They dined, and talked about world affairs.

They drank, and gossiped.

"I've got this guy in Germany. Condit got her caught up in one of these Middle Eastern sex rings," Dunne projected.

Ribicoff and her guests listened—enthralled with the latest chin-wag.

On February 13, Dunne made another appearance on CNN's *Larry King Live*. Again, he relayed his story about the horse whisperer, the procurer, Gary, and Chandra.

He told King: "Condit is running again, and I think this should be brought up and brought up and brought up—and because I believe firmly that he knows more than what he has ever said."

~

Cardoza had ducked every debate.

"He won't show," Chad smirked.

"He'll stand up those kids at the community college but he's not foolish enough to thumb his nose at the League of Women Voters," Gary insisted.

Chad stopped the white Dodge Durango. The car doors opened.

"Monster! LIAR!"

The Klansman and his friends had been waiting for Gary's arrival.

Chad helped him push through the group of protestors. Once inside, Gary walked to where Cardoza sat. The two men shook hands. Lights flashed.

Each candidate was given the opportunity to state their core campaign platform.

Jah Elvis moved off of space shuttles to a simpler message. "Many people are ashamed to say that they are represented by Gary Condit."

Gary's supporters booed. The Klansman and his party snarled approvingly.

Cardoza followed. He talked about the energy crisis in California. "I'd work to lead the delegation of members that went to testify in Idaho before the Federal Energy Regulatory Commission. Because part of this problem was caused by the federal government not having a sheriff in town—we could've sure used some more congressional help during this energy fight last summer. But a lot of folks just weren't around."

Gary bit his lip.

Stockton councilman Ralph White interrupted Cardoza. "I'll bet you a dime against a penny—a dollar against a penny you won't find one thing in there that he used to work for Mr. Condit. You won't find in there that he worked for the congressman and that the congressman helped get him elected. That upsets me. Because you have to tell me the difference between Judas and Cardoza."

The crowd booed.

Gary leaned into his microphone. The crowd quieted. So too did the other candidates.

Gary started, "Each one of these men—with all due respect—will be a freshman, and they'll start from the beginning. Merced, Stanislaus, and Stockton deserve more than a freshman legislator. You want somebody effective, you send Gary Condit back to Congress."

Half of the room cheered, while the other half jeered.

When the debate ended, Chad and Cadee corralled Gary and they made for the front exit. Cadee stopped Gary as the doors opened. More than a hundred rabid protestors and reporters waited outside.

"Gary's rotten, we've not forgotten!" people screamed.

Cadee turned her father around.

"Out the back door!" a protestor yelled.

"You better run—you're the back door bandit!" another protestor squealed.

The protestors and reporters laughed.

"Scary Gary!" they chanted.

When Gary and his kids reached the back parking lot, they moved to a car waiting under a streetlight. They could hear the pounding of footsteps as the mob raced around the building to catch them.

As Chad closed the door to the car a reporter lobbed a question at him. "What are you hearing in the street? Are you hearing Chandra?"

"We're hearing you overreached," Chad replied, then slammed it shut.

—

In lieu of expensive campaign events, Gary's small team of supporters had scheduled sidewalk chats and visits to community centers. He spent his days inside retirement homes and standing at busy intersections waving at passing cars. People honked car horns, shouted words of encouragement, ridiculed him, and threw garbage at his feet.

Surprising politicos, recent polls showed Gary was closing the gap with Cardoza. Not enough to win, but enough so that the early indications Cardoza would trounce him weren't ringing true—particularly in the heart of Condit Country. The latest poll had Gary even with Cardoza in Stanislaus County, and not far behind in Merced County.

His problem was Stockton, where Cardoza held a double-digit lead. Gary had never represented Stockton. It was added to the Eighteenth Congressional District earlier that year, when district lines were redrawn by California's legislature.

In an ironic twist, Gary had helped the Democratic Party redraw his district so that it would be a safe blue seat. The party leadership had asked him to participate in the process, believing, like Gary, that he was likely headed to bigger things and without him the district would be difficult to hold onto because its voters were split almost evenly between Republicans and Democrats.

As Gary advised, adding Stockton—a solid blue area—fixed that.

HUMAN NATURE

On February 25, Gary appeared on *Larry King Live*.

KING: Did you have a relationship with Chandra Levy?

GARY CONDIT: You know, we're not going to go into that.

. . .

KING: I would imagine a person sitting at home hearing a question like that would say, "I'd say 'no' if it's no and I'd say 'yes' if it's yes. But when I say I'm not going to answer it, it means 'yes.'"

GARY: Yes, but there is a whole bunch of people sitting at home saying it's none of my business.

. . .

KING: You voted for the impeachment of President Clinton.

GARY: No. See, you're buying into the media.

KING: It was printed, yes.

GARY: [T]hat's echo journalism . . . But it just seems to me that people ought to focus on what this is. This is not a romantic novel. It's not some silly little game. It's not about people profiteering from a tragedy.

. . .

KING: What do fellow members of Congress say to you?

GARY: [T]here are a lot of members of Congress who would come up to me and, you know, before I made a decision to run and say, you got to run, and you got to win.

KING: Really?

GARY: Because if you don't, we'll never have a life . . . [T]here are no boundaries; they'll always be able to invade our lives.

. . .

KING: So you made a mistake with Anne Marie Smith, you owe it to your wife.

GARY: You owe it to your family, your wife, your church, your God . . . I mean, no disrespect to you, but you're not the church . . . It's not the place to do that, in my opinion . . .

KING: The other side would be: once the public hears something, it doesn't hurt sometimes to come forward, because you're human and people react.

GARY: Well, they know you're human. I mean, we're all human.

KING: Temptation is a thing in front of everybody every day.

. . .

GARY: There's a divine nature and there's a human nature, and they're always struggling with each other . . . There's no one who misses that, Larry. And so I—you know, but I think that probably where we have a little bit of a disagreement here is, I don't think it's appropriate in every case, every time you make a mistake in life, you don't have to call a news conference, even if you are elected. You don't owe that . . . [Y]ou should go to the person you made the mistake against, and that's who you should ask for forgiveness.

Gary held Carolyn in his arms.

"You did good, Gar," Carolyn said. "I can't believe it. All these people have come out to support you."

"We did our best," he answered, feeling that in the moment their dancing conveyed in silence all the thoughts he wanted his friends and family to know.

The banquet room was full of supporters, from all parts of Condit Country. They watched the couple move painlessly across the makeshift dance floor. An American flag covered one wall, and flowers were placed evenly on the tabletops.

"We did," Carolyn answered.

He backed a few inches from his wife, and they kissed, while friends and family cheered.

MARCH 5, 2002

On Acorn Lane, reporters sat in lawn chairs or inside pop-up tents. Garbage littered the ground.

Inside the Condit home friends and family had gathered in the living room. Adrian Condit led them in a long candlelight prayer.

They prayed for the strength to see the final election through.

They prayed for Chandra Levy and her parents.

"Gary's a fighter, Lord. And you've given him the spirit to keep fighting," Adrian said solemnly. "And we know he's fighting for good."

Gary looked over at his grandchildren. *This will follow those boys their whole lives. They'll know Condits don't run away.*

―

Carolyn and Jean put the finishing touches on a vat of homemade chili.

"Take some to the reporters," Carolyn said.

Burl Condit, Gary's cop brother, shot a hard look at his sister-in-law. "We're gonna feed them?"

"I still think we ought to turn the sprinklers on them," Jean Condit insisted.

"They've been out there all day," Carolyn replied. "They're not all bad."

Cadee volunteered to deliver the food.

Reporters jumped out of their seats when she appeared under the willow tree. She waved them over to the Condits' lawn.

"Is your dad with you inside?" a reporter asked.

"You think I'm going to tell you?"

"What kind of mood is he in?"

"Great mood—we're serving you chili," she replied, handing them a box containing individualized bowls of chili.

"Do you have any beer?" a reporter asked.

"Let me see what I can do," Cadee replied.

Cadee returned to the house. She found her mother still in the kitchen, with a concerned look on her face.

"Is there enough? We need to make more?" Carolyn, ever the homemaker, asked.

"Reporters asked for beer," Cadee laughed.

"We don't serve beer," Jean, ever the preacher's wife, interjected.

In the living room, Dayton asked Lynch whether results were coming in.

"It's closer than expected," Lynch responded.

Cardoza had 47 percent of the vote to Gary's 42.5 percent. The national news reports on the election for California's Eighteenth Congressional seat became more regular after the early numbers showed the surprisingly slim margin.

Dayton moved to the back wall and leaned against it. Carolyn came over to where he stood.

"Is it all over?" she asked.

"Not yet," he replied.

Friends and family sat patiently in front of the television. With 43 percent of the vote in, Gary went up by one hundred votes in Stanislaus County, but fell behind Cardoza by a thousand votes in Merced County, Cardoza's hometown. Then the numbers started to come in from Stockton, where Cardoza was outpacing Gary by a margin of two votes to one.

Gary could match and maybe even beat Cardoza in Condit Country, where the people knew him well. But he was going to get slaughtered in areas he hadn't represented before, where voters only knew Gary from what they had read in the recent press.

Within an hour it was clear Gary couldn't catch Cardoza. Gary retreated to his bedroom and changed into jeans and a purple fleece. Chad met him there.

"How are people holding up?" Gary asked.

"They're down. People hope even though we knew this would be the outcome."

"What about Stanislaus County—we got final numbers?" Gary asked.

"It's close. But you're ahead."

Gary smiled, velvet at the edges.

He and Chad rejoined their friends and family.

"No sad faces," Gary instructed as he moved toward the front door. "Don't cry or whine."

At 10:15 p.m., Gary stepped onto his driveway, followed by fifty of his closest friends and family. Nearly one hundred members of the media formed a solid line in front of him, standing between the Condit family and Acorn Lane.

For the first time in six months, not a single reporter yelled or screamed or demanded that he answer a question.

It was a surreal moment.

The night sky was dark, and the crowd's dreamlike silence seemed to brush away the little bit of light put off by the streetlights and cameras.

Here he was, with his family and his antagonists, the faces of the key characters of this melodrama standing together in the final act, and yet he felt almost as if he were standing alone on the Oklahoma panhandle, with nothing but its unending blackness in front of him.

Gary stepped forward, and as soon as he did the crowd erupted in applause.

Up and down Acorn Lane, neighbors stepped onto their porches and front lawns, cheering and crying.

"I want to thank all the people who volunteered. It was a grassroots campaign. All these people standing behind me," Gary said, looking over his shoulder at them. "I appreciate their support and love. I'll never forget that. I want to thank my family. My son and daughter and wife—give them a hand."

The crowd cheered louder.

"I want to thank the voters of the Eighteenth Congressional District for allowing me to serve eleven years—twelve when I finish. I appreciate their support, their love," Gary continued. "I'm going to work hard in the remaining time to make the valley a better place."

"Are you conceding?" a reporter asked.

"We see the trend in the vote," Gary replied, then turned and walked back to the house.

Reporters followed him all the way to the door, asking questions about his future.

Gary stopped at the willow tree and turned. "You guys are making this overdramatic. Things happen to you in life that you can't explain."

When they were back inside the house, Gary's friends said their good-byes, except for Jean Condit, who quietly disappeared to the garage.

"We can sit here and sulk all night. Won't make a difference," Gary said. "I got to be in public service for thirty years. Don't feel bad for me. Put on a smile and go to work. If you want to go work for the other guy—go do it."

He knew that Lynch and others in his operation needed to worry about their own careers. They were as much a part of Condit Country as he was. And they were just as political. To stay in the game, they'd need to work with Cardoza.

"Let me tell you—we've learned that friendships really mean a lot to us. I appreciate your friendship," a campaign worker answered, her voice breaking with the last word.

"Take your pain and give it to God," Adrian said as he wrapped his arms around her.

As reported by the *Los Angeles Times*, fifteen minutes after Gary made his statement on the driveway, "The sprinklers went on, dousing a gaggle of television reporters and cameramen staked out in front of his house."

FATHER

"I go back to DC tomorrow," Gary said. "People don't expect me to but I need to finish this."

"I don't think you owe anyone anything," Chad replied.

The truck stopped at a red light. Gary hung his left arm out the driver-side window.

"We've got boxes of stories. We've tied a lot of things back to sources," Chad said.

"Let it go," Gary replied.

"We should expose the sources."

Gary understood how Chad felt. After sparring with what seemed like ghosts for more than a year, Chad saw an opening to throw a punch. He also knew that if Chad pulled these strings, many of them would lead back to Susan and Bob Levy.

"Be gracious. Once you open the door a crack on someone, the media will bust it down."

"It's not like there's some fucking gentlemen's agreement. Look around," Chad answered, no longer able to hide his hostility with a world that had crashed around him. "You're the only one who believes that."

"Politics is like a prize fight. People throw heavy punches. There are certain things that are understood when you step in the ring. You also understand that you might get carried out."

"You're drawing a line that doesn't exist!" Chad shouted. "It's not what people did. It's what they didn't do."

"I get that," Gary said, trying to assure him. But try as he might, Gary couldn't find the right words. Maybe there weren't any. It was one of those conversations between a father and his son where the son needs answers, but the only right thing for a father to do is tell his son that he loves him.

It is not a father's place to crush the fire in his son's belly. Time will do that.

"Remember the drowning man?" Chad asked.

"I told you that story when you were kids."

"Drowning in a ravine."

Gary stopped the truck in the driveway and killed the engine.

"There are three people on the cliff looking down at you drowning in the water. The first person jumps into the ravine, risking his own life from the fall or you pulling him under with you. The second man runs back to the road and calls for help. What does the third man do?"

"Nothing," Gary answered.

"The most valuable guy is the one who goes for help. The man who jumps is honorable—but dangerous. What did you say about the third man?"

Gary nodded.

"The third man is a coward," Chad replied.

"Chad," Gary started, but was interrupted.

"There is no unwritten rule that says we got to be a bunch of fucking pussies about this," Chad insisted.

"Sometimes the best thing that can happen is to just let something end."

Chad shook his head. "Not like this."

Gary thought about his children, and their careers. *You already jumped into the ravine and tried to save me. I'm afraid I pulled you under with me.*

96 Percent

Gary and Chad Condit sat across from Assistant US Attorney Roderick L. Thomas, inside the US Attorney's Office in DC.

Thomas had called the meeting to "prepare" Gary for the grand jury that had been called later that morning. Information leaked to the press suggested the US Attorney's Office had called the grand jury to seek indictments against Gary for obstruction of justice.

"I've got about 96 percent of this case figured out. I only need about 4 percent more," Thomas explained.

"You issued a subpoena to Gary Condit to testify for 4 percent!" Chad shouted, leaning across Thomas's desk like a junkyard dog.

Thomas, shaken by the violent reaction, fumbled. "I—it's not what I meant."

"Is this 4 percent going to solve the case?" Gary demanded.

"I misspoke. We really, you know . . ."

"No you didn't. This is bullshit," Chad interjected. "You don't have a fucking thing. You called Gary Condit so that you can get on TV."

Chad did not know that some people within the US Attorney's Office still believed Gary and Carolyn had conspired to kill Chandra.

"How much money did you spend on me? How many people did you send after me? Tell me what 4 percent you need. I'll give it to you now," Gary offered.

Thomas backpedaled. "We need you on the stand, Mr. Condit."

Gary's eyes widened. He stood and looked down on Thomas.

"There's something you need to understand. You're fucking with the wrong guy. I don't have to answer your questions, and I am not going to anymore."

Gary was led into the grand jury room and sworn in.

Thomas began asking him questions. Each time Thomas stopped, Gary asserted his Fifth Amendment right under the US Constitution and his right to privacy under the Constitution of the state of California—a right not mentioned in the US Constitution.

The answers angered Thomas.

"You're not going to answer any of my questions today?" Thomas asked.

"I've cited my right to privacy."

Gary doubted Thomas understood why he had asserted a right to privacy. The federal investigators who had chased Gary for more than a year were like interchangeable widgets, each marching to his or her own ambition. Gary and his life were the only constant.

"You don't feel like you should answer my questions?"

Gary didn't feel anything. "That applies to every question. I'm not answering any of them."

—

The Capitol Police force has more than 1,500 officers and protects the two hundred city blocks that immediately surround the Capitol Building.

The events of 9/11 had elevated the importance of the Capitol Police.

On May 10, 2002, Capitol Police chief James Varey retired. By law, his replacement would be chosen by a three-member panel including the sergeant-at-arms of the House, the sergeant-at-arms of the Senate, and the capitol architect, the head of the agency responsible for the US Capitol complex.

The board would take weeks to pick a new Capitol Police chief from a pool of seventy candidates, including Terrance Gainer.

CHAPTER 20

WHAT REMAINS

LOOKING FOR TURTLES

ON MAY 22, 2002, PHILIP Palmer walked his dog through Rock Creek Park, meandering off the Western Ridge Trail trying to find turtle carcasses.

The ground declined rapidly from the Western Ridge Trail to a ravine at the bottom of the hill. The light that made it through the dense treetops darted in slivers over dark shadows.

When he was approximately eighty yards from the top of the Western Ridge Trail, a piece of red clothing caught his eye.

Then a white piece of bone that looked like the top of a sun-bleached turtle shell.

He reached down.

Susan and Bob Levy sat on their living room couch surrounded by cameras for *The Oprah Winfrey Show*. The day signaled the beginning of the first leg of Susan Levy's latest media campaign.

"Do you believe Gary Condit knows what happened to your daughter?" Oprah asked.

"Oh yes," Susan Levy responded. "I think he does."

The *Washington Post*'s Sari Horwitz sat with Terrance Gainer at a cafe table.

She had been a contributor to the *Post*'s July 2001 story alleging Gary had an affair with the teenage daughter of the Levys' gardener, Otis Thomas. She had also covered Guandique's sentencing.

According to Horwitz: "We had heard that there had been serious mistakes and missed opportunities by the police and the FBI. We wanted to hold them accountable and find out precisely how the case went awry . . . With the advent of cable television and the proliferating blogosphere there is more noise and inaccurate information out there than ever before."

Gainer received a page and excused himself to make a call.

He returned a short while later. "Somebody might have just found the remains of Chandra Levy in Rock Creek Park."

In her own words, Horwitz felt a sense of "thrill."

Sergeant Dennis Bosak of the Park Police knelt near a skull covered in dirt and leaves that the man searching for turtle shells had stumbled upon.

Nearby, he found a pair of spotted black underwear, turned inside out, black stretch running pants, a red sports bra, and a black radio cassette player. The pants were knotted at the legs.

Weathered bones scattered around him came into focus, as well as a gray sweatshirt with "Property of USC Athletics" written in red across the front.

On Broad Branch Road, reporters had gathered behind yellow tape. News had spread rapidly that Chandra's remains may have been found near the Western Ridge Trail, not far from the Pierce Mill.

"Are these Chandra Levy's remains?" a reporter asked.

"The remains found earlier today are in fact Chandra Levy," Chief Ramsey declared.

"Is there a case?" a reporter asked.

"There is no indication as to how she died or whether her remains had been at the site since her death or moved there some time later," Ramsey answered.

"Didn't the police search this area of Rock Creek Park last year?"

"It's possible to search and not find."

—

Gary pierced another round green pea with his fork.

Congressman Bud Cramer slid into the chair across from him.

"They found Chandra Levy's body. If you get out the back door you might beat them upstairs," Cramer warned.

When word reached reporters scouring the Capitol for Gary that he was last seen entering the members' dining room, they formed a line twenty yards deep in the hallway outside.

Gary left through the back door. A few dozen reporters confronted him there. He put his head down and pushed them aside, not hearing their questions as he grasped the reality that Chandra was dead.

"You hear," Dayton said as Gary entered the office. "They think they found Chandra Levy in Rock Creek Park. Some guy with his dog. The police said he was looking for turtles."

"Everyone knows I have turtles. Don't you think that's odd?" Gary replied. For many years Gary had kept a pet turtle named Shorty.

In Modesto, Susan Levy's phone rang. She answered, slumped to the floor, and cried.

Perhaps the artistic image of Gary with missiles slamming into his bloodied head and chains clasped around his extremities watched over her as she fell deeper into the twisted misery that had consumed them all.

Chandra was found 386 days after she went missing.

DEFLECTING BLAME

The National Guard brought floodlights into the area of Rock Creek Park where Chandra's remains had been found. The Park Police, Metro Police, and FBI coordinated with forensic archeologists from the Smithsonian, who had been brought in to analyze the weathered bones.

The investigators argued over how they had missed Chandra's remains during searches of the park in 2001.

Jack Barrett claimed that in July 2001 he had ordered his men to search one hundred yards from the roads *and* trails and that his order had been improperly executed because the search teams had stopped whenever they traveled a hundred yards from a road. Experts argued that the distinction was irrelevant, because Chandra's remains were found close enough to where investigators had searched that the cadaver-seeking dogs should have picked up the scent in any event.

Cable news pundits debated whether it was possible Chandra's remains weren't in Rock Creek Park on July 2001 when law enforcement searched the area.

Comparisons, again, were made to another high-profile disappearance: Joyce Chiang.

The Washinton Post

CHANDRA LEVY'S REMAINS FOUND IN PARK BY DOG
By Steve Twomey and Sari Horwitz

The skeletal remains of Chandra Ann Levy were found scattered on a steep, forested slope in Rock Creek Park yesterday, more than a year after her disappearance touched off an investigation that captivated the nation and ended the career of Rep. Gary A. Condit of California . . .

Police found "less of the body than more," they said, possibly because of animals.

The bones were very deteriorated and had no tissue or hair, the sources said. The skull, which was not complete, was cracked, although the cause was unclear . . .

Ramsey said it looked as if the skeleton had been there for considerable time . . .

Staff writers Petula Dvorak, David A. Fahrenthold, Marc Fisher and Allan Lengel, Arthur Santana, Debbi Wilgoren and Clarence Williams and Metro researcher Bobbye Pratt contributed to this report.

Gary read the *Post*'s summation with disgust. The blunt grotesqueness of its contents illustrated with clarity his insignificance to the whole affair. *The Levys shouldn't have to wake up to this. These reporters are ghouls; soulless, arrogant ghouls.*

BONES

A few days after Chandra's remains were found, investigators finished searching the area off the Western Ridge Trail, packed up their equipment, and left.

A week later, the private detectives hired by the Levys stood in Rock Creek Park.

Sari Horwitz of the *Washington Post* had convinced them to let her tag along.

One of the private detectives hit a rake against a hard bone. They called the Metro Police, and detective Ralph Durant arrived a short while later.

"It looks like it came from an animal," Durant concluded.

That evening the medical examiner confirmed the bone was in fact Chandra's left tibia.

News of the miss spread across the networks, kicking up more questioning and ridicule of the Metro Police.

Ramsey and Gainer moved into crisis management mode, issuing the following press release:

It appears that department technicians did not pass over the bone during the original search.

There appears to be a greater likelihood that the bone was reintroduced into the area by wildlife.

Ramsey's defense ignited mockery from some in the press.

Still, he accused the Levys' private detectives of placing the tibia at the scene after his own detectives had left. He and Gainer demanded the Levys' detectives submit to a polygraph examination to prove they hadn't tampered with the crime scene.

The Levy camp refused.

The *Washington Post* turned its ire squarely on the Metro Police, calling the mistakes unacceptable while panning Ramsey and Gainer.

Ramsey and Gainer sent their investigators back out to Rock Creek Park. This time they added a zoologist to track the movement of bones by animals. The additional search took nineteen days. But it was time well spent. They recovered the largest bone in the human body: Chandra's femur.

The Metro Police and its brass faced a storm of renewed criticism.

A light bulb went on in the press, but it wasn't at the *Post*.

Amy Keller, a staff reporter for *Roll Call*, reported that Ingmar Guandique may have been Chandra's killer. Using simple Internet database searches, Keller had discovered Guandique attacked other women in the same area of Rock Creek Park where Chandra's remains had been found.

On a nationally broadcasted interview with Fox News anchor Shepard Smith, Keller stated she believed Guandique could be Chandra's killer.

Smith, after noting "the first one to report on all of this is a reporter for *Roll Call* magazine, Amy Keller," asked Keller whether there were similarities between Chandra's case and Guandique's attacks on other women. Keller answered: "*Roll Call* spoke with one of the victims earlier today. She said that it was spooky to her when Chandra's body was recovered in the Broad Branch Trail area after what happened to her last May in that same area. She said it was scary and eerily similar."

News of a potential suspect that wasn't Gary spread quickly.

The press demanded answers.

Terrance Gainer proclaimed Ingmar Guandique was innocent. If Guandique was in any way involved in Chandra's murder, he told reporters, "The police would have been on him like flies on honey."

Chief Ramsey told reporters Guandique couldn't be the guy because he was behind bars when some of Chandra's bones were moved after the discovery of her remains.

A few days after Keller broke the story, she received a call from a reporter at the *Modesto Bee*.

"Did Mark Geragos—the congressman's attorney—orchestrate that story?" the reporter demanded.

"No, that's not how it happened at all," Keller replied. "I simply used one-part hunch, two cups of research, and one quarter teaspoon of source-based reporting, otherwise known as conversing with the cops. No, Gary Condit's lawyer had definitely not planted this one."

"Well I think—and other reporters do too—that the timing of the story is curious," the reporter for the *Bee* replied.

No doubt, he was referencing his friends at the *Washington Post*.

———

On May 30, the *Washington Post* reported: "Terrance W. Gainer, who became a familiar face on national TV discussing the Chandra Levy case, has been hired as chief of the US Capitol Police."

The *Post* offered no criticism of Gainer's promotion to one of the most significant law-enforcement posts in the nation.

CHAPTER 21

LEGACY

LAME DUCK

THE ODD THING ABOUT LOSING in a March primary election is that you still have half a year remaining in office.

Gary and Dayton dove into the Joint House and Senate Intelligence Committee investigation into the events that led up to the 9/11 attacks.

After the first set of closed hearings, it was clear the intelligence community had failed, catastrophically. Gary joined with House Democrats to demand that the independent commission investigating the events leading up to 9/11 have the greatest degree of independence from the federal government.

In the wake of his experience on the intel committee leading up to and during the war in Kosovo, Gary wanted a full understanding of what the intelligence community knew and didn't know, and what we did or didn't do.

The terrorist attack on 9/11 had galvanized the nation. Gary felt there was a risk, even a likelihood, that the politicians would catapult the nation into a war of retribution before we fully understood what had happened and why, and that the press would be wittingly or unwittingly complicit in going to war prematurely.

News reports disclosed to the public that the National Security Agency had intercepted telephone calls on September 10, 2001, warning that al-Qaeda was on the verge of launching an attack on the United States.

Vice President Dick Cheney fumed, blaming the leak on Congress.

Newly minted attorney general Alberto Gonzales stated his office was considering the possibility of prosecuting the journalists who had been given the information.

"An attorney from the committee will be present for your interviews," Congressman Porter Goss, the chairman of the House Intelligence Committee, informed committee members.

"Is the attorney for the Intelligence Committee our personal attorney? Is he there to protect our rights?" Gary asked.

"The committee attorney represents the committee, the government."

"Why would we want that guy in the room with us if he's not there to represent us?" Gary responded.

A few days later, Gary entered a suite inside the Four Seasons Hotel. His attorney, Mark Geragos, and a team of federal investigators waited for him.

"Who do you talk to in the press?" an FBI investigator asked.

"You can't be serious. Do you think Gary Condit talks to anyone in the press?" Geragos laughed.

Everyone else in the room joined in.

Quietly, Gary was relieved. *People thought I killed a woman. How hard would it be for someone to frame a member of Congress for leaking information?*

—

October 3, 2002, was day seven of the United States Congress Joint House Committee inquiry into the September 11 attacks.

Gary looked down from the dais at a panel of intelligence community leaders sitting behind a table. He leaned into his microphone: "Do you have any idea why we can't reform the intelligence community?"

Lee Hamilton, director of the Woodrow Wilson International Center for Scholars, answered: "Mr. Condit, first of all, substantively, it is just very difficult. You have thousands and thousands of workers and dozens and dozens of agencies. It's very difficult to determine how you put these boxes together and how you put these pieces together. We've never been able to build a consensus. Secondly, the politics of it are very tough."

Later in the hearing, intelligence leaders argued that advances in information-gathering technology would lead to resolving the communication problems between agencies that may have led to a lapse in security leading up to 9/11.

Gary jumped in: "The concern I have is that the technology can be used vastly to improve our way of communicating with each other, but what about people's privacy and civil liberties? What suggestions do you have so that the government can proceed to take advantage of these capabilities without infringing on people's privacy and civil liberties?"

Panelists seemed neither prepared for nor concerned about the question. The polite non-answer seemed acceptable to everyone in the room.

Gary let it go.

As the hearing wound down, Gary took what would be his last shot at a recurring theme: "Mr. Chairman, I can't resist this. I know that it will get a rise out of the panel. I want to go back to the comment the general made about transparency. It just seems to me, what is the problem with opening this up? Everybody knows that everyone is watching everybody, and that we're going to monitor people and so on and so forth. If there was more transparency it just seems to me there would be more openness, more sunshine on the issue. Everybody would be aware of what was going on . . . It seems to me it's an honest approach to protecting ourselves, but doing it in a transparent way so people know we are."

William Odom, the former head of the NSA, answered Gary's question: "If we did that we don't need the intelligence community. That's called a news service. We have a lot now. I'd say 90 percent of the intelligence that affects policymaking in the government comes out of the media."

Gary was speechless.

And, as a lame duck, helpless.

—

On October 7, President Bush warned the world that the first sign of Iraq having acquired weapons of mass destruction "could come in the form of a mushroom cloud."

On October 10, Congress voted to authorize the use of force in Iraq based on intelligence received from the clandestine services and the Bush administration.

Everyone keeps comparing this to the Gulf War. But this isn't the Gulf War. This is Kosovo, Gary thought as he cast his vote.

The resolution authorizing war in Iraq passed the House by a margin of 297 votes in favor to 133 votes against.

Gary voted "No."

Few members of Congress held office long enough to have voted on the resolutions to go to war in Iraq in 1991 and then again in 2002.

Gary is one of a small handful of Americans who can say they voted in favor of the first war in Iraq and against the second war.

GRACE

Gary descended the escalator leading to the tunnel running between the Capitol Building and the Rayburn Building. Illinois congressman Bobby Rush met him at the bottom.

"Hey Bobby. I've been meaning to come by. Congratulations," Gary said.

Rush had just faced an unexpected challenge in his primary election from a young Illinois legislator named Barack Obama.

Rush was among a small, and some said a dying, breed in the Black Caucus. He had marched in the South during the civil rights movement and had founded the Chicago chapter of the Black Panthers. His view of civil rights was rooted in those experiences, and not history books.

Rush was also recently a born again Christian.

"I've been meaning to give you this," Rush said as he handed Gary a copy of a book with the title *Secrets of the Vine*. "Gary, some of us get it."

Later that afternoon, Gary found himself alone in his office. He lay on the couch and opened *Secrets of the Vine*.

As he flipped through its pages, his eyes stopped on a sentence: *"Pruning will intensify as God's shears cut closer to the core of who you are."*

He stood, moved to the closet in his office, and grabbed his copy of a book with the title *What's So Amazing About Grace*.

Gary found Rush in the Capitol Building and handed him the book. He had dog-eared the page with his favorite passage: "The strongest argument in favor of grace is the alternative, a world of ungrace. The strongest argument for forgiveness is the alternative, a permanent state of unforgiveness."

The Potomac's water glowed at the tips of its wrinkled wake. The cherry blossom trees were bare. So too were the banks, left hard and yellow by winter's cold hand.

Farewell messages to Gary had poured in from friends, colleagues, and strangers worldwide. Those caused Gary to truly hurt on the day he left, knowing he would never return to the life of service he had lived for thirty years.

In the wake of 9/11, a resolution by Congress to go to war, the discovery of Chandra's remains, and the identification of her likely killer, many people inside the political game had come to regret not defending him, and told him as much. But he didn't blame them, and told them that as well. Step into the light, and they would have been burned, too.

Dayton pressed the car forward, across the bridge. As he did, the city faded behind them, and ahead appeared an empty gray sky framed by rows of green trees on either side, that seemed endless.

For many people, Gary Condit would be remembered as a playboy or "Congressman Blow-dry." The mainstream media had gone so far as to label him a "backbencher" who was "uninterested in policy."

It was an image backed up by the national media with reference to a decade-old article in the *California Journal* about Gary's involvement in the infamous Gang of Five. The national media didn't care that it was a hit piece. Its truth was ancient history.

On top of that—the world viewed him as a hypocrite. Everyone, it seemed, had believed the stories in the *New York Times* and the *Washington Post* that alleged he had voted to impeach President Clinton.

A do-nothing, a hypocrite, and a man who lied to the cops, Gary reflected. *That's my tombstone.*

Try as he might, he couldn't prevent his mind from thinking about his career and the enemies he had left in his wake. He'd been warned by his mentors that there was a simple rule in politics: all of the people you climb over on your way up the ladder will be waiting to clobber you when you're pulled down.

Sway, Gary thought. *But don't break.*

PART V
CHIEF

CHAPTER 22

CIVIL LIABILITY

PLUNGE

FOR MUCH OF 2003, GARY spent full days alone, disappearing into the Central Valley on his motorcycle, and then into silence when he returned home.

Carolyn didn't protest when he told her he had decided to take a ride north. He packed a small bag and left.

Years before, actor Peter Fonda had told him Red Lodge, Montana, was the most beautiful place in the world. Gary decided to ride there. He stopped only a few times for gas, and to rest.

Fonda hadn't lied.

Gary had never seen skies so blue. *Like Cadee's eyes.*

He had never seen trees so green, as if the envy of every other place had spread over its mountainsides.

He had forgotten silence, and again felt its touch.

When he returned home, Gary put his best front on for the grandkids. Still, he slept a lot when they weren't around.

Carolyn made him lunch. He was never a big eater. But now he ate very little.

She kissed him, but his mind wasn't back from Red Lodge, or wherever it was he had gone.

Gary walked to the backyard and sat in one of the white plastic chairs under the uneven shade of the cypress trees. His face was burnt from the long ride on his bike, cut by the sun and the wind.

He watched the trees sway.

"I'm not going to wrestle with you," he whispered.

Carolyn watched from the doorway. She didn't bother him when he was like that.

—⁓—

Gary stood in the aisle while Carolyn spoke with the pharmacist.

A man brushed by Gary and whispered "murderer" as he passed.

A boy pointed at him.

Eyes darted at him, then away from him.

"You all right, Gar?" Carolyn asked.

"I'm fine."

When they got home Gary retreated to the bedroom.

—⁓—

"I'm not going to wrestle with you," Gary whispered.

He listened intently to the reply.

"It is my choice. Guilt is something other people make you feel. I gave that up a long time ago," Gary insisted.

Carolyn opened the bedroom door.

"Gar," she said.

"Gar," she repeated.

He didn't respond. She knelt down next to him on the bedroom floor.

He was breathing hard and his forehead was damp.

"I'm not going to wrestle with you," Gary answered.

"Who?" she asked. "Who are you talking to?"

Carolyn rolled him onto his back.

His eyes opened, and found her.

MALICE

Gary couldn't pay lawyers. They had to be willing to take on his lawsuits against the media on a contingency basis. The quid pro quo was Gary having to concede to going after the low-hanging fruit. He had little money, and no prospects in his field given how tarnished his name was. His only hope to support his family was to sue the media.

To Gary, that meant giving a pass to the worst of them. But he had no choice.

His lawyers developed a two-prong strategy.

First, Carolyn would bring her own lawsuits. If the lawyers on the other side had doubts about whether they could establish Carolyn was a "public figure," then they'd advise their clients to settle. She'd be a sympathetic plaintiff, and the things that had been said about her were beyond the pale.

Second, Gary would go after the media personalities that either didn't care to hide or lacked the capacity to adequately clothe their spite. As a public person, he'd have to prove actual malice, which would be virtually impossible to do against the likes of the *Washington Post*.

His lawyers zeroed in on two candidates: the tabloids and Dominick Dunne.

David J. Pecker had slicked-back hair and a bushy mustache. He enjoyed taking photographs of himself with a shotgun in his hand and a cigar in his lips. He also owned American Media, which in turn owned the *Star*, *National Enquirer*, and *Globe* magazines.

These tabloids had run dozens of stories covering the Levy scandal, carrying theories that ranged from Gary had killed Chandra during kinky sex and had the Hells Angels dump her body to Gary had a penchant for raping underage women. American Media had even aggregated the "best" of these stories and published them in a book endorsed by Dominick Dunne.

American Media hadn't limited its attack to Gary.

The *Enquirer* had reported that Carolyn verbally attacked Chandra during a phone call shortly before Chandra disappeared. The Metro Police, at Abbe Lowell's demand, had issued a statement debunking the story. Eleven days later, COPS: CONDIT'S WIFE ATTACKED CHANDRA splashed across the front page of the *Enquirer*. One month later, the *Enquirer* repeated the story.

On February 6, 2002, NBC aired its newest episode of the hit television drama *Law & Order*. The plot centered on a politician and his twenty-four-year-old aide, who mysteriously disappears. Throughout, the missing woman's parents demand more media attention. Near the middle of the episode, the politician's wife takes the stand and claims she received a call from the aide shortly before she disappeared. The aide told the wife she was pregnant and the politician was going to start a new family with her. The prosecutor asked the wife, "What did you do?" The wife answered, "I went a little crazy." The episode ended with the revelation that the politician's wife was the real killer.

On February 21, 2002, Carolyn sued the *Enquirer* for libel.

American Media's lawyers deposed Carolyn for more than six hours, trying to establish that she was involved in Gary's political operation.

She didn't break.

Carolyn never wanted to be a political tagalong wife. She clapped for the people in the parades. Her help for those in Condit Country came at bedsides, not in the newspapers.

Because she wasn't a public person, Carolyn would not have to prove "actual malice" to win her lawsuit.

Almost as soon as her deposition ended, American Media made an offer to settle the case, and Carolyn accepted it.

⟶

Gary, Cadee, Chad, and Lin Wood, Gary's attorney, flew to Boca Raton, Florida. Gary was scheduled to be deposed the next morning by American Media's attorneys in connection with his separate lawsuit against the tabloids.

Wood was a pit bull, the last person media outlets wanted to face. He had represented Richard Jewell, the security guard falsely accused of planting the Centennial Olympic Park bomb at the 1996 Olympics in Atlanta, in his lawsuits against the press.

When they arrived, Wood went to his hotel room and called the opposing lawyer.

"You don't have any leverage over Gary Condit because he's perfectly willing to be deposed. But when you do that, and you throw all that garbage at him—and you try and beat him up—he'll never settle this lawsuit—ever," Wood warned. "You need to understand the kind of man you are messing with."

"We'd like to delay the deposition."

"That's not happening," Wood insisted, knowing that American Media's lawyers had thought Gary would fold when faced with the prospect of answering questions about his private life in a taped deposition, and that Gary had surprised them by showing up.

A few hours later, American Media made its first settlement offer. Wood refused it.

An hour after that, American Media called with a higher offer. Wood again refused it.

An hour after that, American Media made a third offer, even higher than the last. This time, Wood said he'd take it to his client.

"I came here to get deposed," Gary insisted when Wood brought him the number.

Wood informed American Media Gary had refused the offer and had no interest in settling.

American Media increased its settlement offer. Wood tried to reach Gary, but Gary had turned off his phone.

By midmorning the next day, American Media's settlement offer had increased again. Gary had correctly guessed that he had become the media's biggest threat: a public figure who felt he had nothing left to lose in the public arena.

Lin Wood stepped into the hotel room. "Can we talk?"

"You come here to tell me the facts of life?" Gary replied.

Wood nodded. "I did."

"You want a cigar?" Gary asked.

"Sure."

They walked to a small patio off the living room.

"We've been going at these guys for a while now," Wood explained.

"It's been a tough fight."

"You'll win in court. And in a best-case scenario they'll calculate your salary and your retirement. You add it up now, and it's a loss to go to court," Wood explained. "They're offering you more in cash than you'll ever get. Much more."

"I don't know if that's true," Gary replied.

"Even the best defamation cases against a public figure are extremely difficult to win. You're a politician. The jury is not going to be sympathetic. The other side will put on all of the stuff said in other newspapers and on television to argue these tabloids alone weren't the cause of your election loss. If the jury accepts that argument you're looking solely at recovering damages for the loss to your reputation. Those awards are hard to predict and not likely to be large."

"I have no reputation anymore. What's that worth?"

"Legally speaking, not nearly as much as what they're offering now to make this go away. Here is how a jury would calculate your damages. I want you to spend time with that," Wood advised, handing Gary a piece of paper on which he and his associates had run the calculations the jury would likely undertake to figure out Gary's lost income and benefits. Just as Wood had explained, the numbers came in well below the settlement offer.

"I've taken a principled position. And I'm not going to back off of that because they're throwing money at me. Tell them I'm ready to be deposed and I'm gonna take this to the end," Gary responded.

"All right."

Wood snubbed out his cigar and left Gary sitting on the patio. He called a meeting with Cadee and Chad, and gave them the same counsel and numbers he had provided Gary.

"He's going to make an emotional decision here. And it's not a good one. Not if he needs the money. I don't think he appreciates how much longer the road will be, and what the risks are," Wood warned.

After hours of arguing with his kids, Gary accepted American Media's settlement.

Wood next set his sights squarely on Dominick Dunne.

HANLON'S RAZOR
2004–2005

Gary had finished his deposition with Dominick Dunne's lawyers. It was now Lin Wood's turn to depose Dunne.

"You can build enough circumstantial evidence that you can prove to a judge that there is a question of fact whether there was reckless disregard to truth and falsehood," Wood explained, "but you are never going to get someone to admit they lied. It's almost impossible to get someone to admit to malice. Let me put it this way: Dunne's lawyers will make sure he doesn't do that."

"He had to have some reason for making that shit up," Gary responded.

"Sure. But he'd have to be dumb enough to admit it."

"I think we might be surprised," Gary insisted.

The next morning, Gary, Wood, and Cadee gathered in a conference room.

Dominick Dunne entered with his attorney, Paul LiCalsi.

Over the next few hours, Wood brought out a rope, tied it in a noose, and then let Dunne hang himself, and his legacy, with it.

WOOD: Once you first heard about Gary Condit, how long do you think—how much time went by before you formed the low opinion of him?

DUNNE: I think when I read the article that was on the Internet that was sent to me, among others, on the Internet by John LeBoutillier. . . . I became friends with a man called Vince Flammini who was a former driver and close friend of Gary Condit. I appeared with him on several occasions on the Geraldo Rivera show. . . .

WOOD: Did you do anything yourself to investigate the truth or falsity of the statements about Mr. Condit that were contained in the LeBoutillier article? . . .

DUNNE: I spoke to John LeBoutillier at a funeral which we both attended, and we talked about it. . . .

WOOD: Do you recall any other characterizations of Mr. Condit, either in the privacy of your own mind or characterizations that you've expressed in public? . . .

DUNNE: He was discussed in public everywhere for months. Everywhere . . . And it was—in the world I move in, he was never spoken of highly or favorably.

American Media had published a book containing its greatest hits about Gary. Dunne had endorsed the book.

WOOD: Did you read it before you agreed to endorse it?

DUNNE: No. . . .

WOOD: Do you have any factual knowledge that you have yourself ascertained to be correct and true that would support a statement that Gary Condit ever rode in any type of motorcycle gang in the Washington, DC, area? . . .

DUNNE: Well, the Washington, DC, area, does that include Luray, Virginia?

WOOD: Yes, sir, if you would like for it to, absolutely.

DUNNE: Yes.

WOOD: You could even let it include the East Coast. . . .

DUNNE: Well, it was my understanding that he was on a motorcycle in Luray, Virginia with—

WOOD: With whom? . . .

DUNNE: Some kind of motorcycle group. . . .

WOOD: Hells Angels?

DUNNE: I know I used the word Hells Angels. I also used the word Haitian motorcycle group.

WOOD: Was that a Hells Angels—Haitian chapter of the Hells Angels motorcycle group that you are referring to?

DUNNE: I don't know.

WOOD: Well, what is the Haitian motorcycle group that you are referring to? Where does that group exist?

DUNNE: In Washington . . . I knew it from Mr. LeBoutillier's first piece.

WOOD: And you knew it to be true?

DUNNE: I believed it to be true. . . .

WOOD: Do you have any factual information that you have confirmed yourself through your investigation to establish the truth of any statement that Gary Condit ever rode his motorcycle with a motorcycle gang anywhere in the United States of America?

DUNNE: Yes.

WOOD: Tell me where you have that information that you have independently verified as being true.

DUNNE: I got it from Vince Flammini, who told me they went to motorcycle rallies, that they shared a motel room. . . .

WOOD: I want to know as a matter of fact whether you have yourself any information, factual information, to establish the truth of a statement that former congressman Gary Condit has at any time ever ridden with any motorcycle gang that is described as Hells Angels or as a Haitian motorcycle gang anywhere in the United States of America. Do you have any such factual information, sir? . . .

DUNNE: Well, on Geraldo Rivera's show, which I was on quite a few times, the motorcycles were discussed, I mean, I don't know, I think mostly from Vince. Yeah. . . .

WOOD: [H]ave you ever at any time sought to undertake any investigation as to whether Mr. Flammini's statements about Mr. Condit, about the rally or the hotel or anything to do with a motorcycle gang, whether those statements are, in fact, true or false?

DUNNE: I talked with a writer who is also a friend of Vince Flammini's from *People* magazine called Champ Clark, and the motorcycle thing came up. I can't remember specifically. . . .

WOOD: Why did you decide to go on the Laura Ingraham radio show on December 20, 2001?

DUNNE: I was reluctant to go on. Quite honestly, I was overpowered by Laura Ingraham. . . .

WOOD: There is a quote: "'Why don't you come on the show tonight,' she asked. I accepted on the spot because I felt like creating some trouble for Condit." Is that true? . . .

DUNNE: Well, he is running for office again and without mentioning this major factor of his life . . . It will be the first line in his obituary that he had an involvement with a girl for a year, a sexual involvement that gave her hope, something, something, and she vanished . . .

WOOD: Did you ever have any information from any source that Gary Condit was going out and engaging in sexual intercourse or sexual activities with prostitutes at a Middle Eastern embassy? . . .

DUNNE: At the time on *The Laura Ingraham Show* . . . Gruner and group were checking that out. . . .

WOOD: Let me see if I understand. Are you telling me that at the time you made the statements that Gary Condit had gone to Middle Eastern embassies that Mr. Gruner and these attorneys, Billy Martin and I guess another lawyer in his office—are you telling me that Mr. Gruner and Billy Martin and . . . Mr. Dyer—were lawyers for the Levy family, right?

DUNNE: Yes.

WOOD: That they were actively investigating whether Mr. Condit had been engaging in sexual intercourse and activities at Middle Eastern embassies with prostitutes when you made these comments about the horse whisperer story on *The Laura Ingraham Show* in December of 2001? . . .

DUNNE: [A]t that time, you see, I had just gotten—at that time, they were investigating that, and I regretted terribly saying that on the air. . . .

WOOD: Did the horse whisperer tell you that Gary Condit was engaging in sexual intercourse or sexual activities with prostitutes at Middle Eastern embassies?

DUNNE: Yes, he did.

WOOD: Did you believe him?

DUNNE: Yes, I believed him, because he described Mike Dayton going with him. Mike Dayton, whom they treated like a chauffeur, they didn't get the same—his—he had incredible details as he told this story. And—well, that's it. . . .

WOOD: The girls that got in—into the country and didn't seem to have to check in?

DUNNE: That was verified by Gruner later, by the way, that was before 9/11 happened. . . .

WOOD: And that is what you told Graydon Carter [editor of *Vanity Fair*] when you wrote him a letter back in October and conveyed to him the horse whisperer story, true?

DUNNE: Yes.

Wood took out a copy of the letter that Dunne had written to Carter.

WOOD: Why did you feel the need to make an addition in this letter where you are conveying the horse whisperer's story to state that "apparently then Congressman Gary Condit was in pig heaven with all the fresh young pussy." Why did you feel the need to make that addition, sir?

DUNNE: Well, this was not to be published. This was not—this was letting my editor, who is my friend, in on the story . . . the "pig heaven" is mine.

WOOD: How about "the fresh young pussy"?

DUNNE: Yeah, that is me. That's me.

WOOD: How often do you embellish on the truth? . . .

DUNNE: That is not embellishing on the—"apparently" is in the sentence. . . .

WOOD: [I]t sounds like you didn't feel Gary Condit acted right; is that what you are saying?

DUNNE: I didn't feel he felt right about her, yes.

WOOD: Did that make you angry?

DUNNE: Yes. . . .

WOOD: In your opinion, he had shown no concern about it from the beginning?

DUNNE: No, more than in my opinion. In the—pretty much the national opinion.

WOOD: And what do you base that statement on?

DUNNE: On every television show he was never treated as anything but—although he was not called a suspect, he was treated on all the television shows, at least all the televisions shows I was on, and all the news reports, as a suspicious character. . . .

WOOD: But as the months went on, I would take it that you became more angry and more disgusted with Gary Condit. . . .

DUNNE: Well, as the months went on, I learned more and more and more about the personal life of Gary Condit, and it was pretty seedy. And I—and I listened to Anne Marie Smith. I listened to Vince Flammini . . . Everything about him was suspicious to me. . . .

WOOD: You didn't find yourself increasingly angry at this man from your viewpoint as a victim's advocate?

DUNNE: Until—until he announced he was going to run again. And it just seemed like the height of chutzpah to me that somebody who had this hanging over his head, a missing woman, that he could announce to run for office and not mention this trouble that he was in. . . .

WOOD: Do you know how much money Vince Flammini has been paid by the tabloids for different stories? . . .

DUNNE: I do not know. I do know that he was never paid by the TV shows that he went on. And he was always free to talk to me. There was never any money involved. . . .

WOOD: Do you know how many varying accounts Mr. Flammini has given of allegedly the same events? . . . Have you ever tried to study that in your search for the victim's rights?

Dunne struggled to respond.

WOOD: When you say that Gary Condit lied to the Washington, DC, police, that is speculation, is it not, sir?

DUNNE: It is my understanding that it was not until the third time he was interviewed by the police— and this has all been in the papers—that he confessed that he had an affair with Chandra Levy.

WOOD: What question was asked of him in the third interview?

DUNNE: This I don't know.

WOOD: What questions were asked of him in the first interview?

DUNNE: I don't know. . . .

WOOD: So since you don't know the questions, you certainly don't know the answers that he gave; do you?

DUNNE: I don't. . . .

WOOD: And you are stating under oath that you know as a matter of fact that Gary Condit denied to the police that he had an affair with Chandra Levy; is that your testimony? . . .

DUNNE: He had lied to the police . . . He did it for several visits. . . .

WOOD: I just would like a simple answer to a simple question. Did you think that by telling the horse whisperer story that you were going to create trouble for Gary Condit?

DUNNE: No. That was not why I told the horse whisperer story. I regretted telling parts of that story which I had never told before. This was not a news show. It was like a chat-gossip show . . . And I . . . regretted that it would interfere with the investigation. I wasn't thinking of him. . . .

WOOD: Who was investigating that information?

DUNNE: Well, I know for a fact that Jerry Gruner. . . .

WOOD: Let me make sure that we agree on this. I thought you had told me this, and I think I am right. Mr. Jerry Gruner was a private investigator that you understood worked for the Levy family by being an employee or working for Billy Martin's law firm, right?

DUNNE: He was described to me by Mrs. Levy as being with the FBI assigned to the team investigating . . . I assumed always that he was. . . .

WOOD: Didn't you think it was odd that an FBI agent was asking you to take certain actions involving some expense to travel to England and just expect that you would pay for it out of your pocket?

DUNNE: Well, I didn't pay for it. I work for a magazine that was thrilled to pay for it. . . .

WOOD: He wanted you, in effect, to do some investigation for the FBI, as you perceived it, right?

DUNNE: Yes.

WOOD: So when you went to England, you were under the clear perception that you, Dominick Dunne, were working, in part, investigating, in part, for the FBI at the FBI's request, right?

DUNNE: That's yes.

WOOD: At the expense of *Vanity Fair*, right?

DUNNE: Yes. . . .

WOOD: Do you remember him ever talking with you in any way that related to him saying that he was an FBI agent?

DUNNE: No. . . . I simply was told he was one by Mrs. Levy. . . .

WOOD: [A]s you sit here today, sir, you now know through an abundance of information that you have received that Monty Roberts is accurately described as an individual who not only is a liar but is a fraud, true? . . .

DUNNE: Well, I don't know that he is a fraud, but he is a liar . . . Now, the liar part, which is certainly true, the liar part came after Chandra Levy's death when I said that I had been hoodwinked by a horse whisperer. . . .

WOOD: Mr. Dunne, do you have any information, factual information, about how Chandra Levy was abducted? . . . You understand when I say factual, I am talking about the difference between factual information—

DUNNE: And theory.

WOOD: And speculation.

DUNNE: And theory. And theory.

WOOD: Yes. Do you have any factual—

DUNNE: I have the theory that—do I have a factual information on that? No. I find it a very logical explanation, however.

WOOD: Which—what explanation is that?

DUNNE: That she went off on the back of a motorcycle. . . .

WOOD: You don't think she might have been abducted by some criminal while she was walking in Rock Creek Park?

DUNNE: I have no idea.

WOOD: I mean, the simple fact of the matter is, you used the word "theory," and I understand, the riding off on the back of a motorcycle is, as you've described it, your theory, right? . . .

DUNNE: Yes. I wasn't alone in that theory, by the way. It was a very popular theory. . . .

WOOD: Is that your theory now about what happened to her?

DUNNE: I don't know that I really have a theory now after this lawsuit . . .

WOOD: Well, it wasn't the horse whisperer story, was it?

DUNNE: It sure wasn't.

WOOD: I mean, you now acknowledge that you got hoodwinked?

DUNNE: I did.

WOOD: That story was bogus, true?

DUNNE: Brilliantly bogus, but bogus.

WOOD: Brilliantly false?

DUNNE: It was.

WOOD: True?

DUNNE: It was the greatest storyteller I ever talked to.

WOOD: But whether brilliantly or not? . . .

DUNNE: Even you would believe him.

WOOD: Well, don't count on that one, but nonetheless, I have a pretty good track record of knowing when I am dealing with an FBI agent and when I'm not.

LiCALSI: Now that's uncalled for. Don't—ask questions. . . .

WOOD: So today what I want to know is do you have a theory about how she was abducted or by whom she was abducted?

DUNNE: I certainly don't know by whom she was abducted.

WOOD: Do have you a theory as to how?

DUNNE: I still think it is possible that she went off on the back of a motorcycle.

WOOD: Do you concede it is equally possible that she was walking or running in the park and some unknown person abducted her and ultimately murdered her?

DUNNE: Well, I have read all the stories of the man . . . who had attacked other women in the park. I do not believe it was he. I can't remember his name . . .

WOOD: When did you investigate this gentleman who is in jail and charged with two other assaults on females in Rock Creek Park? . . .

DUNNE: Well, it wasn't conducting an investigation. I made a lot of calls about the guy to find out about him, if he was a logical person. I talked to Lisa DePaulo, who was really an authority on the case. I talked to my secret source, who was—

WOOD: Champ Clark?

LiCALSI: Objection. We are not—you know, you think—you are having a lot of fun, but, yeah, it's objectionable.

WOOD: . . . I am not here to have fun.

LiCALSI: Well, you seem to be. Why are you grinning and chuckling?

WOOD: Well, because, I mean, Champ Clark is the source, and y'all have admitted it, and it's just . . . I will let *People* magazine know that Champ Clark, who is writing about the Condit case, has been serving as a secret confidential source to Dominick Dunne, and we will find out what *People* magazine thinks about that kind of conflict of interest.

LiCALSI: Yeah, we will. . . .

WOOD: You better believe I will, sport. . . . Mr. Dunne, the person that you say that you did some investigation on or made some calls about, I think were your words actually, Ingmar Guandique, is that the individual?

DUNNE: Who?

WOOD: The man that was in jail that was under suspicion in the Chandra Levy case?

DUNNE: Yes, that is the name, I think. . . .

WOOD: You made reference to the horse whisperer in some *Vanity Fair* columns as well as on Larry King, right?

DUNNE: Uh-huh (affirmative).

Dunne had started to turn pale.

LiCALSI: Are you all right?

DUNNE: Yes, I am fine.

WOOD: And apparently you had some folks fairly spellbound at one of these cocktail parties, do you recall that, with Gore Vidal present?

DUNNE: Yes. It wasn't a cocktail party, but—.

WOOD: I'm sorry. What was it?

DUNNE: A dinner . . . I mean, you got to understand something, Mr. Wood. These are people who go out to dinner every night or six nights a week. You hear the latest news. You know, these are high circles. You hear hot news that is going on. And, you know, they talked about Alfred Taubman for six months. They've talked about Lord Black now for six months. It's the hot—whatever is the hot thing. And then, you know, you hear so much.

Dunne's attorneys filed for a protective order to seal their client's deposition. The motion stated that Dunne was concerned Gary would use the deposition "in an attempt to embarrass" and "demean" him.

Wood moved to oppose the sealing, providing the court with evidence showing LiCalsi had tried the lawsuit in public from the beginning.

The judge refused to grant Dunne's motion.

Dunne extended a settlement offer. This time Wood didn't have a hard fight with Gary. Dunne's deposition had been so thoroughly revealing, Gary felt as though he had received some justice.

Just before the parties were scheduled to sign the settlement agreement, Dunne's lawyers called and informed Wood they would delay signing until after Chad Condit appeared on the Fox News show *At Large with Geraldo*. Chad was scheduled to appear on the show to talk about Gary's lawsuits against the media.

Dunne's lawyers were concerned that in the wake of Dunne's deposition performance Chad would trash him on national television, and they now wanted to condition the settlement on Chad not doing so.

AT LARGE

On March 13, 2005, Chad Condit entered Fox News's studio.

"Mr. Condit, Mr. Rivera would prefer if the interview were done over camera," a producer informed him.

"I'm here in studio. He's here. What's his problem?" Chad replied.

"We can do the interview from green rooms. He'd prefer to do that rather than on set."

"Absolutely not. If he's too chicken to face me like a man, then I'll go home."

Chad had seen enough of the "let us draw our conclusion" television news show world to understand he held all the cards at this juncture. Fox News had widely advertised the interview.

Geraldo Rivera caved.

Less than five minutes before the cameras went live, Rivera skipped onto set. His hair and his mustache had been tailored like a fine suit.

Cameras rolled.

The word "LIVE" came across the corner of television screens followed by the tag "At large W/ Geraldo."

"In 2001, Condit Admitted to Having an Affair with Levy" popped across the bottom of television sets.

Chad started in on Rivera before the host could set his feet. "I just came to tell you you are way off base, anything but fair and balanced, and it's a shame—you should act like a reporter and not an entertainer—and you did that—and it's really discouraging for that to go on in this country, Mr. Geraldo."

"Do you feel better now, Chad?" Geraldo said, smiling.

"No, no, I don't feel better. I feel bad for you being able to go out and do what you did."

"And your dad—you think your dad performed admirably throughout this?"

"Yeah, he performed more admirably than you did in Afghanistan when you went over and put our troops in harm's way—and as a veteran—that was a dirty thing to do."

Rivera had traveled to the Middle East to cover the US-led war on terrorism in Iraq and Afghanistan. During a live telecast from the field in Afghanistan, Rivera knelt and drew the positioning of allied troops in the sand.

"That—that's a bunch of bull!" Rivera yelled.

"That was wrong, Geraldo."

Each man talked over the other, and pointed fingers in the other's face.

"Listen that's a bunch of bull," Rivera again insisted, and rolled his eyes.

"You put the troops in harm's way."

"You're lying," Rivera replied. "You just said something that is so grossly inaccurate."

"No, you put the troops in harm's way."

"You ask the troops if I put them in harm's way," Rivera challenged.

"They said it."

"That's absolute baloney."

"Why'd you get removed?" Chad inquired, referring to Rivera's departure from the war zone shortly after the blunder.

"They did not say it."

"Why'd you get removed?"

"I did not get removed from Afghanistan."

"You trashed my dad on unnamed sources," Chad leveled, hitting Rivera while he was off balance.

"I never got . . . you see what I mean, you're just rambling now, Chad. Do you want to talk about your dad and his lawsuits?"

"No, I want to talk about you—what you did over in Afghanistan."

"Do you think you are helping your father's lawsuits? Or do you want to tell lies about me?" Rivera asked, having no idea that the lawsuit with Dunne had been settled so long as Chad stayed off the topic.

"Do you think you are helping the reporting industry?"

"Is your father for instance going to answer the question?" Rivera asked, referring to the media's new obsession with the fiction planted by Dunne's lawyer, LiCalsi, in the press that Gary would cave under the pressure of a deposition.

Chad tried not to laugh. Rivera was reading the tabloids again, and believing everything in them. He wondered how Rivera would react when in just a few days he learned that Dunne had to settle with Gary, a win that was virtually unprecedented for a public person.

"Are you Jerry Springer or Geraldo Rivera? Which one are you?" Chad asked.

"Is your father going to answer the question—in his deposition?"

"What's the question?"

"Of whether or not he had an affair with Chandra Levy?"

"What does that have to do with who killed Chandra Levy?"

"You don't think it has something to do with it?"

"I heard you on your show . . ."

"Wait—will you answer the question, Chad?"

"What's the question?"

"The question is will your father ever answer the question of whether he had an affair with Chandra Levy."

"He's answered it—he told the police exactly what he needed to tell the police and you reported time and time again."

"That's in his opinion—that's in his opinion."

"And you reported time and time again he lied to the police."

"Who murdered Chandra Levy?" Rivera asked.

"I don't know. You said you were going to find out on your shows when you were on MSNBC—did you do anything about it?"

"I wasn't on MSNBC—I was on CNBC. Let's get the story straight."

"CNBC."

"It doesn't matter. Great—thanks for coming on," Rivera said quickly, putting his hands up in the air as if surrendering to madness.

"Hey—is that it?" Chad asked.

The cameras panned to Rivera's face. He put two fingers to his lips, kissed them, and then stuck the two fingers toward the cameras. "Good night, everybody."

The next day a joint press release was issued announcing that Dunne and Gary had settled the lawsuit for an undisclosed sum.

TYING THINGS UP
2006–2007

On January 31, 2006, Cindy Sheehan took a seat in the gallery above the floor of the US House of Representatives. Her son, a soldier, had been killed in Iraq. She was a guest of Democratic congresswoman Lynn Woolsey. The front of Sheehan's shirt read, "2,245 Dead. How Many More?"

Beverly Young, the wife of eighteen-term Republican congressman Bill Young, sat nearby. As chairman of the Appropriations Committee, Bill Young was an extremely powerful man in Washington, DC.

Beverly Young's shirt read, "Support the Troops."

Capitol Police officers approached both women and asked them to leave. Both women resisted, but were physically escorted by officers from the gallery before President George W. Bush began his State of the Union address.

The media firestorm hit immediately.

"Since when is free speech conditional on whether you agree with the president?" Congresswoman Woolsey stated, as politicians on both sides of the aisle rushed to condemn the action taken by the Capitol Police force.

Congressman Young was furious at the way in which his wife had been treated.

Capitol Police chief Terrance Gainer appeared on CNN and announced the Capitol Police had "made a mistake." He issued apologies to both women.

Sheehan wouldn't accept Gainer's apology and announced she was going to file a lawsuit against the Capitol Police.

Gainer was already in the hot seat over an allegation that he had improperly hired his son-in-law.

Members of Congress were also growing tired of his self-promotion. As one report summarized: "There's also been criticism on Capitol Hill, from staffers and some members, about

Gainer's decision to brief reporters directly, rather than consulting lawmakers about who does the briefing."

On March 4, 2006, Gainer resigned from his post as chief of the Capitol Police.

⚡

On March 11, 2006, Slobodan Milošević died of a heart attack in the middle of the night while sitting inside a prison cell at The Hague.

⚡

On May 25, 2006, Enron's Ken Lay was found guilty on ten counts of securities fraud and related charges. He faced up to thirty years in prison. Less than two months later, Lay unexpectedly died of a heart attack.

⚡

On November 15, 2006, a friend sent Gary a copy of the *Washington Post*.

TERRANCE GAINER NAMED SENATE SERGEANT-AT-ARMS

Former Capitol Police chief Terrance W. Gainer was named yesterday as the US Senate sergeant-at-arms, a job that once again will put him at the forefront of protecting Congress in the age of terrorism . . .

In his new position, Gainer will head the three-member board that oversees the Capitol Police.

⚡

On December 5, 2006, President George W. Bush nominated Assistant US Attorney Heidi Pasichow to be a judge on the Superior Court of the District of Columbia.

⚡

On June 21, 2007, the Federal Energy Regulatory Commission issued its ruling on Enron's involvement in California's energy crisis. FERC determined there was "a plethora of evidence" showing Enron had committed fraud in the wholesale energy market.

Gary called Peace to congratulate him on the decision.

"No, I'm not fucking happy," Peace insisted.

"You don't think it's some vindication?"

"What difference does it make? The press still doesn't get this. It's about derivatives. The geniuses will continue to fail. We're fucked. We're all fucked."

CHAPTER 23

GUILT

WHITE LIES

In 2007, Cathy Lanier replaced Charles Ramsey as the chief of the Metropolitan Police Department. One of Lanier's first orders of business was to reopen the Levy investigation.

—————

In California, Gary and Chad walked into Mark Geragos's law offices in Los Angeles.

Sari Horwitz, a reporter for the *Washington Post*, was working on an investigative piece on the Levy murder. She and her colleague, Scott Higham, wanted to interview Gary for the story. Geragos had asked Gary to meet with them as personal favor to him.

In 2002, Geragos had represented Gary pro bono when the US Attorney's Office called the grand jury to try and charge him with obstruction of justice, and again when the FBI interviewed him after the alleged intel committee leaks to the press during the 9/11 hearings.

Gary was a payback guy. He agreed to meet with Horwitz and Higham, provided the discussion stayed on broad topics and wasn't taped. Horwitz and Higham agreed not to delve into sex.

"Our work is not about that," Horwitz assured Gary. "It's about the mistakes the police made." They gathered around a small table.

"We think we've caught who killed Chandra Levy and we're going to expose him," Horwitz explained, oozing excitement. "I was very involved in this investigation. We've solved the case."

Higham was more reserved, which made Horwitz's giggling and fidgeting all the more maddening.

"I should regret not suing the *Post*, I know that now," Gary started.

The reporters tried to brush off his remark.

Horwitz tried to ask questions about Gary's relationship with Chandra, but he refused to answer them.

"Do you mind if we set up a camera to record this discussion?" Horwitz asked. It was the second time she had pressed to record the interview even though they had agreed not to do so.

Gary had heard enough. "Are you going to deal with the Levys' gardener story the *Post* printed?" he asked, knowing that Horwitz had worked on the salacious and false story spun by Susan Levy and Otis Thomas.

"The guy is a mess. He was on drugs. He wasn't a reliable source. We're not going to deal with that," Horwitz explained.

"Don't you think you need to say that? The FBI interviewed him—he lied," Gary responded.

"No, no, no . . ." Horwitz defended.

Gary shut down the interview and stood up to leave.

"Are you going to write a book?" he asked on his way out.

"We're not going to write a book," Horwitz responded.

"Well good. If I write one, then there's no conflict."

"You're going to write one?" she asked, her response giving her away.

The meeting lasted less than forty-five minutes.

On July 13, 2008, the *Post* published a twelve-part series written by Horwitz and Higham, titled **WHO KILLED CHANDRA LEVY**, as a serial narrative on its website. The series did a bang-up job revealing previously unknown mistakes made by law enforcement and digging up more details about Ingmar Guandique's life.

But it also contained more than a few mistakes of its own.

According to Horwitz and Higham, the series "exonerated" Gary and "identified" Guandique as Chandra's killer, even though many people, including reporters, had previously and publicly identified Guandique as a potential suspect in Chandra's murder.

They also claimed they had conducted an "extensive" and "exclusive" interview of Gary.

For his part, Terrance Gainer told Horwitz there was no physical evidence linking Guandique to the crime, and added that he remained convinced Guandique was not the guy.

Cold case detectives Todd Williams and Tony Brigidini traveled to the Victorville Federal Correctional Institution in Adelanto, California, to execute a search warrant on Ingmar Guandique's jail cell. Inside, they found a picture of Chandra that had been ripped from a magazine.

The detectives moved to an interview room at the maximum security prison. Guandique waited inside, chained to the table. He was covered with tattoos, including the words "Mara Salvatrucha" written on his neck, a picture of a devil on the top of his head, an image of the movie character-doll "Chuckie" holding a knife on his back, and a naked female and the letters "MS" on his chest.

"We have DNA evidence from the crime scene," Brigidini told Guandique. It was a lie, but he hoped it would trick Guandique into admitting he had a connection to Chandra.

"If you have DNA then charge me," Guandique answered through the translator.

"If you didn't attack Chandra Levy, how did we find your DNA on her body?"

"So what if I touched her."

"Witnesses have told us you had cuts on your neck and a fat lip the day Chandra Levy disappeared."

"Two black guys jumped me."

"What about that tattoo on your chest. Don't you think that looks like Chandra Levy?"

ARIZONA

There were no backyard fences, or orchards. The land simply fell into an arid plain that ran in a flat line until it snaked upward into a plateau, spotted along the way by desert trees and black lakes made by isolated clouds.

With the proceeds from the lawsuits, Gary bought two houses next door to one another on a large piece of property outside of Cave Creek, Arizona.

He and Carolyn lived in one of the houses and Chad and his family lived in the other. The property was located at the end of a long dirt road that split off the highway running from Phoenix to the center of Cave Creek. The road was private, and neighbors largely kept to themselves, although they looked out for one another.

Sonny Barger, the founder of the Hells Angels, lived on a ranch just a quarter mile down the road from Gary's house. He had undergone surgery to remove his larynx because of throat cancer. To talk, he had to place a finger over a hole in his neck.

Every few months he and Gary would run into one another, or Gary would stop by Barger's ranch to chat. For both of them it was nice to have someone they could talk to about home and the memories that would fade if not recalled. More than anything, they were two men who had lived, and paid the price of admission. It was rare to find another.

It was here, in Arizona, where I began working with Gary to understand whether he wanted to tell his story, and, if so, how to approach doing so.

—

I looked at Gary, who was sipping coffee.

He had spent the morning finding a new place to park Hop's fifth wheel, a type of camper trailer that is pulled by a pickup truck. They found a good location nearby, but there was a catch. When they arrived, they learned the trailer park was, in fact, a nudist colony. Hop, of course, didn't mind that at all. But Gary had to go to the bank so he could make the payment in cash.

I offered to push our discussion to the next day, but Gary insisted on pressing forward. Chad and Cadee Condit had asked me to help Gary tell his story, and I knew he was afraid that if he stopped he'd never start again. After a year of working together, I had resolved to confront him on his bouts of midday silence.

"What are you thinking about when you drift off?" I asked, taking a seat in a patio chair.

"My family knows. My neighbor Bob knows when I'm like that. They just let me be. I'm not hurt or upset or anything," Gary replied.

"Then what are you?"

"I'll sound crazy if I say this, so don't put it in the book. I've got a good family, and a good life, and I don't want to do a whiny ass book where people think I'm crippled. Someone needs to tell the truth."

"OK."

"Something just comes over me and I talk. I'm not sure what it is. But I don't wrestle it. So I tell whatever it is it can stay, but I won't wrestle."

"What do you think 'it' is?"

Gary cupped his hands together. He looked at me without any pain or pride or shame in his blue eyes. "Probably depression or something like that. We talk and it goes away after a while."

"What do you mean by wrestle?"

"There's something you gotta understand about me. I don't believe in guilt. I gave that up."

"You don't think there's right and wrong?"

"That's not what I mean. I live with my mistakes. Guilt is just something other people make you feel. I don't need to wrestle with judgment anymore. If I did, it would break me."

—

A man in a tattered shirt with long hair pulled into a ponytail behind a leathery face made sweeping brush strokes down the side of a house.

A small radio on the ground played Willie Nelson tunes.

Gary's neighbor paid Hop a weekly allowance to do odd jobs like paint, and to take care of his horses.

It was nearly 100 degrees outside.

"This guy I knew—Stanley Buchanan—he told that to the FBI, 'Hop Condit would do anything for Gary.' And you know what? They said I killed her," Hop explained.

"Yeah, Gary's told me that story," I replied.

"I wasted my life. But Gary, he spent thirty years helping people. That's all he did. Now people will go to their graves—old constituents will die thinking that he had something to do with that woman's disappearance. That's not taking someone's future away from them. That's taking away their past; destroying who they are."

The sound of Gary's diesel truck broke our conversation.

HOP SCOTCH

Going home with Gary Condit is a bit like a game of hop scotch.

He will take you to almond groves outside Ceres and explain how nuts grow, and explain why he voted against NAFTA. He describes a vision he once had of Modesto becoming the world's technology center for agriculture. His tour of Condit Country moves at a frenetic pace, as if to stay ahead of what is not spoken.

It's in the air. The intensity his mere presence creates in a room leaves conversations unbalanced, until that conversation comes, sometimes quicker than others, to the fulcrum of his life.

"That's the market Carol's been telling you about. Adrian's church is right up the street," Gary explained as he stopped the truck at the intersection.

"Why don't you come back more often?" I asked.

Gary put the truck in park and looked over at me. "What happened; it burned out a lot of people. Not just the Condits and the Levys. This whole place sort of had to live all that," he answered. A car behind us honked. Gary put the truck in gear and let his foot off the brake. "When I come back, it's like picking at a scab on a wound that won't heal."

—

Flammini came out the front door of his mobile home, with a large dog pulling at the end of a leash.

"Who are you?" he demanded. "Are you with the press? I don't want to talk."

"I'm not with the press," I replied. "I'm not."

"Are you with the FBI?"

"No."

"Are you with Larry King or Geraldo?"

He let the dog step into the street, a few feet from me.

"I'm a friend of Gary's."

My answer startled him, so I handed him my driver's license.

Flammini looked at me hard. "Steve Peace is your dad?"

"If you know that, you know I'm not lying."

He calmed down.

"I used to arm wrestle," he said without prompting by me.

"I didn't know that."

"I arm wrestled that guy in the movie with Sly Stallone. He was huge. Then I got into bodybuilding. I was Mr. Modesto."

"Gary told me about the bodybuilding."

"Gary and I used to do that together."

We talked, that first time, for nearly two hours. Twenty minutes into our conversation Flammini broke into tears.

"How's Carolyn? She never should have been put through this you know."

"She's fine," I assured him.

"Gary's OK? I've seen him in the news."

"He's fine. He's a tough guy."

"But not as tough as me."

"Sure."

"He treated me the best and the worst in my life. But he left me with nothing. I had no money or job and had to do what I needed to do."

"Is that why you said those things to the press?"

"I had no way to pay for anything."

"You were OK saying those things?"

"I talked with Susan Levy. We're friends; but, the truth is if he wasn't with Chandra she would have been back in California and wouldn't have been killed. So, I don't feel that bad," Flammini rambled. "But I feel bad that he's not in Congress. He was good. And now Dennis Cardoza is in Congress. He was Gary's driver. And Arnold Schwarzenegger is the governor. Gary could have been governor."

"You said Gary hurt people."

"Gary wouldn't hurt a fly."

"But you said awful things."

"I told them to not print those things until I said so."

"And it wasn't true?"

"A lot of it wasn't. But it's not really what I meant to say. They took what they wanted and twisted it."

"They paid you?"

"They'd pay a lot of money for stuff. I wouldn't talk to no one unless they paid me. I told that to the *Washington Post*."

"You needed the money?" I asked.

"I had this photo album, and it had photos of Gary at a motorcycle event. And I flipped by them. The reporter saw the photos, but he didn't say anything. He was hoping that I would give him the photo. There were a lot of things I didn't show people or tell anyone."

"Like what?"

"I know stuff that could put him away."

"Like what?"

"He told me once during a campaign to take down an opponent's sign."

"He did that?"

"Yeah he did, and it's illegal. He could go away for that."

"But I thought you were tougher than Gary? He forced you to do something illegal?"

"He was powerful, you know, when someone powerful says you do something then you got to do it. But I told them, you know, I told the reporters that I didn't ever see Gary with any women."

"But you said a lot of things about Gary and women, and even teenage girls."

"I didn't say anything about teenage girls. The woman from the *Washington Post* asked me about that, and I said 'no way' and then she ran a story saying it anyway."

"Was her name Petula Dvorak?"

"Yeah—that was her. She tried to get me to go to a casino with her."

"You told me you never saw Gary kiss another woman, is that true?"

"I never saw him kiss anyone but Carolyn and probably Cadee. But that doesn't mean I don't know. There were women. I just never saw him making out with anyone. I never saw him with any woman sexually."

"I still don't see why you would tell lies about a friend," I pushed.

At this point Flammini lost his composure, and never regained it.

"I wish I could tell him I'm sorry for some of it. Some of it is his fault. If he wasn't with her she'd be alive. I talked about that with Susan Levy, and she's heartbroken. But he won't talk to me. He probably doesn't talk to nobody."

"He's in Arizona. But he comes to Ceres every now and then to see his parents."

"Does he look all right? He doesn't eat. He eats like a bird," Flammini explained, with tears streaming down his cheeks.

"He's fine. He told me to tell you that he's not mad at you, Vince. But he can't see or talk to you yet and that he hopes you would understand why he feels that way."

"Can you tell him something for me?"

"Sure."

"Tell Gary that when he is ready we'll go fishing without bait."

Gary stopped the truck in front of a family friend's home, a block from Acorn Lane. An older man stood on the sidewalk. He was a healthy six feet four inches tall, even hunched over.

"Irv," Gary said.

"Gary!" Irv replied.

We got out of the truck and followed Irv into his house, where he directed us to seats inside a wood-paneled den that was decorated with hunting trophies and military service awards. Pictures of Irv and his wife, Jan, hung on the wall.

"Are these all yours?" Gary asked, admiring old rifles set in a case in the far corner of the den.

"Sure are," Irv replied, then proceeded to give us the history of each gun.

"You're in Arizona?" Irv asked. "Is that right?"

"I've got a place there near Scottsdale. I've also got some property up in Flagstaff," Gary explained.

They talked quite a while about Gary's high desert home. Irv mentioned the times he had been to Arizona and the places he had seen. The conversation carried on. As it did, I could see the scab getting pulled off, piece by piece.

They're not talking about Arizona. They're just enjoying each other's company without breaking, I realized.

Violent coughing and wheezing erupted from another part of the house. Irv grabbed Gary's hand. "You need to see Jan before you go. She'd get so mad at me if she found out you were here," Irv exclaimed.

The soft smile I'd heard about so often, from so many people, appeared on Gary's face. Irv led Gary into a dark hallway and around the corner to a small bedroom.

I stayed in the den, but through the thin wall I could hear the pained conversation.

"Lord, bless us. Gary!" an old woman's voice sang, followed by wheezing.

"How are you feeling today, Jan?" Gary answered cheerfully.

"What they did to you . . ." she started, struggling to manage the tension between her physical pain and her emotions.

"You don't need to worry yourself about that. It's in the past. We're doing just fine," Gary insisted.

"What they did to you? What they did to us!" Jan continued.

"You don't need to worry about that, you take care of yourself."

The ensuing silence was uneven.

"Promise me you will come around here more often, and the kids. What they did."

The crying grew loud. "God help us!" Jan cried.

A while later, Gary and Irv emerged.

Both men were shaken.

Gary fumbled to escape the discomfort, thumbing through western magazines sitting on a leather recliner.

Irv was smart enough to realize Gary needed to go. He put out his big paw to Gary, bidding him farewell. "We would have fought to the death for you. We still will."

Red and crooked lines penetrated the sides of Gary's eyes. "I know you would. You take care of that wonderful wife of yours. Let us know if there is anything we can do."

Gary isn't the same man I knew as a child, when he and my father, Steve Peace, lived together in Sacramento while they served in the California state assembly.

It's as though he is unable to sit still.

I guess when all of your conversations are carved in jagged emotion, you learn to keep moving so you don't get cut any deeper.

In my view, Gary Condit has been shorn past his core.

PART VI
ACCUSED

CHAPTER 24

COLD CASE

ARREST

ON MARCH 3, 2009, WASHINGTON, DC, mayor Adrian M. Fenty, Metro Police chief Cathy Lanier, and US attorney Jeffrey Taylor called a press conference.

"Today marks a significant step forward in our effort to achieve justice for the Levy family," Taylor declared. "We believe Ms. Levy was a random victim of Ingmar Guandique, who attacked and killed her as she walked through Rock Creek Park."

Sari Horwitz and Scott Higham approached Terrance Gainer to get his view on the break in the case.

"It appears we have the right person now," Gainer said.

Guandique had, allegedly, made a number of jailhouse confessions. The details of his alleged confessions varied. In some versions of events, Guandique told cell mates he acted alone when he attacked Chandra. In others, he claimed a congressman paid him to kill her. But there was a common thread to the jumbled stories—as early as 2002 Guandique had, allegedly, claimed responsibility for killing Chandra in Rock Creek Park.

Horwitz and Higham claimed victory for the *Washington Post*: "We know that our series reenergized the police investigation, which we have been told has been conducted with professionalism and thoroughness unlike the case back in 2001."

Reporters asked Chief Lanier about the sudden breakthrough and whether the *Post*'s twelve-part series had prompted the arrest.

Lanier responded bluntly: "It didn't."

Behind the scenes, the cold case detectives who had quietly built the case against Guandique for the murder of Chandra Levy were growing tired of the *Post*'s act. Their job had been made much harder than it should have been because of the press and, in particular, the *Post*.

—

Everyone wanted to know what Gary Condit felt about the announcement that Ingmar Guandique had been charged with murdering Chandra Levy. The scandal was front page news, again. But Gary had gone completely off the grid.

A cadre of black SUVs stormed down the private dirt road, whipping by cacti and desert rocks.

US Marshals filed out of the vehicles and surrounded the home. A man in a suit banged on the front door.

Chad Condit opened it. "Can I help you?"

"We have a subpoena for Mr. Gary Condit."

Chad wasn't sure what the subpoena was for. He had been in a protracted legal fight with Baskin-Robbins. He and Gary had used some of the money from the lawsuits to purchase two ice cream franchises in the Phoenix area. The franchises proved a dismal failure. As Chad put it, "We weren't very good ice cream men." True as that was, Chad wasn't alone. Baskin-Robbins was in constant legal disputes with beleaguered franchisees for decades before the ice cream giant finally turned to bankruptcy.

"I'm his son. I'll take it," Chad offered as he surveyed the armed men. *This can't be about ice cream.*

The subpoena called for Gary to appear before the grand jury in Washington, DC.

CONTEMPT

"If they think I'm gonna let them stick more knives in me, they're messing with the wrong fucking guy," Gary said.

"They're prosecuting the right guy this time."

"How do we know it's the right guy?"

"Well it's not you."

"Then why the fuck do I need to go to a grand jury?"

"Let me talk to a lawyer we can trust," I replied. "He's the real deal."

"Warn him that I'm gonna do this my way."

I stepped into another room and called Tom Warwick, one of the most respected criminal defense lawyers in California.

"Look he doesn't trust anyone. He thinks the whole justice system is broken and he has good reasons for that view," I explained to Warwick.

"You only get so many chances in your career to fix an injustice. I'll represent him pro bono, but you need to promise me people on his side won't talk to the press," Warwick replied.

"That won't be a problem."

Warwick then called Assistant US Attorney Amanda Haines, the lead prosecutor for the government's case against Guandique. He informed Haines that Gary wanted to cooperate with the subpoena.

"Gary Condit should have had nothing to do with this," Haines replied.

But she had no choice.

⸺

"We could say we're not going to testify and take the Fifth," Warwick explained to Gary. "But if you do that, they'll grant you immunity, in which case you'd be forced to testify. If you're forced to testify and you refuse, you'll go to jail for contempt."

"I get that," Gary responded.

"I'll talk to the prosecutor and get what it is she thinks she needs from you."

"How do you know this new prosecutor isn't just calling me to generate press? They sent all those marshals to Chad's house. I would have handled that different if I wanted someone to cooperate. That's an act of intimidation."

⸺

Sari Horwitz and Scott Higham turned their twelve-part series in the *Washington Post* into a book titled *Finding Chandra*.

Promotion for their "True Washington Murder Mystery" in advance of the trial touted their "extensive" interviews with Gary that never happened.

Finding Chandra begins with the discovery of Chandra Levy's remains in Rock Creek Park, then moves immediately to a self-congratulatory review of Horwitz and Higham, detailing their selfless decision to reopen the investigation.

According to them, Horwitz had to make the tough decision to leave her post covering the important topic of terrorism, to return to the "dangerous, unpredictable life on the streets" as a crime beat reporter.

Horwitz wasn't sure it was "the right move." But Higham convinced her, "Sari, you could solve a murder."

Horwitz allegedly had a secret source. One who would meet her in the evening, on side streets. Apparently, this source warned Horwitz to "be careful" and would slip into her car, provide her with information, and then disappear down the street.

The book then paints Chandra as a naïve Washington intern infatuated with Gary.

The book rehashes the story about an affair between Gary and the teenage daughter of Otis Thomas, the Levys' gardener. The book made no mention of Horwitz's contribution to the original story that was quickly proven to be fabricated either by Thomas or Susan Levy, or by both. Further, while the book noted that Susan still believed Thomas was telling the truth about the affair, it made no mention of what Horwitz had told Gary in Mark Geragos's Los Angeles law office about her view of Thomas—that he was "a mess," "on drugs," and not "a reliable source."

Horwitz's and Higham's criticism of the press was equally self-serving: "Most of the nation's leading newspapers showed some restraint; two months into the story, the *Washington Post* had played it on the front page three times." They, no doubt, wanted to avoid discussing the *Post*'s leading role in feeding the frenzy. Choosing the first two months was clever.

The book compared the Levy story to the following prominent Washington sex scandals:

Representative Melvin Reynolds of Illinois: sex with a sixteen-year-old girl. Representative Barney Frank from Massachusetts: sex with a male prostitute. Senator Brock Adams of Washington: drugging and molesting his staff members and associates. Senator Robert Packwood of Oregon: sexually harassing and groping his staff members and a lobbyist.

CLOWNS

Warwick and Gary flew together to Washington, DC. They spent the flight talking about their families. From bits and pieces, Warwick gathered the depth of Gary's doubts about the justice system, and the sincerity of the current prosecution of Ingmar Guandique.

The plane landed at Dulles after 11:00 p.m., and they took a cab to the Red Roof Inn near Crystal City.

The hotel's night manager didn't want to let them into their hotel rooms without first seeing their IDs—one for each room. After some wrangling, the manager agreed to give them both rooms under Warwick's name.

The next morning, Detective Anthony Brigidini pulled his unmarked police car into the hotel parking lot.

He looked, again, at the room number he had written in a notepad. He hadn't expected to meet a former congressman in a first-floor room at the Red Roof Inn.

The hotel room's door was propped open, and Gary was laying on top of the bed enjoying the breeze.

"Congressman Condit?" Brigidini said as he stood in the empty doorway.

"Gary's fine. Come in."

Gary got to his feet and the two men shook hands.

Brigidini had a barrel chest and big arms. *Reminds me of Burl's boys—strong as an ox*, Gary thought.

"Congressman Condit . . ." Brigidini started.

"Gary."

"Gary—I really didn't think you'd be in here."

"It's the kind of place I stay in if I'm on a motorcycle trip. You park outside the window so you can see at night by pulling back the blinds, or depending on the weather, leaving the door open."

Brigidini laughed. *He's nothing like what I expected.*

Warwick arrived at Gary's room, and Brigidini drove them to the US Attorney's Office.

✐

AUSA Amanda Haines sat behind her desk, typing rapidly.

Warwick and Gary sat in single chairs across from her. Brigidini and the rest of the prosecution team sat behind them, against the back wall.

"I hope you have more than 94 percent this time," Gary joked.

"One hundred percent sure we've got the guy who did this," Haines answered without hesitation.

Haines explained what would happen inside the grand jury room. She had carefully scripted every question. For each area of inquiry, she explained how it fit into her strategy for prosecuting Ingmar Guandique.

Fernando Campoamor-Sanchez, Haines's colleague, interrupted. "We're going to ask you whether you had sex with her."

Gary's mouth clenched. "Look guys, I haven't talked about that for ten years, and I'm not gonna start now."

Warwick intervened before an argument could erupt. "We agreed that question wasn't going to be asked. It isn't going to be asked, and it isn't going to be answered. We flew across country in good faith. He's here to help you."

ACTUAL MALICE

Haines asked Campoamor-Sanchez to step into the hall with her. When they returned, Haines reaffirmed her agreement with Warwick that talking about sex wasn't necessary.

At least not yet.

—

Later that afternoon, Gary spent half an hour inside the grand jury room. The questions he was asked included:

"Do you speak Spanish?"
"Have you ever heard of the gang MS-13?"
"Do you know a man by the name of Costini in the Italian mafia?"
"Do you know a man named Kevin O'Conner, also known as 'the Irishman'?"
"Do you know a carnival guy in North Carolina?"

"You did fine. We appreciate you going through this again," Brigidini said when Gary had finished and emerged in the hallway.

"I never thought I should be in this case," Gary replied. "The law-enforcement people who investigated this the first time weren't professional."

"Those guys are a bunch of fucking clowns. I wouldn't trust them either," Brigidini replied.

INTERFERING

"I just got off the phone with the US Attorney's Office," Roger Chiang said to me over the phone.

AUSA Amanda Haines and her team were also working the open Joyce Chiang case, but didn't know that Roger and Gary were sharing information.

Roger and Gary had mutual friends, who had put them in contact with one another. By the middle of 2009, Roger, Gary, and I talked regularly about the latest information we had received regarding the ongoing investigations. By comparing notes, we were able to make better judgments about whether the US Attorney's Office was on the up-and-up.

"They're close to solving my sister's case," Roger explained.

"Thank God, Roger. Did they say who?"

"They wouldn't say yet. They won't announce anything until after the Chandra Levy trial."

"Why?"

"Amanda said they're not connected. But they need to try and control the press."

"Does that mean he's incarcerated?"

"I'd guess that's the case. I don't know. She had a cold case detective on the line. He just apologized, a lot. He said the people who handled the case the first time messed it up badly. They reopened the case because of the pressure they were getting after opening the Chandra case. The investigators screwed up the forensics, so they've lost a lot of evidence or have evidence they can't use."

"We were told the same thing. Let's hope this leads to answers."

"I asked them about the Gainer problem," Roger added.

The "Gainer problem" referred to the defense Terrance Gainer had handed Joyce's killers by telling the public she had committed suicide.

"How'd they respond?"

"Amanda said, 'We have the same problem in the Chandra Levy trial.'" In this case, the problem was Gainer had repeatedly stated Guandique was not Chandra's killer.

"Shit" was the only response I could come up with.

—

We learned Guandique's defense team from the public defender's office had been calling Vince Flammini to try and place him in Washington, DC, during the time Chandra disappeared.

Flammini told them the truth—he had never traveled to Washington. But the defense team kept calling, trying to get Flammini to place someone else close to Gary in DC and Rock Creek Park.

The defense's strategy was clear: point the finger at Gary Condit.

The "Gainer problem" had reared its head.

—

"There's a high threshold to get in third party culpability defenses," Warwick explained. "I don't think they will be able to meet that threshold for a true third party defense. If they don't, then they can't go into court and point their finger at Gary. But they will still try to argue that Gary's relationship with Chandra is somehow relevant. The prosecution would open that door by calling Gary as a witness. Once they do that the defense will argue that they can attack Gary's credibility as a witness. We all know what they will really be doing is suggesting Gary killed her. They clearly think people still believe Gary did this and are banking on the jury having been poisoned."

"Yeah, well, there's a decade of news stories saying he did," I said.

"And unless the prosecution can keep it out, the defense is going to use the sex question to push Gary. His credibility, which is really his innocence, will all hinge on how that question is handled by the court and by Gary."

"You're kidding."

"Gary might have to decide whether he's going to go there."

"Gary won't see it that way," I responded.

"If the judge agrees with the defense, then Gary will be held in contempt if he refuses to answer whether he had sex with her. If he doesn't answer in court whether he had sex with her or not, he might find himself making little rocks out of big rocks."

WITNESS PREP

On September 17, 2010, Amanda Haines and Chris Brophy, an investigator for the US Attorney's Office, arrived at Tom Warwick's law office in San Diego, California.

We gathered in a cramped conference room.

"Mr. Condit," Haines began, "I feel terrible that we're here asking you to do this. I hope you believe that. What has happened to you is awful. We're trying to fix that."

"I appreciate you saying that," Gary answered.

"Our original strategy in prosecuting Ingmar Guandique was to call three witnesses who could testify to his involvement in Chandra's death. We had to scratch those witnesses because we determined they lacked credibility. Our new strategy—what we are left with—is putting on evidence of numerous inconsistent stories that all lead to the same result, which is that he murdered Chandra. As part of that strategy we need you to testify at the trial."

She paused.

"I'm here," Gary responded.

"We hope you can cover three areas. First, Chandra did not have many friends; you're one of the few people who can help people understand what was going on in her life. We think maybe you know more about her life than her parents do. Second, DC is very critical of you. If you testify we hope to vindicate you in the eyes of the press, and the public. Third, there's no DNA evidence. Press reports are wrong. The case is based on confession witnesses and other women he attacked."

While she talked, Gary wrote a message on a steno pad and handed it to me: "I DON'T NEED TO BE VINDICATED."

Haines caught the movement, but didn't ask to see what he had written.

"One of the witnesses says that Guandique claimed he was approached by a congressman in a car, who gave him a photo of a woman and asked him to kill her while she exercised. He said that he was paid $25,000. He said he saw the woman in the picture on a jogging path in the park, tackled her and dragged her into the woods, stabbing her and covering her body with sticks and weeds. Without the other witnesses, this is our strongest witness because he corroborates the facts of Chandra's killing and he came forward in August of 2001, before they found Chandra's remains in the park."

"That's all you got?" Gary asked. "A bunch of jailhouse confessions?"

Haines acknowledged that they had little forensic evidence that could be used at trial. Much of the evidence had been lost or tainted by investigators.

"The core of each of his confessions—even if they're all different—is that he killed Chandra. We don't have any alternative. We know he's the right guy, but the investigation was done so poorly we lack evidence we otherwise would have."

"That's why I'm here?" Gary demanded. "Is that why I'm getting dragged into this? How are you going to deal with the police? How are you going to deal with Terrance Gainer? What about Chief Ramsey? You all spent years chasing me while he was sitting right there! While he had confessed!"

"That's not me!" Haines insisted.

"What about the prosecutors, your fucking office—the US Attorney's Office—they were out of control!"

"That's not me!"

"Have you read what Kittay did to his wife? The witch hunt she led?" I interjected.

"I work with Barbara Kittay, she's a total bitch," Haines acknowledged.

Over the course of heated exchanges, Haines and Brophy revealed that during the summer of 2001 the US Attorney's Office had actually pegged Carolyn as a prime suspect.

Gary let his anger spill out. "Law enforcement did everything they could to pin this on me. And they couldn't keep from talking to the press, so they did the same thing. If they got what they wanted, I'd be in jail right now and this guy would be walking free."

"That's why we're here. We're here to get the guy who did this, and to vindicate you, Gary," Haines said. "Can't you see that?"

"I don't need to be vindicated," he replied coldly. "You guys tied me up behind a truck and drug me around for ten fucking years."

"Not me . . ." Haines started.

"You fucking come here and tell me that you guys got this wrong, and now you need me to help you fix it? You think I can be vindicated? You've already buried me."

"It wasn't me. You keep saying 'you'!" Haines argued. "We just want to get to the truth, so that people will know the truth."

"How can you get to the truth without putting those assholes on trial?"

"What they did to you was horrible. I know that. We know that. We want people to know that. But it wasn't me. You have to believe that. We're not the bad guys. I know that's hard for you to accept after what has happened, but I'm trying to fix that," Haines pled.

"How are you dealing with the investigators—the original investigators?" I asked, trying to shift the conversation back to the intended target. "There are ten years of lies and mistakes and fraud."

"We're not dealing with them," Haines answered.

Gary jumped out of his seat. Warwick quickly corralled him, concerned that Gary might walk out. Haines explained that the original investigators had screwed up the investigation so badly that the prosecution decided it would be counterproductive to use them or their work. "We can't put Guandique and the investigation both on trial."

"You have the 'Gainer problem,'" I added, wondering if the prosecutors had figured out that Roger Chiang and Gary were talking.

Haines didn't make the connection, but she answered the question. "We know that's an issue. Terrance Gainer has made a lot of statements in the press that aren't helpful to this trial."

"What about the press?" I asked. "You've got the *Washington Post* still pushing false stories and now they're taking credit for solving the case."

Haines and Brophy in unison rolled their eyes.

"Don't get me started on the *Washington Post*," Haines responded. "That book had nothing to do with this."

"I can't believe they'd release a book before the trial. They're just proving they're a bunch of pimps," Gary piled on. "They're continuing to interfere."

"We're not happy about that, believe me," Haines said.

She and Brophy then gave their unfettered and unflattering view of the *Post* and its reporters. "They've been completely used—manipulated—by the Levys," Haines added.

"You know Susan Levy is going to get on her soapbox," I prodded.

"We don't represent Susan Levy or Gary Condit," Haines answered curtly.

"With all due respect, that's a ridiculous position to take," I argued. "You just told me that the *Washington Post* and the rest of the media have created all these problems for you. From the beginning, this case has been tried in the public. This is going to be a circus. How can you ignore Susan Levy if she's going to be out there in the press?"

Haines, again, conceded what everyone knew but nobody wanted to acknowledge—for fear they'd be attacked by the media for having questioned a grieving mother. The media's bread and butter was creating victims and victim's stories. The media didn't like looking back on the unintended consequences of that process.

"She's not stable," Haines declared. "If she wasn't crazy before her daughter went missing, she's crazy now. She still thinks Gary had something to do with this."

"And she's out there saying that—right now—and the *Post* is printing every word of it."

"We can't reason with that woman. She'll say anything and believe it," Haines responded, her frustration with Susan Levy now completely unmasked. "We hope we don't have to call her to the stand. Right now, we don't plan on using her."

"You aren't going to call the mother to the stand in the trial of her daughter's murderer?" I asked.

"We can't prevent her from standing up in court and saying something outrageous. So we aren't planning on using her."

"Meanwhile, the media keeps marching down the Susan Levy path. They're going to trash Gary again—he's going to be the one that is made the bad guy no matter what the outcome is. You've told us you have a 25 percent chance of winning this case but need to pursue it because Guandique is the guy. If you lose this case, the media will blame him for it. Not Gainer. Not Susan Levy. It will be Gary Condit's fault."

"The media has their story," Haines explained. "I don't pay attention to that. I've got to convict the guy who killed Chandra Levy, or at least try."

"The biggest fiction," I started, "is that Gary somehow lied to the cops and to Susan Levy. It's just not true. That telephone call she claims she had with Gary never happened."

"We believe Gary's version of events," Haines replied. "We know a lot of things they said weren't true. It wasn't hard to figure that out."

"Then why don't you put her on the stand and say so?" Gary jumped in. "I'm still struggling to understand why I'm the only one who needs to stand up, take an oath, and testify! What about her? What about Gainer? I'm the only one who did what I was supposed to do during the investigation and kept quiet."

"We need the jury to see that you're not capable of doing this. I wouldn't be here if I didn't think we had to put you on the stand. But you'll need to answer all the questions. Why she died, it's terrible, as a fellow human being . . ."

"Don't put that guilt on me," Gary replied. "Don't put that fucking guilt on me, come out here and put the case on me."

Another heated exchange ensued.

"You've got crooked cops!" Gary shouted. "And they keep getting promoted."

"Nobody trusts the DC police," Brophy acknowledged. "In Maryland, I could take an unrecorded confession and a jury would believe me. In DC, they've been so bad, nobody believes them."

"The press does! Fuck, they don't even need names. And it was your office too!" Gary shouted.

Warwick recommended a break, and everyone agreed.

When we returned to the table, Haines took us step-by-step through the saga that had come to define Gary's life. At each step we corrected inaccuracies or filled in gaps, in the process revealing to Haines and Brophy that Gary had detailed records of his interviews with law enforcement. The more she heard, the more questions she asked. We went like that for a few hours. Eventually, we came to the same place the story always came to.

"You've got to get on the stand and explain the intimate relationship," Haines declared.

"I don't have to do anything," Gary responded.

"We've talked about that," Warwick interrupted.

"How is that relevant?" Gary demanded. "I'm not going to answer that. I've answered that to law enforcement."

Haines tried to explain to Gary that she didn't think it was relevant, but that the defense was going to ask him the question on cross, and they'd use his prior statements to law enforcement where he did answer the question to force him to answer publicly on the stand.

A violent philosophical argument erupted.

"It's going to go real bad if he doesn't admit to having sex with her on the stand," Haines argued. "The defense has his prior statements to the police and FBI where he admitted to having a sexual relationship."

"That's not what this is about. He's never lied. That's all that proves. It's about relevance," I argued.

"It's salacious. But it's out there. The fact of it, the nature of the relationship will be brought up. It will have to be discussed. I don't think I can keep that out."

The argument went back and forth. I could see that Gary hadn't fully grasped that Haines agreed the question should be irrelevant, but that her hands were tied if the judge let the defense bring it in under the guise of pressing his credibility as a witness.

"If the judge thinks it is relevant, then the judge will hold you in contempt if you don't answer."

"The judge can hold me in contempt. I'll go to jail," Gary lashed out. "I'm not going to answer that fucking question. It's totally irrelevant. I'm not going to let them pry into my private life, my family's private life."

"They want you to get upset—they want the jury to see you that way."

"Well—I should be upset, because this is bullshit. I had nothing to do with this. It has no relevance to this case."

"It does," Haines argued.

"No, no, no it doesn't. Two wrongs don't make a right. It's not relevant just because a bunch of newspapers have made it relevant. How does my sex life have anything to do with this man killing Chandra in the park? How!"

More arguing ensued. No legal or philosophical argument put forward by Haines could right the discussion. It had turned adversarial.

"Hold on," I interrupted. "Gary, can I talk to you outside?"

Gary and I stepped out of the room and onto a small landing.

"You good?" I asked, after closing the door.

"I'm fine. But they think they're going to fucking pick into me because they don't have a case? They need to understand I'm not just going to fold because they think they need to answer some sex question. With everything I know and what they've told me, how do I know this isn't just to set me up—to put the final nail in the story that I didn't cooperate and therefore this is all my fault?"

"At this point why does it matter? What you've told the police privately already leaked to the press. You've always talked about justice and right and wrong. What could be a more appropriate venue for stating publicly what your relationship was with Chandra than in a courtroom to convict her killer?"

"That's not justice."

"If people already know, what difference does it make?"

"A big fucking difference. It's my privacy. I'm not going to do it. I've drawn a line."

"Gary, listen."

"I'm listening."

"Are you?"

"I'm listening."

"I think she's being straight with us. I do. You don't need to trust her. She said they're going to try and limit the questioning in advance. If the defense goes there it will be up to the judge to decide if it is relevant or not. Look, we can argue about relevance all day. That's not why you're here. It's not why she's here. Don't forget she needs you. All we're doing today is setting the record straight and seeing if Tom can get her to come around to a position that works for everyone."

"It's been ten fucking years. They think they can put my life on trial. I . . ." Gary started. "Without putting those assholes on trial? They get a pass?"

"Gary, don't be a pussy. Get in there, and we'll help them get their facts right and we'll go from there."

He nodded. "You're right. Being in there—though, it's like being back there again."

We went back into the conference room. For the remainder of the day and the next day, Gary and Haines calmly went through the prosecution's case.

Haines revealed that the analyst who handled the clothing found at the crime scene may have contaminated the samples. She explained that the jewelry Chandra was allegedly wearing was never found. She revealed that the only DNA found at the crime scene was for an "unidentified male." There was no crime-scene DNA match to Guandique or to Gary.

She stated that the Metro Police did not submit to the FBI for analysis the DNA samples taken from Gary and the pair of Chandra's underwear Detective Durant had given to Charles Egan in May 2001 until sometime in 2002. It was unclear what had caused the delay or prompted the sudden submission. Moreover, a report on the comparison of the DNA samples wasn't finalized until March 2004, nearly three years after Chandra went missing. Again, nothing explained either the delay or decision to act, and it was an odd set of facts that contradicted the claim by the Metro police that they had a DNA match in 2001 and had somehow, kept it a "secret" even as they leaked everything else about Gary to the press.

"There is no such evidence," Gary insisted without emotion or clarification. "Why would they wait until 2004? What happened in 2004 that they suddenly decided to test my DNA?"

"We don't know," Haines replied.

"That's a bullshit answer. You don't think it's suspicious? I gave them my DNA in 2001. In fact, they got many samples of my DNA."

Later, at trial, Haines questioned Alan Giusti, a forensic examiner in nuclear DNA at the FBI, about his testing of Chandra's underwear, and Guisti stated, without explanation, that "originally, I did not have any known samples for comparison purposes, but as time went on, I did receive some known samples to do comparisons to." Guisti went on to testify that the DNA profile ultimately matched Gary.

Because Gary wasn't "on trial," the US Attorney's Office never had to explain the contradictions surrounding the DNA analysis or submit anything into evidence.

Haines handed a note to Gary.

It was a love note to Chandra with Gary's name signed at the bottom.

"Do you recognize this?" she asked.

"No," Gary answered.

He handed it to me. "That's not your handwriting," I said. "Not even close."

Whoever had penned the alleged "love note" had used large cursive letters.

"No," Gary reasserted.

I recognized a word was misspelled in the note. I handed Gary a piece of paper and asked him to spell the word.

He spelled it correctly.

I handed the piece of paper to Haines. "Look at that."

She and Brophy smiled, acknowledging that they knew from the beginning it was a fabrication. "That's a woman's writing," Brophy confirmed. Despite our requests, Haines and Brophy wouldn't say who had given the evidence over to authorities.

After nearly two days of in-depth discussion everyone was on the same page, even if it was a very big page. That's when Haines turned to the topic of Gary's 2001 interview with *People* magazine's Champ Clark.

"I took advice and agreed to do the interview with *People* in hopes of trying to put a better face on the situation. The entire process with *People* was a nightmare."

"Your wife did that interview," Haines commented.

"They instantly separated us. They wanted the story that our marriage was falling apart," he responded, his voice unusually weak, soft at the end of the sentence. "What they did to her . . ."

"What does your wife feel about this?"

"The . . ."

Gary paused to compose himself.

"Excuse me," he said. Gary stood, and left the room.

"What's wrong?" Haines asked after Gary had gone. "What did I do?"

"You didn't do anything," I explained. "What they did to Carolyn he'll never forget, he'll never forgive himself for that. You want to see that man come alive, you go after his wife. If you want Gary Condit to help you, you can throw whatever you want at him and he'll take it. You might not like what you get, but he'll handle it. A public defender isn't going to be a match for him. But if he suspects for a fucking second that you or anyone else is going to involve his wife in this, he'll shut you out and shut the whole thing down."

"I didn't mean to . . ." Haines started.

Gary came back into the room, now composed. "Sorry about that."

"Don't be sorry, Gary," Haines insisted.

They're seeing the real Gary. She's trying to figure out how to get this Gary to come out on the stand, I realized.

—

In the weeks that followed, the *Washington Post*'s reporters and Susan Levy hit the morning talk show circuit to pimp their stories in advance of the trial.

Lisa DePaulo wrote a scathing article denouncing Gary and announcing he wasn't owed an apology.

Prime time news specials covered every angle of the decade-old scandal. The calls from Larry King and Oprah to Gary's friends and family doubled down in frequency. For the most part, the media continued to blame Gary for Chandra's disappearance.

But cracks had formed.

On October 18, 2010, Jeffrey Shapiro of Fox News penned an article titled LESSONS LEARNED FROM CHANDRA LEVY'S MURDER. It read, in part:

[I]n 2006, I spoke directly with one of the lead detectives from the Washington, D.C., Metropolitan Police Department who was assigned to the Chandra Levy case. I was intrigued when he told me they had "no interest in Gary Condit as a suspect," and as a result, I pitched a story to several news outlets. To my surprise, no one was interested in reporting it. Maybe that's because vindication isn't as enticing as accusation . . .

RELEVANCE

Just as Amanda Haines had said, the government didn't call Gainer, Ramsey, Durant, Kennedy, Barrett, Kittay, or Pasichow as witnesses. Their appearances would only bolster the defense's position that the investigation was botched at best and corrupt at worst.

But on October 26, 2010, Metropolitan Police Department detective Ronald Wyatt was called to the stand. Wyatt had been removed from the case early in the investigation and replaced by Detective Kennedy.

HAINES: All right. Did there come a time you returned to Ms. Levy's apartment?

WYATT: Yes. The following day, May 10.

HAINES: Now, at that time did you come with anybody in addition to Detective Durant?

WYATT: Yea. We came back, obviously, with a warrant. Had Detective Durant and myself, had a prosecutor from the US Attorney's Office, and two FBI agents and some of our crime scene folks.

HAINES: And is that typical for you to bring a prosecutor and FBI agents to investigate a missing person's case?

WYATT: No, not at all. This was—because this case was getting media attention because a congressman was named as having a relationship with Chandra, this is what grabbed the attention of the command staff. You know, they wanted to know everything we were doing and shadowing, if you will, every step of the investigation . . . I mean it was just—it was like—almost became like a second-guessing of what we were doing by the command staff and people higher rank than I was . . . It was about 30 days into the case, a meeting was called at headquarters. I was to meet with the chief of police, executive chief, one of the FBI agents was there, a new commander of the then CID was present as well as our public information officer.

HAINES: Without telling us what you said at the meeting, how did the meeting end?

WYATT: Well, it ended with the executive assistant chief asking me, he said, "Sergeant," he says, "What is it we can do for you?" . . . And I told him "Chief, what you can do is you can leave me and my people alone and let us investigate this case. You know, and we will give you updates. But this daily, you know, update thing that was going on was not productive to the investigation."

HAINES: Let me stop you there. And who was the suspect, if there was one, at that time in the case?

WYATT: It was Congressman Gary Condit, we were looking at him.

HAINES: And after that meeting?

WYATT: I was immediately removed from the case.

On cross examination, the defense went after Gary, through Wyatt.

PUBLIC DEFENDER SANTHA SONENBERG: Now, also on May 9 of 2001, you actually went to Mr. Condit's condominium on Adams Mill Road, isn't that right? . . .

WYATT: I don't recall the date, but I did go to his apartment, yes.

SONENBERG: And you asked him about his relationship with Ms. Levy, right?

WYATT. That's correct.

SONENBERG: And he claimed that he didn't know Ms. Levy very well, right?

WYATT: He was a bit arrogant and not forthright.

SONENBERG: Okay. So he claimed he didn't know her very well, right?

WYATT: I don't recall the specifics of our—the exact verbiage that we used, but it was very superficial. His relationship with her—he led us to believe it was superficial—you know, and—I mean, I pointedly asked him a straightforward question.

SONENBERG: And the straightforward question you asked him was about whether he had an intimate relationship with Mrs. Levy, right?

WYATT: That's correct.

SONENBERG: And he denied that, right?

WYATT: Yes.

The Metropolitan Police Department brass and the mainstream press had carried the lie for ten years. Gary didn't expect that Wyatt would change his tune now. They knew Gary had detailed records of every one of his interviews with law enforcement except for his first sit-down meeting at the Lynshire with Detectives Durant and Wyatt. It was Gary's word against their claim he had lied to them during that first meeting.

—

Later that afternoon, Dr. Robert Levy took the stand. For the first time, the media listened to Dr. Levy speak under oath, and without his wife at his side.

HAINES: Was she taking anything in the way of birth control pills?

DR. ROBERT LEVY: Yes, she was taking that.

HAINES: How do you know that?

DR. LEVY: Because I got it for her.

HAINES: So when you looked at the phone bill what if anything did you notice?

DR. LEVY: That she had called his number, which we didn't know, several times.

HAINES: What did you do when you saw this number?

DR. LEVY: We called it or tried to get in touch with it.

HAINES: And who did you reach?

DR. LEVY: It was Congressman Condit's office.

On cross-examination, Dr. Levy fell apart.

SONENBERG: Is it fair to say that your daughter was a very private person?

DR. LEVY: Yes.

SONENBERG: In fact, she was even secretive, right?

DR. LEVY: Yes.

SONENBERG: Dr. Levy. Did you tell the police that your daughter didn't like to go out and hike on her own?

DR. LEVY: Yes.

SONENBERG: And did you mention to them that you didn't think she'd be one to go out to a park far from her home that she would know to be unsafe even during the day?

DR. LEVY: Yes. We felt that at the time because we were thinking Condit was the guilty one before we knew about this character here.

SONENBERG: Well, you talked on direct examination about going through the cell phone records, right?

DR. LEVY: Yes.

SONENBERG: And that's how you sort of deduced that one of the phone numbers was the person with whom she was involved.

DR. LEVY: Yes.

SONENBERG: And that was Mr. Condit, right?

DR. LEVY: Yes.

SONENBERG: Did you ever tell the police that she had plans in April, had you not come to DC, that she had plans to go on a trip in April with the person with whom she was involved?

HAINES: Objection, Your Honor.

DR. LEVY: I may have told that.

THE COURT: I overrule the objection. I think at this point though I would just say this. Ladies and gentlemen, with regard to whatever information Mr. Levy provided to the police it's being introduced not for its truth but for what the response to that information was. That is, you cannot conclude from what was said to the police that the facts that Mr. Levy conveyed were in fact true.

SONENBERG: Is it fair to say that you tried to share with the police as much as you could about this relationship in your effort to try to locate your daughter?

DR. LEVY: Yes, I did. I was suspicious of him because of suspicious circumstances of course. He was a primary suspect.

SONENBERG: Okay. I'm just going to ask you a few follow-up questions if I might with respect to things that you shared with the police about that. Okay?

DR. LEVY: Yes.

SONENBERG: Did you tell the police that your daughter was disappointed about being unable to go on a trip with the person with whom she was involved?

DR. LEVY: I may have said that.

SONENBERG: Did you tell the police that your daughter had sort of a 5-year plan that would involve her getting married to the person with whom she was involved?

DR. LEVY: I might have said that but I don't think she actually believed that. But we were mad at Condit at any rate so we just said whatever came to our mind at that time.

SONENBERG: I understand. I'm just trying to find out what you shared with the police at that time.

DR. LEVY: Yes. At that time, I was trying to paint him as the villain.

SONENBERG: Sure. And independently of telling them about a 5-year plan did you tell the police that your daughter was hoping to live with Mr. Condit, move in with Mr. Condit?

DR. LEVY: I might have said that but nothing I knew.

On redirect, Haines clarified for the jury the full extent of what the Levys had done in order to keep their daughter's disappearance in the news. Haines needed to get into the jury's mind the possibility that the Levys, and not Gary, had been the party lying to investigators.

HAINES: Ms. Sonenberg asked you, you gave some information to the police.

DR. LEVY: Yes.

HAINES: Did you have firsthand knowledge, meaning did you actually see all those things with your own eyes or were you repeating things you'd heard?

DR. LEVY: No. Repeating things.

GARY ON TRIAL

Gary and Cadee faced intense stares as they moved through Dulles International Airport. All around them, Gary's face was popping up on television screens.

Gary had insisted on staying at a friend's condo in Crystal City. Even though the fact that he was going to testify at trial had leaked to the press, nobody in the media knew what day had been targeted for his testimony.

Tom Warwick and I stayed at a hotel in DuPont Circle. The next morning was a Sunday. After breakfast, Warwick received a call from Haines asking that we bring Gary to the US Attorney's Office so she could prep him to testify the next day.

I called Gary. Cadee answered.

"Guys, he's not doing good. Going through the airport—as soon as we got to DC he changed. I don't think he will or should go. I think it will do more harm at this point," she said.

Warwick called Haines and pushed back the meeting time, then we took the packed metro to Crystal City.

—

"I don't need to go down there and have them grill me over a table. They already prepped me in San Diego," Gary insisted.

The prior day's questioning of Wyatt and Dr. Levy showed that the defense's strategy was in fact to attack Gary—and to do so by forcing him on the sex question. Gary's fate was in the hands of the judge. If he thought sex was relevant and Gary refused to answer the question, then the judge would have no choice but to hold Gary in contempt of court.

Now, the afternoon before he was set to testify, we faced a new problem.

Chad had sent Gary and Cadee a copy of the latest article in the *Modesto Bee* written by its Washington correspondent, Michael Doyle, under the headline: **GARY CONDIT BIGGEST LOSER IN FIRST WEEK OF CHANDRA LEVY TRIAL IN WASHINGTON**. It read in part:

Beyond a shadow of a doubt, though, the long awaited trial has already soured the names of Gary Condit, past leaders of the Metropolitan Police Department, and individual investigators . . .

The original supervisor on the Levy case, detective sergeant Ronald Wyatt, added under defense cross-examination that he had asked Condit "a straightforward question" about whether he was sexually involved with the much younger Levy.

"He denied it," Wyatt said . . .

If Condit does testify he will expose himself to what could be a reputation smudging cross examination by Guandique's defense attorneys . . .

"They're putting me on trial!" Gary shouted.

Cadee stepped in. "Guys, they won't get the best Gary Condit if they drag him down there today for prep. Just tell them he's not coming and he'll be there tomorrow."

Warwick and I took a cab from Virginia to the US Attorney's Office.

"What are we going to do?" I asked as we sped along.

Both of us knew that things had turned for the worse. Gary was shutting down.

"The only thing you can do when you're in this kind of situation is tell the truth," Warwick answered.

Haines and Brigidini met us at the front of the building.

"Where is he?" she demanded, standing stiffly in blue jeans, a light sweater, and her red tennis shoes.

"He's not coming," I answered.

Haines let out a sarcastic laugh and turned to Brigidini. "Give me your gun so I can shoot myself."

We followed Haines to her office, where we discussed next steps in light of the situation with Gary.

I had forwarded the article in the *Modesto Bee* to her. She pulled the article up on her desktop computer.

"That's not what's happening in there!" she insisted. "That's not even close. Is that what the press is saying?"

"Yes. That's the world he and his family have to live in. This guy was a public servant for thirty years. He never feathered his own nest, never broke the law. Out there, in his world, he's getting put on trial. And as far as he sees it, you're the one doing it."

"If he comes down here I can explain what is actually happening inside the courtroom," Haines offered.

"He won't do that."

"Well he needs to. We need to prep him," she asserted.

The other investigators piled on.

Warwick quietly weighed in. "Amanda, we're here to help. He wants to cooperate. But I've got a client who is held together by duct tape and super glue right now."

"Can we go to talk with him there?" she asked.

"We'll ask," Warwick responded.

I stepped into the hallway and called Gary. He agreed to allow them to drive out to Crystal City and talk with him, so long as they didn't start any interrogation or mock interview.

On the drive over we talked casually. Haines revealed Dr. Levy hadn't just testified that the Levys had made up stories about Gary, but that his testimony directly contradicted what he had said under oath in 2001.

When it came to Susan Levy, Haines gave us a tired look. Susan still believed Gary had something to do with Chandra's death. Haines reiterated what everybody had come to accept about the grieving mother.

Thirty minutes later, we sat around a dining room table, with Gary at one end and Haines at the other.

"We're not putting you on trial. That's not at all what's going on in the courtroom," Haines explained, hoping that it might bring him off the edge.

Within minutes of our arrival Haines had measured the situation and realized that Warwick hadn't overstated the severity of the condition of her key witness. She was now less concerned with preparation and more concerned with correcting Gary's state of mind before they stepped into the courtroom the next morning.

"I want to give you something to look at," she said, handing me a piece of paper.

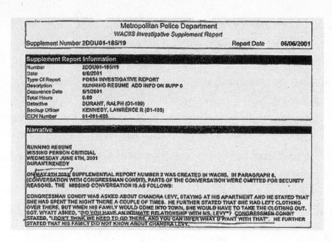

Metropolitan Police Department
WACIIS Investigative Supplement Report
Supplement Number 2DDU01-185/19   Report Date   06/06/2001

Supplement Report Information

Number	2DDU01-185/19
Date	6/6/2001
Type Of Report	PD854 INVESTIGATIVE REPORT
Description	RUNNING RESUME ADD INFO ON SUPP 6
Occurrence Date	6/6/2001
Total Hours	0.00
Detective	DURANT, RALPH (01-109)
Backup Officer	KENNEDY, LAWRENCE R (01-105)
CCN Number	01-091-625

Narrative

RUNNING RESUME
MISSING PERSON CRITICAL
WEDNESDAY JUNE 6TH, 2001
DURANT/KENNEDY

ON MAY 8TH 2011 SUPPLEMENTAL REPORT NUMBER 2 WAS CREATED IN WACIIS. IN PARAGRAPH 6, (CONVERSATION WITH CONGRESSMAN CONDIT), PARTS OF THE CONVERSATION WERE OMITTED FOR SECURITY REASONS. THE MISSING CONVERSATION IS AS FOLLOWS:

CONGRESSMAN CONDIT WAS ASKED ABOUT CHANDRA LEVY, STAYING AT HIS APARTMENT AND HE STATED THAT SHE HAD SPENT THE NIGHT THERE A COUPLE OF TIMES. HE FURTHER STATED THAT SHE HAD LEFT CLOTHING OVER THERE, BUT WHEN HIS FAMILY WOULD COME INTO TOWN, SHE WOULD HAVE TO TAKE THE CLOTHING OUT. SGT. WYATT ASKED, "DO YOU HAVE AN INTIMATE RELATIONSHIP WITH MS. LEVY"? CONGRESSMAN CONDIT STATED, "I DON'T THINK WE NEED TO GO THERE, AND YOU CAN INFER WHAT U WANT WITH THAT". HE FURTHER STATED THAT HIS FAMILY DID NOT KNOW ABOUT CHANDRA LEVY.

"You're kidding me," I said, putting the piece of paper down in front of Gary. The actual Metro Police records showed that Gary had not in fact denied an affair with Chandra. Rather, they supported what Gary had maintained for a decade.

He read it slowly. Color returned to his eyes, and strength to his voice. "Why the fuck isn't he getting prosecuted? Wyatt perjured himself yesterday. Dr. Levy admitted they lied. And I'm the one up there on the stand?"

"Perjury is hard to prove," Warwick explained, knowing that Haines had gone as far as she could. "He'll deny he read the report." Warwick also knew it'd be career suicide for Haines to pursue charges against a cop.

"He'll deny having read his own police report?" Gary demanded. "Why would anybody fucking believe that?"

"The *Washington Post* claims to have all the OASIS notes from the police department," I added. "The *Post* hasn't said anything about Wyatt testifying falsely. Instead we're getting shit like that story in the *Bee*."

"They can't turn back now," Gary said. "Heck, they're trying to convince people that they solved this case."

"I can't fix what the media reports or doesn't report," Haines replied. "But I can help convict the guy who killed Chandra Levy. And I know you want that too."

The morning news announced that American Media had declared bankruptcy.

News vans and camera crews staked out the front of the courthouse.

A mob of reporters had congregated in the hallway outside Judge Gerald Fisher's courtroom.

Inside, Ingmar Guandique sat on the far side of the bar. He was dressed in khaki pants and a turtleneck sweater, hiding the gang tattoos on his neck and the chains that held him to the table. The defense had also managed to cover his other tattoos, including the tattoo of the devil that covered his head.

Warwick and I were taken to reserved seats near the jury box.

Behind us, Susan Levy sat quietly, with a short black hat pulled low on her head.

A short while later, Cadee entered the courtroom and took a seat next to me. She and Gary had been taken into the courthouse through a guarded back entrance.

The room buzzed.

Reporters stepped outside to make phone calls. The word was out. Condit's daughter was there.

Immediately, additional news vans and crews were dispatched to the courthouse, surrounding each of the exits.

People gasped.

Gary Condit—a man who hadn't been seen or heard from in almost a decade—was led to the witness box.

His hair was more gray than sandy blond.

He wore a blue tweed jacket and slacks, but no tie.

In the trial of Ingmar Guandique for the murder of Chandra Levy, the part everyone desperately wanted to see finally started.

BEARING WITNESS

Gary testified for more than two hours. The room hung on every word as Haines systematically walked Gary through the story that now defined his life.

HAINES: Now, Dr. Levy and you had this discussion and you contacted police. What is your thinking as far as where she might be?

CONDIT: I didn't know. You never think. You just don't think this is going to happen to somebody you know. That's the furthest thing out of your mind. You're just hoping that she is somewhere safe.

Haines moved to Gary's first interview with Metro Police detectives Durant and Wyatt, knowing she needed to counter Wyatt's prior testimony that Gary had lied to the police.

HAINES: At the end, did there come a time where they asked you the nature of your relationship with her?

CONDIT: Well, for at least forty minutes Detective Durant asked all of the questions. He just went right down the list. And it was right at the last he sort of tried to wrap up the meeting. And Detective Wyatt said to me, did you have a sexual relationship with Chandra Levy? That's the only question that Detective Wyatt asked. And I said to Detective Wyatt, if you can tell me why that is relevant, I will be happy to answer that question but you need to tell me why it's relevant for our discussion. And he sat there silent and never said another word.

HAINES: Why did you answer the question that way?

CONDIT: I didn't think it was pertinent to the meeting or pertinent to anything. But if he had explained to me why it was relevant at the time I would have been happy to answer the question. Mr. Wyatt said that he asked me and I denied it. That is not correct. What is correct is he asked

me and I asked him to give me the rationale and the justification of why that was relevant. He
refused to do that. He didn't respond. He just sat back and they closed the meeting after that . . .
HAINES: And was it in your mind at the time that she was dead?
CONDIT: No.

Haines showed the jury a picture of cameras pressing up against the windows of Gary's
Modesto office.

Jurors shook their heads as the image recalled the mania of the "Summer of Chandra."

HAINES: What happen with respect to all the media attention on September 11, 2001?
CONDIT: Well, I was in my apartment and my office called and said do you have the TV on. And I said
you know I don't watch TV anymore. I stopped watching TV. And they said turn it on and I turned it
on and we all know what happened, 9/11. I saw the planes flying around and go in the building.
So I went to the . . .

Gary's eyes watered. He paused to collect himself.

Pin-drop silence covered the room. His reaction was raw and unexpected; a jolting con-
tradiction between the man they thought they knew and the one in the witness chair.

It was a remarkable juxtaposition set up by Haines, hundreds of rabid reporters chasing
Gary against 9/11.

A number of jurors cried.

CONDIT: After a few minutes I went to the window and looked down. Before that it was 100 or so
reporters and in 45 minutes they were all gone.

Haines brought Gary a glass of water. He took a sip, and composed himself.

HAINES: Were you ever charged or indicted with perjury?
CONDIT: Never.
HAINES: Did you care about Ms. Levy?
CONDIT: Yes, I did.
HAINES: Why have you never publicly admitted whether or not you had sex with her?
CONDIT: First of all, it's been ten years. I've never spoken publicly of the relationship at all. And it is
purely based on the principle that, as I said to Detective Wyatt, that I don't believe it's relevant.
I do think that we are all entitled to some level of privacy. I think I'm entitled to some level of
privacy. I think my family is. I think Chandra is. And it just seems in this country we've lost our
feeling for common decency.

Her question and his answer, again, jolted the courtroom.

Jurors nodded their heads.

Haines seized the moment.

HAINES: Did you have anything to do with her disappearance?
CONDIT: No ma'am.

HAINES: Did you kill her?

CONDIT: No ma'am

HAINES: I have nothing further, Your Honor.

—⁓—

Public Defender Maria Hawilo handled Gary's cross-examination. She wasted no time, skipping right to sex.

HAWILO: You weren't completely honest with the detectives, were you?

CONDIT: I was totally honest with the detectives.

HAWILO: Well, you said that you were just friends with Ms. Levy, right?

CONDIT: We were friends.

HAWILO: Sir, what you said, you didn't say that you had any romantic involvement with her, right?

CONDIT: No. I didn't say that at all.

HAWILO: And you refused to say during that meeting that you had an intimate relationship with Ms. Levy, right?

CONDIT: I didn't refuse to say that at all.

HAWILO: Sir, you testified that you don't like Sergeant Wyatt very much. Is that fair to say?

CONDIT: I really don't know Sergeant Wyatt. It's not about like. It's about truth.

HAWILO: Well, how is it that you knew Sergeant Wyatt had testified in this trial?

CONDIT: I can read.

HAWILO: Okay. So you've been reading the paper about what's been going on.

CONDIT: Well, I try not to read the paper. I try to read more factual stuff than the papers.

HAWILO: But you had at least read that Sergeant Wyatt had come in and testified and some of what he said, right?

CONDIT: I knew what he said, yes.

HAWILO: Now, on May 9—after that meeting on May 9 when you didn't disclose to the detectives the extent of your relationship with Ms. Levy.

HAINES: Objection.

THE COURT: You haven't established that.

HAWILO: Did you disclose to the detectives the extent of your relationship on May 9?

CONDIT: Yes.

HAWILO: You told the detectives that you had an intimate relationship with Ms. Levy?

CONDIT: No.

HAWILO: Okay. So you did have an intimate relationship with Ms. Levy, right?

HAINES: Objection.

THE COURT: Overruled. You have to answer the question.

CONDIT: I have already stated I'm not going to respond to those kind of questions based on my own privacy, Chandra's privacy, and my family's privacy. Out of principle I'm not going to respond to those questions.

HAWILO: Sir, are you pleading the Fifth on that question?

CONDIT: No, I'm not.

HAWILO: Then can you please answer my question?

CONDIT: No, I don't intend to answer that question. I'm sorry.

HAWILO: Sir, did you have an intimate relationship with Ms. Levy?

THE COURT: Can I ask this question? What's the relevance of that question?

HAWILO: Your Honor, I think the various statements and various impeachments. It goes to credibility.

THE COURT: I think his non-response responds to that.

HAWILO: But at that point of course you hadn't told the police your full involvement with Chandra Levy, right?

Gary paused, looked at Cadee, and gave the same response he had given before.

HAWILO: And of course at that point you hadn't told the police that you had ended your relationship with Ms. Levy in March of 2001?

THE COURT: Again, Ms. Hawilo, there's been no establishment of the former in which to establish the latter. So it's a fact not in evidence.

HAWILO: Sir, had you told the police at that point that your relationship with Ms. Levy had ended?

CONDIT: There was no relationship to end. We were friends. We remained friends. We would have been friends today. She was a friend.

HAWILO: Sir, did you tell the prosecutor at some stage that your relationship, however you character-ize it, with Ms. Levy had ended in March of 2001, right?

HAINES: Objection.

Judge Fisher sustained the objection and called for a lunch break. After the break, Hawilo's cross-examination of Gary continued.

HAWILO: You testified that Ms. Levy had come to your apartment several times, right?

CONDIT: Yes.

HAWILO: And the truth is Ms. Levy had spent the night at your apartment, right?

CONDIT: I am not going to respond to that question.

HAWILO: Sir, if you could please answer the question. Ms. Levy had spent the night at your apart-ment several times?

CONDIT: As I said earlier, there are certain areas that I view as private and who spends the night at my apartment is not relevant.

HAWILO: Sir, in fact, you told the police that Ms. Levy—eventually—first you told the police Ms. Levy never left any clothes in your apartment, right?

CONDIT: Correct.

HAWILO: And then you told police that she had left clothes in your apartment?

CONDIT: No, I did not.

HAWILO: You never told the police that she had left clothes in your apartment?

CONDIT: No, ma'am.

HAWILO: Okay. And so you never told the detectives on that night that you had a sexual relationship with Ms. Levy.

CONDIT: I am not going to respond to any personal or private questions, I am just not going to do that. I've already stated that earlier in my testimony.

HAWILO: Again, sir, are you refusing to respond because you think that the answer will incriminate you?

CONDIT: No. I am refusing to respond because it's not relevant and I believe I have a right of privacy and based on principle and common decency, I am not going to respond to those kinds of questions . . .

HAWILO: And are you denying telling the detectives on July 6 that your relationship with Ms. Levy ended in March of 2001?

CONDIT: I never told detectives that my friendship with Chandra Levy ended at any time.

HAWILO: What about your romantic relationship?

THE COURT: There is no basis for the question. No basis in evidence.

HAWILO: I would ask—sorry, Your Honor, I would ask that the witness respond to whether he had a sexual relationship—

THE COURT: He has declined to answer that.

HAWILO: I don't think he has the right to decline to answer that.

THE COURT: Mr. Condit, can you step down for just a minute?

Gary stepped to the corner of the room. The attorneys gathered at the bench in front of Judge Fisher.

THE COURT: Once again, I am just asking the question, what is the relevance of all this?

HAWILO: Your Honor, it goes to the—it goes to the witness—when the government brings out on direct their relationship, how open he was during the interviews, how long the relationship occurred—

THE COURT: This has nothing to do with quality of investigation. The question is how's the government—if you are trying to prove his opportunity or motive, that's a third party defense, and you said you were not going to pursue a third party defense. And then if this is less than a third party defense, it does not make it more relevant, it makes it less relevant.

As Gary walked out of the courtroom, more than two-thirds of the people in the gallery stood and followed him out.

In less than thirty seconds the crowded courtroom was nearly empty.

⟶

Cloistered in a private room, the investigators informed us that Gary would have to exit the courthouse through the front or side entrance. Either way, the press was going to be waiting with cameras.

Brigidini put a hand on Gary's shoulder and shook his hand. "Gary, if I were on that case at the beginning, none of this would have happened."

"I think you're probably right," Gary replied.

"Ninety-nine out of a hundred people lie when they're confronted with something like that. You were the exception, and you were a congressman. I would have understood what you were saying when you asked whether it was relevant and told me to assume what I needed.

Any good detective would have gotten that—understood the ancillary concerns you would have. We'd worked it out. None of this should have happened this way."

A moment later, we were led out of the courtroom into the main hallway. Reporters lined both walls. Brigidini and another federal investigator flanked Gary, a step ahead of him. Warwick, Cadee, and I followed behind, forming a bubble around him. When the doors to the courthouse flung open, light poured in. So too did the shouts.

"Mr. Condit!"

"Do you have anything to say?"

"Are you flying out today?"

"Why won't you answer the question?"

Cameras were shoved in our faces.

We followed investigators to a car parked in the street. They opened the door. Cadee stepped in first, then Gary followed. The car pulled away.

Warwick and I walked away from the courthouse, intending to find a cab once we were a few blocks away.

"Mr. Warwick!" Michael Doyle, the *Modesto Bee*'s Washington correspondent, shouted. "Mr. Warwick! Will Mr. Condit release a statement? Does he have anything to say?"

Warwick turned. His tall figure moved calmly as he walked straight toward Doyle.

"The judge has issued a gag order in this case. We don't know if it applies to Mr. Condit, but he's going to respect that," Warwick answered.

We turned and crossed the street. Doyle followed, demanding that we give him something more.

Warwick obliged. He turned, pointed his finger at Doyle's chest, and said, "Be accurate."

VERDICT

Having shown Gary wasn't the killer he had been made out to be in the press, Haines now needed to convince the jury Guandique was the killer.

Armando Morales provided Haines with her strongest jailhouse confession witness. Whether she was going to win or lose this case depended now on whether the jury would believe Morales.

On November 4, 2010, Morales took the stand. He revealed that he was a former founding member of the Fresno Bulldogs, a Northern California gang that was part of the same Mexican Mafia family as MS-13. Morales claimed he had dropped out of the gang in 2006 because he was "tired of the game."

Morales testified that he and Guandique were cell mates for four to six weeks at a federal penitentiary in Kentucky

Haines led Morales through a series of questions about Guandique's attacks on women in Rock Creek Park. Morales claimed that Guandique had told him he hid in the bushes until women came by on park paths, then ambushed them.

Morales alleged that Guandique had told him that he would go home to El Salvador and would not seek asylum in the United States when he finished his sentence for attacking women in Rock Creek Park because he thought he would be charged with murder if he stayed.

HAINES: Now, I want to fast-forward a little bit in time. Did there come a time where this topic of Chandra Levy came up again?
MORALES: Yes.

Morales explained that Guandique learned he was going to be transferred to a different prison out west. According to Morales, the gang members in those prisons were more aggressive. Guandique, allegedly, told Morales that while at a prior penitentiary he was suspected by gang members of being a rapist and having something to do with the killing of Chandra Levy. As a result, Guandique was upset when he learned of the transfer, believing he may be targeted if transferred.

HAINES: What did he say?
MORALES: He said, "Homeboy, I killed that bitch, but I didn't rape her."

Morales then testified that Guandique had confessed to him the details of how he had decided to rob Chandra when he saw her walking in the park. According to Morales, Guandique grabbed her from behind, by the neck, and drug her into the bushes. According to Morales, Guandique said he never meant to kill Chandra.

On November 22, 2010, the jury found Ingmar Guandique guilty of two counts of first-degree felony murder.

On February 11, 2011, Judge Fisher sentenced Guandique to sixty years in prison for the murder of Chandra Levy.

CHAPTER 25

WOE

DOUBLE DOWN

IN EARLY MARCH 2011, SARI Horwitz was caught plagiarizing two stories she had published in the *Washington Post*. She was suspended by the *Post* for three months for unprofessional conduct.

During the trial and sentencing of Ingmar Guandique, Horwitz and Scott Higham were finishing and promoting a docudrama based on their book *Finding Chandra* titled *Who Killed Chandra Levy?* The title itself was misleading in the wake of Guandique's conviction.

The main persons interviewed in the program were Linda Zamsky and Horwitz.

Nobody in the Condit camp participated in the docudrama. Because we had organized the facts, the actual facts could now speak for themselves, and Gary was for the first time on offense.

─╼─

I received an advance copy of the script from Roger Chiang, who was now a producer for *America's Most Wanted*. The script for *Who Killed Chandra Levy?* was dated November 28, 2010, and it was stunning in its departure from reality.

The script made no mention of the fact that Dr. Levy admitted to simply making up stories that had been reported by the *Post*. It also simply invented scenes, including one involving Gary and Carolyn in a bar in DC—before Chandra disappeared—and a scene after Chandra goes missing where Carolyn tells Gary, "I don't care in hell if you slept with an intern," and then instructs Gary that he needs to take control of the media to salvage his career.

Below is one particularly interesting scene:

SARI HORWITZ, Co-Author "Finding Chandra" SOT: Every once in a while, Chandra and Condit would sneak out of the city and have dinner at a Thai restaurant in the suburbs. To stay incognito, he would wear a baseball cap, would never take it off.

CHANDRA: You know, you haven't said a word about your wife for a few weeks. When is she coming to town?

CONDIT: Next week . . . for a Laura Bush luncheon. And Carolyn doesn't have anything to do with us.

CHANDRA: But she affects your plans. Our plans.

CONDIT: Chandra. I can't keep telling you. My marriage is a . . . friendship. Really.

CHANDRA: Yeah—but she's the friend you can walk down the street with—or have dinner with without wearing a nasty looking baseball cap.

CONDIT: I told you—we've been together since we were 19. Things can't change in a flash . . .

CHANDRA: Can I ask you something?

CONDIT: OK.

CHANDRA: Did you ever date an 18-year-old intern—a few years back. From Modesto?

CONDIT: Chandra . . . where are you coming up with this? You know the deal. When you're a Congressman, you're in the crosshairs. People make up crap about you all the time.

CHANDRA: Well, what happened?

CONDIT: What happened? How do I know? If it's the case I think, I met a girl in a parade, and before I knew it, her father is calling my office saying crazy things. Again, the crosshairs. I'm just trying to represent my constituents as best as I can.

CHANDRA: Forget the campaign speech.

CONDIT: Chandra. That's all the past anyway. I'm focused on now. And, we have years ahead of us to work things out—

Just then, two WAITERS come in with a small cake with candles on it. Happy birthday. Twenty four— so much more.

He reaches over, slides up the bill on his cap, kisses her, rubs her shoulder gently, then re-adjusts his cap. She bends down, starts to blow out the candles.

With the pro bono assistance of both Lin Wood and famed entertainment attorney Bertram Fields, who was particularly horrified by the *Post*'s behavior notwithstanding his nearly five decades in the news industry, we fired off a letter to TLC notifying the network and its parent of the significant credibility issues associated with one of its "consultants" on the project. The letter also reminded them that Carolyn Condit was a private person.

Scenes involving Carolyn were excised. Carolyn was not a public figure, and therefore would not have to meet the actual malice standard to sue if she chose to do so.

Dramatic fictions about Gary and Chandra were left in. Gary was a public figure, and Chandra was dead.

The docudrama aired on May 1, 2011. Thankfully, for truth's sake, few people watched. That evening, just as *Who Killed Chandra Levy?* was set to air, President Barack Obama announced that the US military had found and killed Osama bin Laden.

The reviews were still brutal:

The Los Angeles Times

Although both Higham and Horwitz provide most of the expository interviews, too much time is spent depicting the affair, and in a soap operatic way to boot . . .

Although Condit is cleared, these scenes manage to imply that he is at least partially to blame for Levy's death . . .

Horwitz suffers particularly; her smiling and energetic explanation of events is at terrible odds with the ominous unfolding of the story, making her appear callous and at times ghoulish when she is clearly neither of those things.

Reporters are not actors, true crime can often become pulp and sex always sells, but when the story revolves around a young woman's senseless murder and the sensationalized reaction to it, more care than this must be taken.

It also announces upfront that it contains "modified or fictionalized" moments, so believe it—or not—when Chandra is shown threatening her married lover, Rep. Gary Condit, by saying, "I wonder what the people in Condit Country would think if they knew about us?"

Billed as a "docu-movie," it pushes further into blurring the documentary/TV movie boundary than almost anything preceding it, and does a shameful disservice to both genres.

The sad part is the Levy case seems timelier than ever, with its mix of tabloid headlines, sex and salacious crime . . .

Mostly, though, "Who Killed Chandra Levy?" provokes a visceral sense of distaste . . .

It's hard not to feel sympathy for Levy's friends and family who participated through interviews, only to have her story exploited in this fashion . . .

"Who Killed Chandra Levy" is a cut-rate example of stooping to conquer.

GARY CONDIT

It was a typical day at Mae Hensley Junior High School in Ceres. Students in the first period physical education class lined up on the blacktop for roll call. Today, they had a substitute teacher, who began reading their names from the class roster.

"Gary Condit," the teacher said.

"Here," the boy replied.

The substitute teacher's double take wasn't unusual. The younger Gary Condit got that a lot from strangers.

"Have you ever looked up your name on the Internet," the teacher asked.

Gary laughed and replied "He's my grandfather," hoping that would end the conversation.

But the substitute teacher let the class roster fall to his side, walked toward him, and asked, "Do you think he did it?"

"Of course not," Gary answered, wondering if his classmates understood the teacher had just asked if his grandfather killed Chandra Levy.

"I didn't pay much attention to the case other than what I saw in the media," the teacher responded.

"That's where you went wrong."

Chad Condit, Gary Matthew's father, dealt with the problem with school administrators. Although it was "fixed" in that moment, the same substitute teacher, to this day, teaches where Gary Matthew goes to school. It's like oil has been thrown on generations, left with a cup of water to wash it off.

LITIGATION PRIVILEGE

During his 2010 trial testimony, Armando Morales stated, under oath, that he had not previously cooperated with law enforcement. In 2015, evidence surfaced that Morales had, in fact, provided law enforcement with key information in at least three different cases prior to 2010.

Guandique's attorneys argued that Morales fabricated their client's confession to curry favor with law enforcement. They also argued that the US Attorney's Office knew in 2010, or should have known, that Morales had a prior history of cooperating with law enforcement, and had withheld that exculpatory evidence from the defense. His attorneys stated that they'd seek sanctions against the prosecutors involved in the 2010 trial, mainly Amanda Haines.

On June 4, 2015, Judge Gerald Fisher set aside Ingmar Guandique's 2010 conviction for the murder of Chandra Levy and granted him a new trial before a new judge and jury.

The outfall was swift. Soon, at least one investigator and two assistant US attorneys, including Haines, were referred to the professional ethics board.

―

Deborah Sines, the lead prosecutor assigned to Guandique's retrial, was older, more direct, and less sure of herself than Haines. She was a career prosecutor, who had no incentive to let personal ambition infect her approach.

Unfortunately, that also meant Sines wasn't going to convict Guandique. Not because she wasn't smart enough—she was as sharp as anyone before her. But if Amanda Haines thought she had a 25 percent chance of winning in 2010, then Sines was playing the lottery.

There still was no hard evidence.

The only convincing confession witness, Morales, now had credibility issues.

And, the government's credibility would be questioned. The defense would try to introduce the fact that the government had withheld evidence in the prior trial, and in doing so would work to find a way to make Haines testify.

―

Sines and Chris Brophy, the investigator with the US Attorney's Office, joined Gary, Cadee Condit, Tom Warwick, and me inside a conference room in San Diego, California.

Sines did her best to explain why Guandique had been granted a new trial. She insisted Haines was not aware the US Attorney's Office had evidence of Morales's prior cooperation in its files during the 2010 trial.

She warned us that this time the defense was going all-in on Gary.

"The defense team is chasing down women. They've talked to Vince Flammini. They interviewed Otis Thomas," Sines explained.

"Who is paying for these people to fly all over the country?"

Gary had received a heads-up from dozens of friends that they were approached by Guandique's attorneys, sometimes at their homes.

"The public defenders' office," Sines explained.

"Taxpayers."

"Yes."

"Do all defendants get this kind of defense?"

"No."

"So the poor black kid in DC gets the $50 defense, and they're spending all this money to defend a guy who has attacked all these women and is in this country illegally?"

"Yes."

By any conservative measure, our government had spent millions of dollars, first trying to prove Gary or someone close to him killed Chandra Levy, and now funding, for a second time, both the prosecution *and* defense of Guandique.

"Tell me why they're interviewing Otis Thomas?" Gary asked.

"They are going to try and put on a true third party culpability defense. Tell the jury you killed her and present their evidence. It's not just you; they have a list of names. One of the guys was not even in the country when Chandra disappeared."

"That's bullshit. What evidence? Statements from these women, Vince, and Otis Thomas?"

"The judge is giving them a lot of room to gather information because of the first trial. I'm disclosing a lot more than I normally would. But I also don't think the judge will ultimately let them go forward with this defense once he sees that these people have no actual evidence."

"Have they reached out to Terrance Gainer?" I asked. "I mean, he twice said Guandique didn't do it."

"We don't know. Our office doesn't talk to Terrance Gainer."

"You aren't going to put the original investigators on the stand?"

"Gainer is not going to tell the truth," Brophy interceded.

"How can we as the government put someone on the stand we know is a liar?" Sines added.

"What if the defense calls Gainer?"

"If the defense calls Terrance Gainer or Charles Ramsey, I'll have a field day. Payback is a bitch," Sines said.

"Durant and Wyatt?"

"We believe Detective Durant and others were kept on the case even after Chandra's remains were found because the people in charge wanted the case to remain with investigators who were not capable of solving it," Sines responded.

"Is the trial on schedule?" Warwick asked.

"Twice Guandique's lawyers told the media they are ready for trial, then they've gone to the bench and asked the judge for a continuance," Sines explained. "They're working the press covering this trial."

"How so?"

"It gives the impression the government isn't ready. All this shit about sex, they're talking about it in court. Then the *Washington Post* reports it. But when they don't want something in the paper they come up to the bench where the reporters can't hear. It was the Levys who hooked Thomas up with the FBI. In one account, Thomas tells the FBI that the Levys offered him $1,000 and gave him a script. But the defense has that discussion at the bench where the reporters can't hear, and it doesn't make it into the paper."

A source inside the US Attorney's Office later confirmed that Thomas had given multiple inconsistent accounts to the FBI of his interaction with Susan Levy. In at least one account, he told the FBI she offered him $1,500 and gave him a script. In a later account, he stated Susan Levy did not in fact do those things.

"Litigation privilege," Warwick explained.

"Exactly," Sines responded.

Litigation privilege allows lawyers to say in a court proceeding what would otherwise be defamatory or libelous so long as the statement has some *relation* to the case. As a result, Guandique's lawyers were free to repeat in court filings and open court hearings whatever salacious thing that had been said about Gary, even if they knew it wasn't true. The media, in turn, could quote Guandique's attorneys in news articles and press reports. This was a core part of the defense's strategy to re-poison the DC jury pool in advance of trial.

Litigation privilege allowed everyone to practice actual malice.

LURING THE PRESS

On May 16, 2016, the public defender's office filed a motion in court, which read in part:

The witnesses the defense seeks to depose all have information regarding Gary Condit, and the relevance of their expected testimony is clear. The government's chief argument is that the noticed witnesses did not know Chandra Levy or Mr. Guandique. But they all know a main suspect in this case: Gary Condit . . .

Mr. Condit was a man of ambition, and with the President Clinton scandal fresh in his mind, Mr. Condit was fully aware of the cost he could pay if his affair with Ms. Levy became public. He therefore had an obvious motive to kill Ms. Levy in order to keep the relationship a secret, and an equally powerful motive to cover-up the circumstances of her death if she died while she was with him—either through his intentional conduct or otherwise . . .

Mr. Condit also repeatedly misrepresented and downplayed the true extent of his relationship with Ms. Levy . . .

Mr. Condit refused to submit to an FBI-administered polygraph examination—like the FBI-administered polygraph test to which Mr. Guandique voluntarily submitted and passed. Instead, Mr. Condit hired his own polygrapher and claimed to have passed, but the results he provided to law enforcement were decried as "useless" and "not credible" by then-Chief of Police, Charles H. Ramsey . . .

W-1

. . . W-1 had a sexual relationship with Mr. Condit in 2001, during the same period of time that Condit had a relationship with Ms. Levy.

The government alleges that Ms. Levy's tights were found near her body in Rock Creek Park, and that each leg of the tights was tied in a knot. The government argued at the first trial that the killer used the knots in the tights to restrain Ms. Levy. According to FBI notes of an interview with W-1, Mr. Condit—only a few months before Levy disappeared—engaged in aggressive sex and scared W-1 by demonstrating a desire to tie up W-1 with items of clothing.

. . . W-1's testimony in this regard would provide a link between Mr. Condit and the evidence near Ms. Levy's body: Mr. Condit's desire to engage in aggressive sex and tie a woman up and the knots in what the government alleges were Ms. Levy's tights found with her remains . . .

W-4

W-4 was Mr. Condit's friend and served as his bodyguard and driver through 2001 . . .

W-4's testimony will link Mr. Condit to Jennifer Thomas.

Susan Levy, Chandra Levy's mother, informed the FBI and the MPD that before Chandra Levy went missing, she received information that Jennifer Thomas had an affair with Mr. Condit, and that Jennifer Thomas went into hiding after the relationship ended because she was afraid of Mr. Condit. Susan Levy learned this information from O.C. Thomas, Jennifer Thomas's father . . .

The motion by Guandique's lawyers was to seek permission to depose Anne Marie Smith, Vince Flammini, and two other female witnesses who alleged to have had a relationship with Gary that ended many years before Chandra disappeared. For each potential witness the defense provided a basis for the person being unable to travel to Washington, DC, to testify at trial, mainly health issues.

If the court agreed that they could be deposed in lieu of testifying at trial, then the defense could use handpicked statements from these depositions to question Gary when he took the stand. None of these people would be subject to cross-examination in front of the jury. Sines would have to rely on her questioning of them during the out-of-court depositions.

Following the defense motion, the *Modesto Bee* declared that Gary's sex life was on trial, repeating what Guandique's defense lawyers had said in court and written in court filings.

The *Washington Post* ran a headline, ATTORNEYS FOR MAN CHARGED WITH KILLING CHANDRA LEVY SAY GARY CONDIT HAS HISTORY OF 'AGGRESSIVE SEX.'

CLOSURE

On July 28, I received an e-mail from AUSA Deborah Sines with no content, just a subject line: "Call me now."

It was nighttime where I was in the United Arab Emirates.

I connected with Sines, and she informed me that the government had decided to dismiss the charges against Ingmar Guandique.

Armando Morales's new girlfriend had alleged she recorded a conversation with him in which he said he was paid to testify falsely by a powerful politician from Arizona.

"Mrs. Levy calls us and tells us this woman has contacted her . . . We get the woman, we get a seven-hour tape she made of Mr. Morales, who had been locked up for thirty years until last month, when he finished his sentence. He apparently was trying to woo her . . . Let me put it this way. In the seven-hour recording I have, he is not saying Gary Condit or a politician in Arizona paid him. She claims that was in other conversations that she taped but she can't explain why it wasn't on the tape I got."

"Does this person even know Gary?"

"Fuck no. She's a hustler. She realizes who he is and she Googled the case. She found Susan Levy on Facebook. Levy calls her, and she tells Mrs. Levy, 'Yeah I think Gary Condit did it too. Here's why, I met this guy. This is what he said . . .' I believe this woman thought this was a paycheck. She's on TV or something. A bit extra like on *House of Cards*."

The woman had a long history of fraud, and this appeared to be another attempt at it.

"What I do know? Morales is on the tape offering to harm people who have harmed this woman. Here is this guy who was supposed to turn his life around due to a life skills program in prison, and that's why he was telling on Guandique. Instead he is right back in the life, and I can't sponsor him as a witness anymore."

"I'm sorry."

"I'd be lying to you if I didn't tell you this is crushing me. This is the part of the job I hate."

"Yeah."

"And I know every reporter in the universe is probably calling Gary."

"Yes."

"And there is nothing I can say to them. I'm not allowed to say I'm 100 percent convinced Guandique did it."

"Why?"

"The way our system works, I can only speak by indictment when it comes to someone's guilt or innocence."

A lead investigator in the Ingmar Guandique case, including direct involvement in the 2010 trial, believes the US Attorneys' Office did not aggressively challenge Guandique's demand for a new trial in 2010. This person believes the US Attorney's Office did not do so because it wanted to avoid putting AUSA Amanda Haines on the stand, fearful of what she might say in open court. This is consistent with information provided by an AUSA involved in the 2016 retrial and decision to dismiss the charges against Guandique. This person claims that shortly after the dismissal, AUSA Amanda Haines visited the 2016 prosecution team and expressed that she was relieved the charges had been dropped against Guandique because she did not want to have to testify about the allegations of misconduct in the 2010 trial.

The US Attorney's Office has repeatedly stated privately that there is no evidence Gary Condit had anything to do with the murder of Chandra Levy. The government blames the press. It has further confirmed that there was rampant misconduct, including potentially criminal conduct, inside law enforcement. It will neither investigate and prosecute the people responsible, nor publicly clear Gary.

EPILOGUE

GUANDIQUE

SHORTLY AFTER THE GOVERNMENT DROPPED its case against Ingmar Guandique for the murder of Chandra Levy, his attorneys contacted US Immigration and Customs Enforcement officials to explore whether Guandique might receive asylum in the United States. This is being done quietly so as not to get leaked to the press.

According to law-enforcement sources, Guandique sexually assaulted a woman in El Salvador before he immigrated to the United States. He allegedly stabbed the woman countless times. It was a miracle she lived. According to these sources, he can't go back to the village he came from because the community, including the woman's brothers, will kill him if he does.

Separately, as a member of MS-13, he will be held in a special facility because of the extremely violent nature of MS-13 in El Salvador and that government's need to control the flow of gang members back into the country.

As an assistant US attorney with direct involvement in the Guandique case put it:

> I don't like sticking him on women in El Salvador either. We had to investigate his run-ins in prison. They almost all involved women. Mainly, as soon as there was a female prison guard his dick was out in his hand or he was violent. This guy is a monster.

JOYCE

The US government now knows what happened to Joyce Chiang that cold January 1999 night she disappeared from in front of the Starbucks in DuPont Circle.

A kidnapping and extortion ring of at least three men grabbed Joyce and put her in the trunk of their vehicle. When they later stopped, Joyce managed to get out of the trunk and run. They caught her from behind, tearing her jacket.

One of the three known suspects is dead.

Another lives in Africa and is now on his deathbed, or is dead.

The third is serving time in a US prison.

Nobody has been charged for the murder of Joyce Chiang.

CHANDRA

Chandra Levy was an intelligent, ambitious, and successful young woman who was taken too soon. In many respects, the world is left with an image of her that is both incomplete and distorted by a version of her so many desperately wanted to be the truth.

Chandra's murder remains unsolved and open.

BIBLIOGRAPHY

BIBLIOGRAPHICAL NOTE

Actual Malice is the product of hundreds of written and recorded sources. The backbone of the book came from Gary Condit's, Chad Condit's, and Abbe Lowell's extensive records encompassing more than twenty banker's boxes of transcripts, detailed memoranda, letters, congressional and legal records, newspaper articles, television news clips, and individual declarations, as well as hundreds of hours of interviews I conducted with primary players in the saga and my own direct involvement with the US Attorney's Office and other investigators in the 2010 and 2016 trials of Ingmar Guandique.

Dialogue in the book is for the most part taken from written contemporaneous records. Where there is no written record, it is re-created from either interviews of all participants, or a combination of interviews with some participants and prior accounts of the conversation from the non-interviewed participants (such as media interview transcripts or press stories). There is a limited set of conversations where one participant's version of what was said or not said had to be chosen over another participant's differing account, whether in an interview or based on available records.

As much as Sari Horwitz and Scott Higham of the *Washington Post* deserve fault for their unwillingness to fully acknowledge the *Washington Post's* and, in the case of Horwitz in particular, her own, central role in the problems that prevented justice for Chandra Levy (including her reporting on the infamous Otis Thomas story), portions of this book benefited from their good work, together with Sylvia Moreno, in investigating the internal dynamics and issues that plagued investigators in the DC Metropolitan Police Department, FBI, and US Attorney's Office from 2001 through 2008. Their work is reflected both in the twelve-part series titled "Who Killed Chandra Levy?" and published by the *Washington Post* online ("the *Post* 12-Part Series"), and in the subsequent book based on that series written by Higham and Horwitz titled *Finding Chandra* (New York: Scribner, 2010) ("*Finding Chandra*"). In many instances, their reporting helped confirm my own understanding based on publicly available records, including extensive press stories, nonpublic records in my possession or which I had been allowed to read by the US Attorney's Office in 2010 and 2016, and discussions with individuals directly involved in the case.

The term "including" as used in this bibliographical note means "including, without limitation."

The following describes the key source materials for each chapter of *Actual Malice* but does not provide a full bibliography. For a complete list of all sources, as well as video footage, the news stories underlying references to "news archives," law-enforcement records, congressional and legal records, court transcripts, and more, go to www.actualmalicebook.com. The extensive bibliography and supporting materials made available there will provide you with the full picture of the extensive record that underlies *Actual Malice*.

Key Materials

Ch. 1, Condit Country. Interviews with Gary Condit, Carolyn Condit, Adrian Condit, Jean Condit, Chad Condit, Cadee Condit, Mike Lynch, Burl Condit, Darrell Condit, Dove Condit-Wilson, and Vince Flammini provided invaluable insight. These interviews were supplemented with Gary Condit's personal and congressional records as well as news archives. Gary Condit's speech at the Condit Country jamboree was captured in the documentary film *Public Service: The Private Campaign of Gary Condit*, directed by Kristina Holland and Aaron Garcia (2002), VHS.

Ch. 2, Public and Private Trust. Interviews with Gary Condit, Burl Condit, Vince Flammini, and Roger Chiang provided invaluable insight. Congressional records together with news archives capture much of the information included in the subsection "Stay in the Box." *My Peace I Offer You: The Disappearance of Joyce Chiang* by Roger Chiang (2008) provided a road map for the subsection "Cold Case Capital." News archives and discussions with law-enforcement officials directly involved in the Joyce Chiang investigation further substantiate the information in this section.

Ch. 3, Warning Signs. Interviews with Gary Condit, Mike Dayton, Vince Flammini, and Mike Lynch provided invaluable insight. Congressional records, including official congressional/ US Department of the Navy CODEL itinerary and photos, helped frame the subsection "Warning Signs." Gary Condit's congressional records, including a contemporaneous office memorandum with attached transcript, provided the raw material for the subsection "Khandet."

Ch. 4, Intern. Interviews with Gary Condit, Mike Dayton, Mike Lynch, Carolyn Condit, Mike Lynch, Willie Brown Jr., Rusty Areias, Gerald Eaves, Steve Peace, Pete Geren, Jimmy Hayes, and Mike Parker provided invaluable insight. Photos referenced in the subsection "Political Field Trip" were provided by the US Attorney's Office and developed from Chandra Levy's camera by investigators. Congressional records and news archives further substantiate Gary Condit's policymaking record. Information in the subsection "Gang of Five" was further supported by *Basic Brown: My Life and Our Times*, Willie Brown Jr. (Simon & Shuster, 2008). Special mention is required for the original naming of the "Blue Dogs" by Jimmy Hayes, which is supported by an extensive interview with Jimmy Hayes and a letter from J. Hayes to Mary Bertaut, Louisiana State Archives, re. "Washington Blue Dog," dated April 14, 2008.

Ch. 5, Turning Points. Interviews with Gary Condit, Cadee Condit, Vince Flammini, Mike Lynch, and Steve Peace provided invaluable insight. News archives substantiate Chandra Levy's e-mails and her interactions with her landlord. News archives, court documents, and discussions with representatives of the US Attorney's Office substantiate the information concerning Ingmar Guandique in the subsection "Inauguration."

Ch. 6, Exchanges. Interviews with Gary Condit provided the basis for much of the dialogue in this chapter. Specific information regarding Ingmar Guandique in the subsection "Tryst" is based on the following sources: the *Post* 12-Part Series, chapter 6; other news archives; *Finding Chandra*, 62–68 (New York: Scribner, 2010); Portillo Trial Transcript, October 27, 2010, 2009-CF1-9230; Sheila Phillips Trial Transcript, October 27, 2010, 2009-CF1-9230; and the Affidavit in Support of an Arrest Warrant, Superior Court of the District of Columbia, Defendant Name: Ingmar Guandique, March 3, 2009, issued by US Attorney's Office ("2009 Guandique Arrest Warrant"). Chandra's e-mail to her landlord in the subsection "Good-bye" is reported in *Finding Chandra*, 25–26 (New York: Scribner, 2010).

Ch. 7, Flotus and Potus. Interviews with Gary Condit, Carolyn Condit, Mike Dayton, Mike Lynch, Rebecca Cooper, and Darrell Condit provided invaluable insight. This chapter is further supported by the following key materials: news archives; a detailed timeline of Gary's activities between April 28, 2001 and May 4, 2001 provided by A. Lowell to law enforcement; law-enforcement records disclosed to author (including Chandra Levy's voice mails); transcripts of media interviews given by Susan and Dr. Robert Levy; and discussions with representatives of the US Attorney's Office. Information regarding Ingmar Guandique in the subsection "A Meeting with Dick" is substantiated by the 2009 Guandique Arrest Warrant and other court records, as well as *Finding Chandra*, 62–68 (New York: Scribner, 2010).

Ch. 8, Fumbles. Interviews with Gary Condit, Mike Dayton, Rebecca Cooper, and Mike Lynch support much of the material in this chapter. This chapter is further supported by the following key materials: law-enforcement records (including Metropolitan Police Dept. WACIIS Investigative Supplement Report No. 2DDU01-185/2, May 9, 2001, and Metropolitan Police Dept. WACIIS Investigative Supplement Report No. 22DDU01-185/19, June 6, 2001); court records (including Detective Ronald Wyatt Trial Transcript, October 26, 2010, 2009-CF1-9230; Officer Charles Egan Trial Transcript, October 26, 2010, 2009-CF1-9230; Gary Condit Trial Transcript, November 1, 2010, 2009-CF1-9230; and Sheila Phillips Trial Transcript, October 27, 2010, 2009-CF1-9230); discussions with representatives of the US Attorney's Office; news archives (including the *Post* 12-Part Series, chapter 6, and Marc Sandalow and Chuck Squatriglia, "Apartment Entered on May 10," *San Francisco Chronicle*, July 19, 2001, re. police officers fail to obtain surveillance tapes from Chandra Levy's apartment); transcripts of media interviews given by Susan and Dr. Robert Levy; "Private and Confidential Memorandum re. GC's Initial Contacts with Police" dated May 2001; and *Finding Chandra*, 56–57 (New York: Scribner, 2010).

Ch. 9, Going National. Interviews with Gary Condit, Mike Dayton, Darrell Condit, Mike Lynch, John Conyers, Jack Russ, Cadee Condit, Chad Condit, Channce Condit, Carolyn Condit, Steve Peace, Adrian Condit, and Jean Condit provided invaluable insight. This chapter is further supported by the following key materials: news archives; court records (including

Officer Charles Egan Trial Transcript, October 26, 2010, 2009-CF1-9230 and the 2009 Guandique Arrest Warrant); transcripts of media interviews given by Susan Levy and Dr. Robert Levy; discussions with representatives of the US Attorney's Office; letter from Joseph Cotchett to NBC News dated June 13, 2001, re. cropped photo with supporting exhibits, together with a response letter from NBC; Confidential Memorandum re. "NBC reply June 14, 2001 letter" dated June 14, 2001 and prepared by Don Thornton of Cotchett, Pitre & Simon (Thornton discussion with J. Baker).

Ch. 10, Tempest. Interviews with Gary Condit, Rusty Areias, and Mike Dayton provided invaluable insight. This chapter is further supported by the following key materials: news archives; discussions with representatives of the US Attorney's Office; and Metropolitan Police Dept. WACIIS Investigative Supplement Report No. 22DDU01-185/19, June 6, 2001.

Ch. 11, Suspect CM. Interviews with Gary Condit, Mike Lynch, Mike Dayton, and Joseph Cotchett provided invaluable insight. This chapter is further supported by the following key materials: news archives; transcripts of media interviews; and "Statement in Response to Inquiries Regarding Anne Marie Smith" issued by Cotchett, Pitre & Simon dated July 3, 2001, together with attachments including letter from *Star* magazine to Gary Condit and e-mail and draft affidavit from D. Thornton to J. Robinson. Susan Levy's collage involving Chandra Levy and Gary Condit is reported in *Finding Chandra*, 247–248 (New York: Scribner, 2010).

Ch. 12, Post Position. Interviews of Gary Condit, Mike Lynch, Abbe Lowell, Mike Dayton, Joseph Cotchett, and Chad Condit provided invaluable insight. This chapter is further supported by the following key materials: news archives (including Anthony York, "Stunned in Sacramento," *Salon.com*, July 14, 2001; Jim Rutenberg, "Levy Case Brings Out Cable's Instinct for the Racy and Repetitive," *New York Times*, July 30, 2001; and Felicity Barringer, "The Lost Privacy of Gary Condit," *New York Times* online, July 8, 2001); transcripts of media interviews; declarations of Walter Hughes dated June 21, 2001, Don Wilcox dated June 21, 2001, Scarlett Parker dated June 20, 2001, and Mike Lynch dated June 20, 2001; congressional records (including letter from M. Lynch to D. LeGrand dated June 8, 2001); and court records (including Dominick Dunne Deposition, September 29, 2004, 02-CIV-9910, and Ronald Wyatt Trial Transcript, October 26, 2010, 2009-CF1-9230).

Ch. 13, Albatross. Interviews with Mike Dayton, Gary Condit, Carolyn Condit, Cadee Condit, Adrian Condit, Jean Condit, Chad Condit, Mike Lynch, and Abbe Lowell provided invaluable insight. This chapter is further supported by the following key materials: news archives; transcripts of interviews with media; *Finding Chandra*, 87–90 (Levys and Martin meet with Metropolitan Police and J. Barrett determines Levys' insistence on pursuing Gary Condit becoming an "albatross"), 97 (Smith meeting with FBI and her comment that Gary "was a decent man"), 122 (J. Barrett version of discussion with A. Lowell at Starbucks), 125–126 (discussion between B. Kittay and J. Barrett and J. Barrett discussion with

C. Ramsey, re. prosecutors, in each case, after the July 6 law-enforcement interview of Gary Condit) (New York: Scribner, 2010); congressional records (including press releases issued by Gary Condit's office each titled "Statement of Congressman Gary A. Condit" and dated June 22, 2001); letter from A. Lowell to H. Pasichow, re. "The Condit Family" dated June 27, 2001; the *Post* 12-Part Series, chapters 5–6; the 2009 Guandique Arrest Warrant and other court documents; *The Daily Howler*, "Our Current Howler (part IV): An ugly, dirty business," August 30, 2001; Confidential and Privileged Memorandum to Attorney File re. "Meeting with Congressman Condit and D.C. Police" dated June 23, 2001; Confidential and Privileged Memorandum to Attorney File re. "Interview of Mrs. Carolyn Condit by U.S. Attorney's Office, FBI and D.C. Police Department" dated July 5, 2001; Confidential and Privileged Memorandum to Attorney File re. "Meeting with Congressman Gary A. Condit, Abbe D. Lowell, Esquire, Detective Commander Jack Barrett, Detective Ralph Durant, AUSA Barbara Kittay" dated July 7, 2001; letter from A. Lowell to Cmdr. J. Barrett, re. "Fox News Press Clip" dated June 26, 2001; letter from Joseph Cotchett to Roger Ailes (chairman and CEO of Fox News Network), re. "Unethical Coverage of Congressman Gary A. Condit" dated June 28, 2001; Metropolitan Police Department WACIIS Investigative Supplement Report Number 22DDU01-185/30, June 23, 2001; and Metropolitan Police Department WACIIS Investigative Supplement Report Number 22DDU01-185/55, July 29, 2001.

Ch. 14, Unreliable Sources. Interviews with Rebecca Cooper, Carolyn Condit, Mike Lynch, Mike Dayton, Vince Flammini, Abbe Lowell, Gary Condit, Cadee Condit, Chad Condit, Adrian Condit, and Jean Condit provided invaluable insight. This chapter is further supported by the following key materials: news archives (including Lisa DePaulo, "Not So Fast, Gary," *The Daily Beast*, February 22, 2009, re. L. DePaulo exchange with J. Greenfield at CNN offices; and Paul Brownfield, "The Condit Saga: To Cover or Not to Cover?" *Los Angeles Times*, July 13, 2001); Howard Kurtz, *Reality Show: Inside the Latest Great Television News War* (Free Press, 2007), 17–18; transcripts of interviews with media (including appearances of Susan Levy, Dr. Robert Levy, Billy Martin, Barbara Olson, Mark Geragos on CNN's *Larry King Live*); Ceres Department of Public Safety, Crime Report File No. 201-04448, dated July 8, 2001 (CNN stakeout of Condit home in Ceres and KFBK radio trespass on Condit property); Confidential Memorandum from M. Lynch to G. Condit re. "The Minister's Daughter Article" dated September 19, 2002; Confidential Memo to File re. "Interview with Vince Flammini" dated July 11, 2001 prepared by Dorene D'Adamo; discussions with representatives of the US Attorney's Office; *Finding Chandra*, 25–27 (Chandra Levy's e-mails) and 157 (misinterpreting URL) (New York: Scribner, 2010); and court records (including depositions of key figures).

Ch. 15, Open Season. Interviews with Gary Condit, Abbe Lowell, Carolyn Condit, Vince Flammini, Mike Dayton, and Mike Lynch provided invaluable. This chapter is further supported by the following key materials: news archives (including Jim Rutenberg, "Why Dan Rather and CBS Limited Coverage of Levy Case," *New York Times*, July 23, 2001; transcripts of interviews with media; records of Abbe Lowell of the search of Gary Condit's condo at the Lynshire building; records of Abbe Lowell of the DNA samples taken of Gary Condit; correspondence with the US Attorney's Office regarding DNA testing related to Chandra Levy; discussions with representatives of the US Attorney's Office; Officer Charles Egan Trial Transcript, October 26, 2010, 2009-CF1-9230; *Reality Show*, 17–18 (Free Press, 2007); Confidential Memorandum from M. Lynch to G. Condit re. "The Minister's Daughter Article" dated September 19, 2002; Confidential Memo to File re. "Interview with Vince Flammini" dated July 11, 2001 prepared by Dorene D'Adamo; letter from A. Lowell to B. Martin, re. "Chandra Levy Investigation" dated July 13, 2001; letter from B. Martin to A. Lowell, re. "Chandra Levy Investigation" dated July 9, 2001; Memorandum to File from Barry D. Colvert re. "01-060 Gary A. Condit Polygraph" dated July 18, 2001, including attached raw results of polygraph examination of Gary Condit; and correspondence from A. Lowell to law enforcement, re. Colvert polygraph examination of Gary Condit.

Ch. 16, Contradictions and Misses. Interviews with Darrell Condit, Vince Flammini, Gary Condit, Abbe Lowell, Mike Dayton, and Mike Lynch provided invaluable insight. This chapter is further supported by the following key materials: news archives (including *The Daily Howler*, "Our Current Howler (part IV): An ugly, dirty business," August 30, 2001 (Billy Martin statements to media, re. pregnancy rumors); *The Daily Howler*, "Our Current Howler (part I): Great American novel," August 27, 2001 (Lisa DePaulo reporting on Chandra Levy's sex life and press statement of Judy Bachrach); Eric Boehlert, "The Ever Changing Stories of Billy Martin," *Salon*, September 7, 2001; Eric Boehlert, "Junk Journalism" *The Nation*, July 27, 2001 (Geraldo Rivera); Associated Press, "CBS Evening News Airs Levy Story," *New York Times*, July 19, 2001; Kenneth R. Bazinet and Helen Kennedy, "D.C. Park Combed for Clues," *Daily News*, July 17, 2001 (search of Rock Creek Park, Gary Condit vasectomy, "clear Condit of siring a son"); Michael Doyle, "Police Follow Trail Left on Laptop," *Modesto Bee*, July 17, 2001 (search of Rock Creek Park); Stephen Braun, "No Landfill Hunt in Levy Case," *Los Angeles Times*, July 18, 2001; Andrew DeMillo and Allan Lengel, "Levy Searchers Turn Up Little in Parks: Bones Are Found, Probably from Animals," *Washington Post*, July 17, 2001 (search of Rock Creek Park); Allan Lengel and Sari Horwitz, "Levy Looked Up Map of a Rock Creek Site," *Washington Post*, July 16, 2001 (Chandra Levy's Internet searches); transcripts of media interviews (including appearances of Susan Levy and Dr. Robert Levy on CNN's *Larry King Live*); copy of the e-mail written by John LeBoutillier, re. "RJ" and Gary Condit; Dominick Dunne Deposition, September 29, 2004, 02-CIV-9910; *Finding Chandra*, 157, 164–165 (search of Rock Creek Park), 197–198 (Mosley tip and follow-up by detectives) (New York: Scribner, 2010); discussions with representatives of the US Attorney's Office; court records (including 2009 Guandique Arrest Warrant); congressional records (including Gary Condit's personal correspondence from Ralph Hall and press release issued July 17, 2001 by Rep. Jane Harman, re. Statement on Police Search for Missing Intern); Privileged and Confidential Memorandum to File from B. Colvert re. "01-060 Gary A. Condit Polygraph" dated July 18, 2001; congressional correspondence, including Ralph Hall; copies of Metropolitan

Police Department and FBI press releases; Privileged and Confidential Memorandum to Condit File re. "Meeting with Law Enforcement" dated July 24, 2001 (detailing A. Lowell's meeting with representatives from the US Attorney's Office, Metro Police, and FBI on July 24, 2001); Privileged and Confidential Memo re. "Chief Ramsey (and Deputy Chief Gainer): Quotes on Polygraph Test (7/13/01 until 7/21/01), Sources: TOP 50 US Newspapers, Newswires" dated on or about July 21, 2001; and Privileged and Confidential Memorandum to File re. "Meeting with FBI and MPD" dated September 7, 2001.

Ch. 17, Fighting Back. Interviews with Gary Condit, Chad Condit, Cadee Condit, Adrian Condit, Jean Condit, Carolyn Condit, Burl Condit, Abbe Lowell, Mike Dayton, Roger Chiang, and Mike Lynch provided invaluable insight. This chapter is further supported by the following key materials: news archives; transcripts of media interviews (including appearances of Chad Condit, Cadee Condit, Susan Levy and Dr. Robert Levy on CNN's *Larry King Live*, Billy Martin on CNN with Wolf Blitzer, and Gary Condit on ABC with Connie Chung); Gary Condit's congressional records (including correspondence with Connie Chung); A. Lowell correspondence to B. Martin; *American Journalism Review*, "Chung v. Condit," October 1, 2001 (Univ. of Maryland) (Connie Chung's impressions during her interview of Gary Condit); court records (including Dominick Dunne Deposition, September 29, 2004, 02-CIV-9910, and Grand Jury Citizen Complaint against Gary Condit, Mike Lynch, and Don Thornton for charges of Criminal Conspiracy and Subornation of Perjury filed by Judicial Watch, Inc. with the Stanislaus County Grand Jury August 27, 20001; Lee Hamilton and Thomas H. Kean, "Chapter Eight: 'The System Was Blinking Red,'" *The 9/11 Report: The National Commission on Terrorist Attacks Upon the United States* (New York: St. Martin Paperbacks, 2010).

Ch. 18, Horse Whisperer. Interviews with Lin Wood, Gary Condit, and Cadee Condit provided invaluable insight. This chapter is further supported by the following key materials: court records (including Dominick Dunne Deposition, September 29, 2004, 02-CIV-9910, and the 2009 Guandique Arrest Warrant, re. selection of Guandique from photo array on September 17, 2001); news archives (including accounts of Dominick Dunne's retelling of the horse whisperer's stories in various settings as well as Dunne's own writings on the matter in *Vanity Fair*); transcripts of interviews with media (including transcripts of Dominick Dunne's many appearances on television and radio shows); *Finding Chandra*, 195–198 (information in subsection "Crimes" regarding Ramon Alvarez and Ingmar Guandique) (New York: Scribner, 2010); and discussions with representatives of the US Attorney's Office.

Ch. 19, Sentencing. Interviews with Mike Lynch, Mike Dayton, Gary Condit, Chad Condit, Adrian Condit, Jean Condit, Carolyn Condit, Cadee Condit, and Burl Condit provided invaluable insight. This chapter is further supported by the following key materials: news archives (including extensive local coverage of Gary Condit's final election, including the candidate debates); Gary Condit's congressional office records (including a memorandum from

M. Lynch to G. Condit detailing the then current campaign cash position and M. Lynch's assessment of the difficulties of running for reelection); court records (including original complaint for defamation filed by Gary A. Condit against Dominick Dunne and Dominick Dunne Deposition, September 29, 2004, 02-CIV-9910, and the 2009 Guandique Arrest Warrant); transcripts of interviews with media (including Dominick Dunne's appearance on the *Laura Ingraham Show* and Gary Condit's appearance on CNN's *Larry King Live*); *Finding Chandra*, 195–204 (information in subsection "Decisions" regarding the polygraph examination and sentencing of Ingmar Guandique); discussions with representatives of the US Attorney's Office; and *Public Service: The Private Campaign of Gary Condit*, directed by Kristina Holland and Aaron Garcia (2002), VHS.

Ch. 20, What Remains. Interviews with Gary Condit provided invaluable insight. This chapter is further supported by the following key materials: news archives (including the *Post* 12-Part Series, chapter 11, re. discovery of Chandra Levy's remains in Rock Creek Park); Michael Grass, "The Forgotten Discovery of Ingmar Guandique's Name," *Washingtoncitypaper.com*, October 25, 2010 (Amy Keller publicly identifying Ingmar Guandique as potential suspect in Chandra Levy murder); and *Finding Chandra*, 207–216 (discovery of Chandra Levy's remains in Rock Creek Park and follow-up search and discovery of bones by Levy family private detectives) (New York: Scribner, 2010).

Ch. 21, Legacy. Interviews with Gary Condit and Mike Dayton provided invaluable insight. This chapter is further supported by the following key materials: congressional records (including personal letters from congressional members to Gary Condit and reports and footage of 9/11 hearings).

Ch. 22, Civil Liability. Interviews with Gary Condit, Carolyn Condit, Cadee Condit, Chad Condit, Lin Wood, Vince Flammini, and Steve Peace provided invaluable insight. This chapter is further supported by the following key materials: court records (including civil depositions of key participants, including Dominick Dunne Deposition, September 29, 2004, 02-CIV-9910); Gary Condit's congressional and legal records compiling the cases against the tabloids; records of tabloid stories and sources collected by Chad Condit; and news archives.

Ch. 23, Guilt. Interviews with Gary Condit, Chad Condit, Cadee Condit, Darrell Condit, Adrian Condit, Jean Condit, Vince Flammini, and Tony Brigidini provided invaluable insight. Additionally, this chapter is based in part on the author's direct involvement in the events. This chapter is further supported by news archives.

Ch. 24, Cold Case. Interviews with Gary Condit, Cadee Condit, Chad Condit, Carolyn Condit, Tom Warwick, Tony Brigidini, and Roger Chiang provided invaluable insight. Additionally, much of this material is based on the author's direct involvement in the events. This chapter is further supported by the following key materials: new archives; discussions with representatives of the US Attorney's Office; review of evidence provided by the US Attorney's Office; and court records (including Detective Ronald Wyatt Trial Transcript, October 26, 2010, 2009-CF1-9230; Dr. Robert Levy Trial Transcript, October 26, 2010, 2009-CF1-9230; Gary Condit Trial Transcript, November 1, 2010, 2009-CF1-9230; and Armando Morales Trial Transcript, November 4, 2010, 2009-CF1-9230).

Ch. 25, Woe. Interviews with Gary Matthew Condit, Gary Condit, Carolyn Condit, and Chad Condit provided invaluable insight. Gary Matthew Condit also contributed to the writing of the subsection "Gary Condit." This chapter is further supported by the following key materials: news archives; discussions with representatives of the US Attorney's Office; and court records (including Motion for Depositions and Supplemental Notice, May 19, 2016 Status Hearing, *United States of America v. Ingmar Guandique* (Case No. 2009 CF1 9230), Superior Court of the District of Columbia, Criminal Division).